Counseling
Addicted Families

An Integrated Assessment and Treatment Model

Gerald A. Juhnke and W. Bryce Hagedorn

Routledge
Taylor & Francis Group
New York   London

Routledge is an imprint of the
Taylor & Francis Group, an informa business

Routledge
Taylor & Francis Group
270 Madison Avenue
New York, NY 10016

Routledge
Taylor & Francis Group
2 Park Square
Milton Park, Abingdon
Oxon OX14 4RN

Printed in the United States of America on acid-free paper
10 9 8 7 6 5 4 3 2 1

International Standard Book Number-10: 0-415-95106-2 (Hardcover)
International Standard Book Number-13: 978-0-415-95106-7 (Hardcover)
Library of Congress Card Number 2005034604

Library of Congress Cataloging-in-Publication Data

Juhnke, Gerald A.
    Counseling addicted families : an integrated assessment and treatment model /
Gerald A. Juhnke and W. Bryce Hagedorn.
        p. cm.
    Includes bibliographical references and index.
    ISBN 0-415-95106-2 (hb : alk. paper)
    1. Substance abuse--Treatment. 2. Family psychotherapy. I. Hagedorn, W.
Bryce. II. Title.
    [DNLM: 1. Substance-Related Disorders--therapy. 2. Family Therapy--meth-
ods. 3. Counseling--methods. 4. Models, Psychological. WM 270 J95c 2006]

RC564.J83 2006
362.29--dc22   2005034604

Visit the Taylor & Francis Web site at
http://www.taylorandfrancis.com

and the Routledge Web site at
www.routledgementalhealth.com

Contents

iii

114482

Preface

What clinician has not thumbed the pages of dozens of family counseling books intently searching for something clinically focused and practical? You know the books. They run the gamut. Some family counseling books are so "minutia focused" and laden with boring historical accounts of who did what when that readers deserve an award for finishing the first few paragraphs. Others posit convoluted pop culture accounts on how to reconnect with pathological parents while terminating one's ineffective family therapist.

This book is different. Our intent in writing this book is to provide readers with a practical, clinically based family addictions model that works. Since the early 1990s we have trained our master's and doctoral students in the Sequential Family Addictions Model. They have successfully utilized the model and have noted its utility with their addicted family clients. Based upon self-report of both master's students and experienced doctoral students, the model is relatively simple to follow and—most important—effective. Its practical applications provide both brief and long-term treatment options that match individual family needs no matter the family's position on the addictions continuum.

Moreover, the book was written to be used in two distinct ways. First as a treatment manual, the book provides more experienced counselors a means to strengthen their current knowledge and augment their clinical acumen. For example, experienced family counselors seeking greater understanding of addictions and desiring effective family interventions will find this no-nonsense book filled with ways to utilize already familiar treatments within a preplanned sequence that changes family addiction patterns. Second, more experienced addictions counselors will find this book helpful as it describes "progressing" family-based interventions that emphasize the importance of family relationships when addressing addictions.

The book's greatest merit, however, is the manner in which it prescribes a sequential movement in treatment. Beginning with "here and now" theories and practices undergirded by the constructs of equifinality and brevity, family addictions counselors learn how and when to move toward more insight-oriented family addictions treatments that are frequently more time intensive and costly. Movement away from briefer family addiction treatment is not perceived as a failure on the part of either counselor or family. Rather, it is understood as a reflection of eloquently presented sequential interventions that match the developing needs of families and their individual system members.

We trust this book will help you attain your next desired proficiency level and commend you for embarking on the journey that you have begun. Above all, we count it a privilege to join you as we serve the needs of addicted families.

Sincerely,
Gerald "Jerry" Juhnke and William "Bryce" Hagedorn

The Definition and Prevalence of Addiction

Impacts on the Family and the Nation

Chapter 1 Learning Objectives

After reading this chapter, you should be able to:

- Define "addiction," including lay and clinical definitions
- Distinguish between chemical and process addictions
- Recognize how the Addictive Disorder definition fully encompasses chemical and process addictions
- Identify the number of individuals impacted by chemical and process addictions
- Identify the impacts of chemical and process addictions, both on a societal and familial level

Introduction

The goal of this book is to provide a practical, hands-on, clinically founded text that will help you facilitate effective family-based addictions counseling. If you have chosen a vocation focused on helping addicted persons and their families, we commend you on selecting a most fulfilling and at times very challenging career. Conversely, if you were "thrown into" addictions counseling either by your clients' needs or by the agency or school in which you work, we sincerely welcome you to one of the most rewarding careers that focuses on helping those in need. But before we get too far into the application of strategies and techniques, it is important to lay the foundation for the challenges that lie ahead. This foundation will be addressed in this first chapter. Here we will begin by wrapping our minds around defining a disorder that has proven to be somewhat ambiguous and fluid: addiction—a clinical disorder that impacts every domain of individuals' lives. Next, we want to firmly establish the societal and personal costs attributable to the disorder of addiction. Finally, and most importantly, we will explore the devastating effects this disorder has on the "family," defined herein as the collection of individuals who live and interact together. The foundation laid here will establish the need for competent and capable counselors to forge comprehensive treatment strategies in their work with addicted individuals and families.

Addiction—A Working Definition

What exactly does the term *addiction* mean? An accurate definition depends not only on who is asking but also on the existence of established criteria for the common set of thoughts, behaviors, and emotions that underlie these disorders. We'll begin by taking a brief look at how we define this disorder, disease, or syndrome and how this definition can be at the same time accurate and contextual for those seeking answers. Then, through a review of the current clinical and diagnostic literature, we will explore the most appropriate means for detecting the disorder's familiar and distinguishing features. We will conclude this section with a call for a more general understanding of addiction that moves beyond the concept of chemical ingestion.

Helping Clients and Families Understand

Say you are conducting a psychoeducational presentation for addicted clients and their families. Whereas a clinical definition may be useful in this setting, a lay definition is often more appropriate and more effective—people want to understand what is happening to them and to their loved ones. One such popular lay definition, adapted from Nakken (1996), states that *addiction is an abnormal love and trust relationship with an object or event in an attempt to control that which cannot be controlled.*

This definition is fairly easy for clients to understand for several reasons. First, most recognize how relationships are *supposed* to work. For example, many believe that a relationship occurs between two people and that this relationship should be based on reciprocal respect, love, and trust. At the same time, most understand that maintaining such a relationship requires consistent and mutual effort, sacrifice, and investment. Finally, many relationships move through predictable stages (e.g., from initial attraction, to romance and passion, to true intimacy, and finally to commitment) with the expressed goal of solidifying and maintaining the connection while honoring the individuality of each individual in the relationship. Sound ideal?

What makes addiction an *abnormal relationship*? First, the relationship is between a person and an *object or event* (e.g., alcohol, sex, cocaine, food, spending). This kind of relationship involves twisted concepts of respect, love, and trust: People come to love and trust the object or event to meet their needs and push away anyone or anything that interferes with that bond. Similarly, this unilateral relationship consists of efforts to satisfy one's personal needs to the exclusion of family, friends, and loved ones, while at the same time demanding painful sacrifice from these same relationships. Finally, the abnormal relationship pathologically progresses through the same stages found in healthy relationships, with the exclusion of intimacy and mutual commitment. Individuals are initially attracted to an object or event because it makes them "feel good," it helps them forget about life for a while, and most importantly, it helps them *feel* like they're in control (of their feelings, of reactions to external events, or of others' reactions). Next, they come to anticipate the next romantic connection with their object or event, they share their object or event with others who are attracted to it, and they begin to form a passion for what the object or event provides them (such as control, a sensation, escape, or avoidance). Unfortunately for them, since an object or event cannot provide true intimacy, and given that the yearning for intimacy remains, individuals often find themselves using more and more of the object or event in a desperate search for an unobtainable connection and fulfillment. Despair tends to follow as individuals (a) find themselves hooked on a cycle of passion and unfulfilled intimacy and (b) find that any semblance of control has been lost (including loss of control of their own feelings, loss of control [and often a worsening] of external events, and a loss of control over others' reactions).

Here is another popular lay definition: *Addiction is an increasing desire for something with an accompanying decreasing ability to satisfy that desire.* When exploring this definition with clients, you might want to refer to the metaphor of digging a hole at the beach. Clients can be asked if they have ever gotten right up next to the incoming tide and tried to dig a hole in the sand. As anyone who has had this experience can attest to, the deeper one digs, the more one tries to keep the incoming water out of that hole, the more frustrated one becomes—the water just keeps on coming. Clients often recognize how their compulsive attempts at getting high through the use of heroin, gambling, the Internet, or exercise approximate that digging experience—the desire to dig the hole and keep it dry is in direct opposition to the ability to do so. Additional lay definitions can be derived from the various theories of addiction. These theories can be explained to addicted clients and their families to assist them in understanding the impact of the addictive disorders. Since we will explore each of these theories in depth in the proceeding chapter, let's move into a discussion of clinical definitions, as this will shape how we conceptualize, assess, and treat these disorders with a comprehensive treatment model.

Clinical Definitions—Can We Agree?

When speaking to clinical professionals (e.g., medical personnel, insurance companies, and other colleagues), a formal definition of addiction is oftentimes most appropriate. The fourth edition (text revision) of the *Diagnostic and Statistical Manual for Mental Disorders* (*DSM-IV-TR*) (APA, 2000) categorizes these addictive disorders into *abuse* and *dependence*. Substance *abuse* is defined by the *DSM-IV-TR* as a maladaptive use of chemicals that occurs over time and that impacts major life domains and responsibilities. Individuals meeting criteria for substance abuse will likely experience one of the following over the course of 12 months: (a) role failure—avoiding responsibilities (with detrimental consequences) in such areas as home, school, or work; (b) chemical use during dangerous situations—for example, while driving a car or operating heavy machinery; (c) legal-related issues—for example, a DUI or expulsion from school; and/ or (d) continue to abuse chemicals even when doing so significantly deteriorates important relationships or impacts social concerns.

When an individual continues to abuse substances compulsively, despite significant negative consequences, substance *dependence* is likely. In this case, the *DSM-IV-TR* notes that individuals meeting criteria for substance dependence will likely exhibit three or more of the following over the course of 12 months: (a) tolerance—they will need more and more of a chemical in order to experience the same "high" or will not get "high" when using the same amount of the chemical over time; (b) physical or psychological withdrawal when they stop using (or lower the amount of) the chemical; (c) more chemical use than planned, or over a longer time period than was intended; (d) unsuccessfully attempts to control, cut back, or stop chemical use; (e) exorbitant amounts of time spent in obtaining the chemical, using their chemical, or recovering from the chemical's effects (i.e., hangovers); (f) sacrifice of activities of a social, occupational, or recreational nature that were once important to them; and/or (g) continued abuse of the chemical even upon recognizing that it significantly impacts their physical or psychological health.

The *DSM* has been an invaluable resource for clinicians who assess and treat chemical abuse and dependency. Like the other disorders listed in its pages, a medical model has been used to delineate the thoughts, feelings, and behaviors that are common to those struggling with obsessive chemical use. Without this resource tool, clinicians would be left with "best guess" diagnoses and prognoses for a disorder that impacts millions of individuals. Unfortunately, whereas the *DSM* does an exceptional job with chemical addictions, it does not address the common process addictions that often exacerbate or complicate the assessment and treatment of chemical disorders. It is to this conundrum that we now turn.

Now to Complicate Matters...

Considerable debate has ensued regarding the appropriate use of the term *addiction*. Whereas some researchers and clinicians in the addictions field believe that the term *addiction* should be applied only to circumstances that involve chemical substances (e.g., Apt & Hulbert, 1995; Barth & Kinder, 1987; Levine & Troiden, 1988; Rachlin, 1990), others have stressed the importance of understanding addiction in a broader context than strictly chemical dependency (Goodman, 1998; Griffin-Shelley, Sandler, & Lees, 1992; Raviv, 1993). Similar diagnostic criteria have been applied to a number of problem behaviors, often called *process addictions*. These addictions include those related to sex (Abouesh & Clayton, 1999; Carnes, 1992, 1994a, 1994b; Fischer, Williams, Byington, & Lonsdale, 1996; Goodman, 1993, 1998, 2001; Levin, 1999), gambling (Buchta, 1995; Griffiths, 1992), eating (Baker, 1995; Sheppard, 1995), work (Robinson, 1998, 2000), television (McIlwraith, 1998), shopping (Lee, Lennon, & Rudd, 2000), exercise (Cockerill & Riddington, 1996), the Internet (Armstrong, Phillips, & Saling, 2000; Young, 1999), and video games (Griffiths, 1991, 1997). Regardless of the chemical or behavior, we contend that a broader definition (as well as accompanying criteria) that addresses the overall addictive process better serves clinicians who work with clients who suffer from multiple addictive disorders.

Another Definition—The Addictive Disorder   Defining addiction as an overarching process has shown continued efficacy. The Addictive Disorder model assumes that compulsive-like behavioral manifestations that meet criteria similar to that for chemical dependency are in fact addictive behaviors (Carnes 1994b; Goodman, 2001). Given that clients seldom present with a singular addictive disorder (Das, 1990; Merta, 2001; Rowan & Galasso, 2000), it seems prudent, as well as cost-effective, to treat multiple addictions simultaneously so as not to repeat therapeutic interventions for each disorder. Since the same interventions used with chemical dependency have proven effective in treating other addictive disorders (Griffin-Shelley et al., 1992), and given that many who are chemically addicted also meet process addiction criteria (Black, Kehrberg, Flumerfelt, & Schlosser, 1997; Carnes, 1992; Delmonico & Griffin, 1997), the diagnostic criteria for the Addictive Disorder provides a comprehensive framework for treatment.

Definitions and Criteria Development for the Addictive Disorder   In creating a definition and corresponding criteria for the Addictive Disorder, several important steps have been taken. First, the disorder must be differentiated from already established disorders that have traditionally encapsulated similar behavior patterns. We will begin with a discussion of similarities and differences between addictive disorders and chemical dependency disorders and conclude with how addictive disorders differ from impulse control and obsessive-compulsive disorders. Between these discussions, we will offer those diagnostic criteria that have been established through the empirical data collected from clinical samples of individuals presenting with similar disorders.

In working toward defining the addictive disorder, Carnes (1992), Goodman (1998, 2001), Levin (1999), and Young (1999) suggested that one begin by identifying the key elements used to identify chemical dependency. Given that neither tolerance nor withdrawal is necessary for designating a behavior or substance as addictive (APA, 2000; O'Brien, 1996; Potenza, Fiellin, Heninger, Rounsaville, & Mazure, 2002), let us explore those conditions that are both necessary and sufficient for the diagnosis of a dependence/addictive disorder.

Goodman (2001) suggested that the two criteria necessary and sufficient for the designation of chemical addiction are "(1) recurrent failure to control the use of one or more drugs, and (2) continuation of drug use despite substantial harmful consequences" (p. 195). To arrive at a concise definition of an addictive disorder, Goodman (a) substituted the word *behavior* for *drug* in the above conditions and (b) added key elements from those arguments asserting that addictive behaviors are better defined within the context of a compulsion or an impulse control disorder. The definition for the addictive disorder actually incorporates many of the key elements from all three disorders (chemical dependency, impulse control disorder, and obsessive-compulsive disorder) and is noted as,

> A behavior that can function both to produce pleasure and to reduce painful affects is employed in a pattern that is characterized by two key features: (1) recurrent failure to control the behavior, and (2) continuation of the behavior despite substantial harmful consequences. (p. 195)

Similar definitions have been successfully applied to designating gambling (Blaszcynski, Buhrich, & McConaghy, 1985; Buchta, 1995; Griffiths, 1992; Potenza et al., 2002), Internet use (Armstrong et al., 2000; Young 1999; Young, Pistner, O'Mara, & Buchanan, 1999), and eating (Baker, 1995; Flood, 1989; Sheppard, 1995) as addictive disorders.

If one accepts the merits of this definition for an addictive disorder, the next step would be to specify diagnostic criteria. In developing such criteria, Goodman (1993), Levin (1999), and Young (1999) began with comparing the *DSM-IV-TR*'s criteria for compulsive gambling with the criteria established for substance dependence. Goodman (2001) combined these criteria and substituted the word *behavior* for the terms *substance* and *substance use* found in the substance dependence criteria. Additionally, "characteristic withdrawal syndrome for the substance" (APA, 2000, p. 197) was replaced with a more universal definition for withdrawal that applied to all addictive behaviors.

We therefore suggest that the following set of criteria be accepted as clinically relevant for diagnosing an addictive disorder:

> A maladaptive pattern of behavior, leading to clinically significant impairment or distress, as manifested by three (or more) of the following, occurring at any time in the same 12-month period:

1. Tolerance, as defined by either of the following:
   a. A need for markedly increased amount or intensity of the behavior to achieve the desired effect
   b. Markedly diminished effect with continued involvement in the behavior at the same level or intensity
2. Withdrawal, as manifested by either of the following:
   a. Characteristic psychophysiological withdrawal syndrome of physiologically described changes and/or psychologically described changes upon discontinuation of the behavior

    b. The same (or a closely related) behavior is engaged in to relieve or avoid withdrawal symptoms

3. The behavior is often engaged in over a longer period, in greater quantity, or at a higher intensity than was intended
4. There is a persistent desire or unsuccessful efforts to cut down or control the behavior
5. A great deal of time spent in activities necessary to prepare for the behavior, to engage in the behavior, or to recover from its effects
6. Important social, occupational, or recreational activities are given up or reduced because of the behavior
7. The behavior continues despite knowledge of having a persistent or recurrent physical or psychological problem that is likely to have been caused or exacerbated by the behavior. (Goodman, 2001, pp. 195–196)

The establishment of such diagnostic criteria would appear to have several merits including, but not limited to, the creation of a common clinical language, a legitimization of process addictive disorders for the purposes of third-party reimbursement, and a step toward a standardized treatment protocol for all addictive disorders.

Before we move on, we believe it is important to address the argument that these problematic and compulsive-like behavioral manifestations are better defined as impulse control (ICD) or obsessive-compulsive disorders (OCD). A brief review of the necessary and sufficient conditions for these diagnoses is presented here in order to more accurately frame the need for the recognition and designation of these behaviors as *addictive*.

The one criterion that best discounts the use of the term *impulsivity* to describe addictive-like behaviors is that an impulsive act is one that is always harmful to the person engaging in the behavior or to others who are impacted by that individual (a necessary and sufficient condition for designating the behavior as an ICD) (APA, 2000). This "designation of harm" is readily seen in such ICDs as intermittent explosive disorder (resulting in serious assaultive acts or destruction of property), kleptomania (stealing objects from others), pyromania (deliberate and purposeful fire setting), and trichotillomania (pulling out one's hair). The one impulse control disorder that warrants recognition as an addictive disorder, namely pathological gambling, has one "harm criteria" that has been used to classify it as such: the possibility of committing illegal acts to finance the behaviors. This criterion may never exhibit itself and yet the disorder is classified as an ICD. Whereas other addictive behaviors *may* cause harm to oneself, many do not, at least not initially. For example, even though sexually addictive behaviors may cause shame and guilt (such as compulsive-like masturbation, homosexuality, and prostitution), they are often not initially harmful to oneself or others (Hagedorn & Juhnke, 2005). The similar lack of harm to self or others can be found in Internet addiction, as well as early stages of eating and spending addictions. It is this "designation of harm" that best describes these behaviors as addictive versus impulsive.

Addictive behaviors have also been compared to those behaviors common to obsessive-compulsive disorders. Granted, criteria are similar in that both disorders include intrusive thoughts, compulsive behavior patterns, and attempts to eliminate or control these thoughts and behaviors. The difference occurs in that whereas addictive behaviors are often utilized to reduce anxiety and other painful affects (a necessary and sufficient diagnostic criterion of compulsive behaviors), they also produce pleasure and gratification, which rules out the diagnosis of compulsion. The American Psychiatric Association (2000) noted this distinction by stating that even though behaviors such as eating, sex, gambling, or substance use have been referred to as compulsive (when individuals engage in them excessively), these behaviors have not been considered to be compulsions as defined by the *DSM-IV-TR* because the individual usually derives pleasure from the activity and may wish to resist it only because of its negative consequences. For these reasons, we believe that the term *addiction* is the more accurate term to use in describing these behaviors.

By offering and endorsing this definition and corresponding diagnostic criteria for the Addictive Disorder, it is not the intention of this book to debate the merits or shortcomings of any one set of criteria. Rather, our objective is to enlighten the minds of those who suffer from, as well as those who treat, addictive disorders to the realities of a likely misdiagnosed impulse control or obsessive-compulsive disorder. Given that several studies have highlighted the process of cross addiction, whereby one addiction (e.g., alcohol) is substituted with another (e.g., exercise) (Buck & Sales, 2000; O'Brien, 1996; Raviv, 1993), it appears imprudent to focus exclusively on the chemical addiction criteria to the exclusion of the process addiction criteria. Similarly, the high comorbidity rates between chemical and process addictions (Das, 1990; Ledgerwood & Downey, 2002; Merta, 2001; Potenza, 2002; Rowan & Galasso, 2000) call for a broader context in which to conceptualize the shared set of problematic behaviors. In approaching the treatment of an addicted family, it is both practical and valuable to cast as wide a clinical net as possible to treat the myriad of disorders that occur within the addicted system.

In addition to defining a disorder by the characteristics common among those who suffer from it, another way is to look at the impacts of this disorder on the individual, family, and nation. In so doing, the need for timely and cost-effective interventions becomes apparent. By noting some of the financial, physical, relational, economic, and societal tolls instigated by addictive disorders, we begin to see that a family treatment approach is the most prudent course of action.

Addiction—Prevalence and Impacts

Addiction is similar to a virus—it infects and spreads into every aspect of the individual's life, including the spiritual, emotional, physical, psychological, familial, social, recreational, and vocational domains. Rather than improving with time, untreated addictive disorders are like untreated heart conditions—given enough time and stress, the individual will suffer an "attack," usually impacting one of the aforementioned domains. Unlike other chronic and yet manageable disorders (e.g., diabetes), the addictive disorder impacts not only the individual addict but also just about every individual who comes in contact with the addict. In this section of Chapter 1, we will explore these impacts in greater detail. First, we will explore the current challenges in determining prevalence figures for both chemical and process addictions. Next, the societal and economic tangible costs will be ascertained, followed by the intangible costs that impact the individual and family. Finally, by investigating the devastating impact of addiction on the family system, we will more concisely define the addictive disorder, the one disorder that by its very nature appears to avoid definition and scrutiny. In so doing, we will set the stage for the importance of addressing these disorders with a comprehensive treatment model.

An Accurate Count—Is It Possible?

One of the most challenging figures to compartmentalize is the number of individuals who struggle with addictive disorders. Accurate and precise figures of addicted individuals have been difficult to ascertain for several reasons. First, prevalence figures are often based on client self-report, that is, on the number of clients who seek treatment or who admit to using/abusing chemicals and behaviors. Given that the social stigma attached to alcoholism and chemical addiction has been greatly reduced, due in part to the national media attention focused on celebrities and athletes who admit to suffering from these kinds of disorders, accurate numbers are more readily ascertained. But these figures are still based on self-report data, which have inherent social desirability components (i.e., respondents often answer affirmatively or negatively about their substance use based on the perceived consequences or benefits of such self-disclosure as well as the anonymity offered).

Unfortunately, the social stigmas associated with process addictions have not declined at the same pace. Given the societal beliefs common to such disorders as sexual addiction (e.g., "he must be some kind of deviant pervert"), spending addiction (e.g., "she writes bad checks all the time—she must be some kind of con artist"), and compulsive overeating (e.g., "look at the size of him—it's a wonder he can get out of bed"), accurate prevalence figures are often difficult, if not impossible, to determine unless affected individuals experience significant negative consequences such as incarceration or physical traumas (Carnes, 1994a; Kafka, 1997). Additionally, as clients often experience shame, guilt, and fear of being identified and labeled a sex, spending, or food addict, even with significant personal or familial crises, the likelihood of their seeking treatment is low (Putnam, 2000).

Another complicating factor to accurate prevalence figures, especially for process addictions, is that such figures are often contingent on defining clients' presenting behaviors as compulsive disorders, impulse control disorders, or addictions (Delmonico & Griffin, 1997; Goodman, 2001; Hollander & Rosen, 2000; Manley & Koehler, 2001). Therefore, if one clinician defines client behaviors as meeting criteria for sexual addiction and another identifies the same behaviors as an issue of impulse control, accurate prevalence figures become muddled. Finally, when addiction symptomatology becomes overwhelmingly severe, clients may initially present dysfunctional behaviors and mood disorders (e.g., marital discord, depression with suicidal ideations, anxiety and panic attacks, physical trauma) that are actually the result of their addiction issues (Carnes, 1994a; Delmonico & Griffin, 1997; Manley & Koehler, 2001; Ragan & Martin, 2000). Therefore the addictive diagnosis may never be recognized and recorded.

That all being said, what work *has* been done to estimate the number of individuals who suffer from addictive disorders? Some authors estimate the number of chemically affected individuals to be between 11 and 58 million people (Page & Bailey, 1995). Notably, there is a huge difference between 11 and 58 million, but remember the aforementioned estimation challenges. Most researchers make attempts at drawing prevalence conclusions based on specific population samples using specific chemicals. For example, Yacoubian and Peters (2005) reported that 10 percent of high school seniors admitted to using MDMA (ecstasy) during their lifetimes. This figure is even more startling when one considers that rave attendees and at-risk youth were not targeted for the study. Another study noted that of the 9 percent of adolescents who report using inhalants (e.g., glue, aerosol spray cans, gasoline, amyl nitrate, Freon, and butane) during their lifetimes, the largest group comprised those of the Native American population (nearly 16 percent) (Mosher, Rotolo, Phillips, Krupski & Stark, 2004). Even among populations that overtly restrict the use of tobacco, alcohol, and nonprescription medications/drugs, such as students who attend parochial or religiously affiliated colleges or universities, prevalence figures have been gathered. Hopkins et al. (2004) noted that 19.8 percent of religiously affiliated college students reported using marijuana during their lifetimes (compared to a national figure of 42.3 percent). Granted, each of the aforementioned studies has its own limitations, ranging from small sample sizes, geographic limitations, and the biases inherent to self-report measures. Nonetheless, these studies, and those like them, highlight the challenges inherent to the prevalence-gathering process.

The U.S. government has made great strides in compiling prevalence figures, likely due to the huge amount of state and national monies that have been allocated to the prevention and treatment of chemical addictions. For example, the Substance Abuse and Mental Health Services Administration (SAMHSA) routinely gathers substance use and abuse prevalence data each year. Some disturbing figures can be gleaned from SAMHSA's (2003a) *National Survey on Drug Use and Health*. For example:

- An estimated 21.6 million persons aged 12 or older in 2003 were classified with substance dependence or abuse (9.1 percent of the total population). Of these:
  - 3.1 million were classified with dependence on or abuse of *both* alcohol and illicit drugs, 3.8 million were dependent on or abused illicit drugs but *not* alcohol, and
  - 14.8 million were dependent on or abused alcohol but *not* illicit drugs.
- In 2003, another 19.5 million Americans aged 12 or older were current illicit drug *users*, meaning they had used an illicit drug during the month prior to the survey interview. This estimate represents 8.2 percent of the population aged 12 years old or older.
- More than one fifth (22.6 percent) of persons aged 12 or older participated in binge drinking at least once in the 30 days prior to the survey in 2003. Binge drinking is defined as five or more drinks on the same occasion at least once in the past 30 days (includes heavy use). This translates to about 54 million people, comparable with the number reported in 2002.
- In 2003, heavy drinking was reported by 6.8 percent of the population aged 12 or older, or 16.1 million people. Heavy drinking is defined

as five or more drinks on the same occasion on at least five different days in the past 30 days. These figures are similar to those of 2002, when 6.7 percent (15.9 million people) reported heavy drinking.

These are some sobering (no pun intended) statistics. By these numbers alone, chemical abuse impacts nearly 50 percent of the U.S. population. And this number does not include those who use/abuse nicotine, the number one addictive drug used in the United States. According to the National Institute on Drug Abuse (NIDA), 30 percent of those 12 years old and older (71.5 million people) used tobacco products at least once in the month prior to being interviewed (2004a).

These aforementioned numbers do not reflect the millions affected by process addictions. Since there is no universally accepted set of criteria for such disorders as sexual addiction, workaholism, and Internet addiction, prevalence estimates tend to be encapsulated within wide ranges based on clinical samples. For example, an estimated 17 to 37 million Americans meet criteria for sexual addiction (Carnes, 1994b; Cooper, Delmonico, & Burg, 2000; Morris, 1999; Wolfe, 2000), another 6 to 15 million struggle with compulsive gambling (Shaffer, Hall, & VanderBilt, 1999; Shaffer & Korn, 2002), 17 to 41 million are addicted to the Internet (Hall & Parsons, 2001; Stanley, 2003; Young, 1999), and approximately 14 million individuals suffer from an eating disorder (Bruce & Agras, 1992; Tenore, 2001). These figures tend to be cited as "stand-alone" statistics, that is, they do not account for those who may have multiple addictions.

Earlier, we stated that chemical and process addictions often occur simultaneously. Several studies have demonstrated these links. For example, associations have been validated among excessive drinking, overeating, and compulsive gambling (Das, 1990); between sexual addiction and comorbid chemical dependency, eating disorders, compulsive working, compulsive spending, and compulsive gambling (Carnes, 1992); between drug dependency and concurrent nicotine addiction, relationship dependency, alcohol dependency, compulsive sexual behaviors, eating disorders, and compulsive gambling (Griffin-Shelley et al., 1992); between sexual addiction and comorbid addictions to drugs, spending, eating, and gambling (Delmonico & Griffin, 1997); between alcohol/drug addictions and compulsive eating, gambling, and compulsive shopping (Merta, 2001); and between gambling and alcoholism (Ledgerwood & Downey, 2002; Potenza et al., 2002; Rowan & Galasso, 2000). As a result of the aforementioned studies and complicating factors, it is extremely difficult to ascertain the actual number of addicted individuals—as we noted, this is a disorder that defies accountability.

How Much Does It All Cost?

Given the prevalence of addictive disorders, it is no wonder that millions of individuals are directly and indirectly affected. In order to recognize the extent of these impacts, we now turn to the discussion of the tangible and intangible costs attributed to addictive disorders. We recognize the ambiguity of the term *cost*: Do we view cost in terms of national dollars spent on treatment? Do we look at economic losses caused by addicted individuals' behaviors? What about the personal expenditures by individuals, big business, and insurance companies? How about the connection between crime and addiction? We believe that in order to accurately describe the severity of these disorders, each of these questions must be addressed and answered.

One mustn't forget about the individual and familial damage done by both chemical and process addictions. Whereas entire books have been written exclusively on the negative impacts of these disorders on society and the family, the reason we wrote this book was that we adamantly believe that addiction is a family disease and that clinicians need a comprehensive assessment and treatment model to work with families in crisis. As a matter of fact, throughout the two authors' clinical work, it has been a rare occurrence when a client's addictive behaviors did not directly affect other important people and situations in his or her life. Similarly, we believe it to be ethically and clinically imprudent to treat recovering addicts without supplying them with the necessary interpersonal skills to address underlying or comorbid family dysfunctions. Therefore one must recognize the pain that inevitably results when addictive disorders touch families. Many of the familial impacts will be addressed in the following discussions involving the impact of chemical/process addiction on the health care system, U.S. economic productivity, the criminal justice system, the social welfare system, and mental health rates. Throughout, we will address the devastating interactions between addictions and the individual family unit through case examples assembled from the second author's clinical work. Like other clinical vignettes used throughout this text, client names and identifying details have been altered to protect the privacy of these individuals and families.

Impacts of Chemical Addictions

The societal costs attributed to chemical addictions are well documented and lamented (French, Roebuck, McLellan, & Sindelar, 2000; National Center on Addiction and Substance Abuse [CASA], 2001; Substance Abuse and Mental Health Services Administration [SAMHSA], 2000a; SAMHSA, 2000b). On a national level, economic costs of drug and alcohol abuse were estimated in 1992 to be $245.7 billion (National Institute on Drug Abuse [NIDA], 2004b). Similarly, in 1998, $81.3 billion of state government monies was spent on substance abuse and addiction programs (CASA, 2001). Included in these estimates are such things as treatment and prevention costs, health care costs, job productivity losses, impacts of drug-related crimes, and social welfare efforts (each of which is reviewed further in this section). The NIDA (2004b) study further identified that more than half (55 percent) of these costs are assumed by local, state, and national governments (i.e., paid through taxpayers), private insurance companies, and victims, whereas the remainder are paid by addicted individuals and their families. To put this into perspective, these numbers are particularly troublesome when one considers that every U.S. citizen (man, woman, and child) pays nearly $1,000 annually due to unnecessary health care costs, increased law enforcement, automobile crashes, crime costs, and lost productivity, all of which are attributable to chemical addictions (Horgan, 1995).

In analyzing the economic costs attributed to alcohol and drug abuse, comprehensive studies by the Office of National Drug Control Policy (ONDCP) are periodically sponsored by the president of the United States, the most recent being published in 2001 and 2004. It is from these and other studies that we can extrapolate the estimated dollar amounts attributed to these disorders. In arriving at the most recent economic figures, Harwood (2000) and the ONDCP studies (2001, 2004) calculated that $184.6 billion is attributed annually for impacts of alcohol abuse and $180.9 billion for drug abuse, totaling $365.5 billion per year. This represents an almost 50 percent increase in economic costs over a 12-year period and clearly indicates that the addiction problem is not going away.

How does one conceptualize $365 billion spent by the United States? Bill Gates, chairman and cofounder of Microsoft, who has been noted as the richest person in world, clears only $46.5 billion (Kroll & Goldman, 2005). Countries like Russia, Argentina, and Taiwan have gross national products less than $365 billion. In fact, if we put $365 billion on a typical credit card that charged an annual interest rate of 18 percent (and didn't spend a cent more), we would end up accumulating as much as the U.S. national debt (currently $7.8 trillion [Bureau of the Public Debt, 2005]) in just 17 years. This being said, perhaps the best way to recognize the dramatic impacts of substance abuse is to break down the different influenced areas and highlight the monies spent therein. For this reason, we will next explore treatment costs, health care costs, job productivity losses, criminal costs, and social welfare costs in more depth and detail. We will also investigate how these costs directly impact families.

Treatment and Prevention   Given that approximately 3.5 million people (aged 12 or older) receive substance abuse–related treatment annually (SAMHSA, 2003a), the U.S. society spends significant monies on preventing and treating addictive disorders. In fact, $18 billion a year is devoted to the prevention and treatment of substance abuse complications (Mark et al., 2005). Even when monies invested in prevention programs appear to cut societal costs (e.g., for every dollar invested in prevention, between $4 and $10 can be saved in treating alcohol and substance abuse disorders) (NIDA, 2003; Pentz, 1998; Spoth, Guyull, & Day, 2002), these monies still must be put forward by individuals, families, the private sector, and the government.

Some treatment modalities are aimed at cost *reduction.* For example, methadone therapy (used in the management of opiate dependence) costs approximately $290 per month, whereas it would cost nearly $3,600 per month to allow an untreated opiate dependent individual to live in the community (NIDA, n.d.1). Similarly, putting the same addict into custody (often seen as a form of treatment) costs approximately $3,300 per month. Significant costs are also assumed by those who seek more traditional forms of treatment. With outpatient treatment costs averaging $75 per hour (SAMHSA, 2003a), inpatient treatment costs averaging upward of $1,000 per day, and traditional 28-day programs averaging $24,000 (Addiction Resource Guide, 2000; Morris, 1999), without a strong insurance policy, many cannot afford the help necessary to combat addictive disorders. Additional monies spent on health care treatment are covered in the following section.

Health Care Costs   Foreign chemicals (i.e., alcohol, cocaine, tobacco, ecstasy, etc.) ingested in mass quantities cause significant trauma and damage to the human body. Overall, more than $18 billion is spent on health care services related to chemical abuse and dependency (ONDCP, 2004). This estimate is actually lower than the actual monies spent due to the difficulty in separating complications attributed to chronic use of legal chemicals (e.g., alcohol and tobacco) versus those ascribed to illegal substance use. Either way, in reviewing the costs incurred by damaged bodies and brains, one must look at both the direct and indirect monies spent. In direct treatment, approximately $5.6 billion is spent for alcohol and another $4.4 billion is spent addressing drug abuse disorders (data compiled from between 1992 and 2002 [ONDCP, 2001]). These dollars include such services as detoxification, rehabilitation, prevention, training providers, and expenditures on research. But the body and mind are severely affected by alcohol and drug abuse. For those health problems exacerbated by alcohol and drug abuse, $13.2 billion is indirectly spent in addressing alcohol-related, and another $5.5 billion on drug-related, disorders (ONDCP, 2001). As an example of how difficult it can be to recognize underlying substance abuse disorders, Weintraub et al. (2001) cautioned that individuals admitted to hospitals for various forms of infection should be screened for disorders related to cocaine, heroin, and other injectable drugs. Similarly, patients who are hospitalized for trauma-related complications may present with underlying alcohol or marijuana abuse. Finally, these same authors note that gastrointestinal disorders are often the result of sustained alcohol consumption but that this same consumption will often go unscreened by medical personnel and unrevealed by many patients.

When considering the impact of drug abuse on health care costs, tobacco is rarely thought of, especially when such drugs as heroin and cocaine capture the majority of media coverage. Nicotine results in $50 to $75 billion in direct medical costs. When you include the loss to productivity and potential earnings, this adds an additional $47 billion (U.S. Public Health Service, 2000), which amounts to more than $100 billion spent each year by the American society. Death rates caused by substance abuse are another medical-related cost. Whereas nicotine remains the leading preventable cause of death (more than 440,000 annually—approximately 1 out of every 5 deaths) (U.S. Public Health Service, 2000), another 132,000 persons die as a consequence of alcohol and drug problems (ONDCP, 2001). Of these 132,000, 107,400 are related to alcohol and 25,500 are related to drug abuse. For individuals between the ages of 20 and 40, deaths related to alcohol and drug abuse include such things as automobile crashes (as well as other causes of traumatic death) and HIV/AIDS infection. For older populations, excessive alcohol consumption appears to be the leading cause of premature death. When one uses these figures to calculate potential losses to lifetime earnings, the estimated costs are $31.3 billion (for alcohol-related deaths) and $14.6 billion (for drug-related deaths) (ONDCP, 2001). This represents an average loss per death of almost $350,000.

Health Care, Treatment, and Families   Consider that one in five adults have either no health insurance or inadequate health care coverage (Centers for Disease Control and Prevention, 1998): This translates to more than 58 million Americans. Even more alarming is the fact that more than half (64 percent) of all individuals seeking health care treatment for substance-related disorders do not have insurance (SAMHSA, 2002). Next, factor in the health care costs assumed by victims of family violence (e.g., spouses and children) where substance abuse is involved. Similarly, children of alcoholics incur more than one and one-half times as many physical injuries as other children (not necessarily related to family violence) and end up accumulating more than 30 percent more in health care costs than children from nonalcoholic families (Nixon & Tivis, 1997).

Having spent many years in emergency rooms performing psychological assessments for individuals seeking substance abuse detoxification and treatment, the second author saw firsthand how devastating the costs of treatment and the coexisting lack of insurance can be to a family. I remember one particular individual who was brought in by his older brother. This 20-year-old patient was indigent at the time, sleeping in dumpsters behind restaurants, eating what he found, and spending every available dollar (some of it stolen) on crack cocaine. It is easy to look at such an individual and assume, "Well, he brought it on himself; he deserves the consequences of his actions"—except when one considers the family he left behind, the family to whom he turned after attempting suicide, the family who now wanted to help this young man obtain treatment for the first time.

Since most patients expect the "insurance question" at the beginning of a psychological assessment, the junior author made it a practice to intentionally leave that question until the end of the interview. This was done so that a therapeutic alliance could be established and so that the patient could feel (momentarily at least) that insurance coverage does not dictate appropriate and courteous human contact and service. But like so many patients before him, as well as those to follow, the insurance question was answered with a resounding, "Look at me, how can *I* afford insurance? And my family ain't got none either! I guess we're done here." Even after exploring the care and treatment available for the uninsured in our county (which involved him being sent to a state facility 3 hours from his home), the patient was ready to leave—he had been insulted by my question and the options I had to present. But before he stepped away, his brother wanted to plead his case with me, even after he understood that I had nothing to do with the allocation of health care coverage and treatment. This man was willing to sell his car, mortgage his home, take on a second job—whatever it took to get his brother into treatment and maintain his sobriety. After carefully providing some reality testing while maintaining the dignity of the individual patient (which amounted to my tactfully attempting to explain the cyclical pattern of substance abuse and treatment and that the family may very well end up losing what they put up as collateral), this brother did what he felt he had to: He provided for his family member. Against my advice, the family was provided with contact information for the best treatment facility in the county. Did the individual complete treatment? Did the family lose all that they owned? I never found out, but the *slightly* cynical part of me (an unfortunate side effect of treating clients with addictive disorders) believes that they might have lost everything. And this is just one story—it occurs all over the United States as families lose millions of dollars trying to finance medical expenses for those whom they love.

Job Productivity Losses Losses related to substance abuse can be devastating and sometimes permanent for individuals and families. Both for those who seek treatment, as well as for those who lose their lives as a result of an addictive disorder, not reporting to work on Monday morning is too often a reality. But for those who do make it to their jobs, what additional costs are incurred?

By far, the biggest drain to the U.S. economy in terms of substance abuse is in productivity losses, to the tune of approximately $129 billion annually (ONDCP, 2004). This figure includes both work *not* performed (i.e., lost earnings) and the lack of household duties completed. Another $29 billion in lost productivity is attributed to alcohol-related motor vehicle crashes (Taylor, Miller, & Cox, 2002). Employers are especially vulnerable to the impact of alcohol-related employee traffic accidents, saving an additional $15 billion if they could eliminate such incidents among their paid drivers (National Highway Traffic Safety Administration, 2004).

An estimated 26 million working-age individuals meet criteria for substance dependence (ONDCP, 2001). It is no wonder that these American workers have more job-related accidents, suffer more job-related fatalities, and miss more days of work than their non-drug/alcohol abusing coworkers. In fact, an incredible 500 million workdays are lost each year due to the effects of alcoholism (U.S. Department of Labor [DOL], 1996). Substance abuse is also a huge factor in workplace violence, rated in the top four reasons for why and how this violence occurs (DOL, 1996). Similarly, drug-abusing workers cost employers more than twice the amount of money in medical and worker compensation claims than their substance-free coworkers (NIDA, n.d.2). Other workplace costs can be attributed to lost wages as a result of incarcerated workers, a topic that better falls under the Crime and Punishment section.

Productivity and the Family Janet and Ricardo presented for couples counseling during the junior author's employment at a community mental health clinic. Among the presenting concerns, Janet complained about Ricardo's lack of job stability and the resulting financial hardship and transitory nature of their lifestyle. Ricardo, on the other hand, bragged that he had held every job known to man. I vividly remember him once commenting, "Doc, no matter what the topic of conversation, I can tell you a story about something that happened to me on one job or another that'll make your hair stand on end" (quite an accomplishment given the author's lack of hair!). As I frequently do with couples, I asked to see each individual separately for the next session so as to determine their perceptions of the presenting concerns. In searching for an underlying common denominator for Ricardo's apparent lack of job consistency, Ricardo offered up the fact that most employers were "jerks" (my word, not his) and that he didn't like to feel controlled by others. He also shared, with prompting, that he had lost more jobs than he had left voluntarily, again attributing his dismissals to managerial blunders and micromanaging. He also shared that he took full advantage of any available unemployment benefits, stating, "These companies have so much money, they can afford to help me out while I'm looking for another job."

The next session with Janet painted a very different picture. It became apparent that Janet compensated for Ricardo, making excuses for him, justifying his bad temper and need for control, and siding with his assessment of his many employers. Given that Ricardo's infrequent use of alcohol had been assessed during the intake interview, I naturally wanted to understand what "infrequent" meant to Janet. She replied, "He only drinks a couple of beers per night." "A couple of beers," I replied. "What kind of beer does he like to drink?" This may appear at first to be a cursory question, but the responses are usually very important. "He likes Olde English, but I can't stand the taste of it." Having worked in the field for a while, I quickly recognized that Olde English was a cheap malt beverage (higher liquor content) that comes in only one size: 40 ounces (versus the regular 12). Well *that* certainly put a different spin on the session! I went on, "Janet, how much do you think Ricardo's drinking has to do with his job history?" She initially replied that she didn't see the connection, but throughout my work with the couple, they were able to determine that his "drinking habits" (as they called it) most likely had an impact on his job performance and history. Over the course of therapy, Janet came to recognize how her enabling behaviors (to be defined and discussed later in this book), such as calling in to work for Ricardo when he had had too much to drink the night before, or flatly accepting Ricardo's interpretations of employers' behaviors toward him as being out of his control, perpetuated the drinking habit. In time, Ricardo also accepted that he needed more intensive treatment for his alcohol consumption and lifestyle choices.

One of the deciding factors for Ricardo finally accepting some responsibility for his behaviors was when he was asked to tally up the amount of money that he had spent on his drinking habits over the course of the last three years. To that amount, I asked him to add the total for such things as lost security deposits (from when the couple had to suddenly move to a new location for a new job), moving costs, auto repairs (as a result of alcohol-induced accidents), and family medical costs (due to a lack of insurance). Finally, to that number I asked him to estimate both the amount of money spent by each *new* company to train him to do the work he performed as well as the amount of money spent by each *previous* employer on unemployment compensation. The final tally surprised him enough to break through some of his minimizations. It was enough to get him to take a serious look at the costs of continued drinking and was enough to get him into a treatment program. Sometimes, clients need to clearly see the *dollar* signs before they accept the other signs of substance-induced losses.

Crime and Punishment   Of the $180.9 billion spent by society to compensate for drug abuse, more than half can be attributed to drug-related crime. The National Institute on Drug Abuse (2004b) noted that more than 20 percent of these costs involve lost productivity of both victims and incarcerated perpetrators of drug-related crimes. Another 20 percent is ascribed to the lost potential of lifetime productivity for career offenders, and almost 19 percent is spent on fighting drug-related crime (e.g., federal drug traffic control, property damage, and police, legal, and correctional services).

It should come as no surprise that alcohol and drugs play a major role in crime rates, particularly violent crime. More than one half of all homicides and assaults are directly related to alcohol and drug consumption (Cychosz, 1996; Martin, 2001). Similarly, 25 to 30 percent of all income-generating crime is drug-related (ONDCP, 2001). In fact, of those juveniles incarcerated at any one time, a stunning 66 percent meet criteria for substance dependency (Office of Juvenile Justice and Delinquency Prevention [OJJDP], 1994). In terms of substance-related crime costs, victims again assume the brunt of the costs: amounting to $11.8 billion. These include lost earnings of homicide victims, medical expenses, and lost time at work, with another $2.6 billion in lost cash and property (ONDCP, 2001).

Besides outright violence and crime, substance abuse, most notably alcohol consumption, costs billions of dollars as a result of motor vehicle crashes. Taylor, Miller, and Cox (2002) were tasked by the National Highway Traffic Safety Administration to determine the economic costs of such crashes, and the results are staggering. First, in 26 percent of all crashes in the United States, alcohol played a significant factor, costing the U.S. economy an estimated $114.3 billion in 2000. This figure included $51.1 billion in direct monetary losses (e.g., lost productivity, medical costs, property damage, and health care) and $63.2 billion in quality-of-life losses (e.g., death, dismemberment, lost loved ones). Of these total costs, nondrinking drivers paid more than half ($71.6 billion). In other words, for each drink consumed in the United States, $1 is drained out of the economy as a result of impaired drinkers, $.60 of which is paid by nondrinking drivers. Sadly, in 2000, more than 2 million alcohol-related crashes killed more than 16,000 people and injured more than 500,000 individuals.

Crime and the Family   Some of the most devastating affects of any addiction are the crimes perpetrated on family members and loved ones. Much research has demonstrated the correlation between substance abuse and family violence. For example, one study found that more than half of all male alcoholics are violent toward their female partners (O'Farrell, Fals-Stewart, Murphy, & Murphy, 2003). Other studies have demonstrated that two thirds of all cases of partner abuse are perpetrated by a partner under the influence of alcohol, whereas the number jumps to three fourths for all spouse abuse cases (Greenfeld, 1998). National studies indicate that more than 90 percent of perpetrators of family violence had used alcohol and other drugs (AOD) the day of their arrests and more than 70 percent had a criminal history of AOD-related offenses (Bureau of Justice Statistics, 2005). Similarly, for those men seeking treatment for a substance-related disorder, partner violence is more than 50 percent more likely than for those who do not abuse chemicals (Schumacher, Fals-Stewart, & Leonard, 2003). Finally, AOD abuse is also a common factor found in most cases of sexual assault (Koss & Gaines, 1993).

Perhaps even more disturbing are the effects of parental substance abuse and crimes against children. More than 40 percent of adults are exposed to family alcoholism as children and more than one in five children are raised by an alcoholic parent (Eigen & Rowden, 1996). Scores of studies have demonstrated the devastating impact of parental substance abuse on children, ranging from neglect, psychological abuse, sexual abuse, and physical abuse (e.g., Bavolek & Henderson, 1990; Dore, Doris, & Wright, 1995; National Center on Child Abuse and Neglect, 1993). As a result, children of substance-abusing parents often develop their own addictive disorders and almost always exhibit emotional and behavioral problems (including aggression and violence) throughout their lifetimes (Claydon, 1987; Fals-Stewart, Kelley, Fincham, Golden, & Logsdon, 2004; Widom, 1993).

One cannot work in the field of substance abuse treatment without encountering victims and perpetrators of abusive or violent family crimes. It is inevitable, and frustratingly enough, the same person can be both victim (e.g., of childhood violence) and perpetrator (i.e., current abuser). To be honest, though I have worked with scores of such clients, without some careful introspection and consultation, I sometimes find myself reacting somewhat negatively to perpetrators of family violence. For example, I remember my first time encountering a violent client while working in an intensive outpatient substance abuse facility. I had been working with an older African American male named Darryl for several weeks. Darryl was a charmer, always on time, always ready with the right answer in group, and always willing to follow directives. However, he was also extremely superficial, always deflecting personal inquiries. One day, before the evening program began, I was paged by the front desk that Darryl's wife had arrived seeking my consultation. I was all prepared to receive accolades for all the terrific work I had been doing with her husband. What I was not prepared for was the battered face and frightened eyes that met me in the waiting room.

Darryl's wife related a long and tearful story of physical and sexual abuse at the hands of her husband, something that she had never shared with anyone. After allowing her to share the details of her husband's behaviors, she said something that continues to haunt me: "Can you guarantee that this program will work for Darryl? Will you promise me that if Darryl gets clean, he won't beat me anymore? Because if he does it one more time, I'm going to leave him and never look back. I want to know if I should stick around." Believe me when I say that, one, I wanted with every bone of my body to make just that promise to her and that, two, I wanted to visit some of my own wrath upon Darryl (just being honest here). But I couldn't do either of these, and I knew it. What I did instead was help her to make safety plans to prepare for the next time that Darryl's mood or drinking escalated (which included referrals for her own safety and therapy) and encouraged her to report any such acts to the legal system. As this was an "unofficial" session, and given that she was neither a client of mine nor a client of the center, I believe that I did the best that I could within the setting and circumstances.

From that point on, I had to be very careful about how I handled Darryl in the remaining days of his treatment—I had to balance my not allowing him to be superficial with my desire to "call him to task" for his violent tendencies at home. I constantly had to evaluate my interactions with him to determine what would be best for his sobriety (this was his first time through treatment) and his home life (trying to teach anger management skills, but in such a way as to not betray his wife's trust). Darryl ended up leaving treatment against medical advice, his wife was contacted, and that was the last that we heard from either of them. As I have learned from so many clients following this lesson, substance abuse and violence are a volatile mix that require strategic interventions and treatment models like the one that we offer later in this text.

Social Welfare Programs   Whereas the U.S. economy once allotted social service benefits to individuals with a primary impairment due to alcohol or drug consumption (paying out $10.4 billion annually), it no longer does so (ONDCP, 2001). A study by the Office of the Assistant Secretary for Planning and Evaluation (1994) found that many of those who received social support also reported illicit drug use in the past month. This included more than 10 percent of those who received Aid to Families with Dependent Children (AFDC), 10 percent of those receiving Medicaid support, and 10 percent of those using food stamps. Progress has been made, but a large percentage of welfare recipients (between 30 and 40 percent) continue to abuse alcohol and other drugs, but not to such a point that it would impair their ability to secure gainful employment if it were sought (ONDCP, 2001).

Another source of social service expenditures is for the homeless population. Approximately half of all homeless individuals have been diagnosed with a substance abuse disorder during their lifetimes, with alcoholism being the largest part of that percentage (as much as 40 percent of the homeless population) (SAMHSA, 2003b). Of those who qualify as chronically homeless (i.e., those who remain homeless over a 7- to 8-month period), most (more than 50 percent) suffer from a co-occurring substance abuse and mental health disorder (Randolph, 2004).

Social Welfare and the Family As noted, many who claim aid for their families abuse chemicals. It should be no surprise then that the majority of welfare worker caseloads consist of families that struggle with substance abuse disorders in one form or another. Within the child welfare system, more than 50 percent of families struggle with chemical dependency (Dore, Doris, & Wright, 1995; National Center on Child Abuse and Neglect, 1993). Similarly, other than the resulting abuse and neglect that was mentioned earlier, another consequence is adolescent runaways, who utilize many forms of social support, with more than 75 percent of such children reporting parental substance abuse (Family and Youth Services Bureau, 1995). Madison was one such adolescent runaway with whom I worked. She was admitted to our residential treatment facility for heroin dependence at the age of 19. Having survived on the street for 4 years, this was Madison's 22nd time through substance abuse treatment, and according to her, our facility (with its therapeutic community) was her last stop before she gave up on life.

Madison, like so many runaway and addicted adolescents, had turned to prostitution to finance her drug habit. Having lost her virginity to her alcoholic stepfather who began molesting her at age 9, Madison hit the streets in search of something better, only to find more of life's cruelties. As a consequence of her prostitution or use of needles, Madison was HIV positive when she sought treatment "one last time." When I began working with her, she had virtually given up on life; suicide appeared like a viable option to her. I remember her once saying, "What use is it for me to go on anyway, I mean, who's gonna want a girlfriend, let alone a wife, who has slept with more guys than she can count and who has AIDS to boot?" Thankfully, Madison's story is a successful one: After connecting her with a strong and supportive community that, among other things, assisted her with obtaining an education and teaching her job skills, Madison found a new lease on life. She actually went on to become a student in a social work program the last time I heard from her.

But I want to revisit the main reason for sharing her story at this point in the chapter: Before coming to our facility, Madison had been through 22 treatment programs, each funded by a governmental, educational, philanthropic, or religious organization. Thankfully, our program worked for her, but there is no telling how many resources were used on her before she finally decided to choose a different path. And she is just one example among millions. But given that a large percentage of all social welfare recipients receive their assistance due to a combination of substance abuse and psychiatric disorders, let us also take a look at the impact of substance abuse on these related disorders.

Mental Health Care Costs　The comorbid and exacerbating effects of addictive disorders on mental health disorders have been firmly established. In fact, it is often extremely difficult to assess for chemical dependency as it is often hidden, intentionally or not, behind other presenting psychiatric issues, such as depression, suicide attempts, or anxiety (Deans & Soar, 2005; Sealy, 1999). Results from the 2002 *National Survey on Drug Use and Health* (SAMHSA, 2003a) indicated a high rate of co-occurrence between serious mental illness (SMI) and substance abuse/dependence disorders. In fact, at least 23 percent of adults with SMI are dependent on alcohol and other drugs. Given that the total expenditures for mental health needs totaled $85 billion (SAMHSA, 2003a), and given the difficulty in teasing out which disorder (i.e., mental health versus substance disorder) is treated as the primary disorder, a possible $19.5 billion of the mental health expenditures is likely due to substance dependence.

Mental Health and the Family　As noted earlier, family members of addicted individuals often develop their own psychiatric and addictive disorders. For example, spouses often develop complications such as depression, anxiety, obsessive-compulsive disorder, suicidality, personality disorders, and sexual and sleep disorders (Brennan, Hammen, Katz, &

Le Brocque, 2002; Schneider, 2000; Whisman, Sheldon, & Goering, 2000), as well as their own addictive disorders to such things as chemicals, food, spending, and sex (DeLucia, Belz, & Chassin, 2001; von Ranson, McGue, & Iacono, 2003; Weinberg, 2001). Not surprisingly, children and adolescents of substance-abusing parents also experience greater addictive and mental health problems than those from non-using families (Lambie & Sias, 2005). In fact, these children and adolescents are many times more likely to be admitted for inpatient hospitalization for substance abuse and mental health concerns throughout their lifetimes (Biederman, Faraone, Monuteaux, & Feighner, 2000; Duncan, Duncan, & Hops, 1996).

In my work with addicted families, it is a rare occurrence to find a family that has members who are *not* experiencing other psychiatric or addictive disorders. One such family comes readily to mind. The Gonzalez family struggled with their eldest daughter's abuse of club drugs, namely ecstasy and ketamine. I met Jasmine and her family after she had been admitted to the intensive care unit (ICU) at the hospital where I worked. Her parents had rushed her to the emergency room after finding her unconscious in her car in their driveway, covered in her own vomit. The attending physician reported that she had stopped breathing in the emergency room, was resuscitated, and was admitted to the ICU where she remained in a coma.

In speaking with the patient's mother, I gathered some background information about Jasmine. At 22 years old, she had just graduated college and returned home to live with her parents until she could secure a new job. The mother reported that the patient's boyfriend of 3 years had recently joined the military and moved out of state, and as a result, Jasmine had been "depressed since he left town." In asking what "depressed" *meant*, the mother reported that Jasmine had been sleeping more than normal, had not been eating more than one small meal a day, and had reported feeling depressed for 3 weeks. In exploring any recent behavioral changes, the mother reported that her daughter had "hooked up" with an old group of friends in the neighborhood and had started attending all-night parties ("she calls them 'raves'") with them. The mother also stated that Jasmine shared the fact that she had taken ecstasy on several occasions ("and something called 'Special K'?"), which was particularly shocking to the mother given that, to her knowledge, Jasmine had never used drugs in high school or college. The first time she used ecstasy, Jasmine slept through the following day of work but didn't think much of it since it was "only one time." In the last month, Jasmine had missed approximately 3 days of work and, as a result, was in jeopardy of losing her job. The mother concluded the initial interview with the following statement: "It doesn't matter how much we fight her about hanging out with those kids, she just answers back with how much she loves how she feels when she is 'rolling' and thinks it is all in fun. I don't know what I'm going to do with her, but if she keeps this up, she can find someplace else to live."

During the next interview I was able to spend more time with Jasmine's mother and father (Jasmine had not yet regained consciousness). I immediately sensed hostility from Jasmine's father, who sat silently throughout the time I spent speaking with her mother. In assessing the family's background, Jasmine's mother reluctantly admitted that there was a family history of marijuana use (Jasmine's brother), alcohol ("her father drinks, but not a *lot*"), and anxiety ("I suffer panic attacks from time to time"). Now granted, I wanted to ascertain what "not a lot of drinking" meant, but I sensed that I wouldn't get much at that point in the interview and wanted to keep the focus on what could be done for Jasmine. Whereas the mother desired to have her daughter admitted to a substance abuse treatment facility, the father spoke up at last with, "She doesn't need that. She just needs to stay at home and not go out with those other kids!" It took several additional meetings with the two of them (Jasmine remained in the coma for 8 days) to help them accept the need for follow-up treatment for their daughter. I believe that their final decision in agreeing to have her admitted was due to the fact that they almost lost their daughter.

The point of this story was to reintegrate the family connection between substance abuse and other psychiatric/addictive disorders. I believed that Jasmine's substance abuse was a medicative response to her depression and that, given the family's use of substances, this must have seemed like an appropriate choice for her at the time. I also assumed that the mother's anxiety disorder went hand in hand with her attempt to control the amount of substances being abused in her home. As with other comorbid disorders, it is often difficult to determine if the anxiety preempted, or resulted from, this substance abuse. Nonetheless, the connection between the two was evident in this family, as well as the other families that I have worked with throughout my clinical experiences.

Impacts of Process Addictions

At this point, we have identified the societal and familial costs of substance abuse disorders. However, scarce data is available concerning the tangible and intangible societal and familial costs of addictions to such things as sex, gambling, eating, the Internet, and spending. One reason for the lack of such information goes back to our argument earlier in the chapter regarding the legitimacy of these disorders. That is, legitimacy leads to funding for research, which leads to empirical data, which leads back to legitimacy of the disorders. Given that the definitions can be unclear and that the prevalence of addictive disorders appears to be increasing rapidly, scholars have been relatively slow to gather timely data. As such, some of the following information is gathered primarily from the clinical versus research arenas and is often reported in the popular press—our hope is that future researchers will gather the resources necessary to corroborate or refute what is being claimed by clinical and anecdotal data. In the following pages, we will briefly highlight some of the projected costs associated with the better-understood, and therefore more costly, process addictions: those to sex, gambling, and the Internet. Following the exploration of such projected societal costs, we will note how these disorders negatively impact families in ways similar to the aforementioned impacts of substance-related disorders.

Costs of Sexual Addiction   Sexually addicted individuals contribute to detrimental societal expenditures in areas such as the workplace, the health care arena, the legal system, and the adult entertainment industry (Benotsch, Kalichman, & Pinkerton, 2001; Carnes, 1992; Delmonico & Griffin, 1997; Goodman, 2001; National Council on Sexual Addiction and Compulsivity, 2000). A brief look at each area is warranted.

Lost Productivity in the Workplace   Similar to the lost hours attributed to employee alcohol and drug use (e.g., employee absenteeism, decreased productivity, job-related injury), those addicted to sex cost employers (and therefore society at large) significant monies. These losses include both lost work hours and litigation resulting from inappropriate workplace behaviors. For example, among issues raised by most employers, restricting employee access to pornographic material while at work has become the number one concern (American Management Association, 2001). Additional facts related to employee use of Internet-based pornography include the following:

- Of the 38,000 respondents to a survey conducted by MSNBC, approximately 20 percent access pornographic materials *primarily* at work (Laino, 2002).
- The U.S. Department of Commerce (2002) concludes that at least 13 percent of U.S. Census respondents access sexual sites at work.
- Internet tracking companies like SexTracker, Vault.com, and Wordtracker.com report that about 70 percent of all visits to pornographic sites occur during normal business hours, with a noted lull during lunch hours (Work & Family Connection, 2001).
- Twenty-five percent of employees admit to visiting a pornographic site at work (Seminerio, 1997).

- Of the disciplinary actions taken against employees with regard to e-mail or Internet use, almost 80 percent were of a sexual matter (American Management Association, 2001).

But accessing and viewing pornography is not the only sexual-related act committed during business hours. Sexual harassment in the workplace, often a large part of sexual addicts' behavior patterns (particularly for those in administrative positions), results in significant legal difficulties (National Council on Sexual Addiction and Compulsivity [NCSAC], 2000). Given that the average cost to litigate a sexual harassment claim is $250,000 and the average cost to settle a claim is almost 10 times that amount (N2H2, 2002), significant financial strain is felt by those industries impacted by these behaviors. Significant costs have also stemmed from malpractice suits and the personal destruction experienced by those who have fallen prey to sexually addicted health care and religious professionals. Many have reported sexual exploitation at the hands of medical doctors, helping professionals (e.g., psychologists, therapists, etc.), and even dentists (Cohen, Woodward, Ferrier, & Williams, 1995; Garrett, 1999; McPhedran, 1996; Penfold, 1998). Similarly, growing numbers of clergy are being charged with various forms of sexually inappropriate behavior (McCall, 2002; Wells, 2003). Granted, all of these individuals may not be sexually addicted, but given that over 50 percent of sexual exploitation cases by professionals are committed by those that *are* sexually addicted (NCSAC, 2000), there exists a high likelihood that addictive tendencies are at play in these cases.

How much of this lost productivity can be attributed to sexual addicts? While the direct answer to that question is beyond the scope of this chapter, the implied answer may be staggering. When Carnes (1992) surveyed 1,000 sexual addicts, 80 percent admitted to lowered job productivity, often as a result of pursuing sexual encounters, sexual fantasy while at work, or exhaustion from staying up too late while engaging in sexually addictive behaviors. Approximately 27 percent revealed that they had lost the opportunity to remain in their preferred career (Carnes, 1990). Come forward in time to the present: With the advances in Internet technology and the resulting increased access to sexually explicit material, lowered job productivity and ruined careers due to inappropriate behaviors implicitly cost society millions, if not billions, of dollars.

Health Care Costs   For the sexual addict, there is an intuitively high risk for obtaining a sexually transmitted disease (STD) (Institute of Medicine, 1997; National Institute of Allergy and Infectious Diseases

[NIAID], 1999; NCSRC, 2000). This includes both direct costs (payments for medical and nonmedical services and materials) and indirect costs (lost wages due to illness or premature death). There are also the intangible costs related to pain, suffering, and diminished quality of life (Institute of Medicine, 1997). Given that Carnes's 1992 study found that 68 percent of sexually addicted individuals had been exposed to AIDS and various STDs, a crude cost can be generated by taking the 68 percent (that is, 68 percent of the 17 to 37 million sexually addicted individuals) and then dividing this number into the annual medical expenditures for the treatment of these diseases. The resulting cost is subsumed by individuals, institutions, and insurance companies.

Sex-Related Crime Costs Like any other addiction, sexual addiction is a progressive disorder. That is, similar to the alcoholic who begins with one beer each night and progresses steadily toward a fifth of whiskey per day, the sexual addict can progress from occasional use of pornography to more intense (and sometimes destructive) sexual behaviors. These behaviors range from the use of prostitution and massage parlors, to more exploitive behaviors such as voyeurism and exhibitionism, to destructive acts such as addictive incest and rape. Although many sexual addicts do not progress past self-indulgent compulsive behaviors, others find themselves driven by the addictive nature of sex to more risky, intense, and exploitative acts (Delmonico & Griffin, 1997; NCSAC, 2000). With these more intense sexual acts come legal ramifications. As many as 58 percent of sexual addicts have experienced such legal consequences (Carnes, 1992). In fact, approximately 55 percent of incarcerated sex offenders meet criteria for sexual addiction (as opposed to those that meet criteria for strictly offending behaviors), with child molesters representing the largest group (71 percent meeting criteria for sexual addiction) (NCSAC, 2000).

In attempting to assign a monetary value to these behaviors, one might begin with the number of incarcerated sexual addicts, multiply that number by the typical length of stay for each offense, multiply that number by the cost of incarceration, and then include judicial system costs such as lawyers, judges, court costs, and police involvement. One can quickly see that the tangible costs accrue quickly.

Adult Entertainment Costs It should come as no surprise that the sexually addicted individual's "drug of choice" is sexually stimulating material. By most estimates, the legal (i.e., not including prostitution and other illicit sexual behaviors) adult entertainment industry earns between $8 and $12 billion annually (Flint, 1996; Sussman, 1999). Additional personal costs might be calculated by including the impact on those who work within the adult entertainment industry, including illicit drug use and overdose, psychiatric disorders such as depression and resulting suicide, and unwanted children.

While there are no estimates as to how much of the adult industry is financed by those who are sexually addicted, given that (a) between 17 and 37 million Americans suffer from this addictive disorder and (b) 50 percent of alcohol sales are consumed by 10 percent of drinkers (Nakken, 1996), one might assume that 50 percent ($6 billion) is spent by sexually addicted individuals for adult entertainment. Given these figures, the financial difficulties experienced by sexual addicts (including the purchase of pornography, the use of prostitutes, telephone and computer service costs, travel for the purpose of sexual contacts, and other sexual activities) can deplete the individual's and family's financial resources, sometimes to the point of bankruptcy (NCSAC, 2000). Carnes (1992) noted that as many as 60 percent of sexual addicts have faced such financial difficulties.

Whereas no empirical data is available to support the final tangible costs attributed to sexual addiction, Hagedorn (2005) asserted that if one tallied the dollars spent on lost productivity, health care, crime, and the adult entertainment industry, a *very* conservative final count would amount to more than $10.5 billion annually. Granted, more research is necessary to substantiate this amount, especially since it appears significantly lower than costs attributed to other addictive disorders that impact smaller numbers of individuals. But the point should be clear at this point: Unmediated sexual addiction costs the U.S. economy money that it doesn't have to spend.

Sexual Addiction and the Family   As one might imagine, sexual addiction has negative impacts for the partners and children of those addicted to sex. Schneider (2000) noted how spouses and partners experience feelings of hurt, betrayal, rejection, abandonment, shame, loneliness, anger, jealousy, and destroyed self-esteem. Carnes (1992) reported that 70 percent experience severe marital or relationship difficulties and that 40 percent lose a partner or spouse as a result of their sexual addiction. Carnes contended that partners of sexual addicts often develop their own addictions and compulsions, including codependence, psychosomatic problems, depression, and other emotional difficulties.

Children also suffer as a result of their addicted parents' behaviors. Children are often exposed to pornography at a young age, are often involved in parental conflicts, and often lack the necessary nurturing attention of the addicted parent. Further, they often have to endure the dissolution of marriage when one partner decides to leave the other (Carnes, 1992; Schneider, 2000). Similar to chemical addiction, sexual addiction is definitely a family disease.

The majority of my private practice work has been dedicated to working with individuals struggling with sexual addiction, the majority of which have been men. Whereas some clients have proactively sought therapy for sexual addiction, the vast majority have done so as a result of "getting caught in the act" by significant others, employers, and law enforcement officers. One example was 57-year-old Erik. Married for 27 years, the father of four children (ages 19 to 25), Erik was very forthcoming as to the extent of the issues for which he was seeking counseling. "My wife caught me looking at pornographic Web sites on our home computer. This was the third time that she has confronted me and she said that I had to get help with this or she was going to seek out a separation." He confessed to being both perplexed and shamed by his behavior.

Over the course of therapy, Erik shared more of his background as it pertained to his sexual addiction. He revealed that he had first seen pornography around his teen years and that it had progressed to daily viewing for the last 8 to 10 years. Whereas he had once viewed what he named "normal pornography," which involved images of women, he had moved on to more explicit material. He had attempted several times to interrupt his maladaptive behaviors (e.g., getting involved in the community, meditation/prayer, exercise, and reading). While these behaviors had been somewhat successful in curtailing his addictive cycle, he had always returned to sexually acting out, particularly when he felt bored, lonely, or angry or when he felt that his wife wasn't sufficiently meeting his sexual and intimacy needs.

In terms of the consequences of his behaviors, he noted that his job performance was likely suffering. Since being caught at home, Erik had begun to view pornography primarily at work, spending up to 2 to 3 hours a day surfing the Internet and masturbating. Admitting to being fully aware that his company collected data on employee Internet use, he noted that this somehow intensified the experience for him: "Avoiding getting caught is just as exciting as actually seeing what's on the screen." The most significant consequence involved the damaged relationship with his wife, whom he brought in on three occasions for couple's counseling. Erik's wife, Marlyne, was confused about his need for sexual stimulation, blaming herself for not being pretty enough and not being responsive to his needs. We spent some significant time exploring the addictive nature of Erik's behaviors, as well as the fact that sex (in and of itself) had very little to do with Erik's current activities (i.e., it wasn't so much the *sex* that met Erik's need for stimulation as it was the increased frequency and intensity of his behaviors). Yet, Marlyne stated that she continued to feel useless and depressed and had taken to compulsive dieting to compensate for her feelings. Whereas the couple believed that the children were not aware of Erik's behaviors, Marlyne once said, "How can you look at those pictures—some of those girls are the same age as your daughters! How would you like it if someone was looking at them like that?!"

In the fifth session, while exploring the progressive nature of his addictive behaviors, Erik shared another aspect of his addictive cycle: "One night I was walking the dog around the neighborhood. I took the same route I always do, trying to clear my head after a real stressful day. And then *bam*—you wouldn't believe it but I saw one of the neighborhood women getting dressed. Why didn't she close her drapes? I don't know why it was such a draw, but it was truly mesmerizing—I couldn't look away. Well, after that first night, I started passing by that house on a regular basis, trying to catch another glimpse." Whereas his behaviors had not progressed to the point where it could be clinically diagnosed as voyeurism, he admitted that he wasn't far from it.

Erik's story is a successful one—after recognizing the impact he was having on his family, he came to desire sexual sobriety at any cost: He did not have to hit the kind of "rock bottom" that many have to experience before getting serious in their recovery. With continued individual therapy, support group attendance, daily accountability, and finally couples counseling, Erik was able to maintain his sobriety. But like other types of addicts, he recognized that he would need to continue "working a program" (i.e., engaging in healthy lifestyle choices instead of turning to addictive behaviors) for the rest of his life.

Costs of Addictive Gambling Gambling, similar to sex, is a socially sanctioned activity that receives support by the media, the legislature, and the entertainment industry. In fact, between 84 and 92 percent of all people in the United States gamble (APA, 2000; Blanco, Ibanez, Saiz-Ruiz, Blanco-Jerez, & Nunes, 2000; Friedenberg, Blanchard, Wulfert, & Malta, 2002). Facts and figures regarding the gaming industry are relatively easy to ascertain, such as the annual earnings of the gaming industry ($41 billion according to McMahon, 2002). Interestingly, this figure is greater than the combined revenues accumulated from movies, spectator sports, theme parks, cruise ships, and recorded music. Other interesting facts gleaned from PBS's *Frontline* (n.d.) public affairs series on the gambling industry include the following: (a) Forty-eight states (excluding Hawaii and Utah) endorse various forms of legal gambling, (b) more than 60 percent of

American adults report gambling on an annual basis, (c) Americans wager more than $480 billion annually, and (d) the fastest-growing industry in the world is Indian gambling, with annual revenues exceeding $27 billion.

While these statistics are interesting (and somewhat surprising!), what is most disturbing is that it is difficult to find statistics that speak to the detrimental impacts of this industry on individuals and families. This may be due to the fact that those governmental agencies responsible for funding such research are often waylaid by political lobbyists hired by the gaming industry who highlight the increased jobs, tax revenues, and entertainment qualities of gambling. As an example, in 1995, the gaming industry hired 74 lobbyists to assist gambling efforts in the state of Texas, amounting to more than two for every state senator and one for every two members of the Texas House of Representatives (PBS's *Frontline*, n.d.). Most likely, the number one reason that so little is known about the negative impacts of gambling is due to the huge financial contributions made to such areas as education, big business, and social reform. Funds for these areas would dry up quickly if problem areas were highlighted in greater detail by the media.

Pathological gambling (the *DSM* designation for addictive gambling) impacts between 2 and 11 percent (6 to 32 million) of Americans (APA, 2004; Blanco et al., 2000; Friedenberg et al., 2002; Shaffer & Korn, 2002). With little known about the direct financial burdens associated with family debt, insurance payouts, medical payments, lost productivity (some estimate that the problem gambler works at only 50 percent capacity), and the criminal justice system, the National Opinion Research Council (NORC) estimated that problem and pathological gamblers cost society in the neighborhood of $5 billion per year and an additional $40 billion in lifetime costs for lost productivity, social services, and creditor losses (NORC, 1999). Others have estimated the societal costs to be much higher, with society spending approximately $13,000 per addicted gambler when one considers treatment costs, lost productivity, criminal activity, and judicial costs (Thompson, 1994). Using the prevalence rates noted above, this amounts to between $78 and $416 billion (quite a difference!). Similarly, approximately one fourth of the annual revenues of casinos and state lotteries result from monies spent by problem and pathological gamblers (PBS's *Frontline*, n.d.), which leads to tremendous financial debt and ruin for individuals and families.

Addictive Gambling and the Family   Several individual and familial costs have been attributed to addictive gambling (APA, 2000; Florida Council on Compulsive Gambling, 2004; Friedenberg et al., 2002;

Lamberton & Oei, 1997; Ledgerwood, Steinberg, Wu, & Potenza, 2005). For example, extensive legal problems are common. In fact, two thirds of compulsive gamblers admit to such acts as claiming bankruptcy, engaging in embezzlement, or committing fraudulent acts to illegally finance a gambling habit. Similarly, skipping out of financial obligations (i.e., bill collectors) occurs frequently. Health problems such as high blood pressure, heart disease, and stroke plague the addictive gambler. Other health concerns occur due to the high comorbidity and exacerbation rates with other psychiatric and addictive disorders (e.g., substance-related disorders, mood disorders, ADHD, binge eating, and obsessive-compulsive disorders) as well as the high suicide rates. In fact, 70 percent of addicted gamblers contemplate suicide and 20 to 40 percent actually attempt suicide—making it the highest suicide rate among those struggling with addictive disorders. Finally, family problems include marital difficulties and low family cohesion (most often due to the strain placed on the family by the addictive gambling and the resulting financial ruin), as well as abuse (physical, emotional, and sexual), neglect (to both children and spouses), and high divorce rates. Although the tangible costs attributed to the aforementioned issues are difficult to ascertain, it should be apparent that gambling has definite negative consequences for individuals and families.

Jorgina and Claude sought premarital counseling to assist with preparing for their wedding. Interestingly, this was their second marriage—to each other! Initially married for 2 years with no children, Claude had left Jorgina when she had sent their small business into bankruptcy as a result of gambling. Owning a cleaning business with Claude, Jorgina had lost more than $35,000 at the casino that had been started in South Florida by the Seminole Indians. Having embezzled the funds, Jorgina spent 6 months in a minimum security prison, during which time Claude had divorced her.

Our first session occurred after they had been divorced for 3 years, had reunited one year prior, and in the interim Jorgina had given birth to Claude's baby daughter. Claude opened with, "Doc [why do clients so often start out that way?], there's no way that I want to go through what we did before—we used to fight like cats and dogs. I want to make an honest woman out of Jorgina, especially since we have a baby girl together. But I want to know how I can make sure she doesn't gamble anymore." Jorgina voiced similar concerns and appeared intent on making this second marriage work. As I've noted earlier, I began the next session seeing each client separately and was able to get more background on Jorgina's gambling addiction.

Jorgina began buying lottery tickets at 18. Before that, she admitted to struggling constantly with her weight, which, when assessed further, turned out to be an undiagnosed and untreated eating addiction (binge-ing). "It was so cool, though," Jorgina shared. "When I started with the lotto tickets, the food thing didn't become so important." After one lottery ticket paid off a large sum of money, Jorgina took her winnings to the horse track, where she quickly doubled her earnings. "And that was it for me—I was hooked! I loved that feeling of winning. I feel like I've been chasing that feeling ever since." She admitted to several negative consequences, including financial ruin (maxing out 13 different credit cards), the loss of her marriage, and the loss of her freedom (jail time). Whereas she hadn't struggled with gambling since her release, she was concerned that it was "just below the surface." Between the couple and me, we decided that con-tinued couple's counseling, in conjunction with support group attendance, was the best path to take. There was no doubt for the two of them that gambling was a problem for the entire family.

Costs of Internet Addictions   Whereas the majority of Internet activity continues to be related to sex (Cooper, 1998), addictive use of the Internet also includes such things as online gambling, spending, day-trading, and information seeking. Although it is difficult to differentiate between (a) those who are addicted to such things as sex or gambling who use the Internet as a medium to feed their addiction and (b) those who are truly addicted to the Internet (independent of the type of online activity), studies indicate that between 17 to 41 million Americans (6 to 14 percent of the general population) struggle with Internet addiction (Griffiths, 2003; Hall & Parsons, 2001; Young, 1999). These addicted individuals spend between 40 and 80 hours per week online and suffer from a variety of negative consequences.

Davis, Flett, and Besser (2002), Hall and Parsons (2001), and Young (1999) cite several detrimental impacts of Internet addiction. For exam-ple, such individuals typically experience decreased work productivity, which includes poor time management and procrastination, resulting in job losses and academic failures. Interpersonal problems, such as serious relationship difficulties with spouses, children, close friends, and other loved ones, are common (53 percent have reported such dilemmas). Physi-cal harm, such as that experienced by interactions with violent individuals met in real time after exchanging personal information online, is a seri-ous consequence. Common comorbid psychiatric-related problems, such as depression, paranoia, poor impulse control, and poor self-esteem, can be exacerbated by the Internet. Similarly, addictive gambling, addictive day-trading, and addictive spending all lead to tremendous financial diffi-culties for this population of Internet users. Legal problems, involving such crimes as online fraud, cyberstalking, sexual harassment, and child por-nography, have significant negative impacts, both on addicted users and on their victims. Finally, physical problems such as backaches, sleep depriva-tion, dry eyes, wrist and finger cramping, and carpal tunnel syndrome are all too common for those addicted to the Internet. To further demonstrate the societal costs of Internet addiction, we'll look more closely at just one of the above-cited negative impacts: lost productivity in the workplace.

The Internet is a valuable and often necessary tool for conducting busi-ness in the 21st century, but when such use gets out of control and begins to negatively impact productivity and success, employers take notice. Lost productivity in workplace settings has become a serious problem, with employers voicing employee non-work-related Internet use as their number one concern in terms of lost revenue (Young, 1999). But how does this lost productivity translate to dollars? One report noted that employ-ees who utilize the Internet for personal purposes (such as e-mail, online trading, shopping, scheduling travel plans, etc.) for just 1 hour a day cost businesses as much as $35 million a year (Snoddy, 2000). The survey results further revealed that 59 percent of Internet use at work was not related to employee projects.

Another report estimated that, on average, employees use the Internet for up to 2 hours per day for non-work-related activities and that one fourth to one half of all e-mail accessed at work is of a personal nature (TechRe-public, 2002). The same study noted that additional costs amounting to $10,000 to $100,000 (per company, per year) result from reductions in net-work efficiency (e.g., file downloading and e-mails with large attachments) and security risks (viruses that come attached to certain downloads and e-mails). Another report proposed the following: If an employee who earns an annual salary of $35,000 spends 20 percent of his or her time (which translates to 2 hours/day for an average workday) on the Internet engaging in non-work-related behaviors, this translates to $7,000 of wasted wages (Foster, 2001). Now, multiply that amount by the number of employees paid at that pay grade and add an additional 20 percent for the company's portion of Social Security payments, unemployment taxes, and worker's compensation insurance, and the results on a national level are staggering. So what is the proposed grand tally? It is predicted that Internet misuse and abuse costs U.S. industries annually between $1 and $54 billion (Cal-houn, 2005). Granted, that range is quite large, so perhaps the average of the two figures is most accurate ($27.5 billion). As a final example of the impact of employee Internet use on U.S. productivity, Calhoun cited the recent (i.e., 2005) 44-minute *Victoria's Secret* online production that was broadcast during the middle of the workweek. Logging just over 2 million viewers (not all of whom were at work), that one event was estimated to have cost an estimated $120 million in lost productivity.

How much of the aforementioned financial losses can be attributed to those addicted to the Internet? Well, currently we haven't been able to calculate that figure—research has been slow to respond to tabulating these figures as debates regarding the legitimacy of Internet addiction continue. But the implied answer must be in the billions of dollars given the number of Internet addicts who must work to support their Internet activities. Besides wasted dollars, other detrimental effects for the addicted Internet user include declined work performance (with increased errors), preoccupation with the Internet (obsessively anticipating the next log-on), late nights spent at work online (which impacts several other life domains), withdrawal from coworkers and friends, job dissatisfaction, and the threat of losing one's job/career.

Internet Addiction and the Family Familial impacts of Internet addiction are relatively easy to understand. If someone is spending more than 10 hours a week of their limited time at home on the computer, relationships with spouses, significant others, and children are bound to be negatively impacted. Young (1999) identified several such consequences on marriages. First, the unequal distribution of home responsibilities is common as the addicted individual withdraws further from such daily chores as child care, grocery shopping, washing the car, cooking, and mowing the lawn. Similarly, activities that were once shared by both individuals, those that helped sustain the marriage (e.g., weekly bridge games, nightly walks, weekends on the boat), are often postponed or canceled by those who become more entangled in the Internet. Whereas some may view increased Internet use as temporary, when the use does not decrease, increased altercations are common as the spouse who has been neglected begins to voice his or her concerns. Addicted individuals often respond with justifications for their online activities, which often increases the emotional distance in the home. Sadly, Internet addiction and cyberaffairs are cited with much more frequency as reasons for divorce and separation (Beard, 2002).

Paul was one such client who had caused his family significant distress as a result of his addictive use of the Internet, as well as other addictive disorders. Once a successful businessman, I met Paul during an intake assessment while working at an inpatient psychiatric hospital. As his presenting concern, Paul listed suicidal ideations and marijuana dependence, but after some initial rapport had been established, he admitted to an underlying daily reliance on the Internet.

Over the course of the last 12 months, Paul's Internet use had soared from 2 hours a week to a current 20+ hours a week. The focus of his computer use had been on trading stocks, as well as (admitted *very* reluctantly) interacting with various women in sexually related chat rooms. Both of these practices had cost him significant distress. First, over time, his compulsive day-trading had cost him and his family more than $45,000 (this was during the dot-com/Internet boom era of the 1990s), which had resulted in their having to sell their home, move to an apartment complex in a less desirable part of town, and his taking up of truck driving as a profession. Had these changes not been enough of a strain to a marriage of more than 17 years, Paul's wife had recently discovered an archive of e-mail from several women whom he had met online. Although Paul had not met with these women in real time, the discovery had been too much for her, and with his two children, she had left him 4 months ago. Since that time, Paul had progressed to daily use of marijuana to medicate a progressively worsening depression. The morning of the intake assessment, Paul admitted to standing in his kitchen with a knife held to his throat.

It should come as no surprise that I couldn't admit Paul with a primary diagnosis of Internet addiction, as that didn't "exist." Similarly, the cannabis dependence doesn't meet inpatient criteria, so we went with depression with suicidal ideations. As the exacerbating condition, I remember listing impulse control disorder not otherwise specified (NOS), but in following up on his case, I learned that it was never addressed during the course of his treatment. Paul was discharged 4 days later, and although that was the end of my contact with him, I suspect that his addictive tendencies with the Internet did not end then and there.

The Final Calculations

As we have hopefully demonstrated, there are significant familial impacts of addictive disorders. However, people tend to focus more on the bottom line. So, are you as interested as we are as to the final societal/tangible costs attributed to addictive disorders? Well, get ready! In terms of alcohol and other drugs (AOD), the U.S. economy spends $365.5 billion per year and Americans themselves waste in the neighborhood of $57 billion on illicit drugs (NIDA, 2004b). The conservative annual cost estimates for the process addictions that we explored include $10.5 billion (remember, that's low!) for sexual addiction, $247 billion for gambling (with Americans wagering more than $480 billion), and $27.5 billion for Internet addiction: Remember that other process addictions were not included in the final estimates. So, by our calculations, more than $1.1 trillion is spent by society and individuals! Just 7 years of allocating these funds elsewhere would result in the elimination of the U.S. national debt! Is it any wonder that we need a comprehensive treatment model that effectively addresses the multifaceted impacts of addictive disorders on individuals and families? In the next chapter we will present the various theories and models that have been developed to help individuals, families, friends, and practitioners understand the origins and pathways of addictive disorders.

Skill Builder

Question 1

In this chapter, we offered three definitions for addiction, two of which were lay definitions and one of which was clinical. Fill in the blanks below and briefly explain how you would use them in your work with addicted individuals and their families.

Definition #1

Addiction is an _____ _____ _____ _____ with an object or event in an attempt to <u>control</u> that which <u>cannot be</u>.

How might you use this definition?

_____

_____

_____

Definition #2

Addiction is an _____ _____ for something with an _____ _____ ability to satisfy that desire.

How might you use this definition?

_____

_____

_____

Definition #3

The _____ _____ _____ _____ for Mental Disorders categorizes addictive disorders into _____ and _____. Substance abuse is defined as a _____ use of chemicals that impacts _____ _____ _____ (out of four) major life domains and responsibilities. Substance-dependent individuals will likely experience _____ _____ _____ detrimental impacts as a result of their disorder.

How might you use this definition?

_____

_____

_____

Question 2

Place a "C" for "Chemical" or a "P" for "Process" next to each of the below items to distinguish between those that can become chemical addictions and those that can become process addictions.

___ Gambling	___ The Internet	___ Spending
___ Alcohol	___ Marijuana	___ Valium
___ Eating	___ Ecstasy (MDMA)	___ Television
___ Steroids	___ Shopping	___ Xanax
___ Sex	___ LSD	___ Nicotine
___ Cocaine	___ Work	___ Video Games
___ Heroin	___ Inhalants	___ Caffeine

Question 3

Identify the missing words below as they apply to the addictive disorder.

- In terms of criteria, neither _____ nor _____ is necessary for designating a behavior or substance as addictive.

- The two criteria necessary and sufficient for the designation of chemical addiction are (a) _____ _____ to _____ the use of one or more drugs and (b) _____ of drug use _____ substantial _____ _____.

- The definition for the addictive disorder incorporates many of the key elements from three other disorders, namely that of _____ _____, _____ _____ disorder, and _____ _____ disorder.

- The one criterion that best discounts the use of the term *impulsivity* to describe addictive-like behaviors is that an impulsive act is one that is _____ _____ to the _____ engaging in the behavior or to _____ who are _____ by that individual.

- The main difference between addiction and compulsion is that although addictive behaviors are often utilized to _____ _____ and other painful affects, they also produce _____ and _____, which rules out the diagnosis of _____.

- Cross addiction occurs when _____ _____ (e.g., alcohol) is _____ with another (e.g., exercise).

Question 4

Match the specific addictive disorder with the number of individuals who are estimated to struggle with that disorder. After this, answer the question.

Chemical addiction	17 to 41 million
Sexual addiction	14 million
Addictive gambling	6 to 15 million
Internet addiction	17 to 37 million
Addictive eating	11 to 58 million

- What are the three challenges associated with gathering accurate prevalence figures for addictive disorders?

_____

_____

_____

Question 5

Fill in the blanks in each of the following sentences, which highlight the major impacts of chemical and process addictions on a societal and familial level.

Impacts of Chemical Addiction

The total economic cost attributed to alcohol and drug abuse is $ _____ billion per year.

- $ _____ billion a year is devoted to the prevention and _____ of substance abuse complications.

- The annual expenditures on health care costs include services such as _____, _____, _____, training providers, and research expenditures.

- _____ is the leading preventable cause of death (more than 440,000 annually—approximately 1 out of every 5 deaths).

- More than 58 million Americans have no _____ insurance or inadequate _____ _____ coverage.

- By far, the biggest drain to the U.S. economy in terms of substance abuse is in _____ _____, to the tune of approximately $129 billion annually.

- More than half of all _____ and _____ are directly related to alcohol and drug consumption.

- For each drink consumed in the United States, $ _____ is drained out of the economy as a result of impaired drinkers.

- More than _____ percent of perpetrators of _____ violence had used alcohol and other drugs (AOD) the day of their arrests.

- Of those who qualify as chronically homeless, most suffer from a co-occurring _____ _____ and _____ disorder.

- Within the public child welfare system, more than _____ percent of families struggle with chemical dependency.

- Almost _____ in _____ adults with serious mental illness is dependent on alcohol and other drugs.

Impacts of Process Addictions

- Data concerning the tangible and intangible societal and familial costs of process addictions are scarce due in part to the lack of _____ afforded these disorders.

- Among concerns raised by most employers, _____ _____ access to _____ material while at work has become the number one concern.

- _____ percent of all visits to pornographic sites occur during normal business hours, with a noted _____ during lunch hours.

- Medical costs for sexually transmitted diseases range annually from $ _____ to $ _____ billion.

- Approximately 55 percent of incarcerated _____ _____ meet criteria for sexual addiction.

- The sexually addicted individual's "drug of choice" is _____ _____ _____.

- The spouses and partners of sexual addicts experience feelings of hurt, _____, rejection, _____, shame, loneliness, _____, _____, and destroyed self-esteem.

- Between 84 and 92 percent of all people in the United States _____.

- Approximately one fourth of the annual revenues of casinos and state lotteries result from monies spent by _____ and _____ gamblers.

- Familial costs attributed to addictive gambling include extensive _____ problems, health problems, _____ difficulties, and low _____ cohesion.

- The addictive disorder with the highest suicide rates (70 percent contemplate suicide and 20 to 40 percent actually attempt suicide) is _____.

- Addictive use of the Internet also includes such things as online sex, _____, spending, _____, and information seeking.

- Addicted individuals spend between __ and __ hours per week online and suffer from a variety of negative consequences.

- The detrimental impacts of Internet addiction include decreased _____ _____, _____ problems, physical difficulties, comorbid psychiatric problems, financial difficulties, and _____ problems.

- Employers voice employee non-work-related Internet use as their number one concern in terms of _____ _____.

- Negative consequences of Internet addiction on marriages include the unequal distribution of responsibilities, lack of _____ activities, increased altercations, emotional distance, and _____.

- The final societal/tangible costs attributed to addictive disorders equal more than $ _____ annually that is spent by society and individuals.

Skill Builder Responses and Answers

Question 1 Responses

In this chapter, we offered three definitions for addiction, two of which were lay definitions and one of which was clinical. Fill in the blanks below and briefly explain how you would use them in your work with addicted individuals and their families.

Definition #1

Addiction is an <u>abnormal</u> <u>love</u> and <u>trust</u> <u>relationship</u> with an object or event in an attempt to <u>control</u> that which <u>cannot</u> <u>be</u> <u>controlled</u>.

How might you use this definition?
<u>This definition's utility lies in its exploration of relationship issues. Explor-</u>
<u>ing such issues (e.g., need fulfillment, trust, romance, passion, intimacy,</u>
<u>and control) with individuals and families is important as it draws out</u>
<u>their stories for how the addiction develops over time.</u>

Definition #2

Addiction is an <u>increasing</u> <u>desire</u> for something with an <u>accompanying</u> <u>decreasing</u> <u>ability</u> to satisfy that desire.

How might you use this definition?
<u>This definition is useful because it explores and explains the existential</u>
<u>emptiness that addicts experience. Clients often recognize how their com-</u>
<u>pulsive use of heroin, gambling, the Internet, or exercise approximates a</u>
<u>vacuum—the drive to fill it is in direct opposition to the ability to do so.</u>

Definition #3

The <u>*Diagnostic*</u> <u>*and*</u> <u>*Statistical*</u> <u>*Manual*</u> for Mental Disorders categorizes addictive disorders into <u>abuse</u> and <u>dependence</u>. Substance abuse is defined as a <u>maladaptive</u> use of chemicals that impacts <u>one</u> <u>or</u> <u>more</u> (out of four) major life domains and responsibilities. Substance-dependent individuals will likely experience <u>three</u> <u>or</u> <u>more</u> detrimental impacts as a result of their disorder.

How might you use this definition?
<u>This definition is important when speaking to clinical professionals, for</u>
<u>example, medical personnel (as many treatment facilities utilize a medi-</u>
<u>cal approach to recovery), insurance companies (for reimbursement pur-</u>
<u>poses), and other colleagues (for consultation purposes).</u>

Question 2 Responses

Place a "C" for "Chemical" or a "P" for "Process" next to each of the below items to distinguish between those that can become chemical addictions and those that can become process addictions.

P	Gambling	P	The Internet	P	Spending
C	Alcohol	C	Marijuana	C	Valium
P	Eating	C	Ecstasy (MDMA)	P	Television
C	Steroids	P	Shopping	C	Xanax
P	Sex	C	LSD	C	Nicotine
C	Cocaine	P	Work	P	Video Games
C	Heroin	C	Inhalants	C	Caffeine

Question 3 Responses

Identify the missing words below as they apply to the addictive disorder.

- In terms of criteria, neither <u>tolerance</u> nor <u>withdrawal</u> is necessary for designating a behavior or substance as addictive.
- The two criteria necessary and sufficient for the designation of chemical addiction are (a) <u>recurrent</u> <u>failure</u> to <u>control</u> the use of one or more drugs and (b) <u>continuation</u> of drug use <u>despite</u> substantial <u>harmful</u> <u>consequences</u>.
- The definition for the addictive disorder incorporates many of the key elements from three other disorders, namely that of <u>chemical dependency</u>, <u>impulse control</u> disorder, and <u>obsessive-compulsive</u> disorder.
- The one criterion that best discounts the use of the term *impulsivity* to describe addictive-like behaviors is that an impulsive act is one that is <u>always</u> <u>harmful</u> to the <u>person</u> engaging in the behavior or to <u>others</u> who are <u>impacted</u> by that individual.
- The main difference between addiction and compulsion is that although addictive behaviors are often utilized to <u>reduce</u> <u>anxiety</u> and other painful affects, they also produce <u>pleasure</u> and <u>gratification</u>, which rules out the diagnosis of <u>compulsion</u>.
- Cross addiction occurs when <u>one</u> <u>addiction</u> (e.g., alcohol) is <u>substituted</u> with another (e.g., exercise).

Question 4 Responses

Match the specific addictive disorder with the number of individuals who are estimated to struggle with that disorder. After this, answer the question.

Chemical addiction	→	11 to 58 million
Sexual addiction	→	17 to 37 million
Addictive gambling	→	6 to 15 million
Internet addiction	→	17 to 41 million
Addictive eating	→	14 million

- What are the three challenges associated with gathering accurate prevalence figures for addictive disorders? <u>Prevalence figure challenges include the fact that they are (a) based on client self-report (unlikely due to the attached social stigmas for some disorders), (b) based on how clinicians define clients' presenting behaviors (either as compulsive disorders, impulse control disorders, or addictions), and (c) often hidden behind other dysfunctional behaviors and mood disorders (e.g., marital discord, depression with suicidal ideations, anxiety and panic attacks, physical trauma) that are actually the result of their addiction issues.</u>

Question 5 Responses

Fill in the blanks in each of the following sentences, which highlight the major impacts of chemical and process addictions on a societal and familial level.

Impacts of Chemical Addiction

- The total economic cost attributed to alcohol and drug abuse is <u>$365.5</u> billion per year.
- <u>$18</u> billion a year is devoted to the prevention and <u>treatment</u> of substance abuse complications.
- The annual expenditures on health care costs include services such as <u>detoxification</u>, <u>rehabilitation</u>, <u>prevention</u>, training providers, and research expenditures.
- <u>Nicotine</u> is the leading preventable cause of death (more than 440,000 annually—approximately 1 out of every 5 deaths).

- More than 58 million Americans have no <u>health</u> insurance or inadequate <u>health</u> <u>care</u> coverage.
- By far, the biggest drain to the U.S. economy in terms of substance abuse is in <u>productivity</u> <u>losses</u>, to the tune of approximately $129 billion annually.
- More than half of all <u>homicides</u> and <u>assaults</u> are directly related to alcohol and drug consumption.
- For each drink consumed in the United States, <u>$1</u> is drained out of the economy as a result of impaired drinkers.
- More than <u>90 percent</u> of perpetrators of <u>family</u> violence had used alcohol and other drugs (AOD) the day of their arrests.
- Of those who qualify as chronically homeless, most suffer from a co-occurring <u>substance</u> <u>abuse</u> and <u>mental</u> <u>health</u> disorder.
- Within the public child welfare system, more than <u>50 percent</u> of families struggle with chemical dependency.
- Almost <u>one</u> in <u>four</u> adults with serious mental illness is dependent on alcohol and other drugs.

Impacts of Process Addictions

- Data concerning the tangible and intangible societal and familial costs of process addictions is scarce due in part to the lack of <u>legitimacy</u> afforded these disorders.
- Among concerns raised by most employers, <u>restricting</u> <u>employee</u> access to <u>pornographic</u> material while at work has become the number one concern.
- <u>70</u> percent of all visits to pornographic sites occur during normal business hours, with a noted <u>lull</u> during lunch hours.
- Medical costs for sexually transmitted diseases range annually from <u>$10</u> to <u>$17</u> billion.
- Approximately 55 percent of incarcerated <u>sex</u> <u>offenders</u> meet criteria for sexual addiction.
- The sexually addicted individual's "drug of choice" is <u>sexually</u> <u>stimulating</u> <u>material</u>.
- The spouses and partners of sexual addicts experience feelings of hurt, <u>betrayal</u>, rejection, <u>abandonment</u>, shame, loneliness, <u>anger</u>, <u>jealousy</u>, and destroyed self-esteem.
- Between 84 and 92 percent of all people in the United States <u>gamble</u>.

- Approximately one fourth of the annual revenues of casinos and state lotteries result from monies spent by <u>problem</u> and <u>pathological</u> gamblers.
- Familial costs attributed to addictive gambling include extensive <u>legal</u> problems, health problems, <u>marital</u> difficulties, and low <u>family</u> cohesion.
- The addictive disorder with the highest suicide rates (70 percent contemplate suicide and 20 to 40 percent actually attempt suicide) is <u>addictive gambling</u>.
- Addictive use of the Internet also includes such things as online sex, <u>gambling</u>, spending, <u>day-trading</u>, and information seeking.
- Addicted individuals spend between <u>40</u> and <u>80</u> hours per week online and suffer from a variety of negative consequences.
- The detrimental impacts of Internet addiction include decreased <u>work productivity</u>, <u>interpersonal</u> problems, physical difficulties, comorbid psychiatric problems, financial difficulties, and <u>legal</u> problems.
- Employers voice employee non-work-related Internet use as their number one concern in terms of <u>lost revenue</u>.
- Negative consequences of Internet addiction on marriages include the unequal distribution of responsibilities, lack of <u>shared</u> activities, increased altercations, emotional distance, and <u>cyberaffairs</u>.
- The final societal/tangible costs attributed to addictive disorders equal more than <u>$1.1 trillion</u> annually that is spent by society and individuals.

References

Abouesh, A., & Clayton, A. (1999). Compulsive voyeurism and exhibitionism: A clinical response to paroxetine. *Archives of Sexual Behavior, 28*(1), 23–30.

Addiction Resource Guide. (2000). *Special populations: Sexual addiction.* Retrieved December 12, 2001, from http://www.addictionresourceguide. com/specpop/sexual.html

American Management Association. (2001). *Workplace monitoring & surveillance: Policies and practices. 2001 AMA Survey.* Retrieved October 17, 2000, from http://www.amanet.org/research/summ.htm

American Psychiatric Association. (2000). *Diagnostic and statistical manual of mental disorders* (4th ed., Text Revision). Washington, DC: Author.

Apt, C., & Hulbert, D. F. (1995). Sexual narcissism: Addiction or anachronism? *Family Journal, 3*(2), 103–108.

Armstrong, L., Phillips, J. G., & Saling, L. L. (2000). Potential determinants of heavier Internet usage [Electronic version]. *International Journal of Human-Computer Studies, 53*, 537–550.

Baker, L. (1995). Food addiction traced to trauma-induced changes in brain. *Psychotherapy Letter, 7*(11), 7.

Barth, R. J., & Kinder, B. N. (1987). The mislabeling of sexual impulsivity. *Journal of Sex and Marital Therapy, 13*, 15–23

Bavolek, S. J., & Henderson, H. L. (1990). Child maltreatment and alcohol abuse: Comparisons and perspectives for treatment. In R. T. Potter-Efron & P. S. Potter-Efron. (Eds.), *Aggression, family violence and chemical dependency* (pp. 165–184). Binghamton, AL: Haworth.

Beard, K. W. (2002). Internet addiction: Current status and implications for employees. *Journal of Employment Counseling, 39*(1), 2–11.

Benotsch, E. G., Kalichman, S. C., & Pinkerton, S. D. (2001). Sexual compulsivity in HIV-positive men and women: Prevalence, predictors, and consequences of high-risk behaviors. *Sexual Addiction & Compulsivity, 8*(2), 83–99.

Biederman, J., Faraone, S. V., Monuteaux, M. C., & Feighner, J. A. (2000). Patterns of alcohol and drug use in adolescents can be predicted by parental substance use disorders. *Pediatrics, 106*(4), 792–798.

Black, D. W., Kehrberg, L. L. D., Flumerfelt, D. L., & Schlosser, S. S. (1997). Characteristics of 36 subjects reporting compulsive sexual behavior. *American Journal of Psychiatry, 154*, 243–249.

Blanco, C., Ibanez, A., Saiz-Ruiz, J., Blanco-Jerez, C., & Nunes, E. V. (2000). Epidemiology, pathophysiology and treatment of pathological gambling. *CNS Drugs, 13*, 397–407.

Blaszcynski, A. P., Buhrich, N., & McConaghy, N. (1985). Pathological gamblers, heroin addicts, and controls compared on the E.P.Q. Addiction Scale. *British Journal of Addiction, 80*, 315–319.

Brennan, P. A., Hammen, C., Katz, A. R., & Le Brocque, R. M. (2002). Maternal depression, paternal psychopathology, and adolescent diagnostic outcomes. *Journal of Consulting & Clinical Psychology, 70*(5), 1075–1085.

Bruce, B., & Agras, W. S. (1992). Binge eating in females: A population-based investigation. *International Journal of Eating Disorders, 12*, 365–373.

Buchta, R. M. (1995). Gambling among adolescents. *Clinical Pediatrics, 34*, 346–349.

Buck, T., & Sales, A. (2000). Related addictive disorders. In *Substance abuse and counseling* (Report No. CG030040). Arizona, U.S.: (ERIC Document Reproduction Service No. ED440345).

Bureau of Justice Statistics. (2005). *Family violence statistics: Including statistics on strangers and acquaintances.* (Report No. NCJ 207846). Retrieved August 23, 2005, from http://www.ojp.usdoj.gov/bjs/pub/pdf/fvs.pdf

Bureau of the Public Debt. (2005). *The debt to the penny.* Retrieved June 14, 2005, from http://www.publicdebt.treas.gov/opd/opdpenny.htm

Calhoun, R. (2005, February 11). Caught in the Web: Internet addiction costs add up in workplace. *San Antonio Business Journal.* Retrieved June 21, 2005, from http://sanantonio.bizjournals.com/sanantonio/stories/2005/02/14/focus6.html

Carnes, P. (1990). Sexual addiction: Progress, criticism, challenges. *American Journal of Preventive Psychiatry & Neurology, 2*(3), 1–8.

Carnes, P. (1992). *Don't call it love: Recovery from sexual addiction.* New York: Bantam.

Carnes, P. (1994a). *Contrary to love: Helping the sexual addict.* Center City, MN: Hazelden.

Carnes, P. (1994b). *Out of the shadows: Understanding sexual addiction* (2nd ed.). Center City, MN: Hazelden.

Centers for Disease Control and Prevention. (1998, July 3). Age- and state-specific prevalence estimates of insured and uninsured persons: United States, 1995-1996. *MMWR Weekly, 47*(25), 529–532. Retrieved August 22, 2005, from http://www.cdc.gov/mmwr/preview/mmwrhtml/00053702.htm

Claydon, P. (1987). Self-reported alcohol, drug and eating-disorder problems among male and female collegiate children of alcoholics. *Journal of American College Health, 36*, 111–116.

Cockerill, I. M., & Riddington, M. E. (1996). Exercise dependence and associated disorders: A review. *Counseling Psychology Quarterly, 9*, 119–130.

Cohen, M., Woodward, C. A., Ferrier, B., & Williams, A. P. (1995). Sanctions against sexual abuse of patients by doctors: Sex differences in attitudes among young family physicians. *Canadian Medical Association Journal, 153*, 169–176.

Cooper, A. (1998). Sexuality and the Internet: Surfing into the new millennium. *CyberPsychology & Behavior, 1*, 181–187.

Cooper, A., Delmonico, D. L., & Burg, R. (2000). Cybersex users, abusers, and compulsives: New findings and implications. *Sexual Addiction & Compulsivity, 7*, 5–29.

Cychosz, C. M. (1996). Alcohol and interpersonal violence: Implications for educators. *Journal of Health Education, 27*(2), 73–77.

Das, A. K. (1990). Counselling people with addictive behavior. *International Journal for the Advancement of Counselling, 13*, 169–177.

Davis, R. A., Flett, G. L., & Besser, A. (2002). Validation of a new scale for measuring problematic internet use: Implications for pre-employment screening. *Cyberpsychology and Behavior, 5*, 331–345.

Deans, C., & Soar, R. (2005). Caring for clients with dual diagnosis in rural communities in Australia: The experience of mental health professionals. *Journal of Psychiatric Mental Health Nursing, 12*(3), 268–274.

Delmonico, D. L., & Griffin, E. (1997). Classifying problematic sexual behavior: A working model. *Sexual Addiction & Compulsivity, 4*(1), 91–104.

DeLucia, C., Belz, A., & Chassin, L. (2001). Do adolescent symptomatology and family environment vary over time with fluctuations in paternal alcohol impairment? *Developmental Psychology, 37*(2), 207–216.

Dore, M. M., Doris, J. M., & Wright, P. (1995). Identifying substance abuse in maltreating families: A child welfare challenge. *Child Abuse and Neglect 19*(5), 531–543.

Duncan, T. E., Duncan, S. C., & Hops, H. (1996). The role of parents and older siblings in predicting adolescent substance use: Modeling development via structural equation latent growth methodology. *Journal of Family Psychology, 10*(2), 158–172.

Eigen, L., & Rowden, D. (1996). A methodology and current estimate of the number of children of alcoholics in the United States. *Children of alcoholics: Selected readings*. Rockville, MD: National Association for Children of Alcoholics.

Fals-Stewart, W., Kelley, M. L., Fincham, F. D., Golden, J., & Logsdon, T. (2004). Emotional and behavioral problems of children living with drug-abusing fathers: Comparisons with children living with alcohol-abusing and non-substance-abusing fathers. *Journal of Family Psychology, 18*(2), 319–330.

Family and Youth Services Bureau. (1995). *Youth with runaway, throwaway, and homeless experiences … Prevalence, drug use, and other at-risk behaviors.* Administration on Children, Youth, and Families. Retrieved August 23, 2005, from http://www.ncfy.com/pubs/compend.htm#Chapter%202

Fischer, J., Williams, K., Byington, K., & Lonsdale, M. (1996). The re-employment of the sexual addict/offender program: An evaluation. *Journal of Applied Rehabilitation Counseling, 27*(1), 33–36.

Flint, A. (1996, December 1). Skin trade spreading across US: High tech fuels boom for $10B industry. *The Boston Globe.* Retrieved November 23, 2000, from http://www.boston.com/globe/

Flood, M. (1989). Addictive eating disorders. *Nursing Clinics of North America, 24*(1), 45–53.

Florida Council on Compulsive Gambling. (2004). *Social effects.* Retrieved June 14, 2005, from http://www.gamblinghelp.org/sections/effects/social.html

Foster, M. (2001, August). Surf's up! But profits are down when employees are caught in a web of Internet misuse. *Insight: The Magazine of the Illinois CPA Society.* Retrieved August 18, 2005, from http://www.insight-mag.com/insight/01/08/col-6-pt-1-WorkForce.htm

French, M. T., Roebuck, M. C., McLellan, A. T., and Sindelar, J. L. (2000). Can the Treatment Services Review be used to estimate the costs of addiction and ancillary services? *Journal of Substance Abuse, 12*(4), 341–361.

Friedenberg, B. M., Blanchard, E. B., Wulfert, E., & Malta, L. S. (2002). Changes in physiological arousal to gambling cues among participants in motivationally enhanced cognitive-behavior therapy for pathological gambling: A preliminary study. *Applied Psychophysiology and Biofeedback, 27,* 251–260.

Garrett, T. (1999). Sexual contact between clinical psychologists and their patients: Qualitative data. *Clinical Psychology & Psychotherapy, 6*(1), 54–62.

Goodman, A. (1993). Diagnosis and treatment of sexual addiction. *Journal of Sex and Marital Therapy, 19,* 225–251.

Goodman, A. (1998). *Sexual addiction: An integrated approach.* Madison, CT: International Universities Press, Inc.

Goodman, A. (2001). What's in a name? Terminology for designating a syndrome of driven sexual behavior. *Sexual Addiction & Compulsivity, 8,* 191–213.

Greenfeld, L. (1998). Alcohol and crime: An analysis of national data on the prevalence of alcohol involvement in crime. *Bureau of Justice Statistics* (Report No. NCJ-168632). Retrieved August 17, 2005, from http://www.ojp.usdoj.gov/bjs/pub/pdf/ac.pdf

Griffin-Shelley, E., Sandler, K. R., & Lees, C. (1992). Multiple addictions among dually diagnosed adolescents. *Journal of Adolescent Chemical Dependency, 2*(2), 35–44.

Griffiths, M. (1991). Amusement machine playing in childhood and adolescence: A comparative analysis of video game and fruit machines. *Journal of Adolescence, 14*, 53–73.

Griffiths, M. (1992). Pinball wizard: The case of a pinball machine addict. *Psychological Reports, 71*, 161–162.

Griffiths, M. (1997). Computer game playing in early adolescence. *Youth & Society, 29*, 223–238.

Griffiths, M. (2003). Internet abuse in the workplace: Issues and concerns for employers and employment counselors. *Journal of Employment Counseling, 40*(2), 87–96.

Hagedorn, W. B. (2005, April). *Sexual addiction: Impacts on society, impacts on your wallet.* Program presented at the national conference of the American Counseling Association, Atlanta, GA.

Hagedorn, W. B., & Juhnke, G. A. (2005). Treating the sexually addicted client: Establishing a need for increased counselor awareness. *Journal of Addictions & Offender Counseling, 25*(2), 66–86.

Hall, A. S., & Parsons, J. (2001). Internet addiction: College student case study using best practices in Cognitive Behavior Therapy. *Journal of Mental Health Counseling, 23*, 312–327.

Harwood, H. (2000). *Updating estimates of the economic costs of alcohol abuse in the United States: Estimates, update methods, and data.* Report prepared by The Lewin Group for the National Institute on Alcohol Abuse and Alcoholism. Based on estimates, analyses, and data reported in Harwood, H., Fountain, D., & Livermore, G. (1998). *The economic costs of alcohol and drug abuse in the United States 1992.* Report prepared for the National Institute on Drug Abuse and the National Institute on Alcohol Abuse and Alcoholism, National Institutes of Health, Department of Health and Human Services. NIH Publication No. 98-4327. Rockville, MD: National Institutes of Health.

Hollander, E., & Rosen, J. (2000). Impulsivity. *Journal of Psychopharmacology, 14*(2), Supplement 1, S39–S44.

Hopkins, G. L., Freier, M. C., Babikian, T., Helm, H. W., Jr., McBride, D. C., Boward, M., et al. (2004). Substance use among students attending a Christian university that strictly prohibits the use of substances. *Journal of Research on Christian Education, 13*(1), 23–39.

Horgan, C. M. (1995, Spring). Cost of untreated substance abuse to society. *The Comminique.* Washington, DC: Center for Substance Abuse Treatment.

Institute of Medicine (1997). *The hidden epidemic: Confronting sexually transmitted diseases.* Washington, DC: National Academy Press.

Kafka, M. P. (1997). Hypersexual desire in males: An operational definition and clinical implications for males with paraphilias and paraphilia-related disorders. *Archives of Sexual Behavior, 26*, 505–526.

Koss, M., & Gaines, J. (1993). The prediction of sexual aggression by alcohol use, athletic participation, and fraternity affiliation. *Journal of Interpersonal Violence, 8*(1), 94–108.

Kroll, L., & Goldman, L. (2005, March). Billion dollar babies. *Forbes.* Retrieved June 14, 2005, from http://www.forbes.com/billionaires/global/2005/0328/027.html

Laino, C. (2002). Click and tell: Distractive dalliances. *MSNBC.* Retrieved January 5, 2003, from http://www.msnbc.com/news/596354.asp?cp1=1

Lamberton, A., & Oei, T. P. S. (1997). Problem gambling in adults: An overview. *Clinical Psychology and Psychotherapy, 4,* 84–104.

Lambie, G. W., & Sias, S. M. (2005). Children of alcoholics: Implications for professional school counseling. *Professional School Counseling, 8*(3), 266–273.

Ledgerwood, D. M., & Downey, K. K. (2002). Relationship between problem gambling and substance use in a methadone maintenance population. *Addictive Behaviors, 27,* 483–491.

Ledgerwood, D. M., Steinberg, M. A., Wu, R., & Potenza, M. N. (2005). Self-reported gambling-related suicidality among gambling helpline callers. *Psychology of Addictive Behaviors, 19*(2), 175–183.

Lee, S. H., Lennon, S. J., & Rudd, N. A. (2000). Compulsive consumption tendencies among television shoppers. *Family & Consumer Sciences Research Journal, 28*(4), 463–489.

Levin, J. D. (1999). Sexual addiction. *National Forum, 79*(4), 33–37.

Levine, M. P., & Troiden, R. R. (1988). The myth of sexual compulsivity. *Journal of Sex Research, 25,* 347–363.

Manley, G., & Koehler, J. (2001). Sexual behavior disorders: Proposed new classification in the *DSM-V. Sexual Addiction & Compulsivity, 8*(3), 253–265.

Mark, T. L., Coffey, R. M., McKusick, D. R., Harwood, H., King, E., Bouchery, E., et al. (2005). *National estimates of expenditures for mental health services and substance abuse treatment, 1991–2001.* SAMHSA Publication No. SMA 05-3999. Rockville, MD: Substance Abuse and Mental Health Services Administration.

Martin, S. E. (2001). The links between alcohol, crime and the criminal justice system: Explanations, evidence and interventions. *American Journal on Addictions, 10*(2), 136–158.

McCall, D. (2002). Sex and the clergy. *Sexual Addiction & Compulsivity, 9,* (2-3), 89-95.

McIlwraith, R. D. (1998). "I'm addicted to television": The personality, imagination, and TV watching patterns of self-identified TV addicts. *Journal of Broadcasting & Electronic Media, 42*(3), 371–387.

McMahon, P. (2002, August 28). Gambling bug bites needy states. *USA Today.* Retrieved August 17, 2005, from http://www.usatoday.com/news/nation/2002-08-28-gambling_x.htm

McPhedran, M. (1996). Sexual abuse in the health professions—Who's counting? *World Health Statistics Quarterly, 49*(2), 154–157.

Merta, R. J. (2001). Addictions counseling. *Counseling and Human Development, 33*(5), 1–15.

Morris, B. (1999, May 10). Addicted to sex. *Fortune, 139*(9), 66–76.

Mosher, C., Rotolo, T., Phillips, D., Krupski, A., & Stark, K. D. (2004). Minority adolescents and substance use risk/protective factors: A focus on inhalant use. *Adolescence, 39*, 489–502.

Nakken, C. (1996). *The addictive personality: Understanding the addictive process and compulsive behavior* (2nd ed.). Center City, MN: Hazelden.

National Center on Addiction and Substance Abuse at Columbia University. (2001, January). *Shoveling up: The impact of substance abuse on state budgets.* New York: NY: Author.

National Center on Child Abuse and Neglect. (1993). *Study of child maltreatment in alcohol abusing families: A report to Congress* (pp. ix–xiv). Washington, DC: U.S. Department of Health and Human Services.

National Council on Sexual Addiction and Compulsivity. (2000). *Public figures and problem sexual behaviors.* Retrieved December 2, 2000, from http://www.ncsac.org/article2.htm

National Highway Traffic Safety Administration. (2004). *The economic burden of traffic crashes on employers: Costs by state and industry and by alcohol and restraint use.* Retrieved June 20, 2005, from http://www.nhtsa.dot.gov/people/injury/airbags/EconomicBurden/index.html

National Institute of Allergy and Infectious Diseases. (1999). *An introduction to sexually transmitted diseases.* Bethesda, MD: U.S. Department of Health and Human Services.

National Institute on Drug Abuse. (2003). *Preventing drug use among children and adolescents: A research based guide for parents, educators, and community leaders* (2nd ed.). U.S. Department of Health and Human Services. Retrieved June 14, 2005, from http://www.drugabuse.gov/pdf/prevention/RedBook.pdf

National Institute on Drug Abuse. (2004a). *NIDA InfoFacts: Cigarettes and other nicotine products.* Retrieved March 21, 2005, from http://www.nida.nih.gov/Infofax/tobacco.html

National Institute on Drug Abuse. (2004b). *NIDA InfoFacts: Costs to society.* Retrieved March 21, 2005, from http://www.drugabuse.gov/Infofax/costs.html

National Institute on Drug Abuse. (n.d.1). *NIDA InfoFacts: Drug addiction treatment methods.* Retrieved June 7, 2005, from http://www.drugabuse.gov/Infofacts/treatmeth.html

National Institute on Drug Abuse. (n.d.2). *NIDA InfoFacts: Workplace trends.* Retrieved June 7, 2005, from http://www.drugabuse.gov/Infofax/workplace.html

National Opinion Research Council. (1999). *The National Gambling Impact Study Commission Report.* Retrieved June 14, 2005, from http://www.gambling-help.org/docs/12.pdf

Nixon, S. J., & Tivis, L. J. (1997). Neuropsychological responses in COAs. *Alcohol Health and Research World, 21*(3), 232–235.

N2H2. (2002). *Internet usage and legal liability.* Retrieved April 22, 2002, from http://www.n2h2.com

O'Brien, C. P. (1996). Recent developments in the pharmacotherapy of substance abuse. *Journal of Counseling and Clinical Psychology, 64*(4), 677–686.

O'Farrell, T. J., Fals-Stewart, W., Murphy, M., & Murphy, C. M. (2003). Partner violence before and after individually based alcoholism treatment for male alcoholic patients. *Journal of Consulting & Clinical Psychology, 71*(1), 92–102.

Office of the Assistant Secretary for Planning and Evaluation. (1994). *Patterns of substance use and program participation.* Washington, DC: U.S. Department of Health and Human Services.

Office of Juvenile Justice and Delinquency Prevention. (1994). *Conditions of confinement: Juvenile detention and corrections facilities: Research report* (pp. 29, 43, 153, 169). Washington, DC: U.S. Department of Justice.

Office of National Drug Control Policy. (2001). *The Economic Costs of Drug Abuse in the United States, 1992-1998.* Washington, DC: Executive Office of the President. (Publication No. NCJ-190636). Retrieved November 3, 2003, from http://www.whitehousedrugpolicy.gov/publications/index.html

Office of National Drug Control Policy (2004). The Economic Costs of Drug Abuse in the United States, 1992-2002. Washington, DC: Executive Office of the President (Publication No. 207303). Retrieved May 27, 2005, from http://www.whitehousedrugpolicy.gov/publications/economic_costs/

Page, R. C., & Bailey, J. B. (1995). Addictions counseling certification: An emerging counseling specialty. *Journal of Counseling & Development, 74*(2), 167–172.

PBS *Frontline.* (n.d.). *Easy money: A report on America's booming gambling industry and its economic and political clout.* Retrieved August 17, 2005, from http://www.pbs.org/wgbh/pages/frontline/shows/gamble/etc/facts.html

Penfold, P. S. (1998). *Sexual abuse by health professionals: A personal search for meaning and healing.* Toronto, ON: University of Toronto Press.

Pentz, M. A. (1998). Costs, benefits, and cost-effectiveness of comprehensive drug abuse prevention. In W. J. Bukoski & R. I. Evans (Eds.), *Cost-benefit/cost-effectiveness research of drug abuse prevention: Implications for programming and policy* (pp. 111–129). NIDA Research Monograph No. 176. Washington, DC: U.S. Government Printing Office.

Potenza, M. N. (2002). A perspective on future directions in the prevention, treatment, and research of pathological gambling. *Psychiatric Annals, 2*(3), 203–207.

Potenza, M. N., Fiellin, D. A., Heninger, G. R., Rounsaville, B. J., & Mazure, C. M. (2002). Gambling: An addictive behavior with health and primary care implications. *Journal of General Internal Medicine, 17*(9), 721–732.

Putnam, D. E. (2000). Initiation and maintenance of online sexual compulsivity: Implications for assessment and treatment. *CyberPsychology & Behavior, 3*(4), 553–563.

Rachlin, H. (1990). Why do people gamble and keep gambling despite heavy losses? *Psychological Science, 1,* 294–297.

Ragan, P. W., & Martin, P. R. (2000). The psychobiology of sexual addiction. *Sexual Addiction & Compulsivity, 7*(3), 161–175.

Randolph, (2004). How many people are homeless? Why? *National Resource and Training Center on Homelessness and Mental Illness, Substance Abuse and Mental Health Services Administration*. Retrieved June 20, 2005, from http://www.nrchmi.samhsa.gov/facts/facts_question_1.asp

Raviv, M. (1993). Personality characteristics of sexual addicts and pathological gamblers. *Journal of Gambling Studies, 9*(1), 17–30.

Robinson, B. E. (1998). Spouses of workaholics: Clinical implications for psychotherapy. *Psychotherapy: Theory, Research, Practice, Training, 35*(2), 260–268.

Robinson, B. E. (2000). A typology of workaholics with implications for counselors. *Journal of Addictions & Offender Counseling, 21*(1), 34–49.

Rowan, M. S., & Galasso, C. S. (2000). Identifying office resource needs of Canadian physicians to help prevent, assess and treat patients with substance use and pathological gambling disorders. *Journal of Addictive Diseases, 19*(2), 43–58.

Schneider, J. P. (2000). A qualitative study of cybersex participants: Gender differences, recovery issues, and implications for therapists. *Sexual Addiction & Compulsivity, 7,* 249–278.

Schumacher, J. A., Fals-Stewart, W., & Leonard, K. E. (2003). Domestic violence treatment referrals for men seeking alcohol treatment. *Journal of Substance Abuse Treatment, 24,* 279–283.

Sealy, J. R. (1999). Dual and triple diagnoses: Addictions, mental illness and HIV infection guidelines for outpatient therapists. *Sexual Addiction & Compulsivity, 6*(3), 195–219.

Seminerio, M. (1997, November 10). Surfing for smut on the clock. *PC Week, 14*(47), 25.

Shaffer, H. J., Hall, M. N., & VanderBilt, J. (1999). Estimating the prevalence of disordered gambling behavior in the United States and Canada: A research synthesis. *American Journal of Public Health, 89,* 1369–1376.

Shaffer, H. J., & Korn, D. A. (2002). Gambling and related mental disorders: A public health analysis. *Annual Review of Public Health, 23*(1), 171–213.

Sheppard, K. (1995). Food addiction deserves to be taken just as seriously as alcoholism. *Addiction Letter, 11*(7), 1–3.

Snoddy, J. (2000, October 18). Bill's up for office surfers. *The Guardian.* Retrieved August 18, 2005, from http://www.guardian.co.uk/business/story/0,,384158,00.html

Spoth, R., Guyull, M., & Day, S. (2002). Universal family-focused interventions in alcohol-use disorder prevention: Cost effectiveness and cost-benefit analyses of two interventions. *Journal of Studies on Alcohol, 63,* 219–228.

Stanley, J. (2003). "Downtime" for children on the Internet: Recognizing a new form of child abuse. *Family Matters, 65,* 22–27.

Substance Abuse and Mental Health Services Administration, Department of Health and Human Services. (2000a). *Summary of findings from the 1999 National Household Survey on Drug Abuse.* Retrieved July 19, 2001, from http://www.samhsa.gov/oas/NHSDA/1999/Table%20of%20Contents.htm

Substance Abuse and Mental Health Services Administration, Department of Health and Human Services. (2000b). Trends in estimated costs to society of alcohol and drug abuse, 1992–1995. *SAMHSA Statistics Source Book.* Retrieved July 19, 2001, from http://www.samhsa.gov/oas/srcbk/TOC.htm

Substance Abuse and Mental Health Services Administration. (2002, November 29). Health insurance status of admissions for substance abuse treatment: 1999. *The DASIS Report.* Retrieved August 22, 2005, from http://www.oas.samhsa.gov/2k2/insuranceTX/insuranceTX.htm

Substance Abuse and Mental Health Services Administration. (2003a). *Results from the 2002 National Survey on Drug Use and Health: National Findings* (Office of Applied Studies, NHSDA Series H-22, DHHS Publication No. SMA 03–3836). Rockville, MD.

Substance Abuse and Mental Health Services Administration. (2003b). *Blueprint for change: Ending chronic homelessness for persons with serious mental illnesses and co-occurring substance use disorders* (DHHS Pub. No. SMA-04-3870). Rockville, MD: Center for Mental Health Services, Substance Abuse and Mental Health Services Administration. Retrieved June 20, 2005, from http://www.nrchmi.samhsa.gov/text_only/HTML%20Blueprint%20for%20Change%20Folder/Chapter%202.htm#C2TocIndividualRisk

Sussman, V. (1999, January 26). Sex sites hot on the Web. *USA Today.* Retrieved April 12, 2000, from http://www.usatoday.com/life/cyber/tech/ctb110.htm

Taylor, D., Miller, T. R., & Cox, K. L. (2002). Impaired driving in the United States. *Pacific Institute for Research and Evaluation* under contract with the National Highway Traffic Safety Administration. Retrieved June 20, 2005, from http://www.nhtsa.dot.gov/people/injury/alcohol/page%202.htm

TechRepublic. (2002, January 31). *Managing content security: Update 2002.* Retrieved August 18, 2005, from http://www.surfcontrol.com/general/assets/whitepapers/trsrvy2002.pdf

Tenore, J. L. (2001). Challenges in eating disorders: Past and present. *American Family Physician, 64*(3), 367–369.

Thompson, W. N. (1994, August). Gambling: A controlled substance. *Pittsburgh Post-Gazette.* Retrieved August 17, 2005, from http://www.pbs.org/wgbh/pages/frontline/shows/gamble/procon/thompson.html

United States Department of Commerce (2002). *A nation online: How Americans are expanding their use of the Internet.* Retrieved September 12, 2003, from http://www.esa.doc.gov/508/esa/nationonline.htm

United States Department of Labor. (1996). *Background information about workplace substance abuse.* Retrieved June 14, 2005, from the National Center on Addiction and Substance Abuse Web site at http://www.jointogether.org/plugin.jtml?siteID=casacol&p=1&Tab= Facts&Object_ID=25988

United States Public Health Service. (2000). *Treating tobacco use and dependence—A systems approach: A guide for health care administrators, insurers, managed care organizations, and purchasers.* Retrieved May 24, 2005, from http://www.surgeongeneral.gov/tobacco/systems.htm

von Ranson, K. M., McGue, M., & Iacono, W. G. (2003). Disordered eating and substance use in an epidemiological sample: II. Associations within families. *Psychology of Addictive Behaviors, 17*(3), 193–201.

Wells, K. (2003). A needs assessment regarding the nature and impact of clergy sexual abuse conducted by the Interfaith Sexual Trauma Institute. *Sexual Addiction & Compulsivity, 10,* (2-3), 201–217.

Weinberg, N. Z. (2001). Risk factors for adolescent substance abuse. *Journal of Learning Disabilities, 34*(4), 343–351.

Weintraub, E., Dixon, L., Delahanty, J., Schwartz, R., Johnson, J., Cohen, A., & Klecz, M. (2001). Reason for medical hospitalization among adult alcohol and drug abusers. *American Journal on Addictions, 10*(2), 167–177.

Whisman, M. A.., Sheldon, C. T., & Goering, P. (2000). Psychiatric disorders and dissatisfaction with social relationships: Does type of relationship matter? *Journal of Abnormal Psychology, 109*(4), 803–808.

Widom, C. S. (1993). Child abuse and alcohol use: Research monograph 24. *Alcohol and interpersonal violence: Fostering multi-disciplinary perspectives.* Rockville, MD: National Institute on Alcohol Abuse and Alcoholism.

Wolfe, J. L. (2000). Assessement and treatment of compulsive sex/love behavior. *Journal of Rational-Emotive & Cognitive-Behavior Therapy, 18*(4), 235–246.

Work & Family Connection. (2001). We're being productive, but at what? *Work & Family Newsbrief,* 8.

Yacoubian, G. S., Jr., & Peters, R. J. (2005). Identifying the prevalence and correlates of ecstasy use among high school seniors surveyed through 2002 Monitoring the Future. *Journal of Alcohol and Drug Education, 49*(1), 55–72.

Young, K. (1999). Internet addiction: Symptoms, evaluation and treatment. In L. VandeCreek & T. Jackson (Eds.), *Innovations in clinical practice: A source book* (Vol. 17, pp. 19–31). Sarasota, FL: Professional Resource Press.

Young, K. S., Pistner, M., O'Mara, J., & Buchanan, J. (1999) Cyber-disorders: The mental health concern for the millennium. *CyberPsychology and Behavior, 2*(5), 475–479.

Helping Clients and Families Understand Addictions
Etiological Theories and Models

Chapter 2 Learning Objectives

After reading this chapter, you should be able to:

- Describe how each of the etiological theories explains the initiation of addictive disorders
- Describe the main principles from each theory that are most useful in working with addicted clients and families
- Recognize how an approach that intentionally integrates all the theories best meets most clients' needs in understanding how addictive disorders occur

Introduction

In the last chapter, we defined addictive disorders and noted the impact these disorders have on individuals, families, and society. We believe that it was important to start with a broad and inclusive definition, to cast as wide a net as possible to help explain these challenging disorders. Similarly, it was necessary to note the tangible and intangible costs associated with addictive disorders in order to demonstrate the importance of treating them with efficient and sufficient modalities. But why are we proposing a model that sequentially progresses through prescribed and intentional counseling interventions that focus on individuals and families? The answer is because we have found that counseling that focuses solely on the addicted individual has diluted potency and fails to capitalize on the available family support and commitment. To fully comprehend our proposed model, it is first necessary to examine the etiology (i.e., foundation) of addictive disorders and the models that have made an impact on how we understand the progression of these disorders.

Throughout our work in training master's- and doctoral-level clinicians, we have found it curious that students "come to an understanding" of addiction in fairly foreseeable ways. That is, many begin their training, especially those with no prior exposure to addictive disorders, with noted confusion and misconceptions for how addictions develop and progress along predictable pathways. Each semester that I teach substance abuse counseling, students inevitably pose questions and make comments such as: "Why don't they just stop drinking/drugging?" "How does it start in the first place?" "Only derelicts take drugs," "That would never happen to me or my family." By the end of the semester, these same students usually come away more "enlightened" as to the predictors, pathways, and perils of addictive disorders.

Another important reason to understand the etiology of addictive disorders is so that you, the reader, can effectively explain the disorders to clients and their families. Oftentimes people get confused between those theories that *explain* versus those that help *guide the treatment* of addictive disorders. Sometimes they are one and the same: For example, as we will see, Psychological Theory offers an explanatory construct while at the same time has specific suggestions for how to approach the treatment process. For the sake of our text, we will offer the etiological theories in this chapter and then provide those theories that guide treatment in the proceeding chapters, for this is what mirrors "real life" in most treatment settings: Clients and families often desire to first understand "why" they drink/drug/act out, then to understand "where" these behaviors originate, and *then* they are more apt to work on addressing the impacts of the disorders. Etiological theories help explain the first two; treatment theories inform the latter.

Granted, the exploration and explanation of addiction's origins may not be so linear a process throughout a client's recovery, but just as we try to assist clients and families through the revelation process, we hope to guide you, the reader, through your own journey of understanding of how addictive disorders develop and how to best address them with comprehensive and holistic approaches. We will begin with a discussion of the utility of theory, specifically for how it can guide intentional interventions. Then we will briefly touch on different ways to organize our conceptualization and discussion of the various theories. In exploring the main theoretical foundations of addictive disorders, we will highlight the history, primary tenets, and advantages of each. We will also offer vignettes taken from the second author's clinical experiences that help to highlight the utility found in each theory. As with the other vignettes offered throughout this text, names and identifying details have been changed to protect the confidentiality of the clients. We will conclude each section with a review of those theoretical principles that we have found to be most beneficial in working with addicted clients and families.

Theory, Theory, Theory ... Why Can't We Just Wing It?

I have found that students are often most interested in discussing the various types of drugs, the most popular treatment modalities, and how addictive disorders impact individuals and families. But whenever I roll out the "theories" lecture, eyes often roll, groans are audible, and the energy in the room decreases noticeably. For years I have asked classes about these reactions, and the answers have been similar: "Why do we need to learn about those boring theories in the first place? Why can't we just jump into the 'meatier' stuff?" My response is always the same: Without understanding *how* individual client issues develop, one cannot feasibly implement appropriate interventions. How issues develop, how they impact individuals, families, and society, and the best way to prevent and treat these issues are all grounded in the discussion of etiological theory.

A thin line exists between the terms *model* and *theory*, and given that the terms are often used interchangeably, we will often refer to one or the other with a primary focus on the processes that best explain the common set of behaviors, thoughts, and feelings found in various addictive disorders (West, 2001). In any discussion of theory, contradictions and arguments often ensue: What is the best theory to use? How can one theory explain a disorder as complicated and intricate as addiction? Truth be told, no one theory is best; no one theory can sufficiently capture and delineate the impacts of these disorders. Rather, it is through an interconnectedness of theories that we can best assist those struggling with addictions. West (2001, p. 6) noted:

Theory should enable prediction of circumstances in which addiction is more likely to occur and give insights into how it can be prevented, controlled or treated. It might seek to predict whether a new drug will be addictive, who among a group of children will be at risk of developing addiction if exposed to particular stimuli, or whether changes in social factors will lead to an increase in the prevalence of particular forms of dependence. It should provide guidance on improved forms of treatment. Moreover, it should do these things better than a simple common-sense view.

Having set the stage for the *purpose* of etiological theories, yet before we actually explore these theories, we want to discuss the importance of using an intentional framework in our conceptualization of clients and client issues. Why, you ask, do we need to ground our interventions in specific theories? Can't we just go where the clients take us? Too often we have found that even though most clinicians have had sufficient training in the theories and models of addictive disorders, they tend to take the "eclectic approach" both when explaining these disorders to clients and throughout the treatment process. Now don't get us wrong, eclecticism *is* the treatment model du jour—in fact, it is probably the *best* answer to a potential employer who asks, "What model do you use to conceptualize clients and presenting issues?" And it *is* important to be able to pick from a multitude of interventions that best meet specific client needs as they surface in session. But with over 200 different theories to pick from, which result in more than 400 clinical techniques (Hubble, Duncan, & Miller, 1999), the key ingredient that appears to be missing from most clinicians' work is that of *intentionality*, which helps organize how we work with clients.

Rollo May described intentionality as a person's inner "structure which gives meaning to experience" (May, 1969, p. 223), noting that all behavior has (and should have) a purpose. Schmidt (1994) noted that intentionality involves the connection between our inner consciousness and our outward behavior, that it guides the selection, purpose, and direction of helping strategies, and that it is one of the main determinants of successful client change. Without intentionality, clinicians tend to "wing it" when it comes to exploring the origins of disorders and in picking interventions, often relying on either "cookie-cutter" approaches (e.g., using one theory to explain how addictions progress for *every* family), favorite interventions (whether or not it is in the best interest of the client), or "let's see what happens when I try *this*" methods. I can personally attest to the fact that a lack of intentionality not only interferes with client progress but also can lead to clinicians feeling ineffective.

I remember my first few years as a counselor. Educated with an eclectic model, I had been provided with a great overview of etiological and treatment theories but had spent little time with the intentional application of said theories. So I resorted to what many beginning-level clinicians do: I "went" where clients wanted to "go." Granted, I remembered that therapeutic techniques account for only 15 percent of client success (the other 85 percent of which is divided among extra-therapeutic factors, relationship factors, and positive client expectations [Lambert, 1992]), but once I found a particular set of theoretical techniques that worked with *most* clients, you better believe that I stuck with them! It appeared to make my job easier—especially during those long days of therapy when I was trying to juggle multiple client issues. The problem came when these techniques did not seem to work, resulting in clients' situations not improving. Similarly, in my psychoeducational discussions of origins, there was always that "difficult" client for whom my etiological model did not appear to fit (how *dare* they question *my* theory!). Another problem would occur when I worked with clients for longer than a few weeks; I had been trained with brief therapy models and had developed my therapeutic repertoire based on the assumption that I had only 3 or 4 weeks to work with someone. When therapy exceeded that time frame, I was at a loss and would go into what I termed "eclectic mode," which meant that I picked whatever appeared best for the moment (but again, without a particular agenda or intention in mind). Unfortunately, steady client progress was often not apparent to me (let alone to my clients) and I would become extremely frustrated, wondering to myself, "Am I helping them *at all?*" I vividly remember the first time a colleague suggested I begin with a specific etiological and treatment framework and then pick intentional interventions based on how I conceptualized clients within that framework. This paradigm just so happened to be Prochaska's Model of Change, something we will discuss more thoroughly in the next chapter. The point is, until I understood my clients' past experiences, conceptualized them with a particular framework, and then intentionally applied appropriate techniques, I was not as effective as I could have been.

Lack of intentionality is particularly easy to do when you work in a setting that promotes one specific approach to etiology and treatment (what I call the "cookie-cutter" approach). For example, I have worked in places where, upon entry, *every* client was educated in the Medical Model and assigned the exact same treatment goals. These goals included (a) completing a First Step (addressing powerlessness and unmanageability), (b) addressing their minimization and denial, and (c) obtaining a support system. Granted, even though the Medical Model definitely has utility, and although these *are* some common and often effective treatment goals, they do not necessarily apply to *every* client struggling with an addictive disorder, particularly if his or her addiction does not fit the Medical Model or if he or she had prior treatment where these treatment goals had been addressed and accomplished.

It is my assertion that, overall, the substance abuse treatment community lacks intentionality. Intentionality initially involves more time and effort: It takes getting to know clients and their unique experiences with addiction, and it involves clinicians coming out of their protective shell of the "same ole, same ole" approaches to individuals with addictive disorders. Granted, addictions counseling is extremely challenging, clients can be demanding (even after all these years, I'm still amazed that clients will lie to me as I try to assist them), treatment depends on funding (which is often difficult to secure), and treatment settings are always under scrutiny by internal and external auditors. But once you learn the importance of intentionality, believe me, it makes the process so much easier and effective; it is something that can be taught to clients to increase their assumption of personal responsibility, it can guide the effective use of external funding, and it can demonstrate to external reviewers that effective client change occurs in your facility. Schmidt (1994) summed up the importance of learning and implementing intentionality, for it is only through intentionality that clinicians can best "choose strategies, plan programs, and establish relationships aimed at relieving pain, solving problems, enhancing environments, and generally behav[ing] in beneficial ways" (p. 3).

Why all this talk about intentionality? First, it is because we want you to be the best clinician possible, the one who uses the best practices in your work with addicted individuals and their families. But more importantly, given that one of the main ingredients to intentionality is recognizing the impact of clients' worldviews and culture, the discussion of intentionality is especially pertinent to our chapters on etiological and treatment models. It is our hope that when you understand the etiology and progression of these disorders, you will be better able to step into your clients' shoes and therefore pick intentional interventions from our suggested treatment regimen.

Moving from Moral to Multifaceted—A Discussion of Addiction Theories

There are several ways to organize the discussion of theories. One classification system suggested by West (2001) was to base theory groupings on underlying processes. This resulted in five major groupings. Theories in group 1 involved those that explored or explained the conceptual understanding of addictive disorders, which involved biological, social, and psychological models. Group 2 theories were grouped by their common exploration of how some substances and behaviors become addictive whereas others do not. Theories listed in this category noted the positive and negative reinforcement qualities of drugs and behaviors. The third group of theories revealed those attributes of individuals that cause them to be susceptible to addictive substances and behaviors. These theories explored genetic, psychological, and social risk factors for developing an addictive disorder. Group 4 theories shared the common goal of determining the environmental and social predispositions that impact the development of addictive disorders. Specifically, these theories seek to explain those factors in individuals' surroundings that make them more or less likely to use a drug or behavior addictively. Finally, the fifth cluster of theories was based on their mutual emphasis on relapse and recovery. Not easily subsumed by the other groups, these theories ranged from those investigating recovery from specific drugs or behaviors to those that were more transtheoretical in nature.

Other authors have made similar attempts at classifying the myriad of etiological theories. For example, Petraitis, Flay, and Miller (1995) grouped theories according to how they best accounted for experimental substance use by adolescents. Their four major headings included cognitive affective theories, social learning theories, conventional commitment and social attachment theories, and interpersonal predisposition theories. On a larger scale, Anderson (1998) identified the dominant substance abuse theories and placed them into eight distinct groups: problem behavior theories, theories of reasoned action, social learning theories, social control theories, self-derogation theories, integrated delinquency theories, social development theories, and theories of multiple influences. Finally, Dean (2001) investigated the unique interactions of theories originating from biology, psychology, sociology, and culture to explain how addictive disorders originate.

The point is that there are numerous ways to organize our discussion of the etiology of addictive disorders. So rather than follow what has already been discussed, I invite you along my personal path of discovery and understanding. I will begin with my own initial questions that arose from the socially ingrained Moral Model, followed by my conceptualizing addiction as a disease, then through an exploration of the psychological aspects of this disorder, into the learning component associated with addictions and how they operate within a system, and finish with an enlightened discussion (I hope) of the multiple interactions of body, mind, relationships, and spirit that cause and perpetuate addictive disorders. Throughout this journey, I will present clinical samples that demonstrate the clinical utility of these theories as well as offer and summarize the attributes from each theory that have been most beneficial to my training of students and in my treatment of clients.

Why Don't They Just Stop?—The Moral Model of Addictive Disorders

Although I do not recall the first time I recognized that someone was addicted to drugs or alcohol, I know that it occurred in my hometown of Chicago. My father would take us for jaunts around the city, exploring the various museums and landmarks of that beautiful metropolis. In a city that size, there was a large homeless population, and depending on the part of town you visited, these struggling individuals often resorted to sleeping on the sidewalks. I vividly remember stepping over people on my way into the Art Institute of Chicago one day and asking, "What's wrong with these people? Why don't they have a place to live?" The answer was a common one: These are the alcoholic and drug addicted derelicts who have chosen to hit "rock bottom" as the result of their addiction.

So, my first encounter with addicted individuals shaped my initial conceptions of the addicted population—these individuals were "street bums, human garbage, dregs of society." All addicts and alcoholics make up their minds to waste all that they possess in search of their next high, they lose everything, they suffer as a result, and then they become an eyesore for the rest of society. Granted, these are definitely not politically correct terms, nor are they necessarily accurate, but they are honest recollections from my youth. And today, I have found that the overwhelming majority of individuals (even well-educated graduate students!) still see addiction as the sole result of individuals' poor choices and that addicts deserve all the misery they invite upon themselves. Research confirms these observations: Even in this day and age, society endorses the view that individuals are addicts due to their own moral weaknesses (Moyers & Miller, 1993).

The Moral Model, as it has come to be called, originated during the temperance movement of the early 20th century. The theory views addiction as a choice, "the result of willful overindulgence and moral degradation [that] can be cured with willpower and a desire to abstain" (Erickson, 2005, pp. 87–88). As noted in this definition, addictive disorders are viewed as sinful practices, reserved for the morally weak, solved only by one's decision to stop drinking/drugging. Other tenets of this model include (a) the emphasis on personal choice as the basis of addiction, (b) individual and obstinate violation of societal norms (from whence the term "acting out" originates), and (c) the idea that individuals lack spiritual direction and need to "get right with God" for abstinence to occur.

The Moral Model has been used to elucidate several types of behaviors and client issues, from alcoholism/drug addiction to criminal behavior in general (Morse, 2004), sexual offending (Morse, 2003), mental illnesses such as depression (Kleinke & Kane, 1998) and dissociative identity disorder (Fine, 1996), and even HIV/AIDS transmission (McCoy, Miles, & Metsch, 1999). All share the common factor of encouraging individuals to assume personal responsibility for their actions and treatment outcomes. Even though the Moral Model is no longer strongly advocated in most treatment modalities, elements of it still exist and can be beneficial to the recovery process, including a focus on personal choices (i.e., responsibility) and the importance placed on seeking a spiritual connection during the recovery process (Morse, 2004; Wikipedia, 2005a).

The underpinnings of the Moral Model, particularly sinfulness and moral weakness, are most often lamented by family members when first confronted by their loved one's addictive behaviors. In fact, in every "family night" that I have ever hosted at a treatment facility, we have always discussed the feelings of parents, spouses, and friends as they relate to the addicted individual. Comments such as, "If she would just recognize how selfish she is!" and "He knows what he's doing is wrong and hurting the rest of us," and "If my son were just stronger, he could resist these terrible impulses" are common.

Clinical Case Example

One particular family comes to mind that had an extremely difficult time accepting anything other than the Moral Model as an explanation for their loved one's behaviors. Arlene, a 63-year-old mother of four and grandmother of nine, had been drinking wine for most of her adult life but solely with dinner. Recently divorced from her husband of 42 years, Arlene increased her wine consumption to the point that she was pulled over one morning and charged with driving while intoxicated (DWI). Her family was shocked by this event, particularly when she admitted that she had been drinking almost every day from dawn to bedtime over the course of the last 6 months. Similarly, she had begun dating a man 19 years her junior, had been spending more and more of her time out at night drinking and dancing, and had been avoiding all family-related functions. These additional facts astonished her family. At first, her family requested an intervention led by the parish priest, who agreed that a spiritual answer was the solution: Arlene was obviously mad at her ex-husband and needed to forgive him. If she could accomplish that, then she wouldn't need to rely on alcohol and could choose a better path. Although these observations were accurate, the intervention failed to produce lasting abstinence and actually resulted in an increase in her drinking. Arlene's family admitted her to substance abuse treatment against her will, citing the fact that her continued driving while intoxicated was endangering her life.

As it turned out, Arlene *was* mad, extremely so. She was mad at her ex-husband, at her children, at God, at the clinical staff, and even at yours truly, her counselor. During one particular group session, Arlene exclaimed, "You all think you know what's best for me. Well, you don't! I wasted most of my life with that SOB and now I want to have a little fun. What's wrong with that? So I got pulled over. That happens to people all the time! I'm not a bad person, even though my family thinks I'm like that old lady who's fallen and can't get up! And now my family, as well as all of you, think you have all the answers. I'm telling you, I can stop when I want to, and I want outta here!" In processing Arlene's statements with the group, many identified similar feelings, both around the idea of being at the mercy of someone else's desires (as most were court-mandated) and the idea of being able to stop whenever they chose. Having discussed models of addiction etiology and treatment in prior psychoeducational groups, the members were able to follow me when I asked, "Who is responsible for your being here, you or someone else?" For most, the "someone else" was chosen, particularly when that someone else was a judge, loved one, or doctor. But for some, specifically those who had been through prior treatment centers, the recognition of personal responsibility was apparent. Arlene was a member of the former group.

Family night brought additional challenges and insights for Arlene; her entire family attended (13 people in all out of a total group of 37 that night). As I noted earlier, we began the discussion about the reasons why people drink/drug (getting at participants' preconceptions). Most family members commented that drinking/drugging was due to a lack of willpower, poor choices, and bad influences. Two of Arlene's adult children, Ted and Jesabel, spoke up. Ted noted, "My mother was a good person, strong, always there for you when you needed her. Then dad took off with his coworker and that obviously was a blow to Mom. But she was strong … but then she met Reuben and everything went to hell. She's not acting like herself, she's let herself go, doing things she's never done before. I'm wondering if that kind of behavior has been just under the surface all the time. Did I not see her correctly?" Jesabel added, "Mom has always been so quiet, so proper. What happened to make her this way?"

Whereas the outcome of the above interactions was favorable, readers should recognize some of the key elements of the Moral Model that underlies these family members comments. For example, in the eyes of her family, Arlene's apparent "fall from grace" was the result of her drinking behaviors. Comments such as "was a good person," "she was strong," "not acting like herself," and "what happened?" indicated the family's adherence to the concepts of willful stubbornness, transgression, and poor decision making. Additionally, Arlene's statements of "I'm not a bad person" and "I can stop when I want to" have definite overtures of the ability to control herself (if she so desired) and her conceptualization of her own behaviors as unusual and sinful.

Summary and Integration

The Moral Model was one of society's, as well as the author's, first ways to conceptualize addictive disorders. It is also the first way that people tend to try and understand the behaviors of clients and loved ones. The key elements from this model that still apply today, particularly those that need to be stressed throughout the therapeutic process, include the power of personal choice and the necessity for addressing client spirituality during recovery. For without choices and spirituality, individuals are locked into an irrevocable moral dilemma, one without exits.

I Can't Help It—I Have a Disease: The Physiological Theory of Addiction

Right from the beginning, we want to address the communal complaint about the utility of the Physiological Theory of addictive disorders, particularly the Disease/Medical Model: Many see it as a way for addicted individuals to avoid taking responsibility for their actions. In fact, who *can't* relate to that same objection? Students, clinicians, family members, and even clients themselves often have difficulty in accepting the belief that addiction is something beyond individual control. Whereas some of this inability to acknowledge the Disease/Medical Model is a holdover from the Moral Model that still underlies our understanding of addictive behaviors, the main deterrent to acceptance is on an emotional level. As children and dad watch mom's refusal to cut back on the eating that is killing her, or as parents watch as their son smokes his scholarship away, or as an employer fires another person caught spending valuable time on Internet pornography, one cannot help but view these all as personally detrimental *choices* rather than predispositions.

Physiological Theory actually encompasses many different theoretical principles, most notably the Disease/Medical Model and Genetic Predisposition Theory. Although empirical evidence supporting these models can be somewhat inconclusive, a closer look is warranted due to the impact of these theories on the treatment and recovery communities.

The Disease/Medical Model

The founders of Alcoholics Anonymous (AA) responded to the detrimental impacts of the Moral Model when they first advocated for the disease concept of alcoholism (Walters, 1992). Unable to stop drinking by sheer determination, these early frontiersmen noted the similarities of their detrimental drinking habits with other brain disorders that also could not be solved by willpower. As a result, AA was one of the first groups to adopt the Disease Model, largely a result of alcoholics' struggle with the stigmatizing and embarrassing outcomes of the Moral Model.

In 1956, the American Medical Association (AMA) responded by passing a resolution stating that alcoholics must be treated like any other patient upon admittance to a hospital. Whereas most believe this was the first time that the medical community noted the disease concept of alcoholism, the diagnosis had actually been recognized by both the medical and psychiatric professions back in 1933 (Mann, Hermann, & Heinz, 2000). Later, the American Psychiatric Association (APA) recognized alcoholism as a disease in 1965, followed formally by the AMA in 1966. From that point forward, the Disease Model has been treated primarily with a medical approach, hence the often interchangeable use of "Disease Model" and "Medical Model" found throughout the literature (and this chapter).

First to conceptualize and popularize addiction as a disease, specifically alcoholism, Elvin M. Jellinek's 1960 work, *The Disease Concept of Alcoholism,* helped to destigmatize a growing problem in the United States (Erickson, 2005; Lyvers, 2000; Moyers & Miller, 1993). Jellinek outlined four distinct phases of the disease of alcoholism (Doweiko, 2002; Walters, 1992). Even before alcoholism develops, the individual uses alcohol in a self-medication fashion to cope with anxiety, stress, anger, or other troubling situations. This was termed the *Prealcoholic Phase,* and it is in this stage that one begins to lose initial control over alcohol consumption. With continued overindulgence, the individual enters the *Early* or *Prodromal Phase,* characterized by such behaviors as clandestine drinking, increased tolerance, chugging or gulping behaviors, and blackouts. Associated emotional/cognitive responses include guilt, preoccupation with drinking, and such distortions as minimization and rationalization. Physical dependence is the hallmark of the third stage, known as the *Middle* or *Crucial Phase.* At this point, the individual has lost control of his or her drinking, as well as experienced significant personality changes. Other common characteristics include (a) sacrificed friends, family, and career opportunities for the sake of continued drinking, (b) protective behaviors of one's supply of alcohol, (c) negligence of physical and emotional health, and (d) decreased self-esteem. Finally, in the *Late* or *Chronic Phase,* morning drinking is common, ethical standards are violated and laws broken, physical tremors and hallucinations are experienced, memory loss occurs, and a turn to alternate substances (e.g., rubbing alcohol, mouthwash, and Sterno) can take place when other alcoholic beverages are unavailable.

Two concepts that run throughout Jellinek's conceptualization of alcoholism as a disease are the alcoholic's inevitable *loss of control* and *inability to abstain* (Lyvers, 2000). In fact, the development of the diagnoses of alcohol abuse and dependence found in the *Diagnostic and Statistical Manual of Mental Disorders* is largely due to his work. Widely accepted in the treatment community, Jellinek's Disease Model continues to be claimed by the 12-step community as one of the primary explanatory constructs of addiction (Davis & Jansen, 1998).

Several underlying hypotheses that support the medical approach to treating the disease of addiction were noted by the National Council on Alcoholism and Drug Dependence in 1992 and have been supported by various authors (Talbott, as cited by Walters, 1992; Tommasello, 2004). In the authors' clinical practice, we have used these "5 P's of the Medical Model" to educate clients and families about the realities of the addictive disorder. First, addiction is a **Primary** disorder—it must be addressed before, or at least in conjunction with, any other disorder. As an example, imagine walking into an emergency room with a compound fractured arm while at the same time suffering a heart attack. Whereas the crushing pain in your chest might make it difficult to breathe, the excruciating pain resulting from the protruding bone in your arm would have you in tears and screaming for relief. Medical personnel would likely attend to the fracture, as it is quickly a recognizable problem. Similarly, your cries for help would direct them toward the arm. Unknowingly treating the fracture, the attending physician might miss the heart attack, which in all likelihood would kill you. So there you are, all patched up and dead on the gurney. Pretty gruesome, huh? This is similar to what happens in therapy. A family comes in with an urgent cry for help—fix "older brother" as he is, once again, in trouble both at school and with the legal system. Something has to be done *now* or he will be suspended and convicted! So off you go, a clinician doing his or her best to address the problem that the family presents. Unbeknownst to you, dad's gambling and alcohol consumption are tearing the family apart, but you do an excellent job and keep junior in school. Unfortunately, the primary problem was not addressed and will soon either kill the family unit or at least bring it back in during another apparent crisis.

The second "P" of the Medical Model is that addictions are **Progressive**, that is, they develop over time. I've never met a client who decided one day to wake up and assume the title of crack addict, or sexual addict, or spending addict. Whereas the motivations that underlie addictive disorders may differ in as many ways as there are individuals who struggle with them, these disorders develop slowly, following a similar (and **Predictable**) sequence to that outlined by Jellinek. Addictive disorders are also **Prolonged**, that is, they worsen over time, which is the third "P." As a matter of fact, addictive use of chemicals have been shown to cause irrevocable changes in the body and brain of addicted individuals, thus lending credence to the idea that this is a physical disease (Lyvers, 1998).

The fourth and scariest "P" of addictive disorders is that they are **Potentially** fatal. Similar to other chronic illnesses, without therapeutic attention, most addictions will eventually lead to one of three conclusions (as noted by the recovery movement): institutions (i.e., psychiatric facilities), prisons, or death. The final of the five "P's" as noted by the Medical Model is the most reassuring: Addictive disorders are **Positively** treatable. With help (and rarely without), individuals *do* recover, their lives become more manageable, and, for some, the lure of addictive use lessens and eventually may fade altogether.

To conclude, most of the attention of the Disease/Medical Model has been given to alcoholism. Does the same model work in understanding and explaining other addictive disorders? The answer is yes. Eating disorders, including obesity, have been examined with a Disease/Medical Model (Frank, 1998 ; Lester, 1997), as have drug use (Carroll, Nich, Frankforter, & Bisighini, 1999; Morse, 2004; Miller, Sheppard, & Magen, 2001), gambling (Grills, 2004; Lightsey & Hulsey, 2002; Wedgeworth, 1998), sex (Cooper, Shapiro, & Powers, 1998; Nixon, 2002; Plant & Plant, 2003), and the Internet (LaRose, Lin, & Eastin, 2003), as well as other mental illnesses (O'Connor, 2003; Zeitner, 2003). It appears that the Disease/Medical Model continues to be a valuable tool in the treatment and recovery communities.

Support for the Physiological Theory: The Impact of Genetics

The influence of genetic research helps support the Disease/Medical Model. Much research and ensuing debate have resulted from the work that has been conducted through the mapping of the human genome. As a result, scientists believe that they have discovered the "addiction" gene, or rather a group of chromosomes that contribute to the development of chemical dependency (Crabbe, 2002). These genes can therefore be passed along to children like any other genetic characteristic. Evidence that contributes to the influence of genetics on the development of addictive disorders includes adoption and twin studies, alcohol sensitivity studies, and neurobiological research.

It is no mystery that addiction runs in families. For example, some studies have noted that 50 percent of alcoholics had fathers who were alcoholics (Craig, 2004). But how does one "tease out" the influence of the environment (the classic nature versus nurture debate) to determine the genetic impacts? Two such methods have been employed. First, researchers have followed the development of addictive disorders in both monozygotic (i.e., identical) and dizygotic (i.e., fraternal) twins. Given that identical twins share the same genetic material, the likelihood of an addictive disorder developing among identical twins should therefore be greater than the development among fraternal twins. And in fact the research has shown just that: Identical twins are much more likely than fraternal twins to share similar alcoholic tendencies (Heath et al., 1997; Mustanski, Viken, Kaprio, & Rose, 2003; Slutske et al., 2002).

The second way to examine the influence of genetics is through the study of children of alcoholics/addicts who are separated from their natural parents and adopted by separate families. If genetics plays a determining role in the development of addictive disorders, there should be higher incidence of such disorders among these children even after they are raised apart from their addicted parent. Several studies, including the landmark research by Goodwin (as cited by Craig, 2004; Goodwin et al., 1974) in the 1970s and 1980s, as well as the more recent studies by Tyndale (2003) and Hopfer, Crowley, and Hewitt (2003), have noted the genetic influence on the development of addictive disorders by their investigation of the high incidence of alcoholism among adopted children.

Whereas the majority of earlier twin and adoption studies relied heavily on an exclusive focus on alcoholism and used predominantly male subjects (Erickson, 2005), current research has included other addictive substances (Tyndale, 2003) and behaviors (Fairburn, Cowen, & Harrison, 1999; Ibáñez, Blanco, de Castro, Fernandez-Piqueras, & Sáiz-Ruiz, 2003) as well as focused on how these disorders affect females (Heath et al., 1997; Slutske et al., 2002). Overall, a plethora of evidence has been collected that clearly demonstrates the value of the genetic component of the Disease/Medical Model through twin and adoption studies (Mann, Hermann, & Heinz, 2000; McLellan, Lewis, O'Brien, & Kleber, 2000).

Studies that note individuals' genetic sensitivity to alcohol also help to perpetuate the Disease/Medical Model (Mann, Hermann, & Heinz, 2000). Individuals differ in their sensitivity to, ability to metabolize, and allergic reactions to alcohol. Sensitivity implies that individuals are genetically predisposed to have lowered responses to alcohol; thus it takes more alcohol to become inebriated (Wall, Shea, Luczak, Cook, & Carr, 2005). Research has shown that alcoholics have a genetic predisposition to metabolize acetaldehyde at much lower rates than nonalcoholics (Nuutinen, Lindros, & Salaspuro, 1983; Quertemont, 2004), which results in a buildup of acetaldehyde. Acetaldehyde, the chemical compound that results from the liver's breakdown of ethanol (i.e., alcohol), is responsible for the hangover experience, as well as the unpleasant withdrawal symptoms. This buildup interacts with the brain's production of natural painkillers, which in turn leads individuals to drink more heavily to counteract the resulting pain and discomfort (Erickson, 2005). Those who drink more heavily therefore have a higher tendency toward alcoholism. The final aspect involved with genetic sensitivity involves research that indicates that some individuals have a predisposition to adverse reactions to alcohol. Some people are born with an abnormally low amount of aldehyde dehydrogenase (ALDH), particularly those of Asian decent (Wall, Horn, Johnson, Smith, & Carr, 2000). This lowered amount of ALDH, which metabolizes ethanol (alcohol), results in increased levels of acetaldehyde (Erickson, 2005). For these individuals, adverse reactions to increased acetaldehyde levels include immediate and unpleasant hangover symptoms. Therefore, these individuals are said to have a genetically based "allergic reaction" to alcohol and tend to avoid alcohol consumption. Interestingly, the drug Antabuse (used in the treatment of alcoholism) has the same effect of keeping acetaldehyde levels high in the recovering alcoholic (Wikipedia, 2005b). Any ingestion of alcohol results in immediate and unpleasant consequences (vomiting, stomach pain, facial flushing, etc.).

The final noteworthy support for the Physiological Theory of addictions involves two aspects of neurochemistry. First, research has demonstrated that neuron activity in the brain occurs in predictable patterns or pathways. The more frequently a behavior occurs, the most solidified the neuropathway in the brain that supports that specific behavior sequence becomes. Addictive use of chemicals and behaviors sets up similar pathways in the brain (Kassel, Stroud, & Paronis, 2003; Roller, 2004). In fact, evidence has pointed to the reinforcing effect of the serotonergic (dealing with the regulation of serotonin) or opioidergic pathways for continued substance and behavioral addictions (e.g., alcohol, heroin, food, and gambling) as a means to avoid withdrawal symptoms (Lyvers, 1998; Modesto-Lowe & Van Kirk, 2002). Similarly, the mesolimbic dopamine pathway (related to pleasurable sensations) is also negatively impacted by continuous addictive use (Lyvers, 1998; Petry, 2002). Finally, monoamine oxidase (MAO) levels, which are responsible for the degeneration of many brain neurotransmitters, particularly dopamine and serotonin, differ from individual to individual. Those with lower levels tend to be more prone to use substances or behaviors to enhance the reward center of the brain.

Research has pointed to lowered MAO levels among those prone to alcoholism (Eklund & Klinteberg, 2005). If there is too little or too much MAO in the system, the brain cannot work effectively, resulting in such disorders as addiction, depression, impulsivity, violence, and attention deficit disorder. It is clear from these studies that brain chemistry can increase the likelihood that individuals will develop addictive disorders, which provides further evidence for the Disease/Medical Model.

All this talk about genetic predisposition, physical sensitivity, and neurochemistry, while very important in understanding the importance of the Disease/Medical Model, will likely not result in your winning "the most interesting person at the party" award. Nonetheless, we have found it crucial to have a thorough understanding of the aforementioned topics so as to explain them in terms that clients and families can most easily digest. We now turn to an example for how this can occur.

Clinical Case Example

Arlen and Irene presented to the Intensive Outpatient Chemical Dependency program where I worked as a substance abuse counselor. Arlen fit the stereotypical "biker" persona, including multiple tattoos, long hair, weighing more than 250 pounds, wearing black leather—the works! On the other hand, Irene appeared more like a stereotypical middle-class housewife—middle-aged with a bun in her hair, wearing a V-neck sweater and Capri pants, quiet and demure. I cannot remember a more dissimilar couple in my experience! Nonetheless, Arlen was quick to admit during the initial assessment that he had a "problem" with drugs and alcohol. Married for just 2 weeks, he noted that his motivation for getting clean was "because the little woman here won't have me unless I clean up my act, and I guess that I'm ready for a change."

Though this was Arlen's first time through treatment, he had spent 6 years in prison for drug trafficking during the 1980s and had attended AA meetings in prison primarily to have some "free time." Consistently "rough" and aggressive in group, Arlen maintained that his drug use was under control, that he could stop any time that he wanted to, and that there wasn't anything anyone could teach him that he didn't already know. Proudly admitting to daily drinking and weekend "speedballing" (dangerously combining cocaine and heroin), Arlen would consistently say, "I'm a big guy: I can handle my liquor and whatever else you throw at me. Besides, if you've seen the kinda things I've seen [he was a Vietnam veteran], you'd use something to take the edge off too!" His lifestyle supported his self-identified impulsivity—he was a car salesman by day and "partied with friends" after work each night. The high-pressure sales, coupled with the intermittent payoffs following these sales, fed his need for intensity, as did his motorcycle riding while under the influence of drugs and alcohol.

Never admitting to having an "addiction" ("overindulging" was all that he ever said), Arlen was deeply in denial. In addition to his time in prison, as a direct/indirect result of his drug use, Arlen had been shot at, stabbed, arrested numerous times, divorced four times, had fathered three children whose names he did not know, had lost more jobs than he could count, and had been in several auto accidents. But regardless of the approach, Arlen was quick to deflect any inquiry of his "addictive disorder." This all changed one memorable Friday night—family night.

As I have noted earlier, the Disease/Medical Model is a very effective way to explore the development and consequences of addictive disorders for family members who are trying to understand their loved ones' behaviors. That night we explored the aforementioned "5 P's" of the Medical Model. With Irene in attendance, Arlen was especially attentive and unusually quiet. As I tended to do, I interactively drew from the clients' experiences to share how their addictions fit the model under discussion. When we got to the progressive nature of addictions, I overheard Arlen admit to his wife, "Whoa, that sounds like what happened to me, all the way from my teen-age years!" And then, one of two major breakthroughs from that evening occurred: In our discussion of the potentially fatal nature of addiction, Arlen admitted to the group, "Hey man, this guy must know what he's talking about because I've been through all three: I've been in prison, I've been close to death [he admitted here to two past, and heretofore undis-closed, overdoses], and now I'm in an institution!"

The "5 P's" discussion was followed with an adaptation of Carnes' (1994a) *Addictive System*. Whereas this model of addictive disorders was developed to explain sexual addiction, I have found it to be extremely effective in outlining the multiple influences on the development and maintenance of any addictive disorder. The model involves three interactive cycles that feed into one another (see Figure 2.1). The top/first cycle involves the Belief System, Impaired Thinking, the Addictive Cycle (which consists of the bottom/second cycle), and Unmanageability. The bottom cycle includes Preoccupation, Ritualization, Addictive Event, and Despair (with the third subcycle of Guilt and Shame). The model does an excellent job of incorporating aspects from several theories, including those from Physiological, Psychological, and Sociological Theories. For the purpose of this evening's discussion, I spent significant time highlighting the neurochemistry that occurs during the ritualization process. For the sake of this text, I share below how the entire cycle is typically explained to clients and their families.

The Addictive System

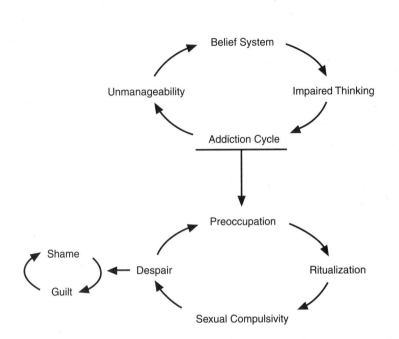

Figure 2.1 The Addictive System. (From Carnes, P. (1994a), *Contrary to love: Helping the sexual addict.* Center City, MN: Hazelden.

Belief System   The Belief System is the window through which we view the world. Through early experiences, primarily in childhood, we come to certain conclusions about ourselves and our relationships with others. If our youth was shaped by pain and inconsistency, or by neglect or poor boundaries, we assume that relationships with people are mostly unreliable. The four beliefs that Carnes (1994a) identified that are common to most addicted individuals are (a) I am basically a bad, unworthy person, (b) No one will love me as I am, (c) My needs are never going to be met if I have to depend on others, and (d) The object of my addiction (sex, alcohol, gambling, food, relationships, etc.) is my most important need. In the presentation about the *Addictive System*, I share that individual and group therapy is the most effective way to explore and challenge these underlying beliefs and to assist in the development of adaptive self-talk and sustaining behaviors.

Impaired Thinking   If our windows to the world are dirty, cracked, or broken, then the information that we receive from the outside world and the messages we send out through these windows are by their very nature inaccurate in most "normal" situations. Therefore, common reactions to the world for the addicted individual include distorted views of reality. This might be in the form of denial (**Don't Even Notice I Am Lying**), rationalizations ("rational lies" used to support arguments, excuses, and justifications), ignoring problems, blaming others, and minimizing behaviors. Sincere delusions, or believing your own lies, are the result, often followed by isolation, suspicion, and paranoia. The result of continued impaired thinking is that the addict cannot see that a specific incident or behavior is a part of a total behavioral pattern—they have lost touch with the reality in which the rest of the nonusing world operates. Group therapy and support group attendance are the most successful modalities to address impaired thinking, as members routinely challenge the "stinking thinking" associated with addictive logic.

Addictive Cycle   As you can imagine, toting a self-depreciating Belief System with a sustaining and impaired cognitive structure is not an easy or pleasurable way to approach life. This is one reason why it is so easy for individuals to succumb to an addictive disorder—they find something that consistently helps them to feel good about themselves or to numb out the realities of their lives. With continued use of a chemical or behavior, the individual finds himself or herself experiencing the Preoccupation, Ritualization, Addictive Event, and Despair found in the Addictive Cycle.

Preoccupation   Obsessively looking forward to the next time one can go to the bathroom at work to sneak a drink, log on to the computer to view pornography, or lay a bet down on the next race are all indicative of Preoccupation. Going through a day in a trancelike mood, addicts lose all sense of time and focus, rational thoughts disappear, and they often have the "thousand-yard stare" of someone lost in their own thoughts. They get fixated on the next time they can use a drug or behavior in order to calm the negative thoughts and emotions running through their heads.

Ritualization   Rituals are, by nature, positive things (e.g., getting up at the same time each morning, driving the same route to work, and practicing one's spirituality) that tend to make us feel comfortable and at ease. But for the addicted individual, rituals heighten the experience or high. Ritualistic behaviors involve three processes: obtaining "it," preparing "it," and using "it" (with the "it" representing the addictive chemical or behavior). Take, for example, someone who wants to purchase his or her weekly supply of marijuana. "Obtaining" rituals might include paging the dealer, waiting by the phone for the return call, driving the same route to the dealer's home, stopping by the same ATM to withdraw money, stopping at the same convenience store to purchase a large drink and a pack of cigarettes, and then haggling over price with the dealer. "Preparing" rituals might involve "cleaning" the marijuana (removing seeds and stems, breaking/ cutting it into usable forms), weighing the larger amount and breaking it into smaller amounts, hiding some for future use, and rolling it all into marijuana cigarettes. Finally, "using" rituals might involve the individual's preferred way of smoking the marijuana, including inviting friends over, watching certain movies, listening to music, playing video games, having junk food readily available, or going out to socialize/work/school.

The power of these rituals has been demonstrated medically and scientifically through the use of magnetic resonance imaging (MRI). While scanning the brains of addicted individuals as they describe their behavioral rituals, researchers have been able to target certain areas of the brain where neurotransmitters such as dopamine and adrenaline are dumped into the system (Lambert, 2000; Volkow & Fowler, 2002). In essence, during the Ritualization process, addicted individuals' brains actually "get high" from the neurochemistry dump before the actual chemical is consumed or the behavior is performed. The intimate therapeutic environment afforded by individual, couple, family, and group therapy can assist addicted individuals in identifying their rituals and to develop more adaptive behaviors to counteract the sequence. Without recognizing one's rituals, and without the strong support to substitute positive behaviors, the addict with a legitimate reason to withdraw money from the ATM to purchase milk at the convenience store may find herself in the midst of a ritualistic cycle that ends with chemical use.

The Addictive Event   I describe the Addictive Event, or as Carnes (1994a) called it, "Acting Out," as the inevitable ingestion of a chemical or engagement of behavior that serves as the end result for Preoccupation and Ritualization. Whether it be the intake of a chemical, a sexual act, a food binge, placing a bet, or logging on to the Internet, the distinguishing characteristic of the Addictive Event is that the individual cannot control or stop his or her behavior. Given the strength of the behavioral sequence, as well as the physiological evidence of chemical and behavioral neuropathways, the likelihood of the Addictive Event *not* occurring following the Preoccupation and Ritualization stages is slim. In order to have any chance of circumventing the predictable event, we have found that an immediate intervention is necessary, most often with a re-directive behavior. Such behaviors include meeting with a sponsor for coffee, immediately attending a support group meeting, calling someone, going to the closest place of worship, or heading to a hospital emergency room. But again, we reiterate that if someone has already completed his or her Ritualistic behaviors, the likelihood of the Addictive Event occurring is great.

Despair The hopelessness and powerlessness that occur following the Addictive Event are what some call "coming down" or "crashing." This black hole–like experience encompasses a subcycle of Shame and Guilt. Shame is inward focused and may include statements such as, "I can't believe I did it again! I am such a coward! I promised myself (my daughter, significant other, etc.) that I'd stay away from it! This is never going to end!" On the other hand, Guilt is directed outward and is focused on the likelihood of getting caught: "Oh, I'm going to suffer for this one! Everyone is going to find out! My significant other is going to leave me! I'm going to jail for sure this time!" Coupled with the physical withdrawal and extreme discomfort that occur following a binge, the emotional anguish that is experienced in Despair are what drive many to contemplate suicide. In fact, the likelihood of successful suicide attempts increases greatly immediately after addictive use of chemicals (e.g., methamphetamines [Callor et al., 2005], cocaine and hallucinogens [Kelly, Cornelius, & Lynch, 2002], and alcohol [Hjelmeland & Groholt, 2005]) or behaviors (e.g., gambling [Ledgerwood, Steinberg, Wu, & Potenza, 2005], sex [Carnes, 1994b], and eating [Stice & Shaw, 2004]).

Preoccupation Revisited Any negative mood state is particularly problematic for the addicted individual (as we will explore in Psychological Theory). Given that no one wants to experience the feelings found in Despair for very long, and since addictive use becomes the primary coping mechanism for the individual, the quickest way to move toward feeling better is to look forward to the next drug/behavior use. There are also several physiological benefits of preoccupation, as research has shown that the anticipation associated with drug use releases such neurotransmitters as dopamine and serotonin (Lambert, 2000; Volkow & Fowler, 2002).

Unmanageability Addicted individuals spend an incredible amount of time and energy struggling to keep their secret life (i.e., the one that supports their addictive behaviors) from affecting their public one (i.e., the one they allow others to see). The more frequently they rotate through the Addictive Cycle, the more evident negative consequences become. From arrests, unmasked lies, disrupted lives, unmet commitments, and failed attempts to explain the unexplainable, addicts are confronted by those closest to them about the realities of their maladaptive and self-destructive behaviors.

This in turn leads addicts to isolate themselves, as the relationship with the drug or behavior soon supersedes their relationships with people. They become alienated from those on whom they once depended; life becomes unmanageable and unlivable without the addictive drugs or behaviors.

Belief System Revisited   When life becomes unmanageable, addicts may begin to reach out for help. Unfortunately for them, many bridges have been burned, people have been exploited, and unmasked lies often leave loved ones angry and confused. So naturally, when addicts turn to those whom they have hurt, they are met with resistance and resentment. This is especially true when the ambivalent behaviors of the addict vacillate between wanting to stop drinking/drugging/acting out and not being "strong enough" to stop. Family and friends are shocked at the behaviors that they see and eventually become reluctant to "put themselves out there" for their struggling loved one/friend to hurt again. These natural by-products of the addict's behaviors then feed back into their core beliefs about themselves. Common statements that we've heard include the following: (a) "Well of course I can't stop. I am a bad and unworthy person. I'll never be able to get beyond this . . ." (which nourishes the first core belief), (b) "Now I've driven away *another* important relationship, just when I was willing to let them know who I really am!" (which feeds back into the second core belief), (c) "I can't trust people. They're always after me to change. 'Change, or I'll leave you!' is all I hear! Who needs them anyway?" (which reinforces the third core belief), and (d) "I might as well just keep doing it [drinking/drugging/acting out]. At least I know that I can depend on it to meet my needs" (which bolsters the fourth core belief).

The reinforced core beliefs then strengthen the impaired cognitive system, which in turn support more addictive use. Each time through the cycle, addicted individuals use larger amounts of the substance or engage in more intense behaviors, their despair becomes more pronounced, and their lives becomes more unmanageable. Unfortunately, it isn't until their lives have become so impossible to maintain (often referred to as hitting "rock bottom") that they are willing to do whatever it takes to break free from the cycle and seek treatment.

It was toward the end of this lecture that I noticed Arlen softly crying in the back of the room. Believe me when I say how shocked I was; Arlen was one tough guy with an apparently impenetrable exterior. But there he was, sobbing softly at first, then more loudly, head on Irene's shoulder, with other clients' hands on his back as he allowed the information to sink in. After allowing him some time to emote, I invited him to share his feelings about the topic. "Doc, I've heard a lot of people tell me what's wrong with me but have never believed it before. Sure, I see how the Disease Model works for my case. Those 5 P's make sense to me. But when I saw you draw *my life* up there on the board with that Systems Model, that really hit home. I guess if they have written books about this stuff, and if they have young guys like you trained in it well enough to explain it to a regular Joe like me, this whole thing has *got* to be real!" This revelation was followed by Arlen acting very different for the next few weeks—he was very active in group, was able to relate to other clients, and spent significant time exploring alternative ways to treat his addictive disorder. For him, the Disease Model demonstrated that his struggles with willpower were never going to be enough to win. To conclude, Arlen once stated, "I mean, how is a guy gonna think his way outta heart disease? That's insanity right there!"

Summary and Integration

Physiological Theory has served numerous clients throughout their recovery program, and given that it is the most prevalent theory in the medical and 12-step communities, it is important that the competent clinician recognize how it can be explained to clients and their families. But like any theory, there are several arguments both for and against conceptualizing addictive disorders with the physiological framework. We have found it very helpful to explore each of these with clients and their families and to invite critical discussions about how each of these applies (or doesn't) to the individuals' addictions. Following this discussion, we will review those aspects of Physiological Theory that are most beneficial to working with families.

Several positive outcomes of Physiological Theory have been noted (Erickson, 2005; Moyers & Miller, 1993). First, it helps remove the moral stigma, embarrassment, shame, and guilt attached to addictive use of chemicals and behaviors. Individuals come to recognize that whereas they may have had a choice at one point to not drink or drug, by the time dependence results, the resulting disease is both beyond their control and beyond a simple statement of "I just won't drink anymore." Another positive outcome is that understanding the theory can increase individuals' motivation for seeking treatment and being responsible for their recovery. Similar to living with heart disease, which usually begins following a heart-related crisis, seeking treatment for addiction is just the first step. One has to maintain those behaviors that keep the disease from reoccurring. For the heart patient, this would involve exercise, healthy eating, stress management, medication compliance, and regular doctor's visits. For the recovering addict, it includes maintaining a support system, engaging in regular accountability, sustaining a balanced lifestyle (including spirituality, exercise, proper nutrition, healthy relationships, etc.), and periodic therapeutic "checkups."

A third beneficial aspect to Physiological Theory is that it offers an explanatory construct for addictive disorders. With the aid of various diagrammed models of addiction (e.g., Patrick Carnes's *Addictive System*, 1994a) and videos and books that explain addiction, as well as through the use of the "5 P's," the debilitating and confounding addictive process can be understood by those who are affected. During the psychoeducational part of inpatient or intensive outpatient treatment, I have successfully used models like Carnes's *Addictive System* to explain to clients and families how addictions begin and progress. Even with the staunchest of clients in denial, an explanatory tool like a diagram can help begin the acceptance process.

The last two advantages of Physiological Theory are that it promotes research and ensures third-party reimbursement. Since the vast majority of the scientific community accepts the Disease/Medical Model, money is allocated both for further research in the efficacy of using this approach for the treatment of addictive disorders and for better understanding the etiology and progression of addiction. Also, given that the medical society advocates a medical approach (as evidenced by the pharmacological approach to detoxification), and since most addictive disorders (at least those to chemicals) are assigned a medical diagnosis, insurance companies will reimburse practitioners who treat these disorders. The outcome of both of these advantages is that the treatment community gets timely and accurate information for addressing these disorders and receives payment to attract competent professionals.

There are also several drawbacks to viewing addictions with a physiological lens (Erickson, 2005; Moyers & Miller, 1993; Walters, 1992). As we already noted, even though it can encourage personal responsibility for treatment and abstinence, it can also absolve individuals from assuming responsibility for their actions. The last thing a hopeful spouse wants to hear from her husband upon returning home from treatment is, "See, I told you. This is a disease that I've got—I can't help it. Now stop nagging me and get me a beer!" Similarly, if the progression or focus of someone's addictive disorder does not fit the Disease/Medical Model, the individual may not seek treatment. For those who are addicted to processes or behaviors (gambling, sex, spending, etc.), a medical approach may not be the most effective etiological explanation or treatment modality. Therefore, a sexual addict might assume, "I'm not addicted to heroin or alcohol like Jimmy down the street who got sober at the local clinic. Therefore, I'm not really an addict." The other side of the coin is also true: Strict adherence to a Disease/Medical Model of treatment, devoid of the consideration of such things as underlying psychological processes, environmental influences, and learned behaviors, is not effective for long-term abstinence and sobriety. The final critique of Physiological Theory is that untreated illnesses such as cancer, heart disease, and diabetes inevitably lead to a worsening of these conditions and often result in death. Conversely, research has demonstrated that some addictive disorders cease to exist, even without treatment, which flies in the face of the Prolonged/Chronic criteria of the Disease/Medical Model.

There are clear advantages and disadvantages to using the Physiological Model to conceptualize addictive disorders. As it is used throughout the majority of treatment settings, clinicians are encouraged to be familiar with the benefits and drawbacks of its use. As a way to conclude this section of the chapter, we want to mention one additional tool that evolved out of Physiological Theory. Since we noted the efficacy of the "5 P's" as a method to explain the Disease Model to clients and families, we want to take this time to briefly reference one of the junior author's proven treatment strategies known as "Hagedorn's 6 P's of Recovery": **Prior Planning Prevents Piss-Poor Performance.** As a U.S. Marine (it *does* have a military ring to it, doesn't it?), I learned that this acronym represented the need to always be prepared for the unexpected. Throughout the years as an addictions counselor, I have reiterated the need for careful planning as a crucial element of successful recovery.

Similar to any other chronic disease, addiction requires proactive planning with a focus on the unexpected. Take diabetes, for example: Those who live with this disease have to have readily available access to insulin, which must be stored in a cool environment (i.e., the refrigerator). If regular use of insulin is a necessary part of an individual's health, he or she should plan for such things as, say, power outages. Coolers, dry ice, generators, and other storage considerations should all be carefully considered in order to maintain one's insulin supply, with a backup plan in case the primary plan fails. This is analogous to the careful planning needed for someone in recovery from alcoholism. In early recovery, the individual might have planned Wednesday afternoons as his or her regular lunch with a sponsor. Then, a "power outage" occurs one Wednesday morning: A fight with a spouse triggers a craving for alcohol. But since lunch is a regular part of the recovery plan, the individual has the necessary incentive to avoid the first drink. But say the sponsor doesn't make it to lunch that day—what's the backup plan? Someone who takes his or her recovery plan seriously would have a list of noontime AA meetings near the restaurant for such an eventuality. Though one might find the "6 P's" a humorous approach to recovery planning, we have found it crucial in the fight against a disease that is cunning, baffling, and powerful, against a disease that can't be out-thought but *can* be out-planned.

Numbing Out—The Psychological Theory of Addictive Disorders

"Life is difficult" are the infamous first three words of M. Scott Peck's *The Road Less Traveled* (Peck, 1978). Anyone who has survived beyond adolescence can attest to the truth of those words: Life is a series of challenges, setbacks, joys, sorrows, pains, and pleasures. Another saying, "When the going gets tough, the tough go shopping," is something I recall one of my friends saying in college. And it rings true—for who *hasn't* turned to some activity or chemical at one time or another to help relieve stress, to "take the edge off" a trying experience, or, as Billy Joel used to sing, to try to forget about life for a while? Whether it be shopping after a long week, eating a bowl (or two) of ice cream after a relationship breakup, happy hour following a hard day, an intense workout following an argument, or surfing the Internet to "veg out" for a little while, most everyone has engaged in similar activities to help them cope with life's challenges. The problem occurs when we continuously turn to such activities as our primary coping mechanism, or worse yet, when our use of chemicals or behaviors becomes a stressor in and of itself.

The Psychological Theory of addiction explains addiction in terms of conscious and unconscious processes that lead to the escape from existential suffering (Ventegodt, Morad, Kandel, & Merrick, 2004). This makes intuitive sense: If you could lessen your pain by taking an aspirin, most would do so. Further, if someone can have a drink to help de-stress after a tough day, why not? But for those who turn to the addictive use of chemicals or behaviors, the stress that drives them to such use is usually greater than a simple headache or hard day. For example, the tremendous amount of childhood abuse that our addicted clients report is beyond the common "I'm having a hard week" kind of stress. Similarly, due to the lack of developed and healthy coping mechanisms found with addicted individuals, escaping through chemical or behavior use has little in the way of checks or balances. That is, for someone who has a supportive network of friends, who has a healthy practice of spirituality, and whose body is disciplined through regular exercise, having an occasional drink may be a nonissue. On the other hand, for someone who is isolated from others, who has experienced significant trauma in his childhood, who is angry with God and distant from any spiritual practice, and who is 50 pounds overweight, one drink may not be enough. Using alcohol, drugs, sex, or gambling may be an effective way to "numb out." But too much numbing hinders individual and relational development, causing significant psychological distress.

In essence, Psychological Theory is an umbrella theory that encapsulates several other theoretical concepts, most notably that of Behavioral Theory, the Self-Medication Hypothesis, and the Addictive Personality. Let's take a closer look at each.

The Influence of Behavioral Theory

The behavioral origin of addictive disorders begins with the classic stimulus–response connection. Wulfert, Greenway, and Dougher (1996) noted that there is a range of addictive-like behaviors (e.g., drinking, sex, gambling), with *normal* use on one end of the spectrum and *addictive* use on the other. Behaviors, they say, will reach the addictive level only if they are reinforced, be it either positively (through encouragement) or negatively (through avoidance). For example, many sexual addicts engage in sexual activity (at least initially) because it has a strong positive reinforcement—it feels good. On the other hand, some sexual activities may be maintained by their ability to alleviate negative mood states (avoidance).

Another way to examine the impact of reinforcements is with the A-B-C explanation of chemical/behavior use. This involves an **A**ntecedent, which is usually a triggering emotion, event, or interaction. This is followed with a **B**ehavior that is used to cope with the event (e.g., ingestion of a chemical, placing a bet on a game, looking at pornography). Following the behavior is a reinforcing **C**onsequence, either one that is pleasurable and encouraging (e.g., the individual gets "high") or one that is avoidant (i.e., resulting in a reduction in tension or stress). This model supports the notion that individuals will engage in their addictive behaviors as long as the consequences meet their need for pleasure or pain reduction. Further, behavioral theory assumes that with repeated use of a substance or behavior, the individual will either (a) experience increased pleasure (which will involve the need for increased amounts or intensity) or (b) experience reduced negative stimuli (e.g., through the use of sex, cocaine, or prescription medications): Both will lead to eventual addictive use. Paradoxically, with continued addictive use, the motivating factor of pleasure *decreases* whereas the motivating factor of pain reduction (e.g., dealing with withdrawal symptoms or alleviating frustrating relationship issues) *increases*.

One final aspect to consider in conceptualizing addictive behavior with the behavioral aspect of Psychological Theory is that of underlying motivations for behavior. Four main reasons exist that explain and sustain behavioral choices: attention, avoidance, tangible reward, and sensory stimulation (Cox Jones, Vallano, Ryan, Helsel, & Rancurello, 1991; Reese,

Richman, Zarcone, & Zarcone, 2003; Sigafoos & Tucker, 2000). Both positive and negative attention, be it from peers, parents, or authority figures, increases the likelihood of repeated behaviors. Avoidance might include the removal of a negative mood or the ability to evade responsibility. Obtaining the tangible involves receiving something of value as a result of behavior, be it money, privilege, or power. Finally, sensory stimulation consists of behaviors that appeal to the five senses.

It is difficult to imagine any behavior that does not fit one of, if not a combination of these motivating factors. For example, what would inspire someone to work long hours of overtime? It might be attention from the boss, avoidance of an unpleasant home environment, or obtaining tangible income. These are the same motivations that perpetuate workaholism (Burke, 1999; Porter, 2001). Similarly, why would someone compulsively use cocaine, even when it is causing her significant personal distress? Perhaps the discipline (attention) she receives from her heretofore inattentive parents (remember that negative attention is "better" than no attention at all) helps her to feel special for once. Or maybe her hangover-like feelings (following a night of bingeing) allows her to avoid the stress of attending her college classes (where she has been studying topics that are of more interest to her parents than to her). Or maybe, due to emotional repression, her cocaine use provides her with the sensory stimulation she craves but is unable to express. As one might imagine, there are multiple potential combinations of these four motivating factors that influence behavior. Given enough time, insight, and support, most clients can identify their individual motivations for continued use of chemicals or behaviors. It is the clinician's job to facilitate this discovery process.

Hiding the Hurt: The Self-Medication Hypothesis

The Self-Medication Hypothesis attributes addictive use of chemicals or behaviors to the lessening of psychological pain (Gelkopf, Levitt, & Bleich, 2002; Greeley & Oei, 1999; Hussong, Galloway, & Feagans, 2005). In this context, individuals use such things as sex, alcohol, eating, work, or cocaine to self-medicate their distress or as an escape from a painful reality. Evidence of the efficacy of this model can be found in the high correlation between substance use and childhood abuse survival. Addictive behaviors are found in large numbers among those who have sustained abuse, particularly sexual, as a means to cope with the resulting emotional trauma and shame (Brems, Johnson, Neal, & Freemon, 2004; Garneski & Deikstra, 1997; Logan, Walker, Cole, & Leukefeld, 2002). Addictive use of chemicals and behaviors by those who suffer from mental illnesses is further evidence of the value of this theory (Harris & Edlund, 2005;

Scheller-Gilkey, Woolwine, Cooper, Gay, Moynes, & Miller, 2003; Weiss, Griffin, & Mirin, 1992). Those who suffer from such disorders as depression, anxiety, and schizophrenia are more likely to abuse mind-altering chemicals or behaviors to regulate their moods and experiences than are those who do not suffer from these illnesses.

Living the Lifestyle: The Addictive Personality

Another tenet of the Psychological Theory is the "Addictive Personality." This concept implies that once individuals form an addictive relationship with a chemical or behavior, they will always be susceptible to forming other addictive relationships. Whereas researchers have spent considerable time exploring the empirical evidence that defines a common set of characteristics and traits for this personality type (e.g., Davis, Katzman, & Kirsh, 1999; Davis & Karvinen, 2002; Johnson, 2003; Seymour, 2003), the evidence is often mixed and inconclusive. Rather, the majority of information that substantiates this phenomenon is clinical and anecdotal. Given that the adage "Once an addict, always an addict" is based on this philosophy, and since it is found throughout the treatment and recovery communities, it warrants a mention here.

One of the primary beliefs underpinning the Addictive Personality is, in essence, that of a split and adversarial personality: the "Self" versus the "Addict" (Nakken, 1996). Nakken explored the addictive personality extensively and asserted, "The Self represents the 'normal,' human side of the addicted person, while the Addict represents the side that is consumed and transformed by the addiction" (p. 25). Addictive use of chemicals or behaviors feeds the "Addict" and allows for the development of destructive and self-perpetuating character traits and behaviors (e.g., pleasure seeking, controlling, selfishness, infantile behaviors, obsessive thinking, all-or-nothing thinking, isolative preferences, delusional thinking, shameful feelings, and dependency). Meanwhile, continued addictive use leads to the destruction of the "Self" and eliminates both the chance to have any real relationships and the ability to maintain any sense of spiritual connectedness.

Walters (1992) noted several behavioral characteristics common to the Addictive Personality, or what he termed the addictive lifestyle. First, those who addictively use chemicals or behaviors demonstrate irresponsibility or pseudo-responsibility. This involves a lack of commitment or accountability with one's loved ones and friends. Whereas the addicted individual may appear to "have it all together" and may be a "functioning addict/alcoholic," maintaining a façade of normalcy is all that can be accomplished. Relationships with people tend to be superficial, and when forced to choose between meeting obligations to the chemical/behavior and meeting obligations to the people in the addict's life, the addict will choose the chemical/behavior. Those struggling with an Addictive Personality will therefore need to closely monitor their ability to create and maintain meaningful relationships with people in order to avoid falling into the trap of irresponsibility or pseudo-responsibility.

Walters' (1992) next behavioral trait, stress-coping imbalance, is exhibited by a cyclical struggle in which one experiences social/environmental stressors, uses addictively to cope with the stressors, and then experiences increased social/environmental stressors. Similar to the self-medication hypothesis, the struggling addict never develops appropriate coping skills or invests enough time in developing supportive relationships to face life's challenges. This lack of emotional maturity is another common factor found in the Addictive Personality. When an individual begins to use chemicals/behaviors to cope with stressors or powerful emotions, their emotional development will freeze at that point. For example, say a 14-year-old tackles school-related pressures with the aid of marijuana, and this chemical use advances throughout the years until she reaches 40. At 40 she enters treatment, and without fully developed coping skills and emotional maturity, she would likely approach life's challenges with the emotional skills of a 14-year-old. She, as well as others with an Addictive Personality, will often need to develop basic coping skills, need to learn stress management techniques, and need remedial communication skills training.

For the Addictive Personality, another component of developing emotional maturity and appropriate coping skills involves learning relationship skills. According to Walters (1992), addicted individuals lack basic interpersonal skills. Attracted to the superficiality of "using" friends, addicted individuals develop rituals and language patterns that support relationships with the common bond of addictive use (noted again when we get to Sociocultural Theory). For example, those who smoke marijuana will tend to seek relationships with others who smoke marijuana, but these relationships will develop only as far as the drug use takes them. Those with an Addictive Personality will therefore need to learn how to be authentic with others, which may include experiencing and expressing emotions, as well as being assertive, "present," and congruent.

Walters' (1992) last noted set of behaviors found in the Addictive Personality includes social rule-breaking or rule-bending. Whereas some drug use or addictive behaviors are primarily maintained by criminal activity (e.g., robbery to support a heroin addiction, embezzlement to pay gambling debts, or voyeurism as part of sexual addiction), many rules and laws are bent or broken as a "natural" part of the addictive lifestyle. Examples include driving while intoxicated, underage drinking, shoplifting, buying and selling drugs, and opening another credit card (for the spending addict) with no intention of reimbursement. Dishonesty, half-truths, justifications, and rationalizations are also a part of the rule-bending found in the Addictive Personality. Total honesty, then, is the goal for recovery, often called "rigorous honesty" throughout the 12-step movement. Individuals in recovery need to learn how to be honest with themselves, honest with others, and honest with society.

For additional information on the Addictive Personality, the reader is encouraged to read Nakken's (1996) *The Addictive Personality*. For the purposes of this chapter, though, we want to highlight the fact that the term and philosophy have been applied to myriad addictive disorders, including drugs and alcohol (Johnson, 2003), food (Seymour, 2003), gambling (Jacobs, 1986), exercise (Davis, Katzman, & Kirsh, 1999), and even self-injurious behaviors (Davis & Karvinen, 2002).

How does Psychological Theory play out in working with addicted individuals and their families? First of all, we have found that family members more readily accept this theory over other theories, especially if they have been privy to the psychological pain of their loved one. For example, with Arlene, most of her family understood that her behaviors were the direct result of her husband leaving her. People can usually connect with the feelings of betrayal and abandonment that drive many to the addictive use of food, with the loneliness and isolation that lead people to spend hours on the Internet, and with the unhappiness brought on by a miserable relationship that causes people to abuse cocaine.

Clinical Case Example

Dwayne was one such client whose pain was evident upon our first meeting. Morbidly obese, 23-year-old Dwayne weighed in the neighborhood of 450 pounds when we first started working together. Always quick with a joke (which always included some type of self-deprecating comment), Dwayne was adamantly against self-disclosing anything below surface-level statements. Having been through treatment programs in the past, Dwayne was cognizant of the fact that his addictive relationship with food replaced his need to trust human relationships. Abused and neglected as a boy, although initially not willing to explore those experiences, he readily admitted that "food is my best friend . . . it never hits me, it always comforts me, and I know it'll be there when I need it."

We explored his eating habits with the A-B-C approach from Psychological Theory. He was able to identify those antecedents (social anxiety, depression, interactions with women, any form of conflict) that always led to bingeing on food. Whereas his eating helped him to feel full, or to fulfill his need for connectedness, in reality the emptiness he experienced as a result of his childhood neglect was so profound that no amount of food would ever be enough to fill the void. The consequence of his eating habits was that it provided him with an extremely large body. The resulting skin and fat helped him to avoid situations where he might have to face his need for affection, attention, and belonging from a hostile world: People were literally unable to get close to him.

Continuing with the motivations for his continued bingeing behaviors, we identified a craving for attention (whenever Dwayne entered a room, all eyes would turn to him). "But that's crazy, Doc," Dwayne would say. "I can't stand it when people look at me. I just want to crawl under a rug!" But with time, Dwayne recognized his need for attention and we were able to devise other, more productive ways for him to get that attention. Similarly, Dwayne's large size allowed him to avoid any responsibilities around the group home where he lived. His resulting health issues (high blood pressure, difficulty breathing, and swollen feet) prevented him from being a productive member of the home. This was addressed by first finding him chores that could be performed with little effort and moving toward more involved activities as his weight decreased. Finally, Dwayne admitted that he relished the sensations involved with eating. This was quite challenging to counteract as eating involves all five senses, but with considerable time, Dwayne learned the value of moderation and delayed gratification.

After 4 months of treatment (which included individual therapy, adherence to an eating plan, attendance at Overeaters Anonymous, and membership in group therapy), Dwayne had started losing weight. But he had also begun "feeling." And feelings for Dwayne were extremely uncomfortable: He had been medicating his early traumatic experiences with food for as long as he could remember. At this point, he would often present in group either in an emotional rage or withdraw totally from the group process. His emotional development was severely retarded and he would often engage in crying fits, temper tantrums, and attempts to split the clinical staff (i.e., playing "mom" against "dad"). Following those sessions that were particularly troublesome for Dwayne, and without his emotional "food bandage," he would remain sullen and depressed. Learning how to experience feelings, how to express them in appropriate ways, and how to seek support throughout these processes were valuable lessons for him.

Since his eating habits were strictly monitored, Dwayne found other "creative" ways to address his emotional pain—and this was when he first revealed his struggle with self-injurious behaviors (SIB—also known as self-mutilative behavior [SMB]); that is, he cut himself with razors, paper clips, and nail files. During one individual session, Dwayne dramatically rolled up the leg of his sweatpants to expose his thigh, crisscrossed with more than 50 cuts and scratches. "What do you think, Doc? Am I one sick puppy or what?" he asked. "Well, Dwayne," I answered, "what is it like for you to share that with me?" "Okay, I guess," he said. "Kinda freaky. I mean, is this stuff normal or am I off my rocker?" "You tell me," I retorted. "Does it help you to deal with your feelings?" "Yeah, I guess it does," he responded. "But I still think it's freaky."

From the Psychological Theory, we explored some of the more common reasons for SIB, which has been likened to an addiction (Davis & Karvinen, 2002). These reasons fall into two broad categories: (a) relief from unpleasant experiences and feelings (such as depersonalization, severe anxiety, intense anger, depression, perceived external/internal flaws, loneliness, emptiness, and insecurity) and (b) social reinforcements (e.g., to gain attention from others or to avoid unpleasant tasks) (Kress, 2003; Nock & Prinstein, 2004). Dwayne readily agreed to the fact that cutting himself helped to redirect his emotional pain (which he felt that he had no control over) into physical pain (which he *could* control). Feeling unworthy of positive comments, experiencing extreme anger directed at authority figures, and suffering from free-floating anxiety, he expressed experiencing tremendous emotional relief whenever he engaged in these behaviors (the medicative factor of SIB), but that this relief was short-lived, often replaced with shame and anger. He concluded the session with the following heartfelt revelation: "If I can't have food, I gotta use something to make myself feel better. Don't take this away from me too."

Following this intensely revealing session, Dwayne continued to make significant progress with his eating behaviors and lost some significant weight. Dwayne was convinced, on his own accord, that he had an addictive personality, especially after he completed a worksheet that asked about other addictive tendencies, where he listed Internet use, video games, shopping, watching TV, and smoking (all of which had caused him significant distress in the past). But he was unwilling to address the secrecy about his cutting behaviors, never admitting to it during the group process where he would have learned that he was not alone. Dwayne ended up leaving treatment prematurely, his progress likely impeded by his lack of disclosure and reluctance to work on his SIB in conjunction with his eating. The clear connection between Dwayne's emotional pain and his addictive use of food and cutting is a prime example of the Psychological Theory of addiction.

Summary and Integration

As a child, I lived adjacent to an expressway. My bedroom window was no more than 50 yards from a bustling highway filled with cars, trucks, construction, emergency vehicles, you name it. You would think the noise would have become unbearable, but that's the interesting point: After a while, I never heard the noise; it had just become a part of my daily routine. This is similar to what has happened with many of the tenets of Psychological Theory; many of the core principles have become so ingrained within the treatment and recovery processes that clients and clinicians do not necessarily note their presence. I would venture to say that no other theory has had such a tremendous impact on our current understanding of addictive disorders.

For example, examining triggers for relapse is an extremely common topic throughout individual, group, and support group modalities. The treatment and recovery processes necessitate gaining insight into the feelings (e.g., boredom, stress, worry, success, anger, sorrow, shame, excitement, frustration), situations (e.g., changes in routine, environmental cues like sporting events or weddings), people (e.g., relationship difficulties, "old drinking buddies," authority figures, parents), sensory input (e.g., smells, sounds, sights, tastes, and tactile sensations), and times/dates (after work, weekends, holidays, anniversaries, etc.) that serve as the antecedents for addictive behaviors. In fact, the acronym HALT (which represents Hungry, Angry, Lonely, and Tired—the most common relapse warning signs) is touted throughout the recovery community as a reminder to those antecedents most likely to re-spark addictive use. Similarly, grasping the primary motivations for continued behaviors, such as attention, avoidance, sensory stimulation, or obtaining tangible rewards, is an important part of the treatment and recovery process. Finally, it is crucial to recognize the consequences that follow addictive behaviors that reinforce the likelihood of those behaviors continuing.

Another principle offered by the behavioral aspect of Psychological Theory includes the necessary steps to both break negative behavioral patterns and establish new and positive sequences. These steps include *identifying exceptions to the pattern*, that is, when the addictive behavior does *not* follow the trigger or when the reinforcing consequence does *not* follow the behavior. Another step, *setting up new behavioral sequences* through the use of modeling, rehearsal, and positive reinforcers is important. *Identifying available resources for change* (supportive people, groups, sponsors, events, etc.) is another step. Determining *how realistic the changes are*, particularly for the individual client, the treatment/recovery setting, and the severity of the presenting problem, is also significant. Finally, *determining clients' readiness to change* and *discussing ambivalence* (e.g., understanding the appropriateness of experiencing two simultaneous thoughts or emotions, such as

"I can't live like this any longer" and "I'm not ready to make a change") is crucial for the new behavioral sequence to generalize to clients' lives.

One part of setting up new behavioral sequences is through using positive self-talk (another principle of Psychological Theory) in the form of recovery slogans. Sayings such as "One day at a time," "Easy does it," "First things first," "Stinking thinking," "Keep it simple," "This too shall pass," "Live and let live," "Let go and let God," "Cultivate an attitude of gratitude," "Time takes time," "Live life on life's terms," "Misery is optional," and "Humility is not thinking less of yourself, but thinking of yourself less" all serve as cognitive reinforcers for interrupting negative behavioral sequences.

The self-medicative aspect of addictive disorders is a common theme throughout treatment. After a client has some significant time in recovery, has some supportive people in his or her life, and has developed some effective coping mechanisms, it is usually appropriate to begin exploring for the presence of any emotional pain that led to the addictive behaviors. Never have I met someone struggling with an addictive disorder who was not also emotionally wounded. Sadly, and all too often, clinicians and treatment centers dig under a client's emotional surface too early in the recovery process. They will try to remove the addictive bandage before the wound is ready to be revealed. Without sufficient time, support, and coping mechanisms, the client usually has just one recourse—a return to addictive use to mask the emotional pain.

One final positive outcome from Psychological Theory is the recognition of the Addictive Personality. Throughout the treatment and recovery communities, individuals come to recognize their tendency to jump from one addiction to another. Some of the more common jumps that we've seen include (a) from stimulant (e.g., cocaine, crystal methamphetamine) addiction to sexual addiction, (b) from smoking to eating, (c) from alcoholism to workaholism, (d) from depressants and cannabis addiction to the addictive use of the Internet, video games, and television, and (e) from addictive gambling to alcoholism or addictive exercise. For the recovering individual, life choices will necessitate a constant evaluative process, where individuals must determine if their behaviors are empowering the Self or enabling the Addict. Increasing awareness of the need for life balance is a crucial step in recovery and treatment—which involves recognizing how to engage in certain behaviors appropriately, such as eating, sex, exercise, work, and the Internet. A final saying common to the treatment community that mirrors this sentiment is "You're either walking toward recovery or toward relapse: You make the choice."

"Where'd You Learn to Drink Like That?"—The Influence of the Environment on Addictive Disorders

If you think about it, how and when do most people take their first drink, smoke their first joint, get introduced to pornography, or place their first bet? The answer: Most everyone first did these things *with* someone else or obtained the material *from* someone else. Be it drinking their first beer at a middle school party, getting high before a high school dance, finding a parent's stash of pornography, or buying scratch-off tickets for mom or dad, most are in the company of peers or family when they experience their first drink/drug/behavior.

The influence of one's environment on behavior development, both productive and detrimental, is nothing new. For example, when it comes to religious preferences, the environment in which one is nurtured has a tremendous impact (Carothers, Borkowski, Lefever, & Whitman, 2005). Similarly, much work has been done on the influence of the environment on individual career choice (Ferry, Fouad, & Smith, 2000; Tracey & Ward, 1998; Whiston & Keller, 2004). On the other hand, the environment also impacts the development of such behaviors as risk taking (Jaccard, Blanton, & Dodge, 2005), aggression and violence (Linder & Collins, 2005; Skopp, McDonald, Manke, & Jouriles, 2005), and of course drug/alcohol use (Graham, Marks, & Hansen, 1991; Larimer, Turner, Mallett, & Geisner, 2004; Petraitis, Flay, & Miller, 1995; Read, Wood, Kahler, Maddock, & Palfai, 2003).

Through several different approaches, be it the family systems approach, social learning theory, or sociological models, the effect of the environment on the development of addictive disorders has been well studied. Given that the family systems approach (which notes the different family roles, the need for homeostasis, and the impact of loose/rigid boundaries) is explored thoroughly in Chapter 4, in this section we will focus more on sociological and learning theories and what they have to say about addictive disorders.

Sociological Theory

To put it simply, the focus of Sociological Theory is to investigate the interaction between human behavior and the environment. Sociological Theory actually encompasses several different perspectives, including Role Theory and Sociocultural Theory (among others). A very brief review of each is warranted for our later discussions.

Role Theory   Role Theory, explained Winick (as cited by Craig, 2004), clarifies the initiation of addictive disorders based on the interaction of three factors: availability of substances, lack of social restraint from their use/abuse, and the presence of role strain. Craig (2004) goes on to note several social groups where substance abuse was/is present. First, Vietnam soldiers were exposed to a variety of drugs that aided them in coping with their surroundings. Marijuana and heroin were available, their use was encouraged by peers, and individuals were under tremendous role strain (i.e., trying to stay alive). Similarly, musicians, whose lifestyle often promotes the use of drugs and alcohol, experience role strain as a result of the heavy burden of travel, sudden financial gain, and strained relationships. Finally, college-age individuals are faced with readily available drugs/alcohol, are encouraged by peers at local parties (one of the major collegiate social events), and experience the role strain involved with both being away from home and maintaining one's academic standing. Other studies have applied similar concepts to other addictive disorders, including gambling (Shaffer, LaBrie, & LaPlante, 2004) and sex (Cooper, Delmonico, & Burg, 2000).

The impact of one's social role(s) on the likely development of an addictive disorder has been well documented. Several authors have noted the mediating factor of social roles and social role changes on alcohol consumption. For example, social roles such as those found with age (older versus younger), gender (male versus female), educational levels (college-educated versus non-college-educated), employment status (employed versus unemployed), and marital status (married, divorced, and single), as well as transitions between these roles (e.g., from married to divorced, from no children to assuming a parental role), have all been shown to influence alcohol consumption (Hajema & Knibbe, 1998; Neve, Lemmens, & Drop, 1997; Robbins, 1991). Therefore, whereas social roles are not the sole determinants, it has been shown that one's role in life greatly influences whether you become addicted to alcohol.

Sociocultural Theory Sociocultural Theory centers on how culture can affect addictive tendencies. For example, Fisher and Harrison (2005) noted how one's culture can inhibit the development of alcoholism. Take the Jewish culture: Low rates of alcoholism are reported in this group, largely due to their moderate use of alcohol. For those raised in the Jewish culture, the use of alcohol is used responsibly and is a normal part of social and religious practices. The same can be found among many European cultures where a glass of wine is found at each meal, with children even consuming watered-down versions (Erickson, 2005).

On the other hand, one's culture can also perpetuate chemical abuse. For members of religious groups that call for total abstinence from alcohol, moderation is never mirrored (Fisher & Harrison, 2005). Therefore, if an individual *does* indulge, this can result in excessive use. As further evidence, Lawson, Peterson, and Lawson (1983) found that whereas 30 percent of children of alcoholics become alcoholics themselves (a recognized statistic), 5 percent of children with parents who drink moderately become alcoholics and *10 percent result from parents who totally abstain.* Lawson (1992) also pointed out how the family culture can influence chemical use patterns. Alcoholics tend to come from those families that are morally rigid, conflict oriented, disengaged, and emotionally repressive rather than those that use alcohol in moderation. We'll talk more about the family's influence on addictive behavior when we get to Social Learning Theory.

The final example of culture's influence on substance misuse involves the social groups to which one belongs. Each of these groups develops its own set of normative behaviors, language, and rituals. For example, among those raised in a culture of poverty, young children and adolescents may learn the value of substance use/misuse. This value is mirrored by those who belong to and maintain the urban drug culture, where easy money, fast cars, flashy jewelry, and expensive stereos are obtained as a result of drug money and are viewed as status symbols (Craig, 2004). The other aspect of sociocultural group membership is the *social feedback mechanism* (Doweiko, 2002). This mechanism occurs as an interaction between the social group and the members of that group. The behaviors of the members of any group are shaped by the group itself, while at the same time the norms of the group are informed by those who belong to it. In terms of addiction, those who use particular chemicals or behaviors will tend to belong to the same group and will often ostracize those who belong to other addictive groups. For example, those who smoke marijuana will seek out others who do the same, which reinforces the rituals and behaviors surrounding marijuana use. These individuals will often experience "instant bonding" with other smokers, sharing the same language (slang), paraphernalia, and even each other's drug supply. Whereas they may venture into other "recreational" drug use (e.g., hallucinogens, ecstasy, or alcohol), they would "find it beneath themselves" to smoke crack or shoot heroin. Similarly, those who *do* use crack or heroin often make snide remarks about those who use "kid drugs" like marijuana and mushrooms. Similarly, adolescent females have been known to form social groups around addictive eating and self-mutilative behavior. From those who binge and purge, to those who restrict food, to those who cut on their bodies, individuals will often boast to one another about how often they vomit, how little they've eaten, or how frequently and deeply they've cut, while at the same time scoffing at those who overeat as a result of *their* addictive disorder. A final example can even be seen in some of the remaining "hard-line" Alcoholics Anonymous groups where alcohol is the only drug spoken of. Even when alcohol has been a part of an addictive routine, some AA members will actually ask those who abuse other drugs to "find an NA meeting that'll better meet your needs."

Roles, culture, families, and social groups all influence the development of addictive disorders. The other aspect to each of these influences is how drug and process addictive behaviors are modeled and learned by those within addicts' inner circles. Social Learning Theory helps to explain how this occurs.

Social Learning Theory

Whereas Social Learning Theory originated in the 1800s, the theory's application to understanding modern behavior can be credited in part to the work of Albert Bandura (Bandura, 1982). There are two primary principles underlying *observational* or Social Learning Theory. First, individuals learn/model specific behaviors by observing others (particularly those whom they admire) and maintain those behaviors that are both attractive and reinforced (Gupta & Derevensky, 1997). Similarly self-efficacy, which is the belief in one's ability to choose actions that best fit one's needs, is based on outcome expectations (i.e., those behaviors that are pleasurable will be repeated versus those that are not will be avoided) (Petraitis, Flay, & Miller, 1995). Environmental stressors, the second component of Social Learning Theory, influence the behaviors that individuals choose to model. A brief review of each, as it applies to addictive disorders, is necessary.

The influence of modeling on the development of behaviors in children and adolescents is well documented: It is the other side of the nature versus nurture argument that we addressed earlier in the genetics discussion. This is particularly true as it pertains to the impact of one's family and peer group. For the initiation of addictive disorders, many authors have noted the influence of parental substance abuse (Biederman, Faraone, Monuteaux, & Feighner, 2000; Bush et al., 2005; Wood, Read, Mitchell, & Brand, 2004), sibling substance abuse (Duncan, Duncan, & Hops, 1996; Petraitis, Flay, & Miller, 1995), and peer substance abuse (Graham, Marks, & Hansen, 1991; NCADI, 2001; Olds & Thombs, 2001). These influences are particularly strong when the role models are respected and revered (Adlaf & Giesbrecht, 1996; Juhnke & Hagedorn, 2003). Additional studies have demonstrated the impact of media-based role models on the development of adolescent substance abuse and other addictive disorders (Bandura, 1982; Brisman & Siegel, 1984; Wakfield, Flay, Nichter, & Giovino, 2003), particularly gambling (Gupta & Derevensky, 1997; Moore & Ohtsuka, 2000) and eating (Markey, Tinsley, Ericksen, Ozer, & Markey, 2002; von Ranson, McGue, & Iacono, 2003).

Using substances or behaviors in response to stressful life events has also been well researched (Hoffman & Su, 1997). Whereas we noted that individuals will engage in certain behaviors to self-medicate their psychological pain, the Social Learning perspective looks at the use of substances by peers and other valued role models as a response to stress. If individuals receive a positive response from their use (e.g., they visibly relax during tense circumstances or receive positive social feedback about their use), then individuals learn the value of this behavior (Petraitis, Flay, & Miller, 1995). As evidence, several authors have investigated the socially reinforced use of substances (Goeders, 2002, 2003; San José, Van Oers, Van De Mheen, Garretsen, & Mackenbach, 2000) as well as addictive behaviors (Cooper, Galbreath, & Becker, 2004; Koff & Sangani, 1998; Lightsey & Hulsey, 2002; Troop, Holbrey, & Treasure, 1998) in response to stress.

Summary and Integration

Whereas we will include a clinical vignette that helps to demonstrate the environment's influence on addictive disorders in the next section, we want to highlight the three areas from Sociological Theory and Social Learning Theory that we have found particularly useful in our work with addicted families. First, as the Medical/Disease Model does not include the impact of one's environment, clients and their families will often bring up the environment's impact themselves during initial discussions of how addictions develop. Be it the family's early financial situation, the impact of a broken family, mom's alcoholism, or brother's gambling problem, clients are often able to identify their personal environmental influences with little prompting. This can also assist clients in recognizing that their addictive disorder is beyond their control, which can be helpful in coming to terms with the acceptance of powerlessness that is involved with most recovery programs. In working with families, it can also be particularly meaningful when parents or siblings recognize their own addictive use and how this has influenced their family members' disorders. Second, addictive disorders rarely develop in a vacuum—that is, understanding how one's social roles, culture, family of origin, and peer relationships have influenced the origination and maintenance of one's addictive disorder is extremely important. Finally, these theories help clients to recognize how important it is to both monitor their future social relationships and develop positive coping mechanisms to deal with the impact of environmental stressors. One of the old sayings from Alcoholics Anonymous is "All you have to change is everything." Although this is quite a daunting task for someone newly in recovery, when it comes to the importance of one's environment, it is particularly crucial to make socially motivated choices that will maintain recovery.

Which Came First, the Chicken or the Egg?— The Biopsychosocialspiritual Approach to Addictive Disorders

I used to believe that I *invented* the Biopsychosocialspiritual Model of addictive disorders. Stop laughing, I'm being serious! After surviving in the addictions field for several years, even before formal training, I noted how insidiously addictions impact every aspect of a person's life. It is not uncommon to see someone first present for treatment with a wasted body, a tormented mind, and a lack of any social support or spiritual connections. It just made intuitive sense to me: Since addictions so negatively impact each and every area of an addict's life, it must also have origins back to each of those areas in the individual's life.

Even though I couldn't claim the quippy title "biopsychosocialspiritual" back in 1997, I truly believed that I had a corner on the new theory market. What I couldn't understand at that point was the direction of impact: Did the affected areas (i.e., the biological, psychological, social, and spiritual) *cause* the development of an addictive disorder, or did the addictive disorder negatively impact each life domain (the classic "chicken or the egg" predicament)?

Sadly, my self-imposed "theory guru-hood" came tumbling down when I learned that 20 years earlier, Engel (as cited by Stroebe, 2000) had noted the need to expand the biomedical explanation of addictions with the inclusion of psychological and social factors. I also found out that it wasn't about determining what caused what, but rather the point was to recognize the reciprocal relationship that one's past and present have on the development and maintenance of an addictive disorder. In fact, Wallace (2003) noted the vicious cycle between the biopsychosocialspiritual influences and the impacts of addictive disorders. When individuals use excessive amounts of drugs and alcohol or engage in more frequent or intense behaviors, detrimental impacts are felt on the body, mind, social network, and spirit. The distress on each of these domains leads to additional use/behaviors, which in turn leads to even greater consequences. Given this interaction between precipitants and consequences, a holistic approach has been noted to be most effective (Laaser, 1996; Manley, 1995; Myers & Willard, 2003). With this new knowledge, I was understandably crushed and therein died my claim to theory fame.

The Biopsychosocialspiritual Model, as it is aptly named, involves the interaction of the biological (brain and body), psychological (mind, mood, and will), social (family, friends, and others), and spiritual (meaning and purpose) domains (Ross, 2005). Addiction is therefore viewed as a multivariate syndrome, with multiple patterns of dysfunctional use coexisting with multiple personality types, resulting in multiple combinations of adverse consequences, and can be addressed with multiple types of interventions (with any number of prognoses) (Dube & Lewis, 1994; Knop et al., 2003; Newcomb & Earleywine, 1996; Shaffer et al., 2004).

In this chapter we have explored the first three components of the Biopsychosocialspiritual Model. The biological piece comprises those precipitants that originate from Physiological Theory, including elements of the Disease/Medical Model, the impact of genetics, and the neurochemistry of addiction. Psychological Theory is also encompassed in this approach. The influence of Behavioral Theory, the Self-Medication Hypothesis, and the Addictive Personality are all considered. Similarly, the role that the environment (through Sociological Theory and Social Learning Theory) plays is incorporated. Learned behaviors, supported roles, the influence of the environment, and responses to stressors are all important parts of this holistic model. The significant piece that this model addresses that we have yet to explore is the impact of spirituality.

Spirituality and Addiction

Whereas the theory was originally designated without the spiritual component (it was once called the Biopsychosocial Model), the importance of addressing the spiritual domain in the assessment, treatment, and recovery processes has been prominent throughout the literature and clinical practice (Brady, Peterman, Fitchett, Mo, & Cella, 1999; Sweder, 1998). Some have even noted the efficacy of using a *spiritual disease* model, combining the biomedical and spiritual approaches to treatment (Garrett, 1998; Hagedorn & Hartwig Moorhead, in press; Sandoz, 2001). While this may be an important step to the incorporation of spirituality, the psychological and social domains still warrant inclusion. Even with the recognized need for spiritual interventions as a part of a client's overall treatment (Chappelle, 2000; Karasu, 1999; McLennan, Rochow, & Arthur, 2001), a client's spirituality is often underconsidered (if at all) during the initial assessment and treatment planning processes, to the detriment of the client (Hathaway, Scott, & Garver, 2004 ; Weinstein, Parker, & Archer, 2002).

The relevance of a spiritual approach to treating addictive disorders is noted for three primary reasons. First, addictions themselves have been conceptualized as spiritual disorders (Hagedorn & Hartwig Moorhead, in press), which result from addicts' failed attempts at filling spiritual voids (Clinebell, 1963; Kurtz, 1979; Sandoz, 2001). As we have noted, two of the primary purposes of spirituality are that it provides individuals with a sense of meaning and connectedness. Interestingly, several authors have discussed how both chemical and process addictions provide users with a felt sense of such purpose and oneness (e.g., Garrett & Carroll, 2000; Glass, 1998; Marzano-Parisoli, 2001; Patterson, Hayworth, Turner, & Raskin, 2000; Yip, 2003). The problem is that whereas substances or behaviors provide initial feelings of wholeness and fulfillment, they are by their very nature temporary substitutes. Worse still, once the chemical or behavior has subsided, individuals are left feeling more empty and disconnected than when they first began, thus resulting in a vicious cycle of attempted fulfillment with resulting desolation. As addiction can be viewed as a spiritual disorder, it only seems prudent to work within the spiritual domain to help resolve these conflicts.

The second reason to utilize spirituality is that it has shown repeated efficacy in the treatment process. Spirituality is effective in preventing addictive disorders in the first place (Hodge, Cardenas, & Montoya, 2001) and serves as a protective factor in alleviating the cravings and risk-taking behaviors linked with substance abuse (Arnold, Avants, Margolin, & Marcotte, 2002). In fact, recovery programs devoid of a focus on the importance of spirituality have been shown to be much less effective than those that do address the spiritual component (Gorski, 1991; Green, Thompson-Fullilove, & Fullilove, 1998; Ng & Shek, 2001; Pardini, Plante, Sherman, & Stump, 2000; Yangarber-Hicks, 2004).

The final reason to include spirituality is that it is connected to every other life domain: "Similar to how one cannot separate the spiritual component from all the other elements that make us human (e.g., physical, emotional, social), one should not discount the importance of a spiritual approach to treating addictive disorders" (Hagedorn & Hartwig Moorhead, in press, p. 31). As a matter of fact, the medical and psychological literature has increasingly noted the importance of the interaction between spirituality and both psychological health and biological well-being (Culliford, 2002; French & Joseph, 1999; Hill & Pargament, 2003; Hodges, 2002; James & Wells, 2003; Miller & Thoresen, 2003; Powell, Shahabi, & Thoresen, 2003; Seeman, Fagan Dubin, & Seeman, 2003). As it often happens, it took theory and clinical practice a while to "catch up" to what has worked for recovering addicts for years: Right from its inception, Alcoholics Anonymous noted the need to look beyond the Disease Model to include the other life dimensions (Miller, 1993), especially the necessity for a spiritual component (Forman, Bovasso, & Woody, 2001).

For the above three reasons, spirituality has become a mainstay in most holistically minded treatment and recovery programs. As a testament to the acceptance of the overall Biopsychosocialspiritual Approach, most treatment facilities now include a psychosocial assessment as a regular part of the intake process. This document usually includes an evaluation of (a) the physical ailments that have impacted (or that have been impacted by) the addictive disorder, (b) the psychological troubles that preempted or are exacerbated by the addictive disorder, (c) key relationships in the individual's life that have had an influence on (or that have been influenced by) the addictive disorder, and (d) the spiritual practices (or lack thereof) that may have an impact on the recovery process. This assessment is vital in obtaining the data necessary to understand the relationship between the addictive disorder and each of the impacted life domains. It is also a crucial piece to use in the development of a comprehensive treatment plan. The case example below demonstrates how the data gathered from such an assessment can be used to work with an addicted couple.

Clinical Case Example

Mario and Carmen presented for couple's counseling at my private practice. In our initial session, I quickly noted how vastly underweight Carmen was and began conceptualizing their presenting concern as the result of her disordered eating. As a couple, they shared that their marriage had reached "an all-time low" and that they were considering getting a divorce. Unable to communicate without verbal altercations, each blamed the other as the source of their stress and discomfort within the relationship.

In separating the couple to explore their individual motivations in pursuing counseling at this time, Mario shared that he was tired of Carmen's eating rituals. "She drives me *crazy* with her food games. First she nags me until I go out and buy her all this junk food, and I just *know* that it's all wasted money—it's gonna wind up in the toilet! I might as well just throw my wallet straight into the crapper and save us the trouble!" In a follow-up with Carmen, she admitted to once being a regular attendee at Overeaters Anonymous and revealed that she had been struggling with overeating followed by purging behaviors for 7 years: a classic example of bulimia. Nonetheless, her addictive rituals were not the only stressor in this relationship.

Carmen's main complaint with the marriage was that Mario was constantly preoccupied with money: "All he thinks about is money, money, money! He wouldn't be so hard up for cash if he didn't worship with it at the track!" It wasn't until the third session that Mario began disclosing his gambling habits, which included weekly trips to the local Indian casinos, daily playing of the state lotto, weekend poker games with his friends, and frequent trips to dog races, horse races, and jai alai. In assessing the total losses that he had accumulated (equaling more that $75,000 in debt) as well as some of the negative consequences that he had experienced (including several lost jobs and 2 months spent in jail as a result of a shoplifting spree, which he had intended to use to pay off debts), I began to recognize the intricate interplay of their addictive disorders and the need for a Biopsychosocialspiritual Approach, most importantly during both the assessment and treatment planning processes.

The Biopsychosocialspiritual Assessment   In performing the initial assessment over the course of our first three sessions, I learned several important facts that impacted the development of our treatment plan. First, in the way of physical impacts of their two disorders, Carmen had lost several of her teeth, a common side effect of continuous self-induced vomiting (which wears away at the tooth enamel). In addition, her physical health had been a continuous concern of her primary care physician, who noted that with her weight below the 85th percentile for her height, Carmen would likely suffer long-term physical consequences if she didn't gain sufficient weight. As evidence of this, her menses had become irregular at first and had recently stopped altogether (it had been 18 months since her last period), she had begun to display early signs of osteoporosis, and she had begun to lose large amounts of her hair (she constantly wore a wig). Carmen's only precipitating physical complaint was that as a child and adolescent, she had been consistently overweight and had suffered from severe acne.

Given that Mario didn't wear his addictive disorder on his sleeve (so to speak), his physical ailments were less pronounced and less noticeable. He appeared to have difficulty concentrating and, when prompted, admitted to having ADHD-like symptoms since childhood. This resulted in his being easily distracted, having difficulty focusing, and being in constant search for external stimulation. At his last physical exam (2 years prior), his doctor had assessed for the presence of any family history of hypertension, noting that Mario's high blood pressure was a concern that would soon necessitate a medical intervention (though Mario had never returned for the scheduled follow-up). Finally, Mario complained of both difficulty staying asleep and frequent night sweats, which were followed by chills. Whereas the doctor could find no physical source for either his intermittent insomnia or nocturnal diaphoresis, Mario believed that it had to do with the "constant tension I'm under to pay off these debts."

Psychologically, both had comorbid (and as yet undiagnosed) psychiatric disorders. Carmen refused to leave the house except in dire circumstances (Mario's threat to divorce her unless she came in for counseling was the current dire circumstance). Her anxiety symptoms met criteria for panic disorder with agoraphobia. Her addictive eating, in turn, supported her anxiety: When she anticipated a panic attack, Carmen would stuff herself with food, and this was followed quickly by horrendous guilt and anxiety about gaining weight, which would prompt a purging episode. Similarly, her refusal to leave home impelled her to hoard food, which she ate compulsively and then made Mario purchase more at every opportunity.

On the other hand, even though he didn't appear so, Mario was clinically depressed. Reportedly, he slept less than 4 hours a night and felt "blue" for the better part of each day; he admitted (*very* reluctantly) that he cried frequently, and during the second couple's session (after we broke into brief individual sessions), he revealed suicidal ideations on a weekly basis. Performing a quick assessment for his intent to self-harm (I used the SLAP acronym: **S**pecific—how specific is the suicide plan? **L**ethality—how lethal is the plan? **A**vailability—does the client have the means to carry out the plan? **P**roximity—are rescuers [e.g., supportive people] close at hand?), I determined that he was not an immediate threat to himself. Mario's addiction to gambling, he admitted, was a perfect way to fight off his depression. "The only problem with gambling is," according to him, "I don't win every time, and when I *don't* win, it sends me into a real tailspin." Always seeking another big win, Mario's preoccupation with the next win distracted him sufficiently enough that he would sometimes forget about his depression. "But it's always waiting for me at night. As I lie there in bed, it feels like wave after wave of dread just sweeping over me. The only thing that helps is to remember the last time I won at cards or at the track."

Whereas we were able to do some work on determining the source of their individual psychological pain, the majority of our time was spent with present and future behaviors that would both support the marriage (a stated goal) and benefit their individual lifestyles of recovery.

The next portion of the biopsychosocialspiritual interview, their social networks, revealed how isolated these two individuals were. Carmen's only contact with the outside world was through either Mario or the local news (which she only allowed herself to listen to, as watching the news increased her anxiety). Whereas she had once had strong family ties, following the death of her alcoholic father, her eating behaviors began to take precedence over her remaining family. Though attempts to connect with her were made by her mother and older brother, these calls and e-mails had become very infrequent. Every attempt of Mario's to bring home friends ("She never lets me have the boys over for poker night!") was met with staunch resistance.

Mario, at first glance, had a bevy of relationships. Both he and Carmen referred to his ability to make friends easily. On closer examination, though, none of these "friends" knew anything about Mario other than his being an apparently "happy-go-lucky guy." Never moving beyond the superficial, Mario's acquaintances centered on his gambling endeavors—the "poker guys," the "track guys," the "guys down at the market where I buy my Lotto tickets," and so on. Even those people with whom he had worked for over 9 years had no idea about his struggles, home life, or his propensity for gambling. When asked whom he could turn to if things got really bad in his life, he retorted, "Come on, Doc, are you serious? You're the first person that I've ever talked to about anything remotely important!"

In completing the three-session assessment, it appeared that both Carmen and Mario had once shared a robust spiritual life. Carmen was raised as a Catholic and Mario came from a Baptist background. While dating, they had decided to attend a nondenominational church that met both their needs. During their first year of marriage, Carmen had miscarried. As a result, she had "lost" her faith, stopped going to church (where she had been active in the children's ministry), and lost her sense of meaning and purpose. Given that feeling connected to her was his main motivation for going to church, Mario also quit attending services. As for any personal practice of their spirituality and faith, neither stated any such tradition.

Without sharing this initially with Carmen, I hypothesized that both her lost sense of purpose and lack of fulfillment in becoming a mother may have had a lot to do with the development of her preoccupation with food. Research has demonstrated that people will eat in order to "feel full" or "full fill" themselves when they are feeling disconnected from God or others, especially when they experience existential pain (Garrett, 1998). I also sensed that part of Mario's search for a "payoff" was an attempt at connecting with the supernatural. His use of rituals and good-luck charms was almost religious in nature, and upon winning, he shared that he experienced a state of transcendence.

The Biopsychosocialspiritual Treatment Plan   In developing a treatment plan with a biopsychosocialspiritual focus, the three of us agreed on utilizing a mantra of "balance." Balance, as defined by Hagedorn and Watts (2002), is a mutually agreed upon conception of wellness. This approach looks at each of the holistic elements of wellness (i.e., physical health, psychological health, social support, and spiritual practice) and considers the meaning-making that the individual assigns to each domain. Rather than choosing interventions that work for *most* people, clients and clinicians choose behaviors that have personal meaning for the client (an intentional focus on wellness). The mantra would entail a continual evaluation by each individual as to how meaningful each behavior was at meeting their physical, psychological, social, and spiritual needs. Questions such as "Is this activity balanced? What else can I do with my time that would be more meaningful?" would need to be asked on a regular basis.

I had three caveats to guide our work together. First, I wanted them to recognize how intertwined their two lives were and how a change in one person's behavior would have repercussions for the other's feelings and behaviors. Anticipating each other's resistance to change would be crucial to the therapeutic process. Second, we agreed that couple's counseling would not be enough in the way of treatment to help them to restructure their lives; adjunct forms of therapy (e.g., possible inpatient hospitalization, group counseling, 12-step support group attendance) would be instrumental in helping them to reach their goals. Finally, we agreed that any one change (let alone the multitude of necessary changes) would be challenging, so we would have to stick to a SMART (as you can see, I'm big on acronyms) plan: Any changes would have to be **S**pecific, **M**easurable, **A**chievable, **R**ealistic, and **T**ime limited.

In terms of physical needs, we agreed that the most meaningful and immediate need was for the two of them to obtain a physical examination, which would occur in the following week. For Mario, we needed to address the likelihood of hypertension and see what dietary and exercise changes might be made to supplement any medications the medical doctor prescribed. I also wanted to have him medically evaluated for the presence of ADHD, though we considered initially avoiding medication as a treatment if it was present (due to some of the addictive tendencies of some commonly prescribed medications). Carmen likely warranted inpatient hospitalization to improve her overall health. Given her lack of health insurance, as well as her reluctance to go that route, we began with a less restrictive approach, which included weekly individual therapy with one of my colleagues who specialized in eating disorders, group therapy with other struggling addicted clients, and continued couple's therapy with me (the total cost of which would be a fraction of inpatient care). In consultation with her medical doctor, her other therapist began working on a careful and intentional eating plan for Carmen that would incrementally increase her caloric intake by 100 calories a day over every 2-week period, eventually attempting to bring her up to the correct amount of calories to support the appropriate weight for her height. For most, since an eating plan involves daily accountability, more than therapy is necessary. This is where a support group like OA would be of benefit. I'll discuss this further in the "social needs" section of the treatment plan.

When we began narrowing down those areas of their psychological health that most warranted attention, all three of us became overwhelmed: So much needed to be changed. Addressing one psychological disorder is challenging enough, but between the interactions of an anxiety disorder with addictive eating, as well as depression coupled with addictive gambling, not to mention how each of these played off the other person's disorders, we had our collective hands full! At this point in therapy, it was necessary to partialize and prioritize their psychological goals, with an intentional focus on meaning-making.

For Carmen, a stated goal of "meeting new friends and regaining family relationships with people who will support me through these changes" was an appropriate way to address her anxiety. But we needed to break that down into achievable and realistic steps. With some work, Carmen verbalized that in the next 2 weeks, she could feasibly attend one OA meeting near her home and obtain two telephone numbers from other women she met at the meeting. As for her family relationships, Carmen decided to begin work on documenting those thoughts and feelings that she would like to share with them once she felt ready. If she was able to achieve these goals, the hope was to capitalize on her successes to help propel her toward future goals.

Mario's depression, particularly with his frequent suicidal ideations, necessitated some careful interventions. His goal to "stop feeling so lousy" first required specificity: What did "lousy" mean to him? He shared, "I feel so sluggish, kinda out of it—I never get out unless it's to the track or to work." When asked what he liked about the track besides the actual race, he mentioned the smells, the fresh air, and the sun hitting his face. "What about walking?" I asked him. He thought that would be easy enough, though it initially sounded silly to him. But he agreed to go for a 20-minute walk twice in the next week and to report back how it impacted him. Believe it or not, the next week his affect was a bit brighter: "Doc, that walking thing is okay. I like being outside, and after a morning walk, I feel a little bit better about my day—I can organize my thinking a little bit as I walk. Who woulda thought?" Granted, walking was not the only intervention employed in our work with Mario's depression, but we needed to start with small steps, allowing him to experience success, as this is crucial to the generalization of behaviors necessary for change.

Social networks and relationships were the next part of our goal. As noted by Sociological Theory, a change in one's environment will often result in a change in one's behaviors. Getting Carmen out of the house would be a huge environmental change, one that we anticipated might involve SLIPs (Slight Lapses In Progress) into old addictive patterns. Preparing for such slips helps to normalize the recovery process and removes some of the resulting guilt and shame in an effort to avoid full relapses. As noted, Carmen's foray into society would begin with a supportive network:

OA. By seeking the telephone numbers of two other women in recovery, Carmen would begin the process of learning more adaptive eating habits by observing how others dealt with anxiety. Therefore, it would be important for her to choose two women whose recovery lifestyles she admired. Her new behaviors would also be reinforced through the OA fellowship, with the accompanying "chip" system and applause for developmental milestones found throughout the 12-step support network.

Mario would be encouraged to attend Gamblers Anonymous for the very same reason that Carmen was referred to OA—increased social support for new behaviors. As the totality of his current relationships supported his gambling, he often found himself joking with his poker buddies about the "lowlifes down at the track" (which is common as a part of the social feedback found among sociocultural groups). Therefore, we decided to make attempts at having him befriend someone new. It just so happened that Mario solved this dilemma on his own. "Hey Doc, there's this old guy that walks in the park at the same time I do. Last week we sat on the bench while he threw a ball to his dog and started talking. He's got a lot of great stories to tell and I don't mind listening. As a matter of fact, I even shared that my doctor suggested I start walking and he said that he'd be willing to meet me whenever I liked. What do you think?" Since interventions that clients choose themselves are much more likely to be continued, I thought that was a great idea.

In picking spiritual treatment goals, both clinician and client need to remember the difference between spirituality and religion. Simply put, spirituality involves such things as a connection with something "Other," transcendence, a faith in the connectedness of events, and the personal practices that support each of these. On the other hand, religion is the corporal practice of spirituality, often organized along denominational lines with specific rituals and beliefs. One can be spiritual and not religious, as well as religious and not spiritual. Given that the focus of our work was to reinstitute meaning and purpose, we had to first determine what each individual found to be particularly meaningful in their prior spiritual practices. For Carmen, a relationship with a loving and personal God had provided her with direction and a sense of peace, up until she had lost her baby. Unable to come to grips with the purpose of this event, she had abandoned her belief structure. Wanting to investigate what God might mean to her during her recovery process, she noted that she would begin this exploration through two avenues. First, she would use OA's 12-step approach to spirituality, namely steps 2 (Came to believe that a Power greater than ourselves could restore us to sanity) and 3 (Made a decision to turn our will and our lives over to the care of God *as we understood*

Him). Accomplishing these steps would take time and the guidance of a good sponsor, someone whom she would identify in the future. The other approach to rediscovery was through reading spiritual books. Over the years I have compiled a list of books that clients and colleagues have suggested, including those that are novels, self-help, and clinically focused. These are organized according to topic, including such things as recovery, depression, relationships, and spirituality. I frequently print a topical list of books from this master list for clients who request it and then they choose what they feel will best meet their needs. In reviewing the list, she picked *The Ragamuffin Gospel*, by Brennan Manning (2000), as her first book. Future sessions focused on what she learned from this text.

Not much of a reader, Mario desired another spiritual practice. Whereas he too recognized that a 12-step recovery program necessarily involves a focus on spirituality, he most desired a feeling of connectedness. We discussed that whereas this sense of unification would flow naturally through his GA participation, he also wanted something that he could begin working on almost immediately. After discussing several spiritual traditions, Mario chose contemplative prayer, a practice where the individual places his entire focus on the presence, will, and love of God. Done in silence, individuals practice clearing their mind as they concentrate on their breathing, each breath punctuated with a word or phrase, for example, "God" on the inhale and "is love" on the exhale. Beginning with 5-minute sessions, Mario would attempt to complete six of these sessions during the next 2 weeks. Given his love of nature, Mario decided to practice this form of meditation while at the park, following his walks. We discussed that one of the likely results might be the quieting of his mind and an increased capacity to focus on the present moment.

Summary and Integration

Wound throughout the Balanced approach to the Biopsychosocialspiritual Model is the need for the creative combination of activities that address multiple life domains (Hagedorn & Watts, 2002). With so much that needs addressing, clients often feel overwhelmed with the amount of changes that need to occur. Therefore, if the counselor and client(s) can cocreate interventions that meet several required changes in one activity, as well as help clients attach meaning to these activities, they tend to follow through more readily. This is why, for Carmen, we coupled her need for accountability on the eating plan, her need for making friends, her need for acceptance and positive role models, and her need to connect with a Higher Power all into her attendance at Overeaters Anonymous. Similarly, for Mario, an intervention like walking could meet his physical need for exercise, his psychological need to be outside and organize his thinking, his social need to connect with other walkers, and his spiritual need to connect with God after his walks. Whereas individuals regularly perform multiple tasks within one activity, they rarely give themselves credit for doing so. For example, the last time you went for a bike ride with your friends, stopped for a bagel and apple juice, and discussed your job-related stress, you inadvertently met your exercise needs, nutritional needs, relational needs, and psychological needs!

At the same time, it is important to not place all of the client's eggs in one basket. For example, if Carmen's anxiety prevented her from attending the OA meeting, and had we based the success of her recovery solely on that event, she would likely experience multiple difficulties. This is why the clinician is encouraged to help clients build in backup plans for each meaningful activity (remember the "6 P's"?). Therefore, the focus of the Balanced approach is to help clients recognize the intentionality behind their activities and build in backup plans, thus resulting in an increase in their self-efficacy for maintaining these activities.

It is also important to help clients assess how each of their goals is being met within the chosen activity and to be ready to help them adjust these activities if they loose meaning. As we've mentioned, gaining success through consistent involvement in the design and implementation of the chosen activity allows them to move on to more challenging goals. Reining in clients' enthusiasm, consistently evaluating how SMART their goals are, processing their SLIPs, and increasing their support systems to create and maintain accountability are all instrumental to the Balanced Biopsychosocialspiritual Approach.

Conclusions

Which theory or model is best for discerning how addictive disorders develop? To complicate the answer to this question, there are a number of etiological theories that we did not discuss. These include, among others, (a) the Characterological Model (addictions develop as a consequence of personality abnormalities), (b) the Temperance Model (addictions exist due to the availability of addictive substances—removal of these substances would end addictive disorders), (c) the Conditioning Model (advocates that addictions are learned and calls for the behavioral approach of counter-conditioning), (d) the Public Health Model (views addictions as the consequence of interactions among an agent, a host, and the environment), and (e) the Educational Model (addiction occurs as a result of a lack of information—if addicts learned the dangers of continued use, they would abstain). The purpose of not exploring these models further was that our focus was to highlight those theories that were both most predominant in the literature and most useful for working with clients and their families. Similarly, most of the above models have been subsumed by the theories we discussed in this chapter.

So then, what method is best for explaining chemical and process addictions? The answer: All of them have their merits and all are useful to describe how the myriad addictive disorders affect individuals and families. So then, the answer is that there is no single answer! Whereas clinicians may have their "favorite" explanatory construct (the Biopsychosocialspiritual Model works most of the time for my clients), they are frequently challenged by those clients for whom their "model du jour" does not work. Even with *my* model preference (said tongue in cheek), whereas clients may understand how three of the four constructs might fit (e.g., the psychological, social, and spiritual), since they do not have genetic links to addiction in their families and the details of their addictive disorders do not fit the principles of the Disease/Medical Model, I am forced to retreat from the confidence I attempt to engender in the Biopsychosocialspiritual Model to a less comprehensive Psychosocialspiritual Model (I didn't even know there *was* one of those!). We need to admit to ourselves (and sometimes to clients!) that even with the bevy of information that we have gathered about chemical and process addictions, we still know very little about how these disorders occur and why they vary so greatly among individuals (Batra, 2004; Nesse, 2002). Similarly, as long as the debates continue about the nature versus nurture origins of addictions (e.g., those who staunchly advocate for a genetic link versus those who note the common life experiences), let alone the disagreements as to what to call these disorders (e.g., addictions, impulse control disorders, compulsions), little forward progress can be made to assist those most in need (Hagedorn & Juhnke, 2005; Nesse, 2002).

Given that no one theory explains addiction for every case, clinicians and researchers alike have been calling for a total reorganization, most notably for an integration, of theories (Futterman, Lorente, & Silverman, 2005; Moos, 2003). One possible outcome of this integration would be that the various professional disciplines that treat addictive disorders (i.e., counselors, psychiatrists, paraprofessionals, medical doctors, social workers, and psychologists) will be able to share a common language that allows for collaboration and improved treatment regimens (Batra, 2004; Kumpfer, Trunnell, & Whiteside, 1990). Similarly, a common language will allow for increased legitimacy for addictive disorders, which in turn may assist with increases in sponsored research, third-party reimbursement, and improved social policies (Gelkopf, Levitt, & Bleich, 2002; Hagedorn

& Juhnke, 2005; Nesse, 2002). Most importantly, though, an integration of theories will better assist struggling individuals and families in coming to terms with these debilitating disorders. Such an integration of theory would therefore necessitate gathering all known data and encapsulating it under one major paradigm. This has occurred recently and has been designated as the Final Common Pathway Theory (FCP) of addiction.

In a nutshell, FCP Theory states that the end of the path (addiction) can be reached through multiple combinations of unique circumstances, leading to multiple explanations for how addictions develop for each individual (Brandon & Brandon, 2005; Cox & Klinger, 1988). Therefore, one must consider how the impact of such things as culture, genetics, the environment, one's emotional and psychological disposition, and spirituality uniquely combine to produce conditions ripe for addictive disorders (Davidson, 2001). This unique combination of factors helps to explain why addictive disorders develop in individuals regardless of race, culture, gender, socioeconomic background, family constellation, psychological state, and spiritual practice. It also clarifies why studies that use addicted animals to predict addicted human behaviors are so inconclusive (Batra, 2004).

Doweiko (2002) noted the intricate interactions of several factors. These factors, which make up FCP Theory, include social forces (e.g., the environment in which individuals are raised, the conditions in which individuals live, the role models that individuals emulate), psychological conditioning (e.g., how we learn to express our needs and feelings), medicating psychological pain (i.e., the Self-Medication Hypothesis), spiritual shortcomings (e.g., a lack of spiritual connections or perhaps a belief in irrevocable sin), genetic-based predispositions (such as those found in the Medical Model), and brain-based pathways (particularly the stimulation of the reward center of the brain [the nucleus accumbens]). This view differs from the Biopsychosocialspiritual Model in that all four domains are not necessarily responsible for the development of chemical or process addictions. Rather, addiction can result solely from one factor, a combination of three factors, or even an interaction of five or more factors. The point is that each individual's path to addiction is unique and the path should be considered carefully as clinicians begin the treatment process.

To conclude, the two most important characteristics that clinicians must possess, especially as they prepare to utilize the multiple theories to assist addicted clients and their families, are flexibility and intentionality. In clinical practice, flexibility and intentionality are crucial, as no one theory explains the intricate disease of addiction. Be prepared to move intentionally (and seemingly effortlessly) from one theory to another to determine which pathway best describes each client's unique circumstances. In a group or family session, we often present data from each theory and ask how it applies to each individual. This may sound as if we are suggesting that the proverbial cart be placed before the horse, and this may be driving the linear-thinking reader slightly batty. There is some credence to this observation: We *are* advocating that clinicians discover how disorders develop for each client and then, with flexibility, pick the theory or group of theories that best explains this process for each individual client. This same process should be utilized in the application of treatment theories (Babor & Del Boca, 2003). As we noted, each etiological theory has merit and value, and this value, in our opinion, lies in how effectively it aids in the recovery process. Granted, theory is crucial to developing prevention efforts and in guiding empirical research, but when it comes to clinical practice, our goal is to help clients understand their disorders so that they are better prepared to battle them.

In the next chapter, we begin the discussion of treating addictive disorders. Additional theories are offered, but these are focused more on alleviating, rather than understanding, addictions. Our hope is that with a firm understanding of etiology, readers are better prepared to begin helping clients and their families through the intricate healing process.

Skill Builder

Question 1

Draw a line between the major etiological theories and their explanatory constructs. Each theory should have three accompanying constructs.

Moral Model   The spiritual domain is considered
                                             important

                                             The power of personal choice

Physiological Theory   Multiple patterns of dysfunctional use

                                             Diverse combinations of precipitating
                                             factors

Psychological Theory   Social roles

                                             Each addictive disorder is unique

Influence of the Environment   The holistic approach

                                             Self-Medication Hypothesis

Biopsychosocialspiritual Approach   Twin and adoption studies

                                             Genetic sensitivity

Final Common Pathway Theory   Parental and sibling use

                                             An integration of theories

                                             Willpower and a desire to abstain

                                             Relapse triggers

                                             A lack of spiritual direction

                                             Addictive Personality

                                             Four distinct phases of the disease

                                             Sociological Theory

Question 2

Fill in the blanks in each of the following sentences, which highlight the major principles from each etiological theory.

Moral Model

- The Moral Model continues to be _____ _____—society, family, and friends tend to hold fast to the belief that addicts are weak and morally degenerative.

- The Moral Model places a lot of responsibility on one's own _____ _____.

- The Moral Model places importance on seeking out a _____ as _____ a part of the recovery process.

Physiological Theory

- The Disease/Medical Model was first advocated by _____ _____ as a response to the detrimental impacts of the Moral Model.

- Elvin M. Jellinek's four distinct phases of the disease of alcoholism are known as the _____ Phase, _____Phase, _____ Phase, and _____ Phase.

- Two of the major principles of the disease concept of alcoholism include an inevitable _____ _____ _____ and an inability to _____.

- One of the major benefits of Physiological Theory is that it removes the moral stigma, _____ , _____ , and _____ attached to addictive use.

- Physiological Theory has been supported by the study of genetics, including _____ and _____ studies, alcohol _____ studies, and _____ research.

- MRI brain evidence has been demonstrated in two parts of Carnes' *Addictive System*: _____ and _____ .

- Another benefit of Physiological Theory is that it promotes _____ and ensures _____ .

Psychological Theory

- Psychological Theory helps explain why individuals use chemicals and behaviors to "_____ Out."

- Psychological Theory highlights the conscious and _____ _____ that lead to the escape from _____ _____.

- Addictions occur if they are reinforced, be it either _____ (through encouragement) or _____ (through avoidance).

- Behavioral Theory explains chemical/behavior use with the **A** (_____)–**B** (_____)–**C** (_____) sequence of behaviors.

- Four main reasons sustain addictive behavior: _____, _____, _____, and _____.

- Psychological Theory notes that addiction is one means to cope with _____ _____ and shame.

- An addictive relationship develops between an individual and a _____ or _____.

- The struggle inherent to the Addictive Personality pits the "_____" versus the "_____."

Influence of the Environment

- Sociological Theory investigates the interaction between _____ _____ and the _____.

- Role Theory notes that addictions develop based on the interaction of three factors: _____ of _____, lack of _____ _____ from their use/abuse, and the presence of _____ _____.

- The study of _____ _____ investigates the impact of one's role in society on the likelihood of an addictive disorder developing.

- Social groups develop their own set of normative _____, _____, and _____.

- The _____ _____ _____ occurs as an interaction between the social group and the members of that group.

- The _____ _____perspective of addictive disorders notes the influence of _____ substance abuse, _____ substance abuse, and _____ substance abuse.

Biopsychosocialspiritual Approach

- The Biopsychosocialspiritual Model, as it is aptly named, involves the interaction of the _____, _____, _____, and _____ domains.

- Research and clinical practice note the importance of addressing the spiritual domain in the _____, _____, and _____ processes.

- Addictions have been conceptualized as _____ _____, resulting from addicts' failed attempts at filling spiritual voids.

- Research has demonstrated the interaction between spirituality and both _____ _____and _____ _____.

- A quick way to assess for suicidal ideations is the SLAP acronym: _____, _____, _____, and _____.

- The best way to create treatment goals is with a SMART plan: Any changes would have to be _____, _____, _____, _____, and _____ _____.

- In order to help normalize the recovery process and remove some of the resulting guilt and shame, clients should be helped to anticipate SLIPs (_____ _____ _____ _____).

- The Balanced approach to the Biopsychosocialspiritual Model calls for the _____ _____ of activities that address _____ _____ _____.

- The Balanced approach helps clients recognize the _____ behind their activities and build in _____ plans, all of which results in an increase in _____ for maintaining healthy activities.

The Integration of Theories

- Though much research has been conducted that helps explain the origins of chemical and process addictions, we continue to know very little about why addictions _____ _____ _____ _____.

- One benefit of integrated theories would be that the various professional disciplines that treat addictive disorders will be able to share a _____ _____ that allows for _____ and improved _____ _____.

- Another benefit of integrated theories is that it promotes increased _____ for addictive disorders, which in turn may assist with increases in _____ _____, third-party reimbursement, and improved _____ _____.

- Most importantly, though, an integration of theories will better assist _____ _____ and _____ in coming to terms with these debilitating disorders.

- _____ _____ _____ Theory states that the end of the addiction path can be reached through multiple combinations of _____ _____, leading to multiple explanations for how addictions develop for each individual.

- The factors that make up FCP Theory include _____ _____, _____ _____, medicating _____ _____, _____ shortcomings, _____ predispositions, and _____ _____ _____.

- The two most important characteristics that clinicians must possess are _____ and _____.

- Clinicians are challenged to discover how disorders develop for each client and then, with flexibility, pick the theory or group of theories that _____ _____ _____ _____ for each individual client.

Question 3

In your own words, explain what intentionality is and why it is important in the choice of etiological theories.

_____

_____

_____

_____

_____

_____

Question 4

Identify and briefly describe the "5 P's of the Medical Model" followed by the "6 P's of Successful Recovery" (and what that statement means to you).

"5 P's of the Medical Model"

Addictions are:

P _____

P _____

P _____

P _____

P _____

"6 P's of Successful Recovery"

P _____ P _____ P _____ P _____ P _____ P _____

Meaning:

_____

_____

Skill Builder Responses and Answers

Question 1 Responses

Moral Model

- The power of personal choice
- Willpower and a desire to abstain
- A lack of spiritual direction

Physiological Theory

- Twin and adoption studies
- Four distinct phases of the disease
- Genetic sensitivity

Psychological Theory

- Addictive Personality
- Self-Medication Hypothesis
- Relapse triggers

Influence of the Environment

- Social roles
- Parental and sibling use
- Sociological Theory

Biopsychosocialspiritual Approach

- The holistic approach
- Multiple patterns of dysfunctional use
- The spiritual domain is considered important

Final Common Pathway Theory

- An integration of theories
- Diverse combinations of precipitating factors
- Each addictive disorder is unique

Question 2 Responses

Moral Model

- The Moral Model continues to be <u>socially ingrained</u>—society, family, and friends tend to hold fast to the belief that addicts are weak and morally degenerative.
- The Moral Model places a lot of responsibility on one's <u>personal choices</u>.
- The Moral Model places importance on seeking out a <u>spiritual connection</u> as a part of the recovery process.

Physiological Theory

- The Disease/Medical Model was first advocated by <u>Alcoholics Anonymous</u> as a response to the detrimental impacts of the Moral Model.
- Elvin M. Jellinek's four distinct phases of the disease of alcoholism are known as the <u>Prealcoholic</u> Phase, <u>Prodromal</u> Phase, <u>Crucial</u> Phase, and <u>Chronic</u> Phase.
- Two of the major principles of the disease concept of alcoholism include an inevitable <u>loss of control</u> and an inability to <u>abstain</u>.
- One of the major benefits of Physiological Theory is that it removes the moral stigma, <u>embarrassment</u>, <u>shame</u>, and <u>guilt</u> attached to addictive use.
- Physiological Theory has been supported by the study of genetics, including <u>adoption</u> and <u>twin</u> studies, alcohol <u>sensitivity</u> studies, and <u>neurobiological</u> research.
- MRI brain evidence has been demonstrated in two parts of Carnes's *Addictive System*: <u>Preoccupation</u> and <u>Ritualization</u>.
- Another benefit of Physiological Theory is that it promotes <u>research</u> and ensures <u>third-party</u> <u>reimbursement</u>.

Psychological Theory

- Psychological Theory helps explain why individuals use chemicals and behaviors to "<u>Numb</u> Out."
- Psychological Theory highlights the conscious and <u>unconscious processes</u> that lead to the escape from <u>existential</u> <u>suffering</u>.
- Addictions occur if they are reinforced, be it either <u>positively</u> (through encouragement) or <u>negatively</u> (through avoidance).
- Behavioral Theory explains chemical/behavior use with the **A** (<u>Antecedent</u>)–**B** (<u>Behavior</u>)–**C** (<u>Consequence</u>) sequence of behaviors.

- Four main reasons sustain addictive behavior: <u>attention</u>, <u>avoidance</u>, <u>tangible</u> <u>reward</u>, and <u>sensory</u> <u>stimulation</u>.
- Psychological Theory notes that addiction is one means to cope with <u>emotional</u> <u>trauma</u> and shame.
- An addictive relationship develops between an individual and a <u>chemical</u> or <u>behavior</u>.
- The struggle inherent to the Addictive Personality pits the "<u>Self</u>" versus the "<u>Addict</u>."

Influence of the Environment

- Sociological Theory investigates the interaction between <u>human</u> <u>behavior</u> and the <u>environment</u>.
- Role Theory notes that addictions develop based on the interaction of three factors: <u>availability</u> of <u>substances</u>, lack of <u>social</u> <u>restraint</u> from their use/abuse, and the presence of <u>role</u> <u>strain</u>.
- The study of <u>social</u> <u>roles</u> investigates the impact of one's role in society on the likelihood of an addictive disorder developing.
- Social groups develop their own set of normative <u>behaviors</u>, <u>language</u>, and <u>rituals</u>.
- The <u>social</u> <u>feedback</u> <u>mechanism</u> occurs as an interaction between the social group and the members of that group.
- The <u>Social</u> <u>Learning</u> perspective of addictive disorders notes the influence of <u>parental</u> substance abuse, <u>sibling</u> substance abuse, and <u>peer</u> substance abuse.

Biopsychosocialspiritual Approach

- The Biopsychosocialspiritual Model, as it is aptly named, involves the interaction of the <u>biological</u>, <u>psychological</u>, <u>social</u>, and <u>spiritual</u> domains.
- Research and clinical practice note the importance of addressing the spiritual domain in the <u>assessment</u>, <u>treatment</u>, and <u>recovery</u> processes.
- Addictions have been conceptualized as <u>spiritual</u> <u>disorders</u>, resulting from addicts' failed attempts at filling spiritual voids.
- Research has demonstrated the interaction between spirituality and both <u>psychological</u> <u>health</u> and <u>biological</u> <u>well-being</u>.
- A quick way to assess for suicidal ideations is the SLAP acronym: <u>S</u>pecificity, <u>L</u>ethality, <u>A</u>vailability, and <u>P</u>roximity.
- The best way to create treatment goals is with a SMART plan: Any changes would have to be <u>S</u>pecific, <u>M</u>easurable, <u>A</u>chievable, <u>R</u>ealistic, and <u>T</u>ime limited.

- In order to help normalize the recovery process and remove some of the resulting guilt and shame, clients should be helped to anticipate SLIPs (<u>Slight</u> <u>Lapses</u> <u>In</u> <u>Progress</u>).
- The Balanced approach to the Biopsychosocialspiritual Model calls for the <u>creative</u> <u>combination</u> of activities that address <u>multiple</u> <u>life</u> <u>domains</u>.
- The Balanced approach helps clients recognize the <u>intentionality</u> behind their activities and build in <u>backup</u> plans, all of which results in an increase in <u>self-efficacy</u> for maintaining healthy activities.

The Integration of Theories

- Though much research has been conducted that helps explain the origins of chemical and process addictions, we continue to know very little about why addictions <u>vary</u> <u>so</u> <u>greatly</u> <u>among</u> <u>individuals</u>.
- One benefit of integrated theories would be that the various professional disciplines that treat addictive disorders will be able to share a <u>common</u> <u>language</u> that allows for <u>collaboration</u> and improved <u>treatment</u> <u>regimens</u>.
- Another benefit of integrated theories is that it promotes increased <u>legitimacy</u> for addictive disorders, which in turn may assist with increases in <u>sponsored</u> <u>research</u>, third-party reimbursement, and improved <u>social</u> <u>policies</u>.
- Most importantly, though, an integration of theories will better assist <u>struggling</u> <u>individuals</u> and <u>families</u> in coming to terms with these debilitating disorders.
- <u>Final</u> <u>Common</u> <u>Pathway</u> Theory states that the end of the addiction path can be reached through multiple combinations of <u>unique</u> <u>circumstances</u>, leading to multiple explanations for how addictions develop for each individual.
- The factors that make up FCP Theory include <u>social</u> <u>forces</u>, <u>psychological</u> <u>conditioning</u>, medicating <u>psychological</u> <u>pain</u>, <u>spiritual</u> shortcomings, <u>genetic-based</u> predispositions, and <u>brain-based</u> <u>pathways</u>.
- The two most important characteristics that clinicians must possess are <u>flexibility</u> and <u>intentionality</u>.
- Clinicians are challenged to discover how disorders develop for each client and then, with flexibility, pick the theory or group of theories that <u>best</u> <u>explains</u> <u>this</u> <u>process</u> for each individual client.

Question 3 Responses

In your own words, explain what intentionality is and why it is important in the choice of etiological theories.

Answers might include:

Intentionality connects one's inner consciousness with one's outward behavior. It guides the selection, purpose, and direction of helping strategies and is one of the main determinants of successful client change. Without intentionality, clinicians tend to "wing it" when it comes to exploring the origins of disorders and in picking interventions, often relying on either "cookie-cutter" approaches, favorite interventions, or "let's see what happens when I try *this*" methods. A lack of intentionality not only interferes with client progress but also can lead to clinicians feeling ineffective.

Question 4 Responses

Identify and briefly describe the "5 P's of the Medical Model" followed by the "6 P's of Successful Recovery" (and what that statement means to you).

"5 P's of the Medical Model"

Addictions are:

- Primary disorders—They must be addressed before, or at least in conjunction with, any other disorder.
- Progressive—They develop over time (predictably).
- Prolonged—They worsen over time.
- Potentially fatal—Without therapeutic attention, most addictions will eventually lead to one of three conclusions: institutions, prisons, or death.
- Positively treatable—With help, individuals *do* recover.

"6 P's of Successful Recovery"

<u>Prior</u> <u>Planning</u> <u>Prevents</u> <u>Piss</u>-<u>Poor</u> <u>Performance</u>

Meaning:

Similar to any other chronic disease, recovery from addiction requires proactive planning with a focus on the unexpected. This is crucial in the fight against a disease that is cunning, baffling, and powerful, against a disease that can't be out-thought but *can* be out-planned.

References

Adlaf, E., & Giesbrecht, N. (1996). The substance use-delinquency nexus. *Addiction, 91*(4), 504–507.

Anderson, T. L. (1998). A cultural-identity theory of drug abuse. In J. T. Ulmer (Ed.), *Sociology of crime, law, and deviance* (Vol. 1, pp. 233–262). Stamford, CT: JAI Press, Inc.

Arnold, R. M., Avants, S. K., Margolin, A., & Marcotte, D. (2002). Patient attitudes concerning the inclusion of spirituality into addiction treatment. *Journal of Substance Abuse Treatment, 23*, 319–326.

Babor, T. F., & Del Boca, F. K. (2003). *Treatment matching in alcoholism. International research monographs in the addictions.* New York, NY: Cambridge University Press.

Bandura, A. (1982). Self-efficacy mechanism in human agency. *American Psychologist, 37*, 122–147.

Batra, A. (2004). Addiction and the search for integrated theory. *Addiction, 99*, 1504.

Biederman, J., Faraone, S. V., Monuteaux, M. C., & Feighner, J. A. (2000). Patterns of alcohol and drug use in adolescents can be predicted by parental substance use disorders. *Pediatrics, 106*(4), 792–798.

Brady, M. J., Peterman, A. H., Fitchett, G., Mo, M., & Cella, D. (1999). A case for including spirituality in quality of life measurement in oncology. *Psycho-Oncology, 8*(5), 417–428.

Brandon, T. H., & Brandon, K. O. (2005). Brother, can you spare a smoke? Sibling transmission of tobacco use. *Addiction, 100*(4), 439–444.

Brems, C., Johnson, M. E., Neal, D., & Freemon, M. (2004). Childhood abuse history and substance use among men and women receiving detoxification services. *American Journal of Drug and Alcohol Abuse, 30*(4), 799–821.

Brisman, J., & Siegel, M. (1984). Bulimia and alcoholism: Two sides of the same coin? *Journal of Substance Abuse Treatment, 1*(2), 113–118.

Burke, R. J. (1999). Workaholism in organizations: Gender differences. *Sex Roles, 41*(5/6), 333–345.

Bush, T., Curry, S. J., Hollis, J., Grothaus, L., Ludman, E., McAfee, T., et al. (2005). Preteen attitudes about smoking and parental factors associated with favorable attitudes. *American Journal of Health Promotion, 19*(6), 410–417.

Callor, W. B., Petersen, E., Gray, D., Grey, T., Lamoreaux, T., & Bennett, P. J. (2005). Preliminary findings of noncompliance with psychotropic medication and prevalence of methamphetamine intoxication associated with suicide completion. *Crisis: The Journal of Crisis Intervention and Suicide Prevention, 26*(2), 78–84.

Carnes, P. (1994a). *Contrary to love: Helping the sexual addict.* Center City, MN: Hazelden.

Carnes, P. (1994b). *Out of the shadows: Understanding sexual addiction* (2nd ed.). Center City, MN: Hazelden.

Carothers, S. S., Borkowski, J. G., Lefever, J. B., & Whitman, T. L. (2005). Religiosity and the socioemotional adjustment of adolescent mothers and their children. *Journal of Family Psychology, 19*(2), 263–275.

Carroll, K. M., Nich, C., Frankforter, T. L., & Bisighini, R. M. (1999). Do patients change in the ways we intend? Assessing acquisition of coping skills among cocaine-dependent patients. *Psychological Assessment, 11*(1), 77–85.

Chappelle, W. (2000). A series of progressive legal and ethical decision-making steps for using Christian spiritual interventions in psychotherapy. *Journal of Psychology & Theology, 28*(1), 43–53.

Clinebell, H. J. (1963). Philosophical-religious factors in the etiology and treatment of alcoholism. *Quarterly Journal of Studies on Alcohol, 24,* 473–488.

Cooper, A., Delmonico, D. L., & Burg, R. (2000). Cybersex users, abusers, and compulsives: New findings and implications. *Sexual Addiction & Compulsivity, 7,* 5–29.

Cooper, A., Galbreath, N., & Becker, M. A. (2004). Sex on the Internet: Furthering our understanding of men with online sexual problems. *Psychology of Addictive Behaviors, 18*(3), 223–230.

Cooper, M. L., Shapiro, C. M., & Powers, A. M. (1998). Motivations for sex and risky sexual behavior among adolescents and young adults: A functional perspective. *Journal of Personality and Social Psychology, 75*(6), 1528–1558.

Cox, W. M., & Klinger, E. (1988). A motivational model of alcohol use. *Journal of Abnormal Psychology, 97*(2), 168–180.

Cox Jones, C., Vallano, G., Ryan, E., & Helsel, W. J., & Rancurello, M. D. (1991). Self-injurious behavior: Strategies for assessment and management. *Psychiatric Annals, 21*(5), 310–317.

Crabbe, J. C. (2002). Genetic contributions to addiction. *Annual Review of Psychology, 53,* 435–462.

Craig, R. J. (2004). *Counseling the alcohol and drug dependent client: A practical approach.* Boston, MA: Pearson.

Culliford, L. (2002). Spirituality and clinical care: Spiritual values and skills are increasingly recognized as necessary aspects of clinical care. *British Medical Journal, 325,* 21–28.

Davidson, R. J. (2001). Toward a biology of personality and emotion. *Annals New York Academy of Sciences,* 191–207. Retrieved October 28, 2005, from http://psyphz.psych.wisc.edu/front/lab%20articles/2001/Toward_a_biology.pdf#search='Final%20Common%20Pathway%20Theory'

Davis, C., & Karvinen, K. (2002). Personality characteristics and intention to self-harm: A study of eating disordered patients. *Eating Disorders: The Journal of Treatment & Prevention, 10*(3), 245–255.

Davis, C., Katzman, D. K., & Kirsh, C. (1999). Compulsive physical activity in adolescents with anorexia nervosa: A psychobehavioral spiral of pathology. *Journal of Nervous & Mental Disease, 187*(6), 336–342.

Davis, D. R., & Jansen, G. G. (1998). Making meaning of Alcoholics Anonymous for social workers: Myths, metaphors, and realities. *Social Work, 43*(2), 169–182.

Dean, A. (2001). Complexity and substance misuse. *Addiction Research & Theory, 9*(1), 19–41.

Doweiko, H. E. (2002). *Concepts of chemical dependency* (5th ed.). Pacific Grove, CA: Brooks/Cole.

Dube, C. E., & Lewis, D. C. (1994). Medical education in alcohol and other drugs: Curriculum development for primary care. *Alcohol Health & Research World, 18*(2), 146–153.

Duncan, T. E., Duncan, S. C., & Hops, H. (1996). The role of parents and older siblings in predicting adolescent substance use: Modeling development via structural equation latent growth methodology. *Journal of Family Psychology, 10*(2), 158–172.

Eklund, J. M., & Klinteberg, B. (2005). Personality characteristics as risk indications of alcohol use and violent behavior in male and female adolescents. *Journal of Individual Differences, 26*(2), 63-73.

Erickson, S. H. (2005). Etiological theories of substance abuse. In P. Stevens & R. L. Smith (Eds.), *Substance abuse counseling: Theory and practice* (3rd ed., pp. 87–122). Upper Saddle River, NJ: Prentice-Hall.

Fairburn, C. G., Cowen, P. J., & Harrison, P. J. (1999). Twin studies and the etiology of eating disorders. *International Journal of Eating Disorders, 26*(4), 349–358.

Ferry, T. R., Fouad, N., & Smith, P. L. (2000). The role of family context in a social cognitive model for career-related choice behavior: A math and science perspective. *Journal of Vocational Behavior, 57*(3), 348–364.

Fine, C. G. (1996). Models of helping: The role of responsibility. In J. L. Spira & I. D. Yalom (Eds.), *Treating dissociative identity disorder. The Jossey-Bass library of current clinical technique* (pp. 81–98). San Francisco, CA: Jossey-Bass.

Fisher, G. L., & Harrison, T. C. (2005). *Substance abuse: Information for school counselors, social workers, therapists, and counselors* (3rd ed.). Boston, MA: Pearson.

Forman, R. F., Bovasso, G., & Woody, G. (2001). Staff beliefs about addiction treatment. *Journal of Substance Abuse Treatment, 21*, 1–9.

Frank, A. (1998). A multidisciplinary approach to obesity management: The physician's role and team care alternatives. *Journal of the American Dietetic Association, 98*(10), S44–49.

French, S., & Joseph, S. (1999). Religiosity and its association with happiness, purpose in life, and self-actualization. *Mental Health, Religion, & Culture, 2*(2), 117–120.

Futterman, R., Lorente, M., & Silverman, S. W. (2005). Beyond harm reduction: A new model of substance abuse treatment further integrating psychological techniques. *Journal of Psychotherapy Integration, 15*(1), 3–18.

Garneski, N., & Deikstra, R. F. W. (1997). Child sexual abuse and emotional and behavioral problems in adolescence: Gender differences. *Journal of the American Academy of Child and Adolescent Psychiatry, 36*(3), 323–329.

Garrett, C. (1998). *Beyond anorexia: Narrative, spirituality and recovery.* New York: Cambridge.

Garrett, M. T., & Carroll, J. J. (2000). Mending the broken circle: Treatment of substance dependence among Native Americans. *Journal of Counseling and Development, 78*(4), 379–388.

Gelkopf, M., Levitt, S., & Bleich, A. (2002). An integration of three approaches to addiction and methadone maintenance treatment: The self-medication hypothesis, the disease model and social criticism. *Israel Journal of Psychiatry & Related Sciences, 39*(2), 140–151.

Glass, S. (1998). Shattered vows. *Psychology Today, 31*(4), 34–42.

Goeders, N. E. (2002). Stress and cocaine addiction. *The Journal of Pharmacology and Experimental Therapeutics, 301*(3), 785–789.

Goeders, N. E. (2003). The impact of stress on addiction. *European Neuropsychopharmacology, 13,* 435–441.

Goodwin, D. W., Schulsinger, F., Moller, N., Hermansen, L., Winokur, G., & Guse, S. B. (1974). Drinking problems in adopted and nonadopted sons of alcoholics. *Archives of General Psychiatry, 31,* 164–170.

Gorski, T. T. (1991). Relapse—issues and answers: Spirituality and sobriety. *Addiction & Recovery, 11*(1), 19–21.

Graham, J. W., Marks, G., & Hansen, W. B. (1991). Social influence processes affecting adolescent substance use. *Journal of Applied Psychology, 76,* 291–298.

Greeley, J., & Oei, T. (1999). Alcohol and tension reduction. In K. E. Leonard & H. T. Blane (Eds.), *Psychological theories of drinking and alcoholism* (2nd ed., pp. 14–53). New York: Guilford Press.

Green, L. L., Thompson-Fullilove, M., & Fullilove, R. E. (1998). Stories of spiritual awakening: The nature of spirituality in recovery. *Journal of Substance Abuse Treatment, 15*(4), 325–331.

Grills, S. (2004). Gambling and the human condition: Transcending the deviant mystique. *E Gambling.* Retrieved August 27, 2005, from http://www.camh.net/egambling/ archive/pdf/EJGI-Issue10/ejgi-issue10-grills.pdf

Gupta, R., & Derevensky, J. (1997). Familial and social influences on juvenile gambling behavior. *Journal of Gambling Studies, 13*(3), 179–192.

Hagedorn, W. B., & Hartwig Moorhead, H. J. (in press). The God-shaped hole: Addictive behavior and the search for perfection. In J. Chauvin (Ed.), *Readings in spirituality and counseling.*

Hagedorn, W. B., & Juhnke, G. A. (2005). Treating the sexually addicted client: Establishing a need for increased counselor awareness. *Journal of Addictions & Offender Counseling, 25*(2), 66–86.

Hagedorn, W. B., & Watts, R. H. (2002, March). *It's all about balance: Creative strategies for the implementation of wellness.* Program presented at the national conference of the American Counseling Association, New Orleans, LA.

Hajema, K. J., & Knibbe, R. A. (1998). Changes in social roles as predictors of changes in drinking behaviour. *Addiction, 93*(11), 1717–1727.

Harris, K. M., & Edlund, M. J. (2005). Self-medication of mental health problems: New evidence from a national survey. *Health Services Research, 40*(1), 117–134.

Hathaway, W. L., Scott, S. Y., & Garver, S. A. (2004). Assessing religious/spiritual functioning: A neglected domain in clinical practice? *Professional Psychology: Research and Practice, 35*(1), 97-104.

Heath, A. C., Bucholz, K. K., Madden, P. A. F., Dinwiddie, S. H., Slutske, W. S., Bierut, L. J., et al. (1997). Genetic and environmental contributions to alcohol dependence risk in a national twin sample: Consistency of findings in men and women. *Psychological Medicine, 27,* 1381–1396.

Hill, P., & Pargament, K. I. (2003). Advances in the conceptualization and measurement of religion and spirituality: Implications for physical and mental health research. *American Psychologist, 58,* 64–74.

Hjelmeland, H., & Groholt, B. (2005). A comparative study of young and adult deliberate self-harm patients. *Crisis: The Journal of Crisis Intervention and Suicide Prevention, 26*(2), 64–72.

Hodge, D. R., Cardenas, P., & Montoya, H. (2001). Substance use: Spirituality and religious participation as protective factors among rural youths. *Social Work Research, 25*(3), 153–162.

Hodges, S. (2002). Mental health, depression, and dimensions of spirituality and religion, *Journal of Adult Development, 9,* 109–115.

Hoffman, J. P., & Su, S. S. (1997). The conditional effects of stress on delinquency and drug use: A strain theory assessment of sex differences. *Journal of Research in Crime & Delinquency, 34*(1), 46–79.

Hopfer, C. J., Crowley, T. J., & Hewitt, J. K. (2003). Review of twin and adoption studies of adolescent substance use. *Journal of the American Academy of Child & Adolescent Psychiatry, 42*(6), 710–719.

Hubble, M. A., Duncan, B. L., & Miller, S. D. (Eds.). (1999). *The heart and soul of change: What works in therapy.* Washington, DC: American Psychological Association.

Hussong, A. M., Galloway, C. A., & Feagans, L. A. (2005). Coping motives as a moderator of daily mood-drinking covariation. *Journal of Studies on Alcohol, 66*(3), 344–353.

Ibáñez, A., Blanco, C., de Castro, I. P., Fernandez-Piqueras, J., & Sáiz-Ruiz, J. (2003). Genetics of pathological gambling. *Journal of Gambling Studies, 19*(1), 11–22.

Jaccard, J., Blanton, H., & Dodge, T. (2005). Peer influences on risk behavior: An analysis of the effects of a close friend. *Developmental Psychology, 41*(1), 135–147.

Jacobs, D. F. (1986). A general theory of addictions: A new theoretical model. *Journal of Gambling Behavior, 2,* 15–31.

James, A., & Wells, A. (2003). Religion and mental health: Towards a cognitive-behavioral framework. *British Journal of Health Psychology, 8*, 359–376.

Johnson, B. (2003). Psychological addiction, physical addiction, addictive character, and addictive personality disorder: A nosology of addictive disorders. *Canadian Journal of Psychoanalysis, 11*(1), 135–160.

Juhnke, G. A., & Hagedorn, W. B. (2003). SUBSTANCE-Q: A practical clinical interview for alcohol and other drug abuse. In J. E. Wall & G. R. Walz (Eds.), *Measuring up: Assessment issues for teachers, counselors, and administrators* (pp. 245–256). Austin, TX: PRO-ED, Inc.

Karasu, T. B. (1999). Spiritual psychotherapy. *American Journal of Psychotherapy, 53*(2), 143–162.

Kassel, J. D., Stroud, L. R., & Paronis, C. A. (2003). Smoking, stress, and negative affect correlation, causation, and context across stages of smoking. *Psychological Bulletin, 129*(2), 270–304.

Kelly, T. M., Cornelius, J. R., & Lynch, K. G. (2002). Psychiatric and substance use disorders as risk factors for attempted suicide among adolescents: A case control study. *Suicide and Life-Threatening Behavior, 32*(3), 301–312.

Kleinke, C. L., & Kane, J. C. (1998). Responsibility attributions for clients working with a counselor, clinical psychologist or psychiatrist on various problems. *Journal of Mental Health Counseling, 20*(1), 77–88.

Knop, J., Penick, E. C., Jensen, P., Nickel, E. J., Gabrielli, W. F., Mednick, S. A., et al. (2003). Risk factors that predicted problem drinking in Danish men at age thirty. *Journal of Studies on Alcohol, 64*(6), 745–755.

Koff, E., &, Sangani, P. (1998). Effects of coping style and negative body image on eating disturbance. *International Journal of Eating Disorders, 22*(1), 51–56.

Kress, V. E. W. (2003). Self-injurious behaviors: Assessment and diagnosis. *Journal of Counseling and Development, 81*(4), 490–496.

Kumpfer, K. L., Trunnell, E. P., & Whiteside, H. O. (1990) The biopsychosocial model: Application to the addictions field. In R. C. Engs (Ed.), *Controversies in the addiction field*. Dubuque, IA: Kendall Hunt. Retrieved October 28, 2005, from http://www.indiana.edu/~engs/cbook/chap7.html

Kurtz, E. (1979). *Not God: A history of Alcoholics Anonymous*. Center City, MN: Hazeldon Educational Services.

Laaser, M. (1996). *Faithful and true: Sexual integrity in a fallen world*. Grand Rapids, MI: Zondervan.

Lambert, C. (2000, March/April). Deep cravings: New research on the brain and behavior clarifies the mysteries of addiction. *Harvard Magazine*, 60–68. Retrieved September 30, 2005, from http://www.dushkin.com/text-data/articles/27237/body.pdf

Lambert, M. J. (1992). Psychotherapy outcome research: Implications for integrative and eclectic therapists. In J. C. Norcross & M. R. Goldfried (Eds.), *Handbook of psychotherapy integration* (pp. 94–129). New York: Basic.

Larimer, M. E., Turner, A. P., Mallett, K. A., & Geisner, I. M. (2004). Predicting drinking behavior and alcohol-related problems among fraternity and sorority members: Examining the role of descriptive and injunctive norms. *Psychology of Addictive Behaviors, 18*(3), 203–212.

LaRose, R., Lin, C. A., & Eastin, M. S. (2003). Unregulated Internet usage: Addiction, habit, or deficient self-regulation? *Media Psychology, 5*(3), 225–253.

Lawson, A. W. (1992). Intergenerational alcoholism: The family connection. In G. W. Lawson & A. W. Lawson (Eds.), *Adolescent substance abuse: Etiology, treatment and prevention* (pp. 41–70). Gaithersburg, MD: Aspen Publications.

Lawson, G. W., Peterson, J. S., & Lawson, A. W. (1983). *Alcoholism and the family: A guide to treatment and prevention.* Gaithersburg, MD: Aspen Publications.

Ledgerwood, D. M., Steinberg, M. A., Wu, R., & Potenza, M. N. (2005). Self-reported gambling-related suicidality among gambling helpline callers. *Psychology of Addictive Behaviors, 19*(2), 175–183.

Lester, R. J. (1997). The (dis)embodied self in anorexia nervosa. *Social Science & Medicine, 44*(4), 479–489.

Lightsey, O. R., Jr., & Hulsey, C. D. (2002). Impulsivity, coping, stress, and problem gambling among university students. *Journal of Counseling Psychology, 49*(2), 202–211.

Linder, J. R., & Collins, W. A. (2005). Parent and peer predictors of physical aggression and conflict management in romantic relationships in early adulthood. *Journal of Family Psychology, 19*(2), 252–262.

Logan, T. K., Walker, R., Cole, J., & Leukefeld, C. (2002). Victimization and substance abuse among women: Contributing factors, interventions, and implications. *Review of General Psychology, 6*(4), 325–397.

Lyvers, M. (1998). Drug addiction as a physical disease: The role of physical dependence and other chronic drug-induced neurophysiological changes in compulsive drug self-administration. *Experimental & Clinical Psychopharmacology, 6*(1), 107–125.

Lyvers, M. (2000). "Loss of control" in alcoholism and drug addiction: A neuroscientific interpretation. *Experimental and Clinical Psychopharmacology, 8*(2), 225–249.

Manley, G. (1995). Healthy sexuality: Stage III recovery. *Sexual Addiction & Compulsivity, 2*(3), 157–183.

Mann, K., Hermann, D., & Heinz, A. (2000). One hundred years of alcoholism: The twentieth century. *Alcohol and Alcoholism, 35*(1), 10–15.

Manning, B. (2000). *The ragamuffin gospel.* Sisters, OR: Multnomah.

Markey, C. N., Tinsley, B. J., Ericksen, A. J., Ozer, D. J., & Markey, P. M. (2002). Preadolescents' perceptions of females' body size and shape: Evolutionary and social learning perspectives. *Journal of Youth and Adolescence, 31*(2), 137–146.

Marzano-Parisoli, M. M. (2001). The contemporary construction of a perfect body image: Bodybuilding, exercise addiction, and eating disorders. *Quest, 53*(2), 216–230.

May, R. (1969). *Love and will.* New York: Norton.

McCoy, C. B., Miles, C., & Metsch, L. R. (1999). The medicalization of discourse within an AIDS research setting. In W. N. Elwood (Ed.), *Power in the blood: A handbook on AIDS, politics, and communication* (pp. 39–50). Mahwah, NJ: Lawrence Erlbaum Associates.

McLellan, A. T., Lewis, D. C., O'Brien, C. P., & Kleber, H. D. (2000). Drug dependence, a chronic medical illness: Implications for treatment, insurance, and outcomes evaluation. *JAMA: The Journal of the American Medical Association, 284*(13), 1689–1695.

McLennan, N. A., Rochow, S., & Arthur, N. (2001). Religious and spiritual diversity in counseling. *Guidance & Counseling, 16*(4), 132–137.

Miller, N. S., Sheppard, L. M., & Magen, J. (2001). Barriers to improving education and training in addiction medicine. *Psychiatric Annals, 31*(11), 649–656.

Miller, W. R. (1993). Alcoholism: Toward a better disease model. *Psychology of Addictive Behaviors, 7*(2), 129–136.

Miller, W. R., & Thoresen, C. E. (2003). Spirituality, religion, and health: An emerging research field. *American Psychologist, 58*, 24–35.

Modesto-Lowe, V., & Van Kirk, J. (2002). Clinical uses of naltrexone: A review of the evidence. *Experimental and Clinical Psychopharmacology, 10*(3), 213–227.

Moore, S., & Ohtsuka, K. (2000). The structure of young people's leisure and their gambling behaviour. *Behaviour Change, 17*(3), 167–177.

Moos, R. H. (2003). Addictive disorders in context: Principles and puzzles of effective treatment and recovery. *Psychology of Addictive Behaviors, 17*(1), 3–12.

Morse, S. J. (2003). Bad or mad? Sex offenders and social control. In W. J. Bruce & J. Q. La Fond (Eds.), *Protecting society from sexually dangerous offenders: Law, justice, and therapy* (pp. 165–182). Washington, DC: American Psychological Association.

Morse, S. J. (2004). Medicine and morals, craving and compulsion. *Substance Use & Misuse, 39*(3), 437–460.

Moyers, T. B., & Miller, W. R. (1993). Therapists' conceptualizations of alcoholism: Measurement and implications for treatment decisions. *Psychology of Addictive Behaviors, 7*(4), 238–245.

Mustanski, B. S., Viken, R. J., Kaprio, J., & Rose, R. J. (2003, May). Genetic influences on the association between personality risk factors and alcohol use and abuse. *Journal of Abnormal Psychology, 112*(2), 282–289.

Myers, J. E., & Willard, K. (2003). Integrating spirituality into counselor preparation: A developmental, wellness approach. *Counseling & Values, 47*, 142–155.

Nakken, C. (1996). *The addictive personality: Understanding the addictive process and compulsive behavior* (2nd ed.). Center City, MN: Hazelden.

National Clearinghouse for Alcohol and Drug Information (NCADI). (2001, November 2). Youth tobacco surveillance: United States, 2000. *CDC/MMWR Surveillance Summaries*. Retrieved November 3, 2002, from http://www.health.org/govpubs/mmwr/vol50/4a1.htm

Nesse, R. M. (2002). Evolution and addiction. *Addiction, 97*, 470–471.

Neve, R. J. M., Lemmens, P. H., & Drop, M. J. (1997). Gender differences in alcohol use and alcohol problems: Mediation by social roles and gender-role attitudes. *Substance Use & Misuse, 32*(11), 1439–1459.

Newcomb, M., & Earleywine, M. (1996). Intrapersonal contributors to drug use. *American Behavioral Scientist, 39*(7), 823–837.

Ng, H. Y., & Shek, D. T. L. (2001). Religion and therapy: Religious conversion and the mental health of chronic heroin-addicted persons. *Journal of Religion and Health, 40,* 399–410.

Nixon, G. (2002). Deconstruction, disability, and sex addiction: Embracing the narrative perspective. *International Journal of Disability, Community, & Rehabilitation, 1*(3). Retrieved September 30, 2005, from http://www.jidcr.ca/VOL01_03_CAN/nixon.shtml

Nock, M. K., & Prinstein, M. J. (2004). A functional approach to the assessment of self-mutilative behavior. *Journal of Consulting and Clinical Psychology, 72*(5), 885–890.

Nuutinen, H., Lindros, K. O., & Salaspuro, M. (1983). Determinants of blood acetaldehyde level during ethanol oxidation in chronic alcoholics. *Alcoholism: Clinical and Experimental Research, 7*(2), 163–168.

O'Connor, R. (2003). An integrative approach to treatment of depression. *Journal of Psychotherapy Integration, 13*(2), 130–170.

Olds, R. S., & Thombs, D. L. (2001). The relationship of adolescent perceptions of peer norms and parent involvement to cigarette and alcohol use. *Journal of School Health, 71*(6), 223–229.

Pardini, D. A., Plante, T. G., Sherman, A., & Stump, J. E. (2000). Religious faith and spirituality in substance abuse recovery: Determining the mental health benefits. *Journal of Substance Abuse Treatment, 19,* 347–354.

Patterson, J., Hayworth, M., Turner, C., & Raskin, M. (2000). Spiritual issues in family therapy: A graduate-level course. *Journal of Marital and Family Therapy, 26*(2), 199–210.

Peck, M. S. (1978). *The road less traveled: A new psychology of love, traditional values, and spiritual growth.* New York: Simon and Schuster.

Petraitis, J., Flay, B. R., & Miller, T. Q. (1995). Reviewing theories of adolescent substance use: Organizing pieces in the puzzle. *Psychological Bulletin, 117*(1), 67–86.

Petry, N. M. (2002). How treatments for pathological gambling can be informed by treatments for substance use disorders. *Experimental and Clinical Psychopharmacology, 10*(3), 184–192.

Plant, M., & Plant, M. (2003). Sex addiction: A comparison with dependence on psychoactive drugs. *Journal of Substance Use, 8*(4), 260–266.

Porter, G. (2001). Workaholic tendencies and the high potential for stress among co-workers. *International Journal of Stress Management, 8*(2), 147–164.

Powell, L. H., Shahabi, L., & Thoresen, C. E. (2003). Religion and spirituality: Linkages to physical health. *American Psychologist, 58,* 36–52.

Quertemont, E. (2004). Genetic polymorphism in ethanol metabolism: Acetaldehyde contribution to alcohol abuse and alcoholism. *Molecular Psychiatry, 9*(6), 570-581.

Read, J. P., Wood, M. D., Kahler, C. W., Maddock, J. E., & Palfai, T. P. (2003). Examining the role of drinking motives in college student alcohol use and problems. *Psychology of Addictive Behaviors, 17*(1), 13–23.

Reese, R. M., Richman, D. M., Zarcone, J., & Zarcone, T. (2003). Individualizing functional assessments for children with autism: The contribution of perseverative behavior and sensory disturbances to disruptive behavior. *Focus on Autism & Other Developmental Disabilities, 18*(2), 89–94.

Robbins, C. A. (1991). Social roles and alcohol abuse among older men and women. *Family & Community Health, 13*(4), 37–48.

Roller, C. G. (2004). Sex addiction and women: A nursing issue. *Journal of Addiction Nursing, 15*(2), 53–61.

Ross, S. (2005). Alcohol use disorders: Special topics. *Primary Psychiatry, 12*(1), 30–31.

Sandoz, J. (2001). The spiritual secret to alcoholism recovery. *Annals of the American Psychotherapy Association, 4*(5), 12–14.

San José, B., Van Oers, H. A. M., Van De Mheen, H. D., Garretsen, H. F. L., & Mackenbach, J. P. (2000). Stressors and alcohol consumption. *Alcohol and Alcoholism, 5*(3), 307–312.

Scheller-Gilkey, G., Woolwine, B. J., Cooper, I., Gay, O., Moynes, K. A., & Miller, A. H. (2003). Relationship of clinical symptoms and substance use in schizophrenia patients on conventional versus atypical antipsychotics. *American Journal of Drug and Alcohol Abuse, 29*(3), 553–566.

Schmidt, J. J. (1994). *Counselor intentionality and effective helping* (Report No. EDO-CG-94-05. 4P). Greensboro, NC: ERIC Clearinghouse on Counseling and Student Services (Eric Document Reproduction Services No. ED378461).

Seeman, T. E., Fagan Dubin, L., & Seeman, M. (2003). Religiosity/spirituality and health: A critical review of the evidence for biological pathways. *American Psychologist, 58*, 53–63.

Seymour, P. M. (2003). Long-term treatment of an addictive personality. *Bulletin of the Menninger Clinic, 67*(4), 328–346.

Shaffer, H. J., LaBrie, R. A., & LaPlante, D. (2004). Laying the foundation for quantifying regional exposure to social phenomena: Considering the case of legalized gambling as a public health toxin. *Psychology of Addictive Behaviors, 18*(1), 40–48.

Shaffer, H. J., LaPlante, D. A., LaBrie, R. A., Kidman, R. C., Donato, A. N., & Stanton, M. V. (2004). Toward a syndrome model of addiction: Multiple expressions, common etiology. *Harvard Review of Psychiatry, 12*(6), 367–374.

Sigafoos, J., & Tucker, M. (2000). Brief assessment and treatment of multiple challenging behaviors. *Behavioral Interventions, 15*(1), 53–70.

Skopp, N. A., McDonald, R., Manke, B., & Jouriles, E. N. (2005). Siblings in domestically violent families: Experiences of interparent conflict and adjustment problems. *Journal of Family Psychology, 19*(2), 324–333.

Slutske, W. S., Heath, A. C., Madden, P. A. F., Bucholz, K. K., Statham, D. J., & Martin, N. G. (2002). Personality and the genetic risk for alcohol dependence. *Journal of Abnormal Psychology, 111*(1), 124–133.

Stice, E., & Shaw, H. (2004). Eating disorder prevention programs: A meta-analytic review. *Psychological Bulletin, 130*(2), 206–227.

Stroebe, W. (2000). *Social psychology and health* (2nd ed.). Philadelphia, PA: Open University Press.

Sweder, G. L. (1998). Coping with serious medical illness: The role of Jewish prayer. *Dissertation Abstracts International: Section B: The Sciences & Engineering, 59*(5-B), 244.

Tommasello, A. C. (2004). Substance abuse and pharmacy practice: What the community pharmacist needs to know about drug abuse and dependence. *Harm Reduction Journal, 1*(3), 1–15. Retrieved October 18, 2005, from http://bmc.ub.uni-potsdam.de/1477-7517-1-3/1477-7517-1-3.pdf

Tracey, T. J. G., & Ward, C. C. (1998). The structure of children's interests and competence perceptions. *Journal of Counseling Psychology, 45*(3), 290–303.

Troop, N. A., Holbrey, A., & Treasure, J. L. (1998). Stress, coping, and crisis support in eating disorders. *International Journal of Eating Disorders, 24*, 157–166.

Tyndale, R. F. (2003). Genetics of alcohol and tobacco use in humans. *Annals of Medicine, 35*(2), 94–121.

Ventegodt, S., Morad, M., Kandel, I., & Merrick, J. (2004). Clinical holistic medicine: A psychological theory of dependency to improve quality of life. *The Scientific World Journal, 4*, 638–648.

Volkow, N. D., & Fowler, J. S. (2002). Application of imaging technologies in the investigation of drug addiction. In K. L. Davis, D. Charney, J. T. Coyle, & C. Nemeroff (Eds.), *Neuropsychopharmacology: The fifth generation of progress* (pp. 1475–1490). American College of Neuropsychopharmacology. Retrieved September 30, 2005, from http://www.acnp.org/g5/p/SC103_1475-1490.pdf

von Ranson, K. M., McGue, M., & Iacono, W. G. (2003). Disordered eating and substance use in an epidemiological sample: II. Associations within families. *Psychology of Addictive Behaviors, 17*(3), 193–202.

Wakfield, M., Flay, B., Nichter, M., & Giovino, G. (2003). Role of the media in influencing trajectories of youth smoking. *Addiction, 98*(1), 79–103.

Wall, T. L., Horn, S. M., Johnson, M. L., Smith, T. L., & Carr, L. G. (2000). Hangover symptoms in Asian Americans with variations in the aldehyde dehydrogenase (ALDH2) gene. *Journal of Studies on Alcohol, 61*(1), 13–17.

Wall, T. L., Shea, S. H., Luczak, S. E., Cook, T. A. R., & Carr, L. G. (2005). Genetic associations of alcohol dehydrogenase with alcohol use disorders and endophenotypes in white college students. *Journal of Abnormal Psychology, 114*(3), 456–465.

Wallace, J. (2003). Theory of 12-step-oriented treatment. In F. Rotgers, J. Morgenstern, & S. T. Walters (Eds.), *Treating substance abuse: Theory and technique.* New York: Guilford Press.

Walters, G. D. (1992). Drug-seeking behavior: Disease or lifestyle? *Professional Psychology: Research & Practice, 23*(2), 139–145.

Wedgeworth, R. L. (1998). The reification of the "pathological" gambler: An analysis of gambling treatment and the application of the medical model to problem gambling. *Perspectives in Psychiatric Care, 34*(2), 5–13.

Weinstein, C. M., Parker, J., & Archer, J. (2002). College counselor attitudes toward spiritual and religious issues and practices in counseling. *Journal of College Counseling, 5*(2), 164-174.

Weiss, R. D., Griffin, M. L., & Mirin, S. M. (1992). Drug abuse as self-medication for depression: An empirical study. *American Journal of Drug and Alcohol Abuse, 18*(2), 121–129.

West, R. (2001). Theories of addiction. *Addiction, 96,* 3–13.

Whiston, S. C., & Keller, B. K. (2004). The influences of the family of origin on career development: A review and analysis. *Counseling Psychologist, 32*(4), 493–568.

Wikipedia. (2005a). Addiction. *Wikipedia: The Free Encyclopedia.* Retrieved September 15, 2005, from http://en.wikipedia.org/wiki/Addiction

Wikipedia. (2005b). Acetaldehyde. *Wikipedia: The Free Encyclopedia.* Retrieved October 18, 2005, from http://en.wikipedia.org/wiki/Acetaldehyde

Wood, M. D., Read, J. P., Mitchell, R. E., & Brand, N. H. (2004). Do parents still matter? Parent and peer influences on alcohol involvement among recent high school graduates. *Psychology of Addictive Behaviors, 18*(1), 19–30.

Wulfert, E., Greenway, D. E., & Dougher, M. J. (1996). A logical functional analysis of reinforcement-based disorders: Alcoholism and pedophilia. *Journal of Consulting & Clinical Psychology, 64*(6), 1140–1151.

Yangarber-Hicks, N. (2004). Recovery model: A Christian appraisal. *Journal of Psychology and Christianity, 23,* 31–39.

Yip, K. (2003). A strengths perspective in working with an adolescent with dual diagnosis. *Clinical Social Work Journal, 31*(2), 189–203.

Zeitner, R. M. (2003). Obstacles for the psychoanalyst in the practice of couple therapy. *Psychoanalytic Psychology, 20*(2), 348–362.

Family Addictions Assessment

Chapter 3 Learning Objectives

After reading this chapter, you should be able to:

- Describe how to conduct a thorough Clinical Family Addictions Assessment Interview including each of the six phases
- Describe what drug detection testing is and the types of drug detection testing most relevant for the addicted family member presenting for family addictions counseling based on the time of last use
- Describe the Marital Satisfaction Inventory-Revised (MSI-R), the Substance Abuse Subtle Screening Inventory–3 (SASSI-3), and the Substance Abuse Subtle Screening Inventory–Adolescent 2 (SASSI-A2), including the implications of high and low scores on each scale
- Understand how to provide effective therapeutic feedback

Introduction

Can anyone truly separate assessment's therapeutic impact from treatment itself? We don't think so. As a matter of fact, we believe assessment and treatment are inseparably intertwined. For us, assessment *is* treatment. Concomitantly, like a single sentence within the context of a paragraph and page, assessment provides vital information about addictions within the context of the family's experiences. In other words, the assessment process helps addicted families better understand addictive behaviors within the context of their family's interactions and the impact addictions have on each member. For example, when working with one addicted family that had multiple generations afflicted with addictions-related symptoms, the mother of an addicted adolescent exclaimed to the senior author, "I get it. So, getting drunk like my mother did is not a good way to cope with my son's drinking." Thus, a well-executed assessment not only commences the treatment process but also provides the foundation on which further treatment is performed and serves as a potent weapon in the family addiction counselors' therapeutic arsenal.

Regretfully, many beginning counselors mistakenly view assessment as a time-squandering, bothersome process "done to" addicted family members. Nothing could be further from the truth. When facilitated correctly, assessment provides addicted families a rare opportunity to review the events of their development and addiction as well. Such review often engenders therapeutic insight and gives addicted families license to exchange encumbering addictions-related dysfunction for freedom. Therefore, a skilled assessment *is* treatment that has the potential to impact both the addicted family system and its members.

Concomitantly, family assessments provide addictions-relevant information from multiple vis-à-vis single sources. Multiple information sources promote the most effective addictions treatments, because they provide the most effective manner in which to understand family addiction concerns. For example, many times addicted family members will inadvertently or intentionally fail to present the full picture of their addictive symptomatology. Here, an addicted family member may provide sufficient information for the counselor to make an initial diagnosis such as alcohol abuse. However, further information provided by the family member's spouse and children may indicate that she did not fully present the severity of presenting symptoms. Such additional information provided by multiple sources might suggest that the diagnoses of alcohol dependence, cocaine abuse, and major depression are highly probable and that inpatient detoxification is likely warranted. Clearly such added information gained by clinical family interviews fosters the most relevant treatment services.

Sometimes, however, addicted families either "cover" for one another or don't recognize the existing addiction problems. For example, we have found it common for some addicted parents to minimize their adolescents' addiction due to their concern that the parents' addiction will be identified. At the same time, we have found that some addicted families have been so immersed in an addicted lifestyle for such an extended time that they are unable to even recognize addiction-related symptoms. Again, family addictions assessment provides counselors the very best opportunity to understand the addiction's dynamics and severity. This in turn increases the probability of successful treatment interventions that are both relevant to the family system and its addicted members.

The Clinical Family Addictions Assessment Interview

The clinical family addictions assessment interview holds the greatest potential for (a) understanding addiction dynamics within the family system, (b) confronting addicted family members within the family system, (c) engendering insight related to self- and others' interactions, and (d) promoting healthy, systems-oriented change. Clearly, the clinical family interview process can be used to evaluate and diagnose via family inquiry.

More importantly, though, the clinical family addictions assessment interview initiates actual family addictions counseling. Because the client family members are present during this assessment process, counselors can concurrently query addicted family members, identify those supporting the pathological addictive behaviors, and support those who are attempting appropriate responses to unhealthy system dynamics related to addiction. A rather recent example of such a situation occurred during a clinical family addictions assessment interview. Basically the cannabis-abusing young adult failed his freshman college year. His failure was primarily due to his (a) being under the influence during most classes, (b) excessive partying with peers, and (c) studying while under the influence. During the clinical family interview, father indicated that he "could not" see a problem with his son's cannabis abuse. When pressed further, father indicated that it would be "hypocritical" of him to reprimand his son. Specifically father indicated, "I used marijuana all the time in high school and college. I can't tell him [son] not to use. It would make me a hypocrite."

Understanding this father's perspective provided an immediate opportunity for the senior author to confront father. It further afforded the senior author an opportunity to align himself with mother and address father's sabotaging her son's school success. Finally, the experience provided an opportunity to reward mother for her healthy behaviors of demanding that son and family enter counseling. Without fully understanding father's position before making other clinical interventions, this family addictions counselor would have been at an extreme disadvantage and could not have successfully treated the family system effectively. Concomitantly, without providing mother the support and praise for doing what was necessary to continue son's treatment, it was evident that father would have persuaded son to discontinue the counseling process.

Now, some of you who are well versed in individual assessments may be thinking, "How is it helpful to concurrently query family members, and why would I want to assess persons other than the addicted client?" Well, individual client interview responses are based on a mixture of client perceptions and beliefs. This mixture is important, because clients' perceptions and beliefs can range from completely accurate to completely inaccurate. Despite potential clinical benefits of understanding even completely inaccurate perceptions and beliefs, it is vitally important to gain a thorough and accurate understanding of the facts about the client's presenting concerns (Doweiko, 1996). Such understanding is central to treatment planning and effective treatment outcomes (Doweiko, 1996).

Clinical family addictions assessment interviews conducted with the immediate family system help compensate for the addicted clients' inaccurately stated perceptions and beliefs (Juhnke, 2000). Therefore, clinical family addictions assessment interviews are crucial to effective treatment and are a critical ingredient to counseling addicted families. Specifically, family members' perceptions of the addicted members and the addicted members' needs enable the counselor to best address the pressing concerns and addiction-related behaviors.

An example of this is illustrated in the following case vignette. Here, an addicted family member initially reports that she drinks to intoxication only one time per week and denies any correlation between her alcohol abuse and other factors. However, her spouse notes that within the last 6 months his wife has been intoxicated most evenings and typically consumes a fifth of vodka every 2 days. Furthermore, her high school–age son reports that mother's alcohol consumption escalates when she perceives her husband is spending greater amounts of time on the job than with her. The son further reports that mother's alcohol consumption increases when she feels she has not sold enough of her paintings to local art galleries. Thus, spouse and son present a mixture of perceptions and beliefs that are starkly different than the addicted family member's. This new information clearly warrants further attention and discussion within the clinical family addictions assessment interview process. Thus, family members lend important information indicating possible spousal and work-related stressors that promote mother's increased dysfunctional alcohol consumption, something that mother either was unaware or chose not to share. Had the counselor not gained this key assessment information before treatment initiation, valuable time and energy could have been wasted addressing the addicted family member's inaccurate beliefs and perceptions mixture.

In other words, without the information provided by family members, the counselor likely would have implemented less efficient treatment. In this case, however, as a direct result of the family members' statements and the ensuing discussion, more efficient treatment can be enacted.

Additionally, clinical family addictions assessment interviews have the potential to engender addicted member insight related to the presenting concerns and, therefore, may promote more effective behaviors. Here, family members can respectfully confront addicted family members regarding inaccurately presented or omitted behaviors. Given that addicted family members often love and trust other family members, conflicting statements are not easily dismissed or ignored. This is especially true when beliefs and perceptions are corroborated by more than one respected family member during the interview process.

Using the previous case vignette as an example, the husband's statements were further corroborated by the son's statements. Thus, their collectively presented beliefs and perceptions would be difficult to deny or ignore. Additionally, given that two people rather than a single person within the family reported the addicted behaviors, the addicted family member may gain insight as to the gravity of her drinking behaviors. Based on our experiences, this is especially true when beliefs and perceptions are respectfully presented and noted as a sincere concern by each family member. Here, for example, each family member may indicate something like,

> "Maria, I love you. I think you married me because you love me too. I believe you have a drinking problem, because you were drunk nearly every weeknight for the past 6 months. There has not been an evening this past week when you haven't been drunk. You are drinking a fifth of vodka every other day. Please don't tell the counselor you're only getting drunk one night a week or that you only drink a little bit, when these statements are not true. You have got to be fully honest, even if it hurts. Our family needs a sober mother. And I need a sober wife."

Many addicted family members we have counseled do not fully understand the severity of their alcohol and other drug (AOD)–abusing behaviors until they are cogently and collectively confronted within the clinical family addictions assessment interview. Until this point, they often do not believe they are AOD-dependent or -abusing, or they deny such dependence or abuse. However, when loved and respected family members provide collaborative beliefs and perceptions, insight related to the severity of the addicted family member's AOD-abusing behaviors is often gained or admitted.

Some readers might now be thinking, "OK, I guess it makes sense to use a clinical family addictions assessment interview, but what does systems-oriented change have to do with my clients' assessments. Why is this important?" Well, the truth is that most AOD-abusing clients that we have counseled during our nearly 25 years of combined addictions counseling work experience their addictions linearly. In other words, they believe that their pathological AOD use is a direct result of an experience or combination of experiences that "cause" them to AOD abuse or some naturally occurring proclivity to AOD abuse. Examples of such cause-and-effect thinking include, "I use marijuana because my father abused me," "You'd drink too if you were married to him," "Memories of Vietnam make me use," and "I have got a chemical imbalance that forces me to shoot up."

More importantly, it is not just the addicted family members who believe their drinking and drugging behaviors are due to some experience combination or proclivity. Family members frequently believe this too (e.g., "My wife wouldn't get drunk and beat her son if he didn't have ADHD"). Often when family members view an addicted member's AOD-abusing behaviors as stemming from a sequela of traumatic experiences or genetic proclivity, family members respond by excusing the client's AOD-abusing behaviors (e.g., "It's not his fault for being a drunk. He's got his father's alcoholic genes.") and repeating the same inappropriate rewarding behaviors that encourage the addicted member's continued dysfunctional responses (e.g., "I am so sorry for not being a better wife. If I had been a better wife and attended to your needs as you had wished, you wouldn't be feeling lonesome and get drunk."). Thus, it is imperative to use the clinical family addictions assessment interview process to assess how family members view the addicted member's behaviors. Concomitantly, counselors need to learn if family members excuse or encourage the member's continued AOD abuse. Enlightening family members about their behaviors' effects on the addicted member enhances effective treatment.

Therefore, this interview process provides family members greater opportunity to gain a larger picture of the presenting issues and learn how both their independent behaviors and their joint, systemic behaviors encourage the continued symbiotic substance abuse within the family system. Concomitantly, the process can challenge family members to independently and systemically orchestrate new, helpful behaviors to address the addicted member's presenting concerns. Stated differently, this interview process teaches family members that they are more than a collection of separate individuals who behave independently within a void. Via the clinical family addictions assessment interview, family members learn that their independently occurring behaviors are interconnected and that their interactive behaviors create a system which has the capacity to promote new healthy behaviors both among each other and within the family as a whole. Hence, if during the clinical family interview one person is noted as continually rescuing the addicted member, the others can encourage new, nonrescuing behaviors.

Here, for example, the addicted family member's husband might gently confront their 16-year-old son regarding the son's attempts to contact art galleries on behalf of his mother when his mother is intoxicated:

> "Geraldo, I know you love your mom and want to protect her when she is drunk. This week you called three art galleries that mom sells her paintings to. You did this to help your mom, because she was too intoxicated to visit those galleries. It may seem as though your calling the galleries is helping mom, but it isn't. Calling the galleries conveys to mom that she doesn't have to be responsible for her behaviors. Will you promise me that you won't call the galleries anymore?"

Encouraging Geraldo to change his typical rescuing behaviors has multiple treatment implications. First, given that Geraldo has been gently and respectfully asked by his father to stop contacting the art galleries for mother and framing the intention behind Geraldo's contacting the art galleries as an attempt to be helpful, it is likely that Geraldo may make a promise to his father to discontinue the rescuing behaviors. In other words, Geraldo will change his behaviors, because he will truly want to help his mother and please his father.

However, Geraldo may not understand what new behaviors he can initiate. Therefore, the counselor can help via the clinical family addictions assessment interview process by teaching Geraldo. In other words, the interview process can be psychoeducational and help Geraldo gain an understanding of new helpful behaviors.

Counselor:	"Geraldo, it sounds like you really want to be helpful to your mom. You certainly have invested a great deal of time and effort in protecting mom from losing her art gallery accounts. Now, I'm hearing dad say that these protecting behaviors may not be best. I wonder what new behaviors you might begin that would be more helpful to mom."
Geraldo:	"Gee, I don't know what I could do. I was only trying to help, but it seems that my efforts weren't doing what was best."

Counselor: "I think your mother is very fortunate to have a son as committed to her as you. Sometimes we don't know what would be helpful to those facing something as scary as addictions, and we need to ask them. I wonder if mom would have any ideas."

Mom: "I haven't got a clue. I like it when Geraldo sells my paintings. He is the ultimate salesperson."

Counselor: "I'm hearing Geraldo say that he would like to be helpful but that he doesn't really know what to do. You and I have discussed the possibility of attending Alcoholics Anonymous. Yet, you were reluctant to go alone. I am wondering, would it be helpful for Geraldo to go with you to those meetings?"

Mom: "Yes, I'm pretty scared of going alone."

Counselor: "Geraldo, would you be willing to attend AA meetings with your mom this week?"

Geraldo: "I sure would. I'd do anything to help."

Counselor: "Dad, what do you think? Do you think it would be a positive thing for Geraldo to attend AA meetings with mom, or do you want to attend those meetings with her?"

Father: "I think it would be a great thing for all of us to go together."

Counselor: "OK, so what I'm hearing dad and mom say is this. Geraldo, don't contact the art galleries for mom. Mom has to make those calls herself. Additionally, I'm hearing that all of you want to go to the AA meetings together this first week. Is that correct?"

Family: "Yes."

Counselor: "Good. Saint Anthony's Church holds AA meetings each weekday at 6 P.M. Can all of you make those meetings?"

Family: "Yes."

This vignette demonstrates how the clinical family addictions assessment interview process can help the system implement new behaviors (e.g., escorting mother to AA meetings).

Furthermore, the vignette demonstrates a second treatment implication occurring as a result of the clinical family addictions assessment interview—an informed system. Here, the system members learn that Geraldo will discontinue his rescuing behaviors and that the entire family will attend AA meetings this week. Maria has learned that her son has agreed not to contact the art galleries for her when she is intoxicated. Thus, the system has announced its intent to change. Finally, Maria has made a commitment to the people she respects and loves indicating that she will attend AA meetings with them. Therefore, a new expectation is placed on Maria. Given that Maria values the people in the system, it would be difficult for her to dismiss their expectations.

Six Clinical Family Addiction Assessment Phases

There are six phases to the clinical family addictions assessment interview. Each phase has its own assessment goals that can be adapted according to the specific treatment milieu in which addicted family members are participating (e.g., inpatient hospitalization, intensive outpatient). The phases are sequenced in a developmental manner designed to (a) empower addicted family members, (b) orient immediate family members to the assessment process, (c) jointly identify the addicted members' strengths and attributes, (d) gather pertinent data related to the addicted members' AOD-related behaviors and confront inaccurate or nonreported AOD-related behaviors, (e) secure family members' commitment to the addicted family member's recovery, and (f) respond to the family's post-interview needs.

During the clinical family addictions assessment interview, members provide historical data (e.g., "The first night Maria ever came home intoxicated was December 11, 2000"), report beliefs and perceptions different from the addicted member's (e.g., "Although you say you have never driven while under the influence, I know you were arrested 2 months ago on a DUI charge"), and identify the addicted family member's strengths (e.g., "Maria is an excellent artist and businesswoman who markets her paintings very well"). Additionally, members may be called on to describe their past or current feelings (e.g., "Geraldo, what was it like for you when your mother came home drunk?"), cognitions (e.g., "Father, what was your first thought yesterday when Maria came home intoxicated again?"), or intended behavioral changes (e.g., "Father, would you be kind enough to tell Maria how you intend to change your behaviors the next time she becomes intoxicated and threatens to hurt Geraldo?").

Each of the six clinical family addictions assessment interview phases is described below. The intent of these descriptions is to familiarize readers with the phases and succinctly outline the distinct differences between them.

Identification Phase   The first goal of this phase is to help the family identify members who should be present. This typically means age-related and older siblings and parents. Member participation depends on a number of important factors including age and family dynamics. For example, when assessing a family system composed of an alcohol-abusing husband, nonusing wife, and two children under the age of 5, it may be determined that the clinical family addictions assessment interview will include husband and wife alone without the children. Children deemed too young to participate would then be allowed to play in an adjacent play therapy room under adult supervision provided by another family member (e.g., grandmother), case manager, or support staff member.

Introduction Phase   The Introduction Phase goal is to reduce family members' anxiety. In most cases, whatever anxiety exists quickly dissipates as the counselor introduces herself, welcomes the family members, and succinctly outlines the purpose of the clinical family addictions assessment interview. The welcome should be brief. Family members are present to help addicted members and themselves. Most are fairly indifferent to the counselor's educational background, credentials, and training. In essence, family members typically just want to know that you've done this kind of work before and to hear that there exists significant hope for a seemingly intolerable situation to improve. We have found it helpful to compliment family members for their attendance and to characterize their role as that of being "knowledgeable consultants" who live with and know their families better than any family addiction counselor possibly could. Therefore, they have an important role in helping us learn how we can be most helpful to their family. Additionally, we encourage family members to make a verbal commitment to each other. Therefore, a typical introduction will likely be similar to this:

> Counselor: "Hello, my name is Jerry Juhnke. I am a counselor here at New Horizons and want to acknowledge your being here as a very positive first step in bringing the changes you want to your family. Your being here today demonstrates your commitment to helping your family and your willingness to support one another as your family enters a new era of starting an addictions-free journey.

The purpose of today's meeting is for me to better understand who each of you are and to learn how I can best help your family. As Maria's family members, you know her best. So, today, I'm asking you to be consultants. Is anyone opposed to helping your family today? Geraldo, is this acceptable to you? Are you willing to help your mom and family today?"

Geraldo: "Sure, whatever I can do to help."

Counselor: "Jesse, you are Maria's husband of nearly 20 years. Are you willing to help Maria and your family participate in this family's recovery?"

Jesse : "Of course I am."

Asking family members to forthrightly comment on the clinical family addictions assessment interview process's acceptability and to verbalize their willingness to help their family is crucial. Such comment provides family members an opportunity to present and address legitimate concerns that may hinder full cooperation. Additionally, the clinical family addictions assessment interview is a means to demonstrate to the addicted family members the commitment they can anticipate from their family member support system. Such verbalized commitment further promotes a united spirit among family members, therefore reducing the probability of someone intentionally or unintentionally sabotaging successful assessment and treatment.

The second goal of this phase is multifaceted. Here, the counselor re-explains limits of confidentiality in greater detail, establishes meeting rules, and responds to voiced concerns. Related to the confidentiality limits and informational meeting rules is our initial assertion that as family addiction counselors we are the only ones bound by professional confidentiality laws. We then explain that the law does not require confidentiality of family members but that it often is therapeutically comforting to know that what is said in family sessions stays confidential except for the immediate family members. We then seek verbal confirmation of this request from each family member present. For example, the counselor might say the following:

Counselor: "Before we go any further, I need to bring up the topic of confidentiality. It is important for you to know that I cannot guarantee that everything you say in this meeting will be confidential. I am unaware of any law which states that you cannot share information or report to others what is said or what happens in today's interview to persons who are not present. In other words, you should be cautious about sharing sensitive information or information that could be potentially embarrassing or harmful. The law clearly states that I am the only one here who is bound by confidentiality. Therefore, I cannot discuss what happens in this room with anyone else unless I have your permission to do so or I believe that you or someone else is in danger. However, knowing the importance of confidentiality and the need to have faith in each other, I am wondering if each of you would be willing to make a confidentiality pledge to one another. Although this pledge may not provide legal recourse for breaking confidentiality and understanding that it may not be legally binding, the pledge would be made by each of us, stating that whatever is said in today's meeting stays between us unless someone is being a danger to herself or is in danger of being injured. Would this be acceptable to you?"

Maria: "I'd really like that."

Geraldo: "Yes, this makes sense."

Jesse: "Certainly."

Counselor: "OK, Maria, Geraldo, and Jesse, I am hearing that each of you is pledging not to report anything that is said or done in this room to someone other than yourselves or me, is that correct?"

Family: "Yes."

Next, the family addictions counselor establishes the informational meeting rules. Although these rules can vary, we have found that seven basic rules are important for the meeting. These include the following:

1. Each family member should be treated with respect—Family members should respect each other by treating each other as they wish to be treated. No one should swear at another, call another derogatory names, or be caustically sarcastic. Threats of violence or implied threats will not be tolerated.

2. Each family member agrees to speak truthfully—Family members promise to speak the truth at all times.

3. Each family member agrees to speak for herself—Family members may describe behaviors that they observed in others (e.g., "I saw Maria consume a fifth of vodka at 8 P.M. last night"), but family members will not speak for others (e.g., "Geraldo is too scared to tell his mother what he really thinks about her drinking") or attempt to interpret observed behaviors (e.g., "I think Maria drinks when she is mad").

4. Each family member agrees to participate—Family members will contribute via their active participation. Nonparticipation suggests an unwillingness to support one another. Thus, it is vital that family members invest themselves in the interview process.

5. Each family member agrees to ask questions—Family members will ask questions and have the right to expect honest and thorough responses. However, parents always have the ultimate authority and therefore the right to decline comments to certain questions that are determined as part of the parents' relationship. For example, if an adolescent asked if mother was having an affair with a neighbor, it may be more appropriate for the response to be discussed among the spouses rather than within the entire family system.

6. Each family member agrees to remain for the entire informational meeting—Family members can leave the informational meeting for short, personal breaks but must agree to return to the interview.

7. Each family member agrees to support the entire family—Family members verbally agree to demonstrate their support of each family member. None should be excluded from support. For example, if daughter is angry at father, she is still asked to agree to support him in his role as parent.

Finally, after the rules are discussed, clarified, and agreed to, the counselor asks family members if there exist any concerns or questions related to the clinical family addictions assessment interview or about anything said to this point.

Strengths Assessment Phase   The primary goal within this phase is to have family members (a) describe healthy ways in which the addicted family member is meeting her current needs, (b) identify ways in which the family and counselor can help the addicted family member be substance-free, and (c) encourage continued positive behaviors toward the addicted family member. This is done by providing family members feedback regarding what they are already doing well, reinforcing these healthy behaviors, and advancing other family members' understanding of even healthier, new behaviors that could be adopted. The result is a collaborative assessment and data-providing venture in which family members and counselor jointly learn what is working and helpful and what will be perceived as helpful in the future. Such a collaborative and positively framed experience is foreign to most addicted family members. Many become emotive and are heartened to hear these other family members say positive things about them. Despite the support occurring within this phase, the intent of the strengths assessment is not to "gloss over" or minimize presented concerns or difficulties. This would be a harmful injustice. Instead, the intent is to learn what is going well and identify how addicted and nonaddicted family members contribute to this recovery process. Thus, the Strengths Assessment Phase encircles the addicted family within a powerful, systems-oriented treatment milieu that continually supports the addicted member's and the family's recovery.

Last, the Strengths Assessment Phase provides an opportunity to establish greater rapport and trust before moving to the next assessment phase. Such opportunities are critical to the assessment process, because family members disclose information regarding their observations and interactions during this upcoming phase. Oftentimes family members will need to respectfully confront incongruent perceptions related to the addicted member and her addictions-related behaviors. In other words, this phase establishes the foundation on which addicted members can be challenged. Therefore, it is imperative that the counselor help the family members affirm and support one another in the Strengths Assessment Phase. This can be accomplished by asking addicted members to respond to supportive statements made by family members during the Strengths Assessment Phase. For example, the counselor may say something like the following:

Counselor: "Mom, what was it like to have Jesse, your husband, say that he loves you?"

Maria (weeping): "I can't fully describe what it was like, because it was so unbelievable. After all the mean things that I've done to him over the last few years, to learn that he still loves me so much is unbelievable."

Jesse: "Oh baby, you know I love you and always will."

Maria: "I know that now, Jesse. But I didn't know that you still loved me until you told me. I had thought you hated me, because I was a drunk and wasn't living up to your expectations of me."

Counselor: "Sometimes when people love us, they don't know how to respond when we are addicted. Jesse, if you could say just one thing to your wife about her committing herself to her sobriety, what would you say?"

Jesse: "Honey, I'd tell you that I know you can beat this thing. You are as strong-willed as your own mother. I know you can be sober and stay sober. More importantly, though, Maria, I'll do everything I can to support you. But I won't lie to you. If you begin drinking again, I'll get right in your face and call you a drunk again and tell you that you need counseling."

Counselor: "What do you hear your husband saying, Maria?"

Maria: "I hear him saying that he believes I can beat my addiction."

Counselor: "I hear him saying that, but I also hear him saying something else too."

Maria: "What's that?"

Counselor: "I hear Jesse saying that he loves you, that you can successfully beat your addiction, and that he will support you in every way possible. But I also hear him saying that he is going to be truthful and call things the way he sees them. Do you hear him saying that?"

Maria: "Yes, I do. That's the way he does things."

Counselor: "Does that mean he doesn't love you or that he is not trying to be helpful when he tells the truth?"

Maria: "Of course not. It merely means that he is trying to be helpful and knows telling the truth will help me face my addiction."

This vignette demonstrates two central elements of the latter half of this phase. First, it promotes an opportunity for wife and husband to further build rapport and establish trust. This is done by emphasizing husband's statement that he loves Maria and by encouraging Maria to report what hearing this means to her. Second, it inoculates Maria from responding inappropriately to truthful, confrontational statements in the upcoming phase. Thus, not only is husband indicating that he will make truthful statements, but also wife is encouraging such statements and indicating that the purpose of husband's statements is to help Maria successfully combat her addiction.

Drinking and Drugging History Phase In this phase, the chief goal is to promote the counselor's understanding of the addicted family member via the other family members' observations. Thus, the counselor will seek information from all members, unless the counselor perceives that such truthful statements could place others in jeopardy. For example, it may be therapeutically powerful for mother to hear her 7-year-old describe what it was like for her to watch her mother drink to the point of intoxication most weekend nights. However, should the counselor suspect that any potential retaliation or harm could come to the 7-year-old as a result of her truthful statements, the child should not be allowed to make comments. Concomitantly, should this be a concern, we would question whether or not it is therapeutically appropriate for this young child to participate in this portion of the family counseling. In other words, it might be better to have just wife and husband participate in this phase.

When the counselor perceives no harm and no potential for retaliation for younger and more vulnerable members of the family system, the family addictions counselor will solicit information related to the addicted member's past and current AOD abuse. In addition, the family addictions counselor will seek information related to the addicted family member's cognitive functioning, mood and affect, insight and judgment, interpersonal skills and social interactions, vocational history and marketable work skills, and the home environment. Therefore, this phase might begin with the counselor first lauding the addicted family member and then asking addictions-related questions. An example is presented below.

Counselor: "It is readily apparent that Maria is invested in this assessment process and the treatment which she has willingly entered with this family. Furthermore, it seems that Maria is most fortunate to have family members who are so supportive and committed to her recovery. One thing that we've heard today is that Maria wants each of you to be truthful and help provide information to the best of your recollection. Is that right, Maria?"

Maria: "Yes. Please be truthful."

Counselor: "Now, speaking truthfully doesn't mean being disrespectful or mean-spirited. However, it does mean providing accurate information about what you know. So, I would like to ask some general questions and then move to questions about things that you possibly observed or experienced with Maria. Is that all right with you, Maria?"

Maria: "Certainly."

Counselor: "OK, Jesse, as the father of this family and someone who has known Maria before you had children together, would you mind if we start with you?"

Jesse: "By all means."

Counselor: "Jesse, how long have you known Maria?"

Jesse: "Well, I've known Maria since our freshman year in college. We started at State and we began dating about a year later."

Counselor: "Can you tell me about the first time you saw Maria drink alcohol?"

Jesse: "It was about 3 years ago. I had been away on business travel, and when I came home, Maria was drinking straight out of a vodka bottle. I asked what was wrong, but she was so blitzed she could barely respond. Her drinking really scared me. I had never really seen her like that ever before."

Counselor: "When did you realize that Maria had a drinking problem?"

Jesse: "About that same time, it seemed that she was drinking most days and nights and was often intoxicated when I came home from work. Geraldo is our only child and he reported that his mom was 'drunk' by the time he got home from school in the afternoons. I think this was the first time I realized that Maria's drinking was problematic."

Counselor: "Did you ever see or suspect that she was using other substances like marijuana, cocaine, hash, or LSD?"

Jesse: "No, I'm quite sure she doesn't use any of those things."

The clinical family addictions assessment interview continues until both counselor and family believe an accurate and representative description of the addicted family member's addiction has been created, and the phase naturally leads to the Reestablishing Phase.

Reestablishing Phase   The primary goals within the Reestablishing Phase are to (a) ensure that the addicted member and family believe that sufficient data gathering has occurred to generate a thorough and accurate understanding of the addicted member's substance abuse and establish effective treatment goals, (b) teach addicted members how to ask family for help, and (c) communicate and reestablish family members' commitment to one another and a family independent from addictions. Therefore, this phase begins with a scaling question (Cade & O'Hanlon, 1993; O'Hanlon & Weiner-Davis, 1989). Scaling questions allow the addicted family member and other family members to assign numerical values to the assessment process and the final appraisal picture. These numerical values reflect the family members' perceptions related to the addicted family member and her substance abuse. Thus, the counselor might ask the following:

Counselor: "On a scale of 1 to 10, with 1 indicating not at all accurate and 10 indicating a perfect reflection of Maria's addiction, what score would you assign related to our new, joint understanding of Maria and her current degree of substance abuse?"

Each family member would provide a score. Should all family members indicate a fairly high score, such as 8 and above, the counselor might respond by saying something like this:

Counselor: "So it sounds as though we all agree that we have a pretty good understanding of Maria's current degree of substance abuse."

Should all family members agree that this statement is true, the counselor would likely ask Maria if she believed that the family members truly understood her current substance abuse. If Maria affirmed the family members' perceptions, the counselor would merely ask Maria if there was anything further the family members needed to know. If nothing was identified by Maria, the family addictions counselor would move to the next scaling question.

Counselor: "Maria, everyone here believes we have a pretty good understanding of your current use of alcohol. Do you believe this is true?"

Maria: "Yes, these are my family members. They know everything about me and about how I drink."

However, should Maria report that there was further key information that her family members needed to understand, she would be asked to provide the information. If further information was provided by the addicted member, the original scaling question would be restated and the process would be repeated until all family members and Maria believed an accurate assessment picture reflecting Maria and her alcohol abuse had been provided.

Contrastingly, should one or more family members indicate low scaling question scores, the counselor might ask what further information would be required to move the family member's scores higher.

Counselor: "I'm hearing Jesse say that he would assign a score of 3. Therefore, Jesse is indicating a concern that we may have a relatively inaccurate understanding of Maria's addiction and the addictive substances she uses. Jesse, help us understand what things we need to learn about Maria's addiction and the addictive substances she uses before we conclude today's interview."

Once Jesse identifies the specific information he needs to perceive his wife's addiction, Jesse will be instructed to query Maria until he feels relatively comfortable.

Asking for Help   When all family members acknowledge a satisfactory understanding of the addicted member's substance abuse, the counselor will ask the member to behaviorally describe how her family members can be helpful to her as she begins her recovery process. Here, it is incumbent upon the family addictions counselor to help the addicted member request behaviorally anchored descriptions that are *small, realistic, and completely attainable*. This can be challenging, as addicted family members often do not know what to ask or are unaccustomed to making requests understandable. Requests should be made to one specific family member at a time. It should be clear that everyone needs to understand the requests and know that requests may be denied. An example is provided below.

Counselor: "Maria, both Jesse and Geraldo have demonstrated their desire to help by being here today. What they need to know now is how to help. There are two things you need to understand before you ask for help. First, Jesse and Geraldo have the right to consider or turn your requests down. In other words, they may be unable or unwilling to fulfill your requests. Many times people turn down requests because other obligations exist which inhibit them from being able to help as they want. Additionally, some requests may be inappropriate given your son's age and the fact that you are the parent and not your son's peer. So, should Jesse and Geraldo turn down your request, it would not necessarily mean that they don't like you or don't want to help. Is that correct, Jesse and Geraldo?"

Jesse: "Yes. We want to help."

Geraldo: "Uh-hmm."

Counselor: "Second, for Jesse and Geraldo to fully understand your request, it has to be made in a way that is specific. In other words, they need to know exactly what the behavior will look like. For example, instead of saying something like, 'I want you to communicate with me,' it would be important to say, 'When I get back from selling paintings at 7 P.M. on Tuesday and Thursday nights, I would like you both to ask me questions about my day.' Given what I have seen you do so far today, I know that you are able to make very specific requests, Maria. Are you ready to ask Jesse and Geraldo for help?"

Maria: "Yes. I really need their help."

Counselor: "OK, why don't you turn toward Jesse, look him straight in the eyes, and ask for his help."

Maria: "Jesse, I really need your help."

Counselor: "Good, now tell him what you want."

Maria: "Jesse, I want you to be there for me."

Counselor: "OK, Maria, good job. However, I don't know if we really understand what you fully mean. Look at Jesse and tell him what 'being there for you' will look like."

Maria:	"I don't know. I guess it means that he will listen to me when I need to talk."
Counselor:	"Good, now ask him if he will be willing to listen to you when you need to talk."
Maria:	"Will you listen to me when I really need to talk with you?"
Jesse:	"You know I will, Maria."
Counselor:	"Maria, how will you let Jesse know when you really need to talk? I know that some people simply call their husbands at work and say, 'I need to talk.' Others ask their husbands out to lunch and ask for their help then. Others convey their need to speak in yet other ways. How will you specifically indicate to Jesse when you need to talk so that he understands beyond a shadow of a doubt that you need to speak with him?"
Maria:	"I would just say, 'Jesse, I need to talk. Will you listen to me?'"
Counselor:	"What if Jesse is in the middle of doing taxes or something and just can't speak with you at that time. How will you handle it then?"
Maria:	"I don't know."
Counselor:	"Could you say, 'It sounds like this is a bad time for you to talk. When can we talk, because I really need to talk soon?'"
Maria:	"Sure, I could say that."
Counselor:	"OK, let's practice this. Turn to Jesse and say, 'When can we get together, because I really need to talk soon?'"
Maria:	"So, when can we get together, because I really need to talk soon?"
Jesse:	"I can't talk until tomorrow."
Maria:	"But I can't wait until tomorrow. You said I could talk with you anytime I needed and I need to talk tonight."
Counselor:	"Good, you are letting him know that you need help right now. Excellent work, folks."

Communicating Commitment   After the addicted member has asked her family members for help with her most pressing issues and her family members have responded, the counselor reestablishes the verbal commitment between the family members. Again, scaling questions are used. This time, however, instead of using scaling questions to determine whether or not the family members understand the addicted member's substance abuse, family members are asked to identify their levels of commitment to the member and her recovery.

> Counselor: "Jesse, you wouldn't be here unless you were committed to Maria and her recovery. Would you look at Maria and tell her on a scale from 1 to 10, with 1 indicating not at all committed and 10 indicating completely committed, how committed you are to both Maria and her recovery?"

Should the family members indicate average to high commitment (e.g., scores between 5 and 10), the counselor should then ask family members to describe behaviors that the addicted member will see suggesting such commitment. Here, the intent is to encourage new, helpful behaviors that will promote abstinence. Additionally, responses by family members further serve as demonstrations of their commitment. Thus, whenever the addicted family member observes the noted "commitment behaviors," the addicted member will be reminded of the commitment that the family has toward her recovery. It has been our experience that when addicted members observe such noted commitment behaviors by family members, the addicted members are heartened and rededicate themselves to the recovery process.

> Counselor: "You report a score of 8, indicating that you are very committed to Maria, her recovery, and your family. What things will Maria see you doing that will demonstrate your significant commitment to her?"
>
> Jesse: "Frankly, I hadn't thought about it . . . well, she will see that I ask her at least twice a day to learn what I can do to be helpful for her."
>
> Counselor: "Do you really mean that? I mean, after all, if you don't ask her twice a day, Maria may believe that you are abandoning her or that you have forfeited your commitment to her and her recovery."

Jesse:	"I wouldn't say something if I didn't mean it."
Counselor:	"Maria, what do you hear Jesse saying?"
Maria:	"I hear Jesse saying that he is committed to me and my recovery and that he is going to take an active role in my recovery by asking me at least twice a day how he can be helpful to my recovery."
Counselor:	"Is that correct, Jesse?"
Jesse:	"Yes."
Counselor:	"Maria, I hear Jesse saying that he is very committed. But what happens if Jesse catches the flu and has a lot of things going on and accidentally forgets to ask you? What would that mean to you?"
Maria:	"I don't think he would forget, but if he did, I might think that he isn't committed to me or my recovery anymore."
Counselor:	"Jesse, given what you've said, it certainly doesn't sound to me as though you are going to forget to ask Maria what you can do to help her recovery. However, if the worst-case scenario occurred and something came up stopping you from asking Maria about what she needs to maintain her recovery, should it suggest to Maria that you are no longer committed to her or her recovery?"
Jesse:	"Of course it wouldn't . . . but, if something did happen and Maria feared that I wasn't committed to her, Maria should ask me, 'Are you still committed to me?'"
Counselor:	"Maria, what do you hear Jesse saying?"
Maria:	"I hear Jesse saying that he doesn't plan on forgetting, but if he does forget or if I think he is no longer committed to me or my recovery, I just need to ask."
Counselor:	"Jesse, is this correct?"
Jesse:	"You've got it exactly correct, Maria. If I don't ask or if you have any question related to my commitment to you, let me know immediately so we can talk. I love you and want you to know that I will do everything I possibly can to help you beat your addiction."

If, however, the family indicates low to below-average scaling question responses related to commitment (e.g., scores between 1 and 4), the counselor should seek clarification related to the low scores and identify what new behaviors the addicted member will need to observe by the family to increase the addicted member's commitment.

Counselor:	"Jesse, you've indicated that on a scale between 1 and 10, your level of commitment is 3. This suggests that you have some commitment but that your commitment level is not very strong. Can you help me understand your response?"
Jesse:	"Sure, we've all been through this at least a dozen times with Maria. She says she is going to stop using, then within a month she is back on the bottle and is worse than ever. I attended Al-Anon and learned that I don't control other people's behaviors. If Maria wants to quit, she will. I can't make her."
Counselor:	"Agreed, you can't make her, but I don't think that is the question here. The burden for Maria's recovery is upon Maria, not you. However, I also know that unless addicted persons have support from their family members—people such as yourself who are extremely important to Maria—the process is even more challenging and the probability for full recovery is less likely. Maria can recover without anyone's help, but your commitment to her is vital, and she is asking for your help. What I'm hearing you say is that Maria has attempted recovery before and that you have found the process frustrating or difficult when she is unsuccessful. My guess is that Maria probably has experienced these frustrations and difficulties as well. I think what we are doing today is working to ensure the greatest potential for Maria's success. Are you committed to helping Maria attain that highest probability of a successful recovery?"
Jesse:	"Yes, but I am not willing to sacrifice myself for Maria and her recovery."
Counselor:	"Good, because neither Maria nor I want you to sacrifice yourself for Maria. However, I'm wondering what things

	you would need to begin seeing Maria doing to increase your commitment from a 3 to a 5."
Jesse:	"Listen, if I could see Maria really being committed, you know like attending AA on a daily basis or stopping her alcohol use, I would increase my commitment to a 10."
Counselor:	"So, I'm hearing you say that when you begin seeing Maria attend daily AA meetings and discontinue her alcohol use, you will increase your commitment to her."
Jesse:	"Yeah, that's it."
Counselor:	"Maria, what are you hearing Jesse say?"
Maria:	"Jesse is saying that he's been there for me in the past and that he's committed. However, he has to see me start working my program before he will be able to move his commitment from a 3 to a 5."
Counselor:	"Jesse, is that correct?"
Jesse:	"Yes, all I've got to do is see her really work her program for the next month and I will become even more committed to her."

These vignettes demonstrate how the counselor can challenge both addicted members and their families in constructive ways to encourage their recovery commitment.

Conclusion Phase   The purpose of this phase is to help family members gain a sense of closure related to the family members' participation, provide a brief recap of the session's positive highlights and agreements, and discuss any further thoughts or concerns. Additionally, the family addictions counselor encourages the family members to apprise each other and the counselor of any changes, concerns, or progress. Given the high degree of suicidal behaviors among substance-abusing clients (Rogers, 1992), the counselor also describes high-risk factors that may indicate suicidal ideation and appropriate intervention guidelines. In addition to the counselor's business card with telephone number, all family members are given the local 24-hour help-line number and are informed that if they believe that any of the family members are suicidal or a danger to someone else, they should immediately contact the help-line number. Furthermore, they are reminded that they may always contact the 911 emergency services dispatcher or take a family member to a local hospital emergency room should they perceive imminent danger. Finally, the counselor makes a few last closing comments related to the visible support and caring demonstrated by the family members. An example vignette is provided below.

Counselor: "We have accomplished much today. We've learned that Maria is committed to her abstinence from alcohol and each of you has echoed your commitment to her via this process. Furthermore, each of you has identified ways in which you are going to support Maria and her recovery. For example, Geraldo will attend daily AA meetings with Maria, and Jesse will ask Maria twice each day how he can be helpful to Maria's continued recovery and abstinence. Your being here today clearly demonstrates your support of Maria, as well as Maria's commitment to addressing her addiction. Before we conclude, however, I want to encourage each of you to speak with one another related to any progress or concerns that might become apparent to you. So, should you believe that Maria is doing a great job attending her AA meetings, tell her as well as the rest of us. Too often people only convey the bad things or what is going wrong. Maria, who do you think will be the first to let you know how well you are progressing?"

Maria: "Geraldo . . . he always is the first to tell me how well I'm doing."

Counselor: "Jesse, it sounds as though you will need to act quickly to tell Maria how well she is doing before Geraldo tells her. I'm glad Maria can count on both of you to provide her with support regarding her progress. Conversely, however, speak with each other, and should you ever believe that Maria is beginning to drink again or you have other concerns, jointly ask her. We may be able to meet at that time to discuss such potential concerns and ensure that Maria is making the progress that she wants. Next, let me talk about something that no one likes to discuss but is very important. This is the issue of suicide and violence. Addicted persons are at high risk for harming themselves and others. If Maria states that she is thinking about killing herself or someone else, or should you believe she is in danger of harming herself or others, simply ask her, 'Mom, are you thinking of hurting or killing yourself?' When you ask, you are showing you care. Asking the question won't cause Maria to commit suicide. Rather your question provides Maria an opportunity to let us know if she needs help. Maria, if Jesse, Geraldo, or I asked whether you were thinking about killing yourself or not, will you become angry?"

Maria: "No, I would think you were just trying to help."

Counselor: "Even if Maria would get angry, her anger is not the issue. The issue is keeping her alive. If you believe she is thinking about suicide, ask her. It may save her life."

Geraldo: "What happens if I think she is going to kill herself, but she says she's not?"

Counselor: "On the back of my business card is the local 24-hour help-line telephone number. Call them. They are very helpful and can help. If they say they can't or if you believe she needs immediate help, call the 911 emergency services dispatcher or take Maria to the hospital emergency room."

Maria: "Hey, I don't want people to send me to some psycho-hospital. I'm not going to kill myself. I want to live."

Counselor: "I don't think you are a danger to yourself, Maria. And I'm sorry if I've conveyed in any way that you are currently a danger. As a matter of fact, just a very few moments ago I heard you say that you are not going to kill yourself. However, we want you to live and not die. What I'm talking about is a situation in which someone believes you are seriously thinking about killing yourself. Should this ever happen, I want people to know how to intervene to save your life. Each family member here has indicated that you are important and they support you."

Maria: "OK, I just don't want you to think that I'm crazy."

Counselor: "I don't. As a matter of fact, I think that you are quite healthy and moving forward on your road to recovery. Crazy people don't realize they need help and continue drinking and drugging. I sincerely commend you on taking this opportunity to speak with these family members that you love and who love you. Despite potential concerns and fears about how family members might respond to the interview, you asked Jesse and Geraldo to help. As I've listened and interacted with each family member here, I have truly come to appreciate their clearly visible dedication and love for you. Each wishes to help. This is something that doesn't always happen, Maria. Additionally, not only have you asked for help, but you have done so in a manner that deserves much credit. Not once did you point a finger at anyone or condemn others for telling the truth or for their attempts to help. I am most impressed and sincerely believe the behaviors I have seen here suggest investment on the part of those who love you and a dedication on your part to successfully live alcohol-free. Thank you for allowing me to work with you. Are there any further concerns or issues that need to be discussed?"

Jesse: "No."

Geraldo: "Not from me. I just want mom to know that I love her and will help in any way I can."

Maria: "I think we are all set."

Drug Detection Testing and Specialty Assessment Instruments

By this point within the clinical family addictions assessment interview, it will be evident whether or not sufficient information has been gathered to begin the actual Sequential Family Addictions Counseling Model presented in the following chapter. There are times, however, when sufficient information has not yet been obtained or there exists a question regarding a family member's actual substance use. We have found this especially true when parents describe a picture of an AOD-abusing adolescent, yet the youth actively denies any AOD use. In such situations, we have found it useful to gain additional information via drug detection testing and specialty assessment instruments. For this reason, we will first address drug detection testing and then specific assessment instruments that we have found particularly useful with addicted families. The use of these tests and instruments is invaluable in providing necessary information regarding potentially addicted family members and the family system's dynamics.

Drug Detection Testing

Five different drug detection tests are most frequently available and often utilized by family addictions counselors. These include urine, hair, blood, saliva, and breathalyzer tests. The primary purpose of these tests is to determine the presence of psychoactive substances in family members presenting for addictions counseling. Most drug detection test purveyors, other than those who supply breathalyzers, sell a basic drug detection option that evaluates test samples for five of the most commonly abused psychoactive substance categories. The categories include cannabinoids (e.g., marijuana), cocaine (e.g., crack), amphetamines (e.g., speed), opiates (e.g., heroin), and phencyclidine (e.g., PCP). These substance categories are often referred to as the "NIDA Five." This is because the federal government, via recommendation of the National Institute on Drug Abuse (NIDA), requires employers of commercial-class truck drivers to have substance abuse policies that periodically screen drivers for these five psychoactive substance categories.

Additionally, most purveyors offer expanded drug detection test options and allow purchasers to select additional tests to determine the presence of other psychoactive substance categories such as barbiturates (e.g., phenobarbital), benzodiazepines (e.g., Valium), and ethanol (alcohol). Costs can significantly increase when purchasing such expanded drug detection tests. Therefore, the use of such expanded detection tests must be carefully chosen. Since most addicted families will have described the potentially addicted member's substances of choice via the clinical family addictions assessment interview, such expanded drug detection tests may be of limited utility unless the family addictions counselor needs to continually screen the abusing member for psychoactive substance categories outside the NIDA Five. Here, for example, if the addicted family member had previously indicated barbiturate abuse and the counselor's initial or provisional diagnosis was related to barbiturates, continual random barbiturate screenings would be a logical choice. However, if the diagnosis was related to psychoactive substance categories contained within the NIDA Five, little benefit can come from the expanded detection tests.

No matter which drug detection test is used, family addictions counselors must be aware of required and standardized procedures that promote reliable and accurate drug detection. These standardized procedures follow strict specimen collection and appropriate notification processes. Specifically, the specimen collection process should ensure that specimens have little chance of being adulterated and the notification process should occur within a time period that ensures adequate detection.

Urine (Immunoassay)   Urine drug detection testing is typically used when concerns arise about immediate past drug use (e.g., 6 hours to 4 days). Depending on the suspected psychoactive substance used within the immediate past, urine drug detection testing can be a cost-effective and easily administered means to testing addicted family members. Contrary to popular belief, parents do not have to directly observe their adolescent urinate into a vial or container. Instead, temperature strips attached to the specimen vial can be used to ensure that samples are genuine (i.e., the adolescent's actual urine sample) and unadulterated (i.e., not mixed with any of a variety of products commonly sold specifically to mask or evade psychoactive drug detection). Although some drug detection laboratories require urine specimens to be measured via digital thermometer with a temperature range between 96 and 99 degrees Fahrenheit, these exacting requirements likely are too strict for home urine test kits. As a matter of fact, federal agencies such as the Substance Abuse and Mental Health Services Administration (SAMHSA) have broader collection standards and indicate that specimens can range between 90 and 100 degrees Fahrenheit and suggest that the more rigorous 96- to 99-degree temperature range need not be the threshold for indicating attempted adulteration attempts. In other words, especially for home urine analysis kits, temperature specimen ranges between 90 and 100 degrees Fahrenheit likely present a sufficient threshold to identify attempts to deceive the tests. Thus, should an addicted family member attempt to add masking contents into a submitted specimen or attempt to use someone else's urine, the person receiving the specimen will be alerted, because the urine specimens will likely not match the temperature standards.

The senior author was informed of such a situation in which an alcohol-abusing adolescent attempted to dilute his urine with tap water. His intent was to deceive a home urine test. Previously, this adolescent's mother told him that she would test him if she believed he had again been drinking. Reportedly, the adolescent smelled of beer and marijuana when he returned home late one weekend evening, and mother required a urine sample. The home urine test kit's container had temperature strips attached to its side. According to mother, when son provided the specimen container, the temperature strips failed to mark even room temperature. She accused the son of attempting to "cheat" the test and brought him to the clinic the very next day. The therapeutic part of this experience was not that the mother *caught* the adolescent. Instead, the therapeutic part was that the son realized that his alcohol consumption did not go unnoticed and that his mother loved him so much that she was unwilling to allow him to continue his drinking and drugging behaviors. In other words, this adolescent learned that contrary to his previous beliefs, his drinking could be detected and he was accountable for his drinking behaviors.

Additionally, in the case of family members who have agreed to random urine screens (except in the case of alcohol) and who have been notified that specimens are due, the specimens must be submitted within 24 hours of the notification. Should addicted members submit specimens later than 24 hours, the members may well have simply waited until the drug was completely metabolized out of their bodies. Thus, the addicted members would merely pass the urine test without detection.

In the instance of alcohol, a urine test should be completed within 6 hours of notification. This is because depending on the amount of alcohol consumed, urine tests may only detect alcohol consumption up to 12 hours from the last use. So, the general rule here is if alcohol is the expected substance, collection must occur within 6 hours of use.

Another complicating factor regarding the use of urine detection tests with addicted family members is that the test results will simply indicate immediate past use. However, the urine results cannot indicate whether or not the member was under the influence or indicate the blood alcohol levels attained as a result of the alcohol consumption. In other words, unless the addicted family member is a minor or is required to be alcohol-free by the courts, merely knowing that alcohol was consumed within the preceding 12 hours does little good.

Most nonemergency, ambulatory, medical care facilities as well as hospitals with occupational medicine programs and laboratory facilities will provide urine drug detection testing. Additionally, there exist many relatively inexpensive over-the-counter home drug detection kits sold at local pharmacies. Most of these kits sell for less than $60. Some kits are even Federal Drug Administration (FDA) approved (e.g., Dr. Brown's Home Drug Testing System) and can provide results within 3 to 9 days from submission.

Hair (Radioimmunoassay)   Werner Baumgartner developed hair drug detection testing in 1978 (Minnesota Poison Control, 2001). In 1986 hair drug detection testing became available for commercial use, and currently it is utilized by the courts and corrections systems to ensure that parolees and probationers remain substance-free (Jordan, 1988; Minnesota Poison Control, 2001). The central premise of hair drug detection testing is that once psychoactive substances enter the bloodstream, substances or metabolites contained within the blood are deposited on individual hair shafts. Thus, this process creates a historical record of recently used drugs. Given that hair typically grows half an inch each 30 days, a one-and-a-half-inch hair sample is painlessly cut from the crown of an addicted family member's head and tested to determine whether or not AODs were used within the preceding 90 days. As with urine detection testing, hair drug detection testing is used when concerns arise regarding past psychoactive substance use. However, hair drug detection testing, unlike urine drug detection testing, provides a much longer window. Thus, it is especially useful when concerns reflect substance use within the last 8 to 90 days. Additionally, unlike other forms of drug detection tests, it was uniquely created "to show whether drug use is frequent, or occasional, light or heavy" (Jordan, 1988). Because addicted family members are not required to urinate into a vial or have blood extracted, hair drug detection testing is less "personally invasive" and therefore likely more comfortable than urine or blood drug detection testing.

As with the case with urine drug detection testing, hair drug detection testing cannot determine if an addicted family member has consumed alcohol to a point of intoxication or indicate the addicted family member's blood alcohol level at the time of consumption. And although hair drug detection testing can usually identify psychoactive substances used within 90 days, it cannot typically identify psychoactive substances used within the last week. Hair detection drug tests completed at an on-site laboratory facility typically cost between $130 and $200 per test and therefore are more costly than urine drug detection tests. However, there are a number of hair detection tests sold online that cost less than $50. These home tests require parents to cut a sample of their child's hair and forward the hair sample to a laboratory for analysis. Results can often be returned within 7 to 10 days and can provide a detailed description of the substances used.

Frankly, in treatment, we have found hair detection drug tests invaluable. It is our first choice in drug detection tests. The reasons for this are clear. Hair detection drug tests are inexpensive and simple to purchase online. Specimen collection is easy and relatively unobtrusive. They are highly reliable. They have a quick turnaround time and provide a 60- to 90-day drug history window. Furthermore, when you combine both the urine analysis and the hair detection tests, you are likely to have sufficient information to either confirm a family member's abstinence or clarify the frequency of her drug abuse.

Parents often bring their adolescents or young-adult children and suggest that the family member is using substances. In nearly all cases, the drug use is adamantly denied. It is at this time that we typically offer a quick solution—for less than $100, mom and dad can have the youth participate in a drug detection test to prove the youth is telling the truth. About 10 percent of the time, the tests will come back negative and support the youth's statement that she does not use. However, about 40 percent of the time, the youth will indicate immediately prior to participating in the test, "Well, I did have one drink yesterday" or "I was at a friend's house, and they were toking. Even though I didn't use, I'll probably test positive for secondhand smoke." And about 50 percent of the time, the youth will agree to participate in drug detection testing and anticipate that the only test used will be urine analysis. Given that addicted family members typically are brought to our offices 24 hours or longer after their drug use, addicted youth anticipate that the urine analysis will completely miss their alcohol use. However, immediately following the urine analysis, when their parents then pull out the scissors to neatly trim about a pencil's diameter of hairs, their youths quickly realize that a much longer window of use will be detected.

Not long ago we had such a case. Mother and father were paying for their son's college tuition. Son failed his fall freshman semester at his father's alma mater. Son blamed the university's well-known rigor for his failure and returned to living at his parents' home. However, his parents suspected that the son's failure was related to his "heavy partying." The parents enrolled their son at a local college. Within 2 months he was again failing. His schedule included sleeping until afternoon, leaving home, and returning home in the early morning hours or returning 1 or 2 days after leaving. His parents had experienced enough. They told him on a Thursday that he would need to participate in counseling and submit to a drug test. The alternative was that they would discontinue paying his college tuition and end his home residency. Son agreed. However, he failed to show up for his scheduled drug detection test and instead returned 3 days later—the day of the scheduled family counseling session. At that meeting, son reported that he had "forgotten" about the scheduled drug test and had spent the weekend with friends at the beach. Then he confidently stated, "But I would be happy to do a pee (urine) test now!" Mother and father were elated. So was son, until he learned that the process would include both urine and hair analyses. Immediately son refused to participate in the hair analysis. Months later, toward the end of his treatment, when son had been abstinent for over 60 days, he divulged that he knew he couldn't pass the initially scheduled drug test and had spent that entire weekend drinking 4 quarts of herbal tea and assorted fitness drinks each day. He had also purchased a $40 synthetic urine substitute to "fool" the urine test. However, he was unprepared for the hair test.

Again, it is imperative to remind parents that the drug tests are merely a tool for accountability. Having a loved family member test positive on her hair analysis is nothing to celebrate. It is, however, an important way of demonstrating to family members that testing will occur and that if they use, there exists a high probability that their use will be identified and have consequences.

Blood   Although the most intrusive and expensive drug detection testing type, blood drug detection testing is the most accurate. Unlike urine and hair drug detection testing, blood drug detection testing is used to detect immediate psychoactive substances within the family member's body. In other words, this test is typically used to determine the specific amount of psychoactive substance present at the time of testing (e.g., blood alcohol levels) and can indicate whether a family member *is* under the influence. Often this method includes using gas chromatography (GC) to separate the psychoactive substances and compounds (e.g., masking agents used by persons attempting to adulterate urine samples) within the blood sample and then mass spectrometry (MS) to identify the isolated psychoactive substances (R. Silverman, personal communication, June 19, 2001). Because it is the most expensive and the most invasive drug detection testing method, it is used less frequently than the other types of testing.

Saliva   Saliva drug detection testing has gained popularity in recent years and, depending on the online source, costs between $20 and $75. The use of saliva testing is quite unobtrusive when compared to other drug detection types. Often saliva testing can detect more recent substance use. However, as of yet, there are no nationally accepted concentration thresholds for this testing type, which means each individual purveyor and laboratory establishes its own cutoff concentrations. This could have an impact on result reliability. Overall, saliva testing is more reliable in detecting methamphetamine and opiates and less reliable for THC or cannabinoids.

Breathalyzer   Breathalyzers come in many different types and, like blood drug detection testing, are used to assess current intoxication levels. Stated differently, breathalyzers indicate if an addicted family member is currently under the influence. Breathalyzers are frequently used by law enforcement following vehicular accidents when drivers are perceived as intoxicated. Two of the most frequently used breathalyzer types include disposable "blowpipe" alcohol detectors and digital handheld breathalyzers. Typically, blowpipes are purchased to identify a specific alcohol percentage (e.g., .08 percent) and can be used to detect breath alcohol from .02 percent to .10 percent. Usually, the counselor will break a plastic ampoule within the blowpipe and the addicted family member will be required to blow through one end of the plastic tube for a period of 10 to 20 seconds. Next the counselor will shake the blowpipe and allow the crystals in the ampoule to change color. Blowpipes are relatively inexpensive and usually can be purchased in quantities for under $5 apiece.

Digital handheld breathalyzers are also easy to administer and read. Often these units will have LCD displays indicating the addicted family member's breath alcohol level from .00 percent to .15 percent. They are small, about the size of a computer mouse, and run on batteries. When used, addicted family members are required to blow a steady stream of air through a straw-like tube for approximately 10 to 20 seconds. Often this type of breathalyzer will emit a tone when enough air has been blown into the instrument to provide a reading. The breathalyzer will then provide via the LCD display the addicted family member's breath alcohol level.

Other Drug Detection Testing Methods   A number of other drug detection testing methods exist. However, their use is not as prominent or is relatively recent. For example, there are aerosol products that can be sprayed onto backpacks, clothing, computer keyboards, or desktops which change color to indicate cannabis or cocaine residual. Certain swab-type drug detection tests are similarly used. Here someone would swab items that the addicted family member touched and then forward the swab to the test's maker for analysis. Additionally, there are bandage-type "patches" with tamperproof seals designed to absorb perspiration. After being worn for approximately 1 week, the perspiration patch is sent to a lab for analysis to determine which psychoactive substance residues or metabolites were excreted via perspiration.

Therapeutic Use of Drug Detection Testing   The overall intent of drug detection testing with families is threefold. First, at the onset of family addictions counseling, drug detection testing is used to identify which psychoactive substances family members have recently used and to further substantiate abstinence claims. Knowledge about the abused substances is vitally important and aids in creating a treatment plan for the entire family system.

Second, drug detection testing can be used if a counselor suspects that a family member may have been using or is currently under the influence. Part of the therapeutic use of drug detection testing contained within this second area revolves around the issue of accountability. For example, it is not all that uncommon for addicted family members to abuse alcohol or sedative hypnotics just prior to their family counseling sessions. This often is done to reduce their pre-session anxiety. Although these addicted family members may deny any AOD use since their most recent family counseling session, they may have the aroma of alcohol "about them" and emanating from their breath, clothes, and perspiration. Additionally, they may have slurred speech, be unusually gregarious, and have dilated pupils. At this point, the counselor may then ask other family members about the addicted member's physical and emotional presentation. Should the family also believe that the member is under the influence of alcohol, for example, she would be asked to use a breathalyzer to determine her alcohol intoxication level. In cases like this, it can be exceptionally therapeutic for the entire family to discuss the occurrence. Using the previous example of Maria, the family counseling session might go something like this:

Counselor:	"Maria, there seems to be the smell of alcohol on your clothing and breath."
Maria:	"What are you saying?"
Counselor:	"There seems to be the smell of alcohol on your clothing and breath. I am wondering if you drank alcohol or used drugs before you came to session."
Jesse:	"I've been with her the entire afternoon and I haven't seen her drink."
Maria:	"See, I told you I haven't been drinking. If I had been drinking, Jesse would know it."
Counselor:	"I'm sorry, Maria and Jesse, but this is what I see and smell. Maria, your pupils appear dilated, you seem rather clumsy, and your speech seems slurred and erratic. I also smell alcohol in the room. Jesse, do you smell the alcohol?"
Jesse:	"Now that you mention it, I do. And, before we came, Maria used a lot of mouthwash and breath mints in the car."
Counselor:	"Maria, sometimes people are scared to say they have been drinking when they have been drinking. Most of the time, people say they haven't been drinking, because they don't want to let their loved ones down. And sometimes people haven't been drinking even though I think that they present as though they have been drinking. In any case, I am wondering whether you would be willing to take a breathalyzer. All you need to do is blow into a small tube. By doing that, you will demonstrate that I was incorrect and we can begin session."
Maria:	"Well, I've had this bad cold and have taken some cough syrup that might have alcohol in it."

Counselor:	"No problem. That is one thing nice about how advanced and accurate breathalyzers have become. They can pretty accurately demonstrate that you've just taken the prescribed dosage of cough syrup or if you likely have a score suggesting a low, moderate, or high blood alcohol level. Let's merely show that you only had a little cough syrup so that we can use our counseling time wisely."
Geraldo:	"Hey, you're not being fair to my mom. She said she hasn't used. Leave her alone."
Counselor:	"Mom, your family is really working hard to protect you. Is this what typically happens when you say you haven't been using?"
Maria:	"I told you I have used cough syrup with alcohol in it, so leave me alone!"
Counselor:	"OK, let's just have you use the breathalyzer and clear things up."
Maria:	"I can't."
Counselor:	"Because?"
Maria:	"Because I was really scared of coming to session today and everybody has been watching me to make sure I don't slip, I couldn't help it. I had to drink to make it here today!"

As demonstrated, the purpose is not to argue with the addicted family member about whether she has or has not used. Instead, it is to train the entire family to identify the physical indicators of her use (e.g., smell of alcohol in the room, Maria's slurred speech).

Accountability is important within addicted families. Regretfully, often the concept is foreign to addicted members. From a family systems perspective, if I don't hold you accountable for your addicted behaviors, you can't hold me accountable either. Stated differently, consciously or unconsciously family members who don't confront the addicted member's abusing behaviors are attempting to be released from others' expectations of them at a later time. In other words, family members are "buying" each other off. The appropriate use of drug detection testing can teach accountability among family members and help them better understand that ignoring the addictive behavior is part of the problem, not the solution.

Finally, drug detection testing can be used for monitoring continued abstinence and rewarding recovering members for their success. Such rewards are exceedingly helpful to recovering members who are in the early and middle recovery stages. Often these members are nagged by concerned others who mistakenly believe their nagging promotes continued recovery. Thus, the intentions are good. However, their continued badgering tends to both provoke the recovering member into stressful, defensive posturing (e.g., arguing with the accuser, returning to old substance-using friends to escape the perceived surveillance) and further suggest that the member is doomed for relapse (e.g., "If she really thought I could be substance-free, she wouldn't be so worried about me").

Drug detection testing can be integrated into contingency contracting (Rinn, 1978)—or, as we call it within our clinics, "sobriety contracting"—as a means of addressing such nagging. Here the emphasis is on successful monitoring of the family member's continued abstinence. In other words, the family member is told that the objective is to "catch you being clean." The goals are to support the member's abstinence and to let the family know that they do not have to nag. The upcoming chapter will go into greater detail on the use of contingency contracting. There, we will describe how to integrate contingency contracting into sequential family counseling treatment, something we have found especially helpful with recovering adolescents and their parents.

We would like to make one final note regarding drug detection testing. All one has to do is visit the Web or talk with any group of substance-abusing persons to learn of the various myths and realities surrounding drug detection testing. From the products that can be placed in urine samples to ways of blowing into breathalyzers, it seems nearly everyone has an idea of how to beat the tests. Surprise is the ultimate method of ensuring that the samples taken are unadulterated and original. Thus, if an alcohol-abusing family member is asked to provide a urine sample at 6 P.M. on Saturday night, another sample may be requested later that evening after the football game. AOD-abusing family members often do not anticipate being asked to provide two or more samples on a given day. Choosing times immediately following when the family member is potentially at risk for using is key. Additionally, choosing a laboratory that alerts the counselor to substances commonly used to "clean" urine samples is important. The common rule we have with our addicted families is that if they take the time, effort, and money to purchase a product or substance that is added to their urine sample, it is the same thing as sending in a positive sample.

Specialty Assessment Instruments

Okay, you have learned how to conduct thorough clinical family addictions assessment interviews and how to use drug detection testing. We next want to shift our focus to specialty assessment instruments. Numerous sources within the professional literature indicate both the importance of using assessment instruments within the counseling process and multiple benefits of using assessment instruments to establish pertinent and client-relevant treatment goals (Donovan, 1992; Doweiko, 1996; Evans, 1988; Juhnke & Hovestadt, 1995; Lewis, Dana, & Blevins, 1988; Nelson & Neufeldt, 1996; Vacc, 1982; Vacc & Juhnke, 1997). The most recent published survey of all Master Addictions Counselors (MACs) certified by the National Board of Certified Counselors noted a number of standardized specialty instruments identified as frequently used and important to addictions professionals (Juhnke, Vacc, Curtis, Coll, & Paredes, 2003). Participants in this survey were seasoned addictions professionals who minimally held a master's degree in counseling or a related professional field and had 3 years post-master's addictions counseling experience. Clearly, based on the outcome of that article and the sheer number of addiction instruments being utilized within the treatment community, there exists a number of worthy addictions specialty assessment instruments from which one can choose. However, we have identified three specific instruments that should be fundamental to all family addictions counselors. The first is the Marital Satisfaction Inventory–Revised (MSI-R). We use this instrument regularly and believe that, when properly interpreted, the results provide crucial information related to marital partners as well as a window into the addicted family's dynamics. The second and third instruments were identified in the Juhnke et al. (2003) article as the sine qua non addictions instruments. These include the Substance Abuse Subtle Screening Inventory–3 for adults and the Substance Abuse Subtle Screening Inventory-Adolescent 2 for adolescents. These are the cornerstone addictions instrument on today's market.

In essence, these three specialty assessment instruments provide important information regarding individually addicted family members and the families in which they reside. Such information augments information gleaned from both the clinical family addictions assessment interview and drug detection. These specialty assessment instruments also provide baseline data that can be used as pretreatment scores for both addiction-related behaviors (e.g., frequency of intoxication) as well as marriage- and family-related topics (e.g., marriage satisfaction) that are so relevant when counseling addicted families. When used to provide baseline data, counselors can note clinical progress or the lack thereof. This is accomplished by readministering these same specialty instruments at a later time. For example, some counselors choose to readminister specialty instruments such as the Substance Abuse Subtle Screening Inventory–3 at specific intervals throughout treatment (e.g., weeks 8 and 16) or at the end of treatment.

Moreover, specialty instruments can be used to support the assessing counselor's initial diagnoses and treatment recommendations. Remember, many family members deny the existence of addiction or its impact on their families. Assessment specialty instrument authors often have developed scales or other standardized response analyses that alert counselors to family members' attempts to present themselves in a favorable, nonaddicted light. Thus, even if the addicted family member and family manage to deceive the counselor, standardized specialty instruments can provide credible evidence that alerts the counselor to the deception potential. Therefore, family addictions counselors can use specialty instruments as (a) a means to gain further understanding of the addicted member and the family system, (b) a baseline to identify individual and family improvement, (c) a method to detect deceitful familial presentations, and (d) collaborating evidence for the family addiction counselor's clinical judgment and diagnoses.

Marital Satisfaction Inventory-Revised

General MSI-R Overview   Snyder developed the MSI-R to help identify "the nature and extent of relationship distress with couples considering or beginning conjoint therapy" (Snyder, 1997, p. 1). The instrument was not specifically created for use with addicted couples but has great utility when counseling families adversely impacted by addiction. Specifically, this assessment will provide clear indications of the couples' individual and joint perceptions of the marriage as well as relationship "hot spots" that warrant immediate attention. Thus, the instrument is an invaluable tool when counseling addicted couples and families.

The MSI-R is composed of 150 question stems with corresponding "true" and "false" response options. Couples without children complete only questions 1 through 129; those with children complete all 150 question stems. These last 21 questions deal specifically with perceptions related to the couple's children and parenting (e.g., disciplining, child rearing workloads). A combination of 13 unmarked or "double-marked" responses (where the respondent endorsed both "true" and "false" responses) suggests the profile to be "unscorable" (p. 6). According to Snyder, persons taking the instrument "should be instructed to respond to the inventory items *separately and without collaboration*" (p. 6). In other words, this is not a project that the couple completes together. The instrument takes approximately 25 minutes to complete and requires a sixth-grade reading level (p. 1). The MSI-R was developed for persons 16 years of age and older (D. Snyder, personal communication, September 27, 2005) and can be ordered online from Western Psychological Services at www.wpspublish.com.

MSI-R Reliability and Validity Test–retest reliability coefficients ranged between .74 and .88 with a mean coefficient of .79 (excluding the Inconsistency Scale) (Snyder, 1997, p. 55). In other words, MSI-R scales appear stable over time. Cronbach's alpha coefficients of internal consistency for all MSI-R scales except the Inconsistency Scale ranged between .70 and .93 with a mean coefficient of .82 (p. 55). Such coefficients confirm the internal consistency of the MSI-R. Related to validity, each of the instrument's 13 scales was able to differentiate between clinical and nonclinical couples at the $p < .001$ level. Concomitantly, other research studies comparing "broad-band multidimensional measures of psychopathology and personality functioning in adults and children or adolescents" (p. 68) suggest concurrent validity with appropriate and corresponding scales on the Minnesota Multiphasic Personality Inventory and the Personality Inventory for Children.

Scales Especially because this assessment instrument was not specifically developed for use with addicted couples or for couples presenting with addictions-related concerns, it would be foolish to suggest, for example, that *all* addicted couples will score high or low on certain scales. Additionally, any attempt to group all addicted persons or families suffering from addictions together into one measurable population that would respond in only one direction on specific testing instruments would be clinically and theoretically indefensible. More often than not, variance within specific populations is robust. Addicted families are no different. They are composed of the stereotypical unemployed, impoverished, Euro-American couples that reside in rural North Carolina as well as the nonstereotypical affluent, college-educated, executive, gay-married, Hispanic couples that reside in Alaska.

However, as one reviews the MSI-R's individual scales, it becomes increasingly evident that specific endorsement response types may be reflective of couples experiencing similar addiction-related concerns. For example, based on clinical experiences with addicted families and understanding of the overwhelming financial costs of chronic, long-term cocaine dependence, one would anticipate that most middle-class, cocaine-dependent couples would endorse at least some financial stressors on an instrument such as the MSI-R. Thus, the intent of this MSI-R scale review is not to suggest that all addicted couples will score in one direction on individual scales but to encourage you to better understand the potential dynamics of addicted couples presenting for treatment.

This said, as we describe the individual MSI-R scales, we have included some generalized statements related to our assessment experiences with addicted couples who have completed the MSI-R. These generalizations relate directly to our experiences and are not suggesting that *all* addicted couples will present with the same endorsements or score types (e.g., "high" or "low"). So, as you review the scales below, remember that any specialty instrument is just one piece of the overall assessment process.

Are you ready? Here we go. The MSI-R is composed of 13 scales. Two of these scales are validity scales; one is a global affective scale. The first validity scale, Inconsistency (INC), reports random or careless responses, which may also be indications of confusion or deliberate noncompliance (Snyder, 1997). High scores on the INC suggest random or careless scoring, whereas low scores may indicate an overall investment in the testing process and potentially a more positive perception of most relationship domains (e.g., communications, finances). The second scale, Conventionalization (CNV), reports the clients' "tendencies to distort the appraisal of their relationship in a socially desirable direction" (p. 20). High scores on this scale suggest defensiveness or resistance to discussing conflict within the relationship. Thus, when we have counseled addicted couples mandated into family counseling by Child Protective Services, they sometimes surprisingly present inflated CNV scores. To the novice clinician, this may seem to make little sense, because it is as if they are saying, "Everything in the relationship is fine." However, what they are really saying is, "We don't need your help. Leave us alone." Low scores conversely are often associated with moderate overall relationship distress. Here, addicted couples are reporting concerns within their marriage.

The Global Distress (GDS) Scale reports "overall dissatisfaction with the relationship" (p. 21). High scores suggest significant relationship dissatisfaction that likely has existed for a significant time period. We have noted such high scores when counseling couples where one presents with an addictions dependence diagnosis (e.g., cocaine dependence) and the other does not fulfill either abuse or dependence diagnoses (e.g., alcohol abuse or cannabis dependence). Such scores may be due to the addicted spouse's continuing addiction and reoccurring relapses, combined with typical, comorbid, addiction-related marital dysfunction (e.g., communication and financial challenges resulting from a husband's drinking and drugging behaviors). Furthermore, the nonaddicted spouse may well view the other as both critical and uncaring—again, descriptors commonly used by our nonaddicted client spouses when describing their addicted partners. The chaos and dysfunction of living with an addicted partner is quite noticeable when the nonaddicted spouse compares her marriage to other marriages void of addiction and dysfunction. For example, the senior author recently heard an addicted family member report, "My younger sister whose husband is stranger than Pee-wee Herman has a better marriage than mine!"

Another instrument scale is the Affective Communication (AFC) Scale. The AFC Scale is the "best single measure of emotional intimacy experienced" by the couple (p. 21) and reflects dissatisfaction related to perceived partner affection and understanding. High scores denote extensive dissatisfaction related to expressed love and affection within the relationship. Alternatively, low scores suggest that the couple experiences their relationship as happy and fulfilling and their spouses as loving and supportive. In general we have found that when both partners are addicted, these scores tend to be more moderate than one might initially anticipate. In other words, although the addicted client spouses may not be endorsing feelings of great affection and support, they do tend to report feeling understood by each other. Upon further review, we have noted that their conceptualizations of mutual disclosure and partner understanding are more often than not their joint efforts to obtain and use substances of first choice. In other words, these addicted couples often believe that their coaddicted spouse knows exactly what they are experiencing—the effects of withdraw and the desire to jointly use substances with them.

The Problem-Solving Communication (PSC) Scale measures the "couple's general ineffectiveness in resolving differences and measures overt discord rather than underlying feelings of estrangement" (p. 22). Addicted couples scoring high on this scale are reporting chronic arguing within the marriage. Often these client couples are unable or unwilling to look at voiced partner complaints through their spouse's eyes. We have found that most of our addicted couples presenting with high PSC scores perceive their spouses as rigid and intentionally caustic. By contrast, addicted couples presenting with low PSC scores appear invested in their marital relationship and display behaviors or make statements suggesting they want or expect the relationship to improve. In our experience, addicted couples endorsing low PSC scores are those in which the addiction onset or marriage is relatively recent.

One of the most often inflated scales we experience with addicted client couples is the Aggression (AGG) Scale. This scale reports intimidation and physical aggression. When people are under the influence, they often act impulsively and lack an ability to control their behaviors or tempers. Concomitantly, with the use of certain substances that enhance anger and bravado (e.g., cocaine, methamphetamines) or are linked to increased rage (e.g., anabolic steroids), it is clear why such a correlation exists. High scores on this scale denote "at least moderate levels of intimidation (threats of physical harm) as well as low levels of physical aggression (pushing, grabbing, or slapping)" (p. 23). Lower scores suggest an absence of physical aggression or intimidation.

We have found that the Time Together (TTO) Scale can also have somewhat unusual implications for our addicted client couples. The scale assesses "the couple's companionship as expressed in terms of the time they spend together in leisure activity" (p. 23). We have found that when our client couples fulfill similar AOD abuse or dependence diagnoses related to the same substance of choice (e.g., alcohol abuse, alcohol dependence) and their scores on this scale are low, drinking and drugging is often the focal point for their shared leisure interactions. For example, an older addicted couple we counseled reported spending significant leisure time together. Initially, we thought this time together would be a positive, drug-free opportunity that could be used to strengthen their relationship and their joint recovery. Upon further assessment, however, it was learned that this leisure time revolved primarily around consuming alcohol together with mutual friends. Playing cards and bingo were also part of this leisure time experience. And based on the couple's descriptors of their mutual friends, it seemed highly plausible that the friends qualified for addictions-related diagnoses. Therefore, what originally appeared to be a score reflecting something positive instead reflected something quite different with this addicted couple.

Low TTO scores for some of our younger couples can suggest drinking and drugging as their primary leisure time together as well. For example, some of our younger couples addicted to cocaine or who abused substances like ecstasy endorsed low TTO scores. In essence, they interpreted their leisure time as time spent together combining their substance abuse as well as sexual and partying activities. One younger couple recently reported their shared leisure activity as "raving"—that is, attending rave parties, using ecstasy and other designer drugs, dancing until the early morning hours, and participating in sexual activities with other couples. As the 19-year-old mother of one reported, "We live to party on the weekends. It's not what you think. We work regular jobs during the week, save our dough, and then give the kid to my mother on the weekends. Then we rave our weekend away." Another reported camping trips where the couple would spend significant leisure time together, but with drugging as the focal point of the experience. Thus, when TTO scores are low, we now make it a general practice to investigate if the addicted couple is drinking or drugging during their time together.

High TTO scores can have significant ramifications for addicted couples too. Specifically, we have found that high TTO scores are frequently noted when one spouse is addicted and the other is not. In other words, the addicted and nonaddicted partners have little in common related to drinking and drugging behaviors. Often this means that the addicted spouse spends time with other addicted persons, at places where others are participating in similar addictive behaviors. Often this means people and places the nonaddicted spouse has little desire to interact with. This seems especially true when the addicted or substance-abusing partner is surrounded by work peers who are using.

The Disagreement About Finances (FIN) Scale reports relationship disharmony resulting from financial management. Given AOD's financial costs and the lack of financial trust that most spouses have toward their addicted partners (e.g., "Will she use my paycheck to pay the bills or purchase cocaine?"), addicted couples typically present with an inflated FIN Scale score. High scores indicate financial concerns, lack of confidence in the partner's money management, and frequent arguments over money within the relationship. Low scores suggest agreement in the way money is managed.

Another scale within the MSI-R is the Sexual Dissatisfaction (SEX) Scale. According to Snyder (1997), this scale "reflects the respondent's level of discontent with the frequency and quality of intercourse and other sexual activities" (p. 24). High scores suggest "extensive dissatisfaction" (p. 25) related to the sexual relationship and frequency of sexual activities, and low scores suggest a generally positive sexual relationship. We have found that many of the addicted couples with whom we have worked surprise us with low to moderate scale scores. According to our addicted couples who abuse the same substances of first choice, they either have very frequent sexual interactions—especially while under the influence—or do not care to have sex, because they are too busy pursuing or experiencing their buzz. In other words, many of the addicted couples with whom we have administered the MSI-R do not find sexual frequency an issue. This is because they are so frequently under the influence that sexual interactions are clearly less important than their addiction habits. Additionally, many of our addicted clients, even married addicted clients, sell their bodies for drugs or money to purchase drugs. Thus, the frequency of sexual relations is not perceived as problematic. The bigger sexual issues for our addicted couples appear to revolve around two areas: (a) the quality of affection displayed during sex and (b) an inability for partners to sexually perform due to the effects of their repeatedly being under the influence.

The Role Orientation (ROR) Scale is not necessarily a scale noting marital discord but rather a scale that can report incongruence between partners' perceptions of traditional vis-à-vis nontraditional family roles. Here, high scores indicate a belief in more contemporary parenting and marital roles; low scores indicate more traditional parenting and marital roles. Thus, discord can result if spouses have highly differing expectations, assumptions, and beliefs related to how one and one's spouse will participate in such roles.

The Family History of Distress (FAM) Scale reports "disruption of relationships within the respondent's family of origin" (p. 25). High scores on the FAM Scale suggest significant family-of-origin conflict and dysfunction. Low scores suggest that the addicted family member likely experienced a fairly positive family-of-origin experience. More often than not, our severely addicted clients who present with chronic AOD histories endorse high FAM scale scores and indicate highly disrupted family-of-origin experiences with extensive AOD use by at least one of their parents.

The remaining two scales measure concerns about children and parenting. The Dissatisfaction with Children (DSC) Scale measures "emotional and behavioral adjustment of their children, quality of the parent-child relationship and negative impact of child rearing demands" (p. 25). High DSC scores suggest "greater levels of distress in respondents' relationships with their children" (p. 26). Addicted client couples endorsing lower scores typically indicate overall satisfaction with their children.

One of the most notable commonalities that we have found on the MSI-R occurs when the adult parents are in the beginning or initial recovery stages and notice behaviors they believe signify the onset of AOD-abusing behaviors in their children. These parents often seem to endorse higher DSC scores and verbally note their perceived failures both to model more appropriate non-substance-abusing behaviors and to extinguish their children's drinking and drugging interests. As one addicted family member so eloquently put it, "My parents failed me, now I'm failing my daughters. It's a family curse that my daughters will pass down. How could I have done this to them?" This addicted family member later relapsed under the burden of her recovery struggle and the emotional pain experienced when her oldest daughter's full-blown addiction manifested itself. During family counseling, her daughter shouted, "I hate you [mother]! You want me to do what you couldn't!" The daughter of course was referring to mother's inability to maintain her recovery for little more than a few months at a time.

The final scale is the Conflict Over Child Rearing (CCR) Scale. Unlike the parent–child relationship addressed in the DSC Scale, the CCR measures the conflict between parents due to child-rearing practices. High CCR scores suggest "extensive conflict in the partners' interactions regarding children" (Snyder, 1997, p. 26). In other words, there likely exists discord between spouses related to the way one or both spouses discipline or rear children in the home, or discord related to the distribution of child-rearing responsibilities. Low CCR scores suggest the opposite: satisfaction with one's spouse's child-rearing responsibilities and disciplining of the children. We have noted three common scenarios related to the CCR Scale with addicted families.

First, when one spouse is addicted and the other is not, the couple will often post moderate to high scores. This is because the addicted spouse is often under the influence and failing to invest time or energy with the kids. Concomitantly, the addicted spouse, when fulfilling a substance-dependent diagnosis, will often impulsively and haphazardly discipline out of frustration and anger when experiencing physical and emotional distress associated with withdrawal. Similar behaviors are demonstrated when the addicted spouse is in search of securing his drug of choice. Additionally, moderate to high scores occur when the addicted spouse enters treatment and the nonaddicted spouse is again stuck with the entire immediate responsibility of child rearing. This tends to be especially true when the addicted parent is hospitalized for detoxification and has ample insurance that provides inpatient hospitalization for a week or more. However, we have found that such CCR scores can also be high when one spouse enters intensive outpatient counseling. Here again, the time invested in daily treatment is inordinate and removes the recovering client from an active parenting role. Thus, the immediate child-rearing burden is placed on the other spouse.

MSI-R Example: Karen and Tim   Karen (23) and Tim (25) have been married for 3 years. The couple met at a college dorm beer party. Karen reports that at the party "things became incredibly sexual between Tim and me." A week later, Karen moved into Tim's apartment. Karen became pregnant during the semester and discontinued her college studies. Tim continued classes until he was suspended due to his failing grades. The couple wed 2 months after Karen learned she was pregnant, and Tim began working at a local tool and die company. Tim reports that Karen "lost the kid" in her first trimester following an all-night drinking and drugging binge. Karen and Tim both fulfill DSM-IV-TR criteria for alcohol abuse and cocaine abuse. The couple reported significant marital discord and dissatisfaction and were administered the MSI-R to better identify the nature and extent of their marital distress. Their MSI-R Profile Form (Figure 3.1) is found below. A summary of the couple's responses is also noted below.

Both Karen and Tim responded to all required test questions on their respective MSI-R instruments. Examination of the couple's scores on both the Inconsistency and Conventionalization Scales supports further interpretation of the remaining instrument scales. Their Inconsistency Scale scores were in the moderate range and suggest that both partners attended to item content but may have mixed sentiments regarding various aspects of their relationship. Neither spouse appears to report distorted appraisals of their marriage in an unrealistic, positive manner.

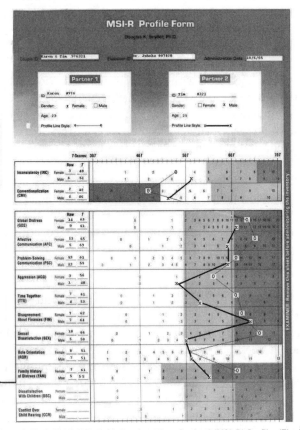

Figure 3.1 Karen & Tim's Marital Satisfaction Inventory-Revised (MSI-R) Profile. (The Marital Satisfaction Inventory-Revised is published and copyrighted by Western Psychological Services and is not to be reproduced in whole or in part without written permission of Western Psychological Services. All Rights Reserved by WPS, 12031 Wilshire Blvd., LA, CA 90025-1251.)

Clinical Scores These spouses both endorsed a high number of Global Distress Scale items. Such scores are typically indicative of extensive relationship dissatisfaction. Concomitantly, such scores often suggest long-term relationship conflicts across a wide range of relationship areas and interactions. Quite frequently spouses presenting with such scores perceive their partners as uncaring and overly critical. These scores are typical for spouses who have experienced substantial disappointments in their relationships and doubt whether or not the relationship can be sustained.

Tim's Affective Communication Scale scores suggest that he is experiencing at least moderate distress regarding the amount of affection he perceives from Karen and that Tim may feel emotionally distant, unappreciated, or misunderstood by his spouse. Karen endorsed all but one of the Affective Communication Scale scores, suggesting extensive dissatisfaction with the amount of love and affection expressed within the relationship. Given her high scores, it is likely that she may be reticent to share intimate feelings with Tim and may feel that Tim is emotionally distant, uncaring, and unsupportive.

The couple's Problem-Solving Communication Scale scores suggest that the couple experiences general ineffectiveness in resolving relationship differences and suggests that there likely exist underlying feelings of estrangement. Tim's scores suggest a protracted history of relationship difficulties characterized by frequent arguments and disagreements. Karen's scores suggest an extensive history of unresolved relationship conflicts with frequent arguing. Couples similar to Karen and Tim often have a difficult time acknowledging each other's point of view and typically have a long accumulation of unresolved differences.

Aggression Scale scores presented by the couple suggest at least a somewhat minimal level of incongruence of perception. The number of Aggression Scale endorsements made by Tim suggests that he perceives a relative absence of physical aggression or intimidation by his partner. Karen's scores suggest that she may experience perceptions of nonphysical intimidation as well as low levels of physical aggression within the marriage relationship. Such low levels of physical aggression may include screaming or yelling, directing violence against an object, or threats by Tim to hit or grab Karen.

Scores endorsed by the couple on the Time Together Scale suggest that Tim may perceive that he and Karen lack sufficient time to enjoy common interest areas together. Persons with scores similar to Karen's, however, typically note a lack of common interest or friends with their spouses and often report feelings of emotional distance from their spouses as well as significant disruption of positive interactions with their partners.

Both spouses endorse a high number of items on the Disagreement About Finances Scale. Here Karen's and Tim's scores suggest a couple that likely experiences significant disagreements or arguments about finances and likely view finances as a major source of conflict within the marriage. Couples presenting with such scores often experience their partners as selfish and irresponsible. Many times these spouses are also perceived as lacking a commitment toward resolving the couple's financial difficulties.

Sexual Dissatisfaction Scale scores are different for these partners. Tim's scores on this scale reflect only modest concern regarding his sexual relationship with Karen, dissatisfaction with the sexual relations frequency as well as nonsexual expressions of intimacy and affection. Karen endorsed a greater number of Sexual Dissatisfaction Scale items. Spouses presenting with scores such as Karen's indicate extensive sexual relationship dissatisfaction and extensive dissatisfaction with the frequency of sexual behaviors with their spouses. Often persons endorsing such a high number of scale items report their spouses as unaffectionate.

Role Orientation Scale scores endorsed by these spouses reflect somewhat similar moderate-range scores. These scores often reflect flexibility in sharing of traditional roles. Women with scores similar to Karen's are likely to espouse greater opportunities for women outside the home, although they may stop short of advocating role reversal. Men endorsing scores similar to Tim's are more likely to share decisions with their partners, although they may assert final authority in decisions perceived as important.

Tim's Family History of Distress Scale score suggests that he likely had conflicted relationships with his parents or siblings and that Tim likely experienced tensions in his family of origin and that his parents' marriage may have had difficulty resolving differences or expressing affection. Karen's Family History of Distress Scale score suggests extensive conflicts in her family of origin with feelings of alienation from parents or siblings.

Computer-Generated Interpretive Reports vs. Hand Scoring Western Psychological Services provides three computer scoring options. These include mail-in scoring, fax-in scoring, or microcomputer-based scoring. Each provides graphic individual spouse and couple profiles and a narrative Test Interpretation area. The MSI-R can also be easily hand scored, and it provides one of the clearest depictions of the individual spouses' and joint couple's graphic profile. The profile uses graduated shading intensity to help addicted couples more easily understand their individual scores on each of the scales and what such scores suggest based on individual T-scores.

Substance Abuse Subtle Screening Inventory-3

General SASSI-3 Overview The standardized substance abuse specialty instruments indicated as most frequently used by and important to addictions professionals were the Substance Abuse Subtle Screening Inventories (i.e., the SASSI-II and SASSI-Adolescent) (Juhnke et al., 2003). The current adult version is the SASSI-3. The SASSI-3 was authored by Miller and Lazowski in 1997 and is the newest version of the original SASSI, which was published in 1988 (Miller, Roberts, Brooks, & Lazowski, 1997). The SASSI was designed to "identify individuals with a high probability of having a substance dependence disorder, even if those individuals do not acknowledge substance misuse or symptoms associated with it" (Miller et al., p. 2). The SASSI-3 was developed for persons 18 years of age and older with a minimum of a 4.4-grade reading level (F. Miller, personal communication, July 3, 2001). It takes approximately 15 minutes to complete (F. Miller, personal communication, July 3, 2001) and is composed of 93 questions. The instrument can be ordered directly from the SASSI Institute (1-800-726-0526; e-mail: sassi@sassi.com).

Side 1 of the instrument contains 26 face-valid items. These items are highly transparent and directly relate to AOD use. They provide information regarding the extent to which the addicted family member acknowledges AOD use and define the extent and nature of the AOD problem. The second side of the instrument contains 67 question stems to which the addicted family member endorses either "true" or "false." Unlike side 1's obvious questions, side 2's questions are typically nontransparent and subtle. Thus, addicted family members may not identify their responses as being directly related to their AOD use.

SASSI-3 Reliability and Validity Test–retest reliability for the Face-Valid Alcohol Scale was 1.0, test–retest for the Face-Valid Other Drug Scale was 1.0, and test–retest for the various subscales ranged between .92 and .97 (F. Miller, personal communication, July 3, 2001). The alpha coefficient for the entire instrument was .93 (F. Miller, personal communication, July 3, 2001).

Miller reports that the SASSI-3 has a positive predictive power of 98.4 percent (personal communication, July 3, 2001). Positive predictive power indicates the ratio of true positives to test positives. In other words, 98.4 percent of the time, the SASSI-3 correctly identified persons who actually had an AOD problem. The instrument also demonstrates exceptionally high concurrent validity. For example, the SASSI-3 matched the addicted family members' clinical diagnoses 95 percent of the time and demonstrated concurrent validity with a number of instruments including the (a) Michigan Alcohol Screening Test (MAST), (b) Minnesota Multiphasic Personality Inventory–2, and (c) MacAndrew Scale–Revised (MAC-R) (Lazowski, Miller, Boye, and Miller, 1998).

Scales   The SASSI-3 has 10 scales. Two of these scales are face-valid scales that require addicted family members to describe the extent and nature of their AOD use. One of these scales is related to alcohol (Face-Valid Alcohol) and the other is related to all other psychoactive substances (Face-Valid Other Drug). Persons endorsing high Face-Valid Alcohol or Face-Valid Other Drug scores are likely openly acknowledging AOD misuse, consequences resulting from such use, and loss of control related to their AOD use (Miller, Roberts, Brooks, & Lazowski, 1997). High scores on either or both of these two scales may suggest the need for supervised detoxification (Miller et al., 1997).

The Symptoms Scale asks addicted family members to endorse symptoms or problems resulting from their AOD abuse (Miller et al., 1997). Those with high Symptom Scale scores are likely to be heavy users and be part of a social milieu (e.g., family, peers) where AOD use is prevalent. Thus, it may be difficult for these persons to perceive the negative aspects of remarkable AOD use. In other words, given that their friends and family likely use, they may consider abstinence abnormal rather than typical.

The Obvious Attribute Scale indicates the degree to which the addicted family member acknowledges characteristics typical of AOD-using clients (Miller et al., 1997). In other words, persons endorsing a high number of these scale items are indicating a high number of behaviors and characteristics typically indicated by persons who are substance-dependent or in recovery from their substance use. High scores suggest that addicted family members are receptive to clinical intervention (e.g., group counseling) and able to identify with the experiences of other substance-dependent persons. Conversely very low Obvious Attribute scores suggest addicted family members who are reticent to acknowledge characteristics commonly associated with substance-dependent persons or personal flaws.

The Subtle Attributes Scale denotes persons who either may be attempting to present themselves in a most favorable light by denying their substance dependence or may not recognize their behaviors as problematic or associated with AOD use (Miller et al., 1997). Persons who have endorsed a high number of Subtle Attributes Scale items, especially when the number of these items is greater than the number of their Obvious

Attributes Scale items, find it challenging to admit the degree to which AOD is prevalent and problematic within their lives.

Two other scales that directly complement one another and enrich the assessment process are the Defensiveness and Supplemental Addiction Measure Scales. As is the case with all assessment instruments, the scores and clinical profiles are used in conjunction with the counselor's clinical judgment to ensure appropriate assessment and intervention. The SASSI-3 Defensiveness Scale identifies persons who may respond defensively. However, the counselor must use her clinical judgment to determine if the defensiveness revolves around AOD abuse issues or other issues (e.g., addicted family member personality traits, immediate life circumstances). Those endorsing a high number of Defensiveness Scale items are attempting to present themselves in a favorable light and minimizing "evidence of personal problems" (Miller et al., 1997, p. 36). When the Defensiveness Scale is used in conjunction with the Supplemental Addiction Measure Scale, counselors can better assess if the addicted family member's defensiveness relates to AOD abuse or other areas. Thus, when both the Defensiveness Scale and the Supplemental Addiction Measure Scale are elevated, there is increased evidence that the addicted family member's defensiveness revolves around his or her AOD abuse. However, the counselor must weigh all evidence to make this determination and use her best clinical judgment when making the final clinical diagnosis.

Another important aspect of the Defensiveness Scale is related to low scores at or below the 15th percentile. Such low scores may be indicative of self-abasing or overly self-critical clients. These addicted family members may have problems related to low self-esteem and have "feelings of worthlessness and hopelessness, loss of energy, and suicidal ideation" (Miller et al., 1997). Given the robust correlation between feelings of hopelessness and suicide, it would be important to assess such addicted family members for suicidal ideation and to provide appropriate intervention.

The Family vs. Control Subjects (Family) Scale identifies persons who may not be AOD-abusing themselves but who likely have family members or significant others who are AOD-abusing (Miller et al., 1997). In essence these are likely family members who have agreed to participate with their AOD-abusing family members who entered addictions counseling. The Family Scale should not be used as a codependency scale. Rather, it should be used to assess whether or not the addicted family member is overly focused on others and their needs rather than on the addicted family member's personal needs. Persons scoring high on this scale may benefit from counseling goals that include establishing appropriate and healthy boundaries.

The Correctional Scale indicates the addicted family member's "relative risk for legal problems" (Miller et al., 1997, p. 39). Although the scale was not created to identify specific antisocial psychopathology, it does identify persons who, even if they discontinue their AOD abuse, may potentially require additional counseling services related to areas such as anger and impulse control. Persons scoring high on this scale may also have a checkered history of difficulties with the legal system.

The final scale is the Random Answering Pattern Scale. This scale suggests that the addicted family member's scores are likely suspect or invalid if the addicted family member has a Random Answering Pattern Scale score of 2 or more. Such scores may also be indicative of persons who are unable to read at the required level or who do not speak English as their primary language.

SASSI-3 Example: The Gonzalez Family   Marie (38) and Edwardo (40) have been married for 15 years. They have two children, Eddy (21) and Angel (19). Marie works as a cashier for a local grocery store chain; Edwardo works as a maintenance supervisor for a large city-owned housing authority. Both children live at home and attend a local university. Edwardo has a chronic history of alcohol abuse and received two driving-under-the-influence offenses within the last month. Edwardo reports "extreme embarrassment" resulting from the last offense, during which his daughter and son observed him being placed in a patrol car after failing a sobriety test. Following the second offense, he was mandated into an intensive outpatient treatment program where Edwardo and his counselor identified family addictions counseling as his preferred counseling intervention. Marie, Eddy, and Angel have agreed to attend these sessions. Part of Edwardo's assessment included a SASSI-3 (see Figure 3.2). A summary of Edwardo's SASSI-3 is provided below.

Edwardo's Random Answering Pattern (RAP) score of 0 suggests that he has not answered the SASSI-3 in a haphazard or random fashion. Additionally, a review of Edwardo's endorsements indicates that he has answered all questions.

Clinical Scores   Edwardo's high Face-Valid Alcohol and Symptoms Scales scores suggest that Edwardo acknowledges extensive alcohol use with accompanying negative consequences. Whereas Edwardo's low Face-Valid Other Drugs Scale scores indicate that he denies the use of nonalcoholic substances, this matches his self-report to the family addictions counselor and family members. The high Obvious Attributes Scale score combined with his high Subtle Attributes Scale score suggest that Edwardo may

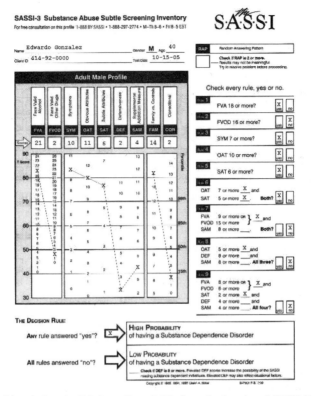

Figure 3.2 Edwardo Gonzalez Substance Abuse Subtle Screening Inventory-3 (SASSI-3). (The Substance Abuse Subtle Screening Inventory-3 is published and copyrighted by The SASSI Institute and is not to be reproduced in whole or in part without written permission of The SASSI Institute. All Rights Reserved by SASSI, 201 Camelot Lane, Springville, IN 47462.

be open to seeing similarities between himself and other substance-dependent people but that he may be unable to see the full implications of his current problematic alcohol abuse. Edwardo's low Defensiveness Scale score suggests that he may be experiencing shame, hopelessness, or other depressive symptoms. Because of Edwardo's high Face-Valid Alcohol and high Obvious Attributes Scale scores, further assessment is warranted to determine whether or not he warrants detoxification. Furthermore, in view of the fact that Edwardo's Defensiveness Scale score is below the 15th percentile, it is very likely that he tends to view himself in an overly self-critical manner. Thus, further assessment for possible consequences and correlates to such self-critical thinking such as depressed affect, suicidal ideation, and potential suicide monitoring is warranted. Edwardo's score on the Family vs. Control Subjects Scale suggests that Edwardo may tend to focus on other people's needs rather than his own. Concomitantly, persons scoring in this manner often have difficulties establishing a sense of personal power and setting limits with others.

Computer-Generated Interpretive Reports vs. Hand Scoring   Narrative reports provided by the SASSI Institute are thorough and provide the addicted family member's graphed profile. Hand scoring of the SASSI-3 is quite easy as well and can be completed within a matter of minutes. Templates are used to identify the number of potentially addicted family member positive endorsements for each scale. These raw scores are then circled and plotted on the profile sheet, and the counselor merely checks each of the nine decision rules and the Random Answering Pattern rule on the profile sheet to determine if the potentially addicted family member has a high or low probability of having a substance dependence disorder. The plotted profile can be easily shown to addicted family members and their families. Furthermore, the displayed percentile markings make it easy for addicted members and families to understand how they scored in comparison to others.

Substance Abuse Subtle Screening Inventory-Adolescent 2

General SASSI-A2 Overview   The SASSI-A2 replaces the original SASSI-A, which was first published in 1990. The SASSI-A2 underwent 4 years of research and development and was normed on 2,326 adolescents between the ages of 12 and 18 (SASSI Institute, 2001). These adolescents came from 48 treatment and correctional programs and five school systems. The SASSI-A2 was developed to "identify individuals who have a high probability of having a substance use disorder, i.e., substance abuse and substance dependence" and was developed for adolescents ages 12 to 18 years old (SASSI Institute, p. 1). The instrument is composed of 100 questions, takes approximately 15 minutes to complete, and requires a 4.4-grade reading level (F. Miller, personal communication, July 3, 2001). The SASSI-A2 can be ordered directly from the SASSI Institute (1-800-726-0526; e-mail: sassi@sassi.com).

Twenty-eight questions comprise the SASSI-A2's side 1. Similar to the SASSI-3 adult version, these items are highly transparent and ask how frequently addicted family members "have had certain experiences that are directly related to alcohol and other drug use" (SASSI Institute, 2001). Seventy-two question stems are contained on side 2. Addicted family members can endorse either "true" or "false" for each of the questions. These question stems configure into one of four areas: (a) symptom-related (AOD use acknowledgment), (b) risk (substance misuse degree of risk),

(c) attitudinal (attitudes and beliefs regarding AOD use), or (d) subtle items (nontransparent, unremarkable items that identify AOD-abusing addicted family members).

SASSI-A2 Reliability and Validity   The overall SASSI-A2 2-week test–retest coefficient yielded a .89 with six of the instrument's scales having coefficients between .85 and .92. The range for all SASSI-A2 test–retest reliability coefficients was .71 to .92. To demonstrate validity, Miller and Lazowski again used statistical analyses to demonstrate the SASSI-A2's positive predictive power.

Overall Accuracy, Sensitivity, and Specificity   Correspondence with the clinical diagnoses of substance use disorders in their studies resulted in a combined sample positive predictive power of 98 percent (Miller & Lazowski, 2001). Positive predictive power indicates the ratio of true positives to test positives. Thus, in their combined sample of 1,244 subjects, 98 percent of the time the SASSI-A2 correctly identified persons who actually had a substance use disorder (Miller & Lazowski, 2001). The instrument also demonstrated a positive predictive power of 99 percent among participants who had a Defensiveness Scale score of 7 or less (Miller & Lazowski, 2001). Finally, as previously mentioned, the SASSI-A2 has an area of questions noted as subtle items. Rules pertaining to these subtle items demonstrate robust efficacy in correctly identifying adolescents with substance use disorders. Specifically, 10 of these decision rules demonstrated 97 percent accuracy or better (Miller & Lazowski, 2001). Four of these noted 10 decision rules accurately identified adolescents presenting with substance use disorders 100 percent of the time. Additionally, Miller and Lazowski (2001) purport that the SASSI-A2 has face validity. They state, "As with all prior versions of the SASSI, the SASSI-A2 includes face valid scales that are composed of items that clearly address substance misuse" (p. 5). A brief review of the instrument certainly supports their claim.

Scales   The SASSI-A2 has 12 scales (SASSI Institute, 2001). Similar to the SASSI-3 adult version, the Face-Valid Alcohol, Face-Valid Other Drugs, Symptoms, Obvious Attributes, Subtle Attributes, and Supplemental Addiction Measures Scales are again used in the SASSI-A2. However, this time the scales were normed on an adolescent population. Interpretation of scores on these items is similar to the information provided on the SASSI-3 above.

Four new scales have been added to the SASSI-A2. One of these is the Family–Friends Risk Scale. Addicted family members scoring high on the

Family–Friends Risk Scale are "likely to be a part of a family and social system that may promote rather than prevent substance misuse" (SASSI Institute, 2001, p. 31). Because they are part of a social milieu in which substance use may be promoted or perceived as typical, it is important to ensure that these addicted family members have sufficient supervision and support by non-AOD-abusing persons.

Another new scale is the Attitudes Scale. This scale assesses the addicted family member's AOD attitudes and beliefs. Addicted family members who endorse a high number of items on this scale

> are likely to be defensive if they are confronted regarding the consequences of their substance use. If the diagnosis and severity of the substance use warrants treatment, it is likely that adolescents who have elevated . . . scores will need a great deal of structure, supervision, and support to make significant changes in their substance use. (SASSI Institute, 2001, p. 32)

The remaining two new scales are the Validity Check and Secondary Classification Scales. The Validity Check Scale is used on the SASSI-A2 instead of the SASSI-3's Random Answering Pattern Scale. This scale provides further information when the counselor's assessment of the diagnosis differs from that of the instrument. The Secondary Classification Scale helps differentiate between the two substance use disorders—substance abuse and substance dependence.

SASSI-A2 Example: The Arnold Family   Mike (42) and Polly (42) have been married for 14 years. This is a second marriage for Polly. Regina, Polly's 15-year-old daughter, moved from her biological father's home 3 years ago and now resides with Mike and Polly. According to Regina, "I was too hot for my dad to handle."

During the intake, Mike states, "Regina's personality has drastically changed in the last 6 months." Mike and Polly report that Regina has begun "hanging around the wrong crowd," and they have found drug paraphernalia, as well as marijuana, in her backpack. The family was mandated to get substance abuse counseling for Regina following her intoxication at a school dance. Regina flatly denies any alcohol or other drug (AOD) abuse: "Who me? Never." Regina's SASSI-A2 Profile Form (Figure 3.3) is found below. A summary of Regina's SASSI-A2 is also provided below.

Validation Scores   Regina answered all SASSI-A2 questions.

Clinical Scores   Regina's Face-Valid Alcohol and Face-Valid Other Drugs Scale scores are low; thus she is not endorsing AOD abuse. However,

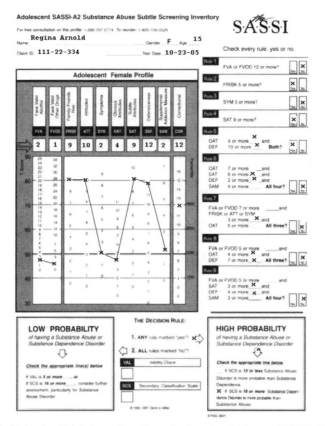

Figure 3.3 Regina Arnold Substance Abuse Screening Inventory-Adolescent 2 (SASSI-A2) Profile. (The Substance Abuse Subtle Screening Inventory-A2 is published and copyrighted by The SASSI Institute and is not to be reproduced in whole or in part without written permission of The SASSI Institute. All Rights Reserved by SASSI, 201 Camelot Lane, Springville, IN 47462.)

one should remember that these scale questions are highly transparent and one can easily determine how to present oneself in a favorable, "nonabusing" light on these scales.

Regina's Family–Friends Risk Scale score is high, suggesting that Regina may be part of a family or social system that may promote rather than prevent substance misuse. Adolescents with scores similar to Regina's on the Family–Friends Risk Scale often have difficulty recognizing and accepting AOD abuse consequences and may be particularly resistant to accepting limits imposed on them by authority figures.

The Attitudes Scale score presented by Regina is also high. Such high scores are often indicative of adolescents who are defensive if confronted regarding the consequence of their AOD abuse. Persons with such scores, depending on the specifics of their situations, often require highly structured, highly supervised, and highly supportive interventions.

Regina's Symptoms Scale score and Obvious Attributes Scale score are low. Thus, she is not divulging AOD-abusing behaviors, and she may not recognize that she has a problematic behavior history similar to those who have an AOD abuse pattern. Combining these scale scores with Regina's high Subtle Attributes Scale score, one sees a clustering of data that again supports the possibility that Regina lacks awareness and insight related to her AOD abuse. A high Subtle Attributes Scale score like Regina's suggests the possibility of problems or characteristics that often accompany AOD abuse. If one again looks at Regina's high Family–Friends Risk Scale score in conjunction with her high Subtle Attributes Scale score, one may conclude that it is probable that she tends to focus exclusively on her friend's AOD abuse while avoiding introspection of her own potential AOD abuse.

Regina's Defensiveness Scale score is high. Thus, it is likely that she has responded to the SASSI-A2 in a defensive manner. Such a high Defensiveness Scale score may suggest that her defensiveness may extend beyond AOD abuse and may reflect a larger tendency to avoid acknowledging, and possibly recognizing, personal limitations or problems.

Finally, Regina's Correctional Scale score is moderately high. One should be cautious not to over-pathologize such a score. Clients with elevated Correctional Scale scores typically have responded to the SASSI-A2 in a fashion similar to persons who have violated the law. Regina's score suggests that further assessment may be required to determine if she is at risk for potential encounters with the criminal justice system related to things like low impulse control, anger management, or a lack of parental supervision.

Computer-Generated Interpretive Reports vs. Hand Scoring Computer-generated interpretive reports and hand scoring for the SASSI-A2 are similar to those of the SASSI-3. As with the Adult Substance Use Survey, the raw scores are summed and plotted on the Adolescent Substance Use Inventory.

Therapeutic Feedback

Sincere Accomplishment Reviews and Compliments

Most people remember taking written examinations and returning the following class period to learn one's fate. Often the major concerns did not revolve around learning. Nearly everyone studied, attended lectures—at least to some degree—and learned something. Rather, the key anxiety-provoking components frequently revolved around the professor's interpretations of one's written responses, concerns regarding course failure, and, ultimately, rejection by the institution and significant others. Addicted families have similar concerns and often have been maligned because of their addiction. Thus, family members are often hypersensitive to negative assessments.

The vast majority of persons living within addicted families present themselves in a fairly accurate light. However, their concerns typically revolve around the interpretation of their assessment responses, failure to achieve their goal (e.g., obtaining help, getting their children back from Child Protective Services), and rejection by the counselor. Many fear they will be identified as "crazy" or "inferior." Thus, the first task after analyzing the assessment data is to help family members feel at ease and to help dispel potential fears. One way of engendering comfort is to review the addicted members' and families' accomplishments via the assessment process and compliment all members on their dedication to the addicted members.

For example, in the case of Maria, the counselor might begin by stating the following:

Counselor: "You and your family have accomplished much today. You and your family have told me about your experiences with alcohol and the problems resulting from those experiences. These are major accomplishments, Maria. It truly is a privilege to work with someone so devoted to making her life better and with a family dedicated to helping their wife and mother."

Maria: "I don't think it was anything. I've got a long way to go."

Counselor: "But the truth is you have done some very important things and you're making progress. A lot of people might have given up or refused to participate so fully. Not you, Maria—you and your family fully participated and are consciously choosing to commit to getting better."

In this exchange, we see that the counselor reviews the work that the addicted member and her family have accomplished and gives a clear compliment. Maria and her family have invested themselves in the assessment process and have successfully utilized the assessment experiences. Maria at first belittles her behaviors and dismisses the compliment. Instead of accepting her self-abasing statement, the counselor responds by indicating that others might have given up but that Maria and her family are consciously choosing to make progress. Thus, the counselor reminds Maria and her family of Maria's attained progress and her active abstinence commitment. Concomitantly, the counselor demonstrates that Maria and her family will be confronted should they choose to inappropriately belittle noteworthy accomplishments.

Conversely, it would be inadvisable to give hollow compliments or false statements. For example, if the addicted family member had refused to participate, a compliment like the one above would be at best negatively perceived. The addicted member and family would likely feel as though the counselor were attempting to manipulate her or, worse yet, that Maria had fooled the counselor. Either perception could negatively impact the counseling relationship.

In most situations the addicted family member has at least minimally participated in the experience. Thus the counselor should be able to positively reframe at least some portion of the member's behaviors into a compliment. Here, for example, the counselor might say the following:

Counselor: "Becky, based on what you've stated, I know this family session has been challenging for both you and your family. You've indicated on a number of occasions that you didn't want to be here."

Becky: "Yeah, this whole thing stinks. My mom and dad made me come."

Counselor: "Yes, but the point is that you did come with your family and you participated. You didn't give up, Becky."

Becky: "Big deal . . ."

Counselor: "It is a big deal. You've come today and you've worked with your parents and sister on helping me understand your alcohol and cocaine use. This suggests to me that you really want things to get better."

Again, the goal is not to argue with an addicted family member or to give an inappropriate compliment. Rather, the intent is to merely review what the addicted member and family have done and provide a sincere compliment.

If the addicted family member's standardized instrument responses have been highly suspect or invalid due to the number of blank responses and the individual has refused to either retake the instrument or change responses accordingly (e.g., complete the previously unanswered questions), the counselor can return to the unanswered questions and ask about specific questions to determine if an underlying theme exists.

Counselor: "Toni, although you originally agreed to take the SASSI-3 and you answered some of the questions, I am unable to provide feedback until you complete all the items that remain unanswered. Let's complete those unanswered questions now, so I can provide the best possible feedback in helping you."

Toni: "Let's not. I'm tired of answering test questions."

Counselor: "It is a long and tiring process. However, you have already taken the time to answer most of the questions. Help me help you by just looking at the questions that you didn't answer before and let's see how many of those you can respond to right now."

Toni: "No. I'm done reading the questions and filling in circles."

Counselor: "Reading the questions and filling in circles is a long and tedious process. How about if I just read the questions? Certainly you can tell me your answers?"

Toni: "I'm tired of reading the test questions and responding."

Counselor: "OK, instead, then, let's just take a few moments to discuss some of the questions that you did not respond to. I noticed that one of the questions to which you didn't respond asked whether you have ever consumed more alcohol than you originally intended."

Toni: "Yes, so what?"

Counselor: "Would you say that question is mostly true or mostly false?"

Toni: "I guess that is mostly true."

Counselor: "Thank you for your response, Toni. Let's go on to the next question."

This verbal interchange demonstrates two important question review techniques. First, the counselor continues to encourage the addicted member to respond to the unanswered questions. For example, the counselor begins by indicating that most of the questions have already been answered. This implies that the addicted family member has completed the majority of the work and that the major energy output is over. Moreover, it implies that she can complete the task with little effort—especially when compared to the energy already invested. Additionally, an invitation to complete the questions was made. Often such an invitation is sufficient, and family members will complete previously unanswered questions without further haggling.

Furthermore, when the family member indicates that she is tired of reading and answering the test questions, she is neither threatened by the counselor (e.g., "If you don't finish the test, I won't be able to score it and that will look bad for you") nor belittled (e.g., "Can't you answer a meager 100 questions?"). Instead, the counselor agrees that the process is tedious and offers a compromise. The counselor will ask the questions and the family member can verbally respond. Finally, the addicted member agrees to participate. Most of the time, such compromises can quickly and easily occur. Whatever you do, just continually keep throwing options out and look for a win-win opportunity for the addicted family member and the family.

When Perceptions Don't Match

Sometimes the perceptions of addicted family members, nonaddicted family members, and the family addiction counselor do not match. For example, the person identified by the family system as being addicted or abusing substances flatly denies AOD abuse. Here, the use of specialty addictions testing is critical for addressing both the addicted member and the family in a helpful way. The next chapter describes how to effectively utilize motivational interviewing to help the addicted family member and family better understand the presenting concerns and the impact of these concerns on the entire family system. For now, let's just say that when the specialty testing suggests AOD abuse, the objective is not to batter the addicted family member or family with scores and results. At this point, it is better to tuck the information away and return to the information at a later time. This increases the probability that the addicted family member will return with the family to address his or her AOD use.

Summary

This chapter has described what a clinical family addictions assessment interview is, potential benefits of such an assessment, and how to facilitate the assessment. Readers have further learned about each of the clinical family addictions assessment interview's six clinical phases and how each phase relates to addicted family systems. Additionally, readers have learned about the five primary drug detection tests that can be utilized by family addictions counselors. Finally, the chapter has described three specialty assessment instruments perceived by the authors as fundamental to the family addictions assessment process. These include the Marital

Satisfaction Inventory-Revised (MSI-R), the Substance Abuse Subtle Screening Inventory-3 (SASSI-3), and the Substance Abuse Subtle Screening Inventory-Adolescent 2 (SASSI-A2).

Skill Builder

Question 1

Name and describe the six clinical family addiction assessment phases.

_____   _____

                        _____

                        _____

_____   _____

                        _____

                        _____

_____   _____

                        _____

                        _____

_____   _____

                        _____

                        _____

_____   _____

                        _____

                        _____

_____   _____

                        _____

                        _____

Question 2

Identify the five major drug detection tests reported in the book and indicate their corresponding window of use history.

_____   _____

_____   _____

_____   _____

_____   _____

_____   _____

_____   _____

Question 3

Please select the best answer regarding the following MSI-R scores:

A. This score would reflect extensive relationship dissatisfaction and suggest that conflicts are likely to be of long duration and to be generalized across diverse areas of the couple's interactions.
  (1) A high Global Distress Scale score
  (2) A low Global Distress Scale score
  (3) A low Time Together Scale score
  (4) A high Time Together Scale score

B. This score would reflect a lack of common interests or friends with one's partner, feelings of emotional distance from one's partner, and absence of behavioral intimacy.
  (1) A high Global Distress Scale score
  (2) A low Global Distress Scale score
  (3) A low Time Together Scale score
  (4) A high Time Together Scale score

C. This score would reflect extensive conflict in the partners' interactions regarding children and suggests that children are likely viewed as major stressors in the couple's relationship. Additionally, there will likely be negative sentiment toward the partner specific to child-rearing responsibilities.
  (1) A high Dissatisfaction with Children Scale score
  (2) A low Dissatisfaction with Children Scale score
  (3) A high Conflict over Child Rearing Scale score
  (4) A low Conflict over Child Rearing Scale score

Question 4

Please select the best answer regarding the following SASSI-3 scores:

A. This score would reflect someone presenting himself or herself in a favorable light.
   (1) A high Obvious Attributes Scale score
   (2) A high Subtle Attributes Scale score
   (3) A high Defensiveness Scale score
   (4) A high Supplemental Addiction Measure Scale score

B. This score would reflect that a person may focus on other persons' needs.
   (1) A high Obvious Attributes Scale score
   (2) A high Family vs. Control Subject Scale score
   (3) A low Obvious Attributes Scale score
   (4) A high Correctional Scale score

C. This score would reflect that a person tends to relate to and identify with substance-dependent people, including those in recovery.
   (1) A high Obvious Attributes Scale score
   (2) A high Family vs. Control Subject Scale score
   (3) A low Obvious Attributes Scale score
   (4) A high Correctional Scale score

Question 5

Please select the best answer regarding the following SASSI-A2 scores:

A. This score tends to reflect adolescents who are part of a family and social system that may promote rather than prevent substance misuse.
   (1) A high Family–Friends Risk Scale score
   (2) A low Family–Friends Risk Scale score
   (3) A high Attitudes Scale score
   (4) A high Symptoms Scale score

B. This score would reflect a lack of awareness and insight and suggests the possibility of problems or characteristics often accompanying substance misuse.
   (1) A high Family–Friends Risk Scale score
   (2) A low Family–Friends Risk Scale score
   (3) A high Attitudes Scale score
   (4) A high Subtle Attributes Scale score

C. This score would reflect the self-endorsement of alcohol use and indicate the extent of usage that clients are willing to acknowledge.
   (1) A high Family–Friends Risk Scale score
   (2) A high Face-Valid Alcohol Scale score
   (3) A high Attitudes Scale score
   (4) A high Subtle Attributes Scale score

Skill Builder Responses

Question 1 Response

Six Clinical Family Addiction Assessment Phases

Identification Phase	Identify which family members should be present for the assessment.
Introduction Phase	Reduce family members' anxieties, describe the family assessment process, describe confidentiality limits, and establish rules.
Strengths Assessment Phase	Describe healthy ways for addicted members to meet their needs, identify how family members and counselor can help the addicted member stay substance-free, and encourage continuing positive behaviors among family members.
Drinking and Drugging History Phase	Gain an understanding of the addicted family member's addiction history.
Reestablishing Phase	Ensure that sufficient information has been obtained to provide treatment, teach addicted family members how to ask for help, and reestablish commitment among family members.
Conclusion Phase	Provide a sense of closure and recap the session's highlights.

Question 2 Response

Urine (immunoassay)	6 hours to 4 days
Hair (radioimmunoassay)	8 to 90 days
Blood	Immediate
Saliva	Recent
Breathalyzer	Immediate

Question 3 Response

A. A high Global Distress Scale score would reflect extensive relationship dissatisfaction and suggest that conflicts are likely to be of long duration and to be generalized across diverse areas of the couple's interactions. Thus, the answer is:

(1) A high Global Distress Scale score

B. A high Time Together Scale score would suggest a lack of common interests or friends with one's partner, feelings of emotional distance from one's partner, and absence of behavioral intimacy. Thus, the answer is:

(4) A High Time Together Scale score

C. A high Conflict Over Child Rearing Scale score would reflect extensive conflict in the partners' interactions regarding children and suggests that children are likely viewed as major stressors in the couple's relationship. Additionally, there will likely be negative sentiment toward the partner specific to child-rearing responsibilities. Thus, the answer is:

(3) A High Conflict over Child Rearing Scale score

Question 4 Response

A. A high Defensiveness Scale score would reflect someone attempting to present himself or herself in a positive light. Thus, the answer is:
(3) A high Defensiveness Scale score

B. A high Family vs. Control Subject Scale score would suggest that the person tends to focus on other persons' needs rather than his or her own needs. Thus, the answer is:
(2) A high Family vs. Control Subject Scale score

C. A high Obvious Attributes Scale score suggests that one is able to relate to and identify with substance-dependent people, including those in recovery. Thus, the answer is:
(1) A high Obvious Attributes Scale score

Question 5 Response

A. A high Family–Friends Risk Scale score reflects adolescents who are part of a family and social system that may promote rather than prevent substance misuse. Thus, the answer is:
(1) A high Family–Friends Risk Scale score

B. A high Subtle Attributes Scale score reflects a lack of awareness and insight and suggests the possibility of problems or characteristics often accompanying substance misuse. Thus, the answer is:
(4) A high Subtle Attributes Scale score

C. A high Face-Valid Alcohol Scale score reflects the self-endorsement of alcohol use and indicates the extent of alcohol usage that clients are willing to acknowledge. Thus, the answer is:
(2) A high Face-Valid Alcohol Scale score

References

Bubenzer, D. L., Zimpfer, D. G., & Mahrle, C. L. (1990). Standardized individual appraisal in agency and private practice. *Journal of Mental Health Counseling, 12*, 51–66.

Cade, B., & O'Hanlon, W. H. (1993). *A brief guide to brief therapy.* New York: Brunner/Mazel.

Coll, K. M., Juhnke, G. A., Thobro, P., & Hass, R. (2003). A preliminary study using the Substance Abuse Subtle Screening Inventory-Adolescent Form as an outcome measure with adolescent offenders. *Journal of Addictions & Offender Counseling, 24*, 11–22.

Donovan, D. M. (1992). The assessment process in addictive behaviors. *The Behavior Therapist, 15*, 18–20.

Doweiko, H. E. (1996). *Concepts of chemical dependency* (3rd ed.). Pacific Grove, CA: Books/Cole.

Evans, W. N. (1988). Assessment and diagnosis of the substance use disorders (SUDSs). *Journal of Counseling and Development, 76*, 325–333.

Jordan, R. (1988). Hair analysis: A new turn in drug testing. *Risk Management*, 68–69.

Juhnke, G. A. (2000). *Addressing school violence: Practical strategies & interventions*. Austin, TX: Pro-Ed.

Juhnke, G. A., & Hovestadt, A. J. (1995). Using the SAD PERSONS Scale to promote supervisee suicide assessment knowledge. *The Clinical Supervisor, 13*, 31–40.

Juhnke, G. A., Vacc, N. A., Curtis, R. C., Coll, K. M., & Paredes, D. M. (2003). Assessment instruments used by addictions counselors. *Journal of Addictions & Offender Counseling, 23*, 66–72.

Lazowski, L. E., Miller, F. G., Boye, M. W., & Miller, G. A. (1998). Efficacy of the Substance Abuse Subtle Screening Inventory–3 (SASSI-3) in identifying substance dependence disorders in clinical settings. *Journal of Personality Assessment, 71*, 114–128.

Lewis, J. A., Dana, R. O., & Blevins, G. A. (1988). *Substance abuse counseling: An individualized approach*. Pacific Grove, CA: Brooks/Cole.

Miller, F. G., Roberts, J., Brooks, M. K., & Lazowski, L. E. (1997). *SASSI-3 user's guide: A quick reference for administration and scoring*. Bloomington, IN: Baugh Enterprises, Inc.

Miller, F. G., & Lazowski, L. E. (2001). *The Adolescent SASSI-A2 Manual: Identifying substance use disorders*. Springhill, IN: SASSI Institute.

Minnesota Poison Control. (2001). Retrieved from http://www.mpoison.org/drug_testing_kit.htm

Nelson, M. L., & Neufeldt, S. A. (1996). Building on an empirical foundation: Strategies to enhance good practice. *Journal of Counseling and Development, 74*, 6009–6015 .

O'Hanlon, W. H., & Weiner-Davis, M. (1989). *In search of solutions: A new direction in psychotherapy*. New York: Norton.

Rinn, R. C. (1978). Children with behavior disorders. In Hersen & A. Bellack (Eds.), *Behavior therapy in the psychiatric setting*. Baltimore, MD: Williams & Wilkins.

Rogers, J. R. (1992). [Current Trends] Suicide and alcohol: Conceptualizing the relationship from a cognitive-social paradigm. *Journal of Counseling and Development, 70*, 540–543.

SASSI Institute. (2001). *The Adolescent SASSI-A2 user's guide: A quick reference for administration & scoring*. Springville, IN: Author.

Snyder, D. K. (1997). *Marital Satisfaction Inventory, Revised (MSI-R): Manual* (2nd ed.). Western Psychological Services. Los Angeles, CA: Author.

Vacc, N. A. (1982). A conceptual framework for continuous assessment of clients. *Measurement and Evaluation in Guidance, 15*, 40–48.

Vacc, N. A., & Juhnke, G. A. (1997). The use of structured clinical interviews for assessment in counseling. *Journal of Counseling and Development, 75,* 470–480.

Vacc, N. A., Juhnke, G. A., & Nilsen, K. A. (2001). Community mental health services providers' codes of ethics and the Standards for Educational and Psychological Testing. *Journal of Counseling and Development, 79,* 217–224.

Watkins, C. E., Jr., Campbell, V. L., & McGregor, P. (1988). Counseling psychologists' uses of and opinions about psychological tests: A contemporary perspective. *Counseling Psychologist, 16,* 476–486.

The Sequential Family Addictions Counseling Model

Chapter 4 Learning Objectives

After reading this chapter, you should be able to:

- Describe common family counseling terms and constructs
- Describe the Sequential Family Addictions Counseling Model
- Understand how each of the model's stages seamlessly "sequences" into the next

Introduction

Every counselor knows it. There is no one best way to counsel addicted families. Each family presents with unique needs, characteristics, desires, and external and internal stressors that impact treatment. Effective family addictions counselors further understand that if treatment is to be effective, religious, cultural, ethnic, and gender domains must be adequately investigated and respectfully addressed within ways acceptable to individual family members and the family system itself.

Our experiences have been that many entry-level family counselors adopt a single counseling theory that matches their personalities or fits their perceptions of what counseling should be. Then, despite the specific idiosyncratic needs of the individual addicted family system and its particular addicted members, entry-level counselors indiscriminately apply their preselected theory to each addicted family. This is akin to a physician prescribing the same medication to each patient despite differing needs. As one can imagine, the results of utilizing a single, blanket theory for every client family even before understanding the system's dynamics or needs can be disastrous for counselors and families alike.

An example of such disastrous outcomes occurred in the early 1990s while the senior author was directing a counseling program's doctoral research and training clinic and conducting "supervision of supervision." This process is where an advanced supervisor provides clinical supervision to a less experienced supervisor-in-training, who in turn is providing supervision to a counselor. In this case the supervisor-in-training was a doctoral student supervising a counselor treating a court-referred family. The family struggled with multiple members' long-term addictions and addictions-related dysfunction. The counselor facilitating treatment was enamored with Behavioral Family Therapy. Needless to say, the family was not. The harder the counselor attempted to force behavioral and contingency contracts upon the system's individual members, the harder the system defended itself. In the end, the system won. The family refused to return to counseling, the novice counselor questioned her future as a counselor, and the budding clinical supervisor felt as though he had failed both supervisee and family. For the senior author, the painful supervisory experience incited changes in how he trained supervisors and counselors. Specifically, he began requiring all of his clinical supervisees and advanced addictions and family counseling students to become proficient in the use of a sequential family addictions model that guaranteed that the theories employed clearly matched the presenting family's immediate and long-term needs.

For many experienced counselors, the need for such a sequential family addictions model exists as well. Here, the situation is typically somewhat different. We have found that, for the most part, more experienced family counselors craft their own family addictions treatment models. Often these models focus on one or at most two basic family theories such as Structural-Strategic Family Therapy or Cognitive-Behavioral Family Therapy. These family theories have proven records and are used either separately or in conjunction depending on the counselor's preferences and perceptions of family needs. When this type of treatment works, it works well. However, when treatment is ineffective, some experienced counselors respond by utilizing more of the same intervention techniques. Of course, doing more of the same within treatment is for clients similar to customers complaining about a restaurant's distasteful entrée. If the customer originally found the entrée distasteful, clearing the plate and serving a second larger serving of the same entrée makes little sense.

We have further found that often when treatment is ineffective many experienced family counselors have difficulty articulating their intended treatment progression or describing why they are utilizing newly introduced intervention techniques. In other words, their therapeutic map fails to provide adequate directions for the detour that they have encountered. Then, irresponsibly, they continue speeding down the same interstate without seeking input from those who have been there before.

Therefore, the challenge facing both entry-level and experienced family addictions counselors is how to effectively and efficiently engender healthy individual and family change via a seamless treatment model that ensures goal continuity. Furthermore, this sequential model must to be constructed in such a way that counselors begin treatment with the most cost- and time-effective interventions. Only when these initial interventions prove powerless to the system or the system's needs should the counselor progress to the next treatment stage—a somewhat more costly and time-consuming intervention that will build on the previously implemented counseling stages and congruent counseling techniques.

Why Family Counseling?

Families have power. They can promote change and support new nonabusing, nonaddictive behaviors, or they can utterly sabotage success at every turn. Counselors can either employ families as allies or observe them erode their clients' forward progress. The trick is getting families to quickly commit to addicted clients and the client's recovery.

Families have a unique influence on all persons. In particular, families have a very impactful influence on abusing and addicted persons. Specifically, we have found that many clients are ushered into addictions counseling via their families. Addicted persons often do not perceive their addictive behaviors as severe enough to warrant treatment. Family members do. An ultimatum frequently results: Get addictions counseling now or leave the family. Even when addicted persons finally realize that their addictive behaviors are problematic enough to warrant treatment, they often either do not know how to access affordable treatment or are unable to get themselves into treatment due to the severity of their addiction symptoms. Many times families become the resource that identifies treatment options and even transports clients into treatment.

One of the most remarkable examples of family support experienced by the senior author occurred in 1986 when more than 12 extended family members arrived at his office. In fact there were more family members present than waiting room chairs. Family members who could not find chairs sat on the floor. Others leaned against waiting room walls. Some waited in the hallway and two even waited with the client in a van located in the parking lot. They told a story about an adult cousin who had arrived in the early morning hours approximately 2 months earlier. He had traveled nearly 1,300 miles from a western state to come back to family. According to family members, the cousin was addicted and needed help.

Family members had banned together and attempted everything they knew to help this cousin beat his multiple addictions. They had monitored his activities and required him to attend daily NA meetings. When that didn't do the trick, they required him to attend Sunday morning and evening worship services. Then they required Wednesday evening church services. Finally, they held "Bible study" with him two nights a week. When these attempts proved futile, they made an appointment with the senior author and now brought their cousin to counseling. Once they told their story, the senior author agreed to meet their cousin. Family members escorted him from the waiting room to the counseling office. When the senior author spoke with him individually, he reported that his initial reason for coming back to his hometown was to "live off" his extended family. However, he reportedly never expected the love and compassion demonstrated toward him.

Although originally frustrated when confronted by family members about his addictions, he finally agreed to counseling when family used a tough-love approach and informed him that he would be abandoned if he continued using. Then family members began to monitor him and drove him to daily NA meetings. According to him, he realized he could not continue to use when he overheard two elementary school–age cousins initiate a prayer vigil for him. What a powerful experience for this client. Even when he did not have the strength to secure addictions counseling for himself, his family did. More importantly, their unified behaviors and active interventions helped this client realize both his need for counseling and the support his family would offer should he commit himself to an addiction-free life.

Existing literature clearly supports the authors' clinical experiences as well. Numerous seminal studies support the efficacy of different types of family therapy with addicted clients (Bennun, 1988; Bukstein, 2000; Cadogan, 1973; Catalano, Gainey, Fleming, Haggerty, & Johnson, 1999; Cunningham & Henggeler, 1999; Diamond, Serranon, Dickey, & Sonis,

1996; Friedman, Terras, & Kreisher, 1995; Liddle & Dakof, 1995, McCrady & Epstein, 1996; McCrady, Paolino, Longabaugh, & Rossi, 1979; O'Farrell & Fals-Stewart, 2000; Shapiro, 1999; Stanton & Shadish, 1997; Walitzer, 1999; Zweben, Pearlman, & Li, 1988). As a matter of fact, as early as 1974 the U.S. National Institute on Alcohol Abuse and Alcoholism (NIAAA) identified family therapy as "one of the most outstanding current advances in the area of psychotherapy of alcoholism" (Keller, 1974, p. 161). We believe Walitzer (1999, p. 147) best summarized the need for including family therapy when treating addicted persons. Specifically Walitzer purported that overall family functioning can either subtly maintain addictions or create "an environment conducive to abstinence" (p. 147).

What Is Family Counseling?

Kaufman and Yoshioka (2004, p. xvi) state, "Family therapy is a collection of therapeutic approaches that share a belief in the effectiveness of family-level assessment and interventions." In other words, there is no one family therapy. Instead family therapy is composed of many differing theories and models that share a common belief. This belief is that the most effect counseling occurs when one treats the family system. A few of the most widely recognized family therapies include Psychodynamic, Multidimensional, Brief-Strategic, Structural, and Behavioral Family Therapies. Each may have somewhat differing views regarding the specific reasons for abusing or addictive behaviors.

Additionally, there may exist some incongruence among the treatment techniques used by the different family theories. A broad example of such technique incongruence may be whether or not the family therapy model employed utilizes interventions designed to engender change via insight alone or via techniques designed to promote behavioral change without the need for insight. Thus, instead of a single family counseling paradigm, family counseling is typically composed of a number of commonly shared foundational points related to the family system.

Specifically, family theory focuses on family relationships and holistically views the family system as a whole that is greater and more powerful than its individual members. These views are especially important to addicted persons and suggest that the system itself has the potential to create change that is more powerful and lasting than change undertaken by a single addicted family member alone. Furthermore, this systems perspective suggests that addictions cannot be adequately addressed without understanding both the relationship interactions within the family system and the addicted family member's life and interactions within that system. Therefore, family counseling theories do not typically endorse intrapsychic psychopathology (e.g., what is flawed or wrong within the person) as the underlying reason for addictive behaviors. Instead most family addictions counselors focus on interpersonal or relational dysfunction occurring within the family. Hence, family addictions counselors seek to determine what the family system is doing that promotes or continues the individual member's addiction and potential benefits to the family system to have an addicted member.

Change, according to family therapy, revolves around a central theme of modifying behaviors, roles, rules, and relationships within the family system to decrease or eliminate addiction and addictive behaviors. According to Kaufman and Yoshioka (2004), two main purposes of family counseling with addicted persons include using the family's strengths and resources to develop and find ways to effectively function without abuse or addiction and to reduce the negative effects of abuse or addiction on both the client and the family.

Common Family Therapy Terms and Constructs

Before embarking on a description of the Sequential Family Addictions Counseling Model, there exist a number of common terms and constructs utilized within family therapy that warrant review. It is important to note that not all family theories espouse each of these terms or constructs. However, knowledge of these terms and constructs will be beneficial in understanding the underlying foundation of the Sequential Family Addictions Counseling Model. Therefore a succinct list of common terms and constructs is presented below.

Equifinality

Equifinality is a crucial construct within many family theories. One of the major tenets of this construct suggests that families have the opportunity and potential to obtain their ultimate goals in different ways. Some ways of obtaining the family system's ultimate goals may be more time-, energy-, and cost-efficient than others. However, even if the family system chooses to use less efficient means to secure their ultimate treatment goals, less direct and less efficient ways can be utilized to accomplish this feat.

So, what does this mean? Well, if your ultimate goal was to fly from your hometown to Chicago, Illinois, you might simply hop a nonstop flight that would take you directly to Chicago. Equifinality, or "equal finality," which implies the same end point via different means, suggests that you could ultimately arrive in Chicago by less direct or less efficient means. Therefore, instead of the direct and very efficient flight previously mentioned, you could instead fly from your hometown to Miami, Florida, and then hop a direct flight to Chicago. Or, for a more convoluted and energy-draining trip, you could fly to Paris, France, on your way to Chicago. However, instead of boarding a direct flight from Paris to Chicago, you could instead choose to fly to Los Angeles. Once in Los Angeles you could visit Disneyland in Anaheim and then drive to New York City by way of Canada. Finally, you could board a boat in New York City and proceed up the Atlantic Coast through the Great Lakes and arrive at your ultimate destination—Chicago. No matter the route chosen or the travel methods used, the ultimate Chicago destination is achieved. Hence, "equal finality" or equifinality has occurred. Of course, the first method of simply hopping a direct, nonstop flight is the most time- and energy-efficient method.

Similar to the above example, some addicted families immediately initiate their pathway to success with little wasted energy or direction. Others, however, become encumbered with what can seem like minutia to the counselor but is of extreme importance to the family. No matter the path and methods taken, effective family addictions counselors keep their families focused on the final goal—whatever that looks like for them.

Equifinality is crucial to the Sequential Family Addictions Counseling Model. It reminds family addictions counselors that addicted persons and their families can use multiple counseling means to reach their treatment goals. For example, some families respond well to Solution-Focused Family Therapy, while others do not. Still others seem to respond more quickly to Cognitive-Behavioral Therapy. It does not matter. The point to remember is that you merely begin with the most time- and energy-effective interventions. If these do not work, move in an intentional manner to the next efficient treatment strategy in the model.

Homeostasis

Another key family therapy construct is homeostasis (Jackson, 1957). This construct is all about balance within the family system. Behavioral patterns within the family system create a balance or homeostasis within the system. Similar to a rapidly spinning plate precariously balanced atop a stick by a circus clown, a family system experiencing accepted behaviors, roles, and rules has homeostasis. However, anything that threatens this homeostasis will result in the plate wildly wobbling in an effort to rebalance itself and continue the system's homeostasis.

Addicted families create family patterns that promote homeostasis via ineffective and dysfunctional means. The senior author worked with one such addicted and dysfunctional family where the family adopted dysfunctional roles for the children and an addicted, highly dependent, single-parent father. Here, the addicted father parentified the oldest daughter at an early age and gave her the role of primary caregiver to father and her biological siblings. The children encouraged father to continue a dependent, childlike role within the family, even to a point where the children, not the father, managed the family's basic needs related to paying bills, washing clothes, and purchasing groceries. When they entered family counseling, all three children were entering adolescence and dad's attempts to end his drinking and drugging were met with significant resistance by the children.

The eldest daughter, who had been placed in the parentified role, feared that the family system would "disintegrate" if she allowed father to become sober. In session she stated that father's newly experienced sobriety would end her familiar "mother role" and destroy the family system that she had established. She reported little intent to relinquish the powerful family system role she had become accustomed to and rewarded for.

Further, she and her siblings acknowledged a concern that the family system would suffer irreparable harm if father again attempted sobriety and failed once more. They reported that on the previous half dozen occasions when father had become sober and then relapsed, father had become acutely depressed and suicidal. These adolescents told horrific accounts of living with a depressed, nonfunctioning, and suicidal father that ultimately ended after relative long-term foster care placements.

At the same time, the younger adolescent siblings enjoyed the freedom of having an addicted father. There were relatively few rules imposed by the eldest sibling, so the younger adolescents could stay out late with peers and had few responsibilities at home. These younger adolescent siblings feared father's potential sobriety, because the sobriety would eventually end their freedom.

When father initiated his recovery, the dysfunctional homeostasis of the family system was disrupted. Instead of embracing and supporting father's recovery, the adolescents acted out by arguing with father, stealing, and running away from home. One of the adolescents even replaced father's favorite alcohol in an attempt to sabotage father's sobriety.

Although these adolescent behaviors initially seem irrational and irresponsible, they actually were attempts to restore the familiar dysfunctional homeostasis. Similar to novice sailors who panic and quickly scramble to the high side of a sailboat when the sails fill with air, persons in a family system sensing homeostasis jeopardy panic and scramble to restore familiar family balance. Family addictions counselors realize that the void left from removing dysfunctional family dynamics needs to be quickly replaced with new, healthy patterns that restore or create healthy family homeostasis.

Family Roles

Family roles are another construct important to the understanding of addicted families. Familiar and predictable family roles are the bedrock to the homeostasis described above. Most people are familiar with typical family roles such as father, mother, daughter, grandfather, and great-grandmother. Homeostasis occurs when family members understand their various familiar roles and follow the roles imposed by the system. Remember this could be functional homeostasis if the roles are healthy and allow for flexibility to meet the needs of maturing family members, or it could be dysfunctional homeostasis if roles are inflexible and hinder opportunities for healthy change.

Family roles are greatly influenced by ethnic, religious, gender, economic, and sociocultural factors. South Texas, for example, is a place where many first-generation Mexican American families are resolutely committed to the Catholic faith (A. Valadez, personal communication, August 25, 2005). Concomitantly, these South Texas Mexican American families tend to have a patriarchal power structure where older males have greater power and privilege than younger family members or females. Therefore, homeostasis could potentially be threatened should younger females within the family system earn greater incomes than older males. In other words, threats to established family roles can potentially impact familiar homeostasis, and the family may respond by attempting to oppose even healthy change.

A different type of role that can significantly impact and alter an addicted family's homeostasis and structure was proposed in the early 1980s. Wegscheider (1981) identified six general roles commonly assumed by members within addicted families. Each role serves as a defense against threats from the toxic addicted family environment. Identification and adoption into these roles by individual family members and encouragement for individual family members to continue in these assigned roles by the family system itself promote the dysfunctional homeostasis discussed earlier. These roles are described below:

The Chief Enabler   This person frequently is the spouse or partner of the primary addicted person within the family system. However, the Chief Enabler can also be a parent who protects an addicted child from full responsibility and sanctions her drinking and drugging behaviors. This person often feels afraid to confront the addicted or abusing person(s) within the family system and feels hurt by the addicted person's behaviors and by the system's unwillingness to "forgive and forget" transactions by the addict. The Chief Enabler also commonly acknowledges feelings of guilt for not being able to stop the addicted person from using.

The Family Hero   Often, but not always, the Family Hero is the oldest child. Her identity is founded upon demonstrations of achievement and success. Family members may use the terms "super sibling," "golden-haired child," "the perfect one," "overachiever," or "perfect daughter/son" to describe this person. Those outside the family system often are amazed by the Family Hero's remarkable accomplishments—especially since she comes from an addicted family. The Family Hero frequently uses such achievements to cover or hide feelings of inadequacy, loneliness, and pain. Unfortunately for the Family Hero, her accomplishments rarely if ever provide true feelings of accomplishment or success. In addition, many Family Heroes feel that their accomplishments pale in comparison to others' successes.

The Family Mascot   The Family Mascot typically is the youngest child within the system. The Mascot is a master at distracting family members and the system away from painful or threatening subjects. She typically is quite fun to be around and has a lightning quick sense of humor that provides welcome relief to family members. Deep within their fun-loving presentation, Mascots hide their need to rescue family members from addictions' pain and trauma. Often they feel quite insecure and frightened and use their humor as a means to address these feelings.

The Dependent   The Dependent family member has the ability to present in a couple of ways. Initially, this person may present as rather charming and able. However, upon more frequent interaction, her anger, perfectionism, and sometimes grandiose sense of being will become strikingly apparent. Many Dependent family members have underlying feelings of hurt, shame, and guilt.

The Scapegoat   The Scapegoat, often refereed to as the black sheep by family members within the system, is frequently the person who is initially the identified patient. She often will present with drinking or drugging problems, school-related behavioral problems, or legal problems. Scapegoats have an uncanny ability to ensure that the addiction or dysfunction within an addicted family system is never fully addressed. Specifically, when topics close to family addiction or dysfunction arise, Scapegoats grab the family's focus via acting out behaviors. Like others within addicted systems, they frequently report feelings of loneliness, anger, rejection, and hurt.

The Lost Child   The Lost Child typically focuses on being a "nonproblem" player within the family system. She often is unseen and unheard. Lost among the Family Hero's awards and recognized accomplishments, the Mascot's attention-seeking behaviors and jokes, and the Scapegoat's trouble with school and the police, the Lost Child frequently withdraws into the camouflaged recesses of the family system or escapes into the bland, unremarkable domains outside the family. Feelings of inadequacy, loneliness, and abandonment mark the Lost Child.

Family Boundaries

Finally, although there exist many terms and constructs common to family therapy that could be included in a family addictions book, any book would be incomplete without describing the important construct of boundaries. All families have boundaries. In general, boundaries occur between (a) individual family system members (e.g., father vs. mother), (b) different subsystems within the family (e.g., parents vs. children), and (c) the family system and society (e.g., the family system as a whole vs. the school system). In addition to the existence of boundaries between persons and systems, Minuchin (1974) identified three different boundary types that exist on a continuum between extremely rigid to extremely porous. Boundaries at either extreme (i.e., being either rigid or porous) can be highly dysfunctional.

Most addicted families present rigid boundaries. This type of boundary dysfunctionally serves the family system by isolating the family from those who could potentially help. Often such isolation occurs in an attempt to keep others from learning that addiction is occurring within the family system. Here, family members keep others at a distance from the family and especially the addicted person. The intent is to protect the family secret—that someone is addicted.

In the previous family example, the eldest daughter and siblings refused to seek external help for their father. This was because they did not want others to become aware of their father's addictions or the addictions-related problems occurring within the family system. Additionally, they refused to talk with each other about father's alcoholism. Denial was the focus. When father sought treatment, the adolescents initially denied problems resulting from their father's addition. In essence they told father and his counselor that father should be left alone to continue his drinking behaviors. Furthermore, they attempted to shelter father and the family system from the impact of external interactions with the counselor. In other words, they denied the existence of father's alcoholism or problems resulting from his alcohol abuse, and they attempted to isolate the family from having outsiders engage with either the addicted family member or the system.

Alternately, some addicted families present with extremely porous boundaries. These families essentially lack boundaries both between family members and between the family system and society. Often family counselors will find that members within this system are highly enmeshed. That is to say that there exists little opportunity for individuality or uniqueness within the family. Instead, member conformity is prized.

Metaphorically speaking, should one member within such an enmeshed and porous boundaried family system be kicked in the knee, all members would grab their knees in pain and hop on their other leg. Bowen (1961) utilized the term *undifferentiated family ego mass* to describe such family members who were so emotionally fused. Like raspberry granules of gelatin that dissolve in water and then congeal into a single raspberry gelatin dessert, it is virtually impossible to separate individuals from such enmeshed family systems.

Healthy family systems present in the center of this continuum halfway between rigid and enmeshed. Essentially, these systems value healthy individuality within a supportive and flexible family system. In other words, members within these systems are encouraged to maximize their potential and strengths and then in return support the system without sacrificing self. Here, there exist sufficient boundaries and rules to help protect members from dysfunctional persons and external systems.

There. You now know the fundamental terms and constructs necessary to understanding the basic Sequential Family Addictions Counseling Model contained later in the book. However, before proceeding to the model, there is another topic that warrants discussion.

Domestic Violence and Addicted Families

Family addictions counselors who have worked in the field for even the briefest time understand the dangerous trifecta of addictions, domestic violence, and family dysfunction. The convergence of this trifecta puts families and counselors in harm's way. Domestic violence complicates the counseling scenario and mandates that even the purest family systems model be sufficiently compromised to ensure family and individual safety. The intent of this chapter is not to describe therapeutic interventions designed to change domestic violence perpetrators. We will leave such writing to our respected professional colleagues who thrive in that specialization and enjoy working with perpetrators. Instead, we will present how the Sequential Family Addictions Model addresses perpetrators and nonperpetrating family members.

Mothers Call the Shots The nonperpetrating partner's decision of what is best for self and dependents is where we will begin. Stereotypically, the nonperpetrating partner is female and the family's dependents are her children. Clearly this is not always the case. However, such clinical scenarios have been the most prevalent situations we have encountered over the years, and for reading ease we will utilize such a stereotypical scenario.

Like many of you, we have learned from our clinical experiences those practices that work well and those that do not. One of the most challenging situations family addictions counselors face is when an addicted partner is physically or sexually abusive. Stereotypically, this means a male partner drinks or drugs, rules others via intimidation and brutality, and simply scares the living daylights out of family members as well as those intending to help mother and children. It is not uncommon for these abusive and addicted men to continue their reign of terror over their partners and family dependents even while the family is participating in counseling.

Jacobson and Gottman (1998) clearly warned family counselors to keep perpetrators out of family counseling until it is evident that the perpetrator would neither pose a safety threat nor sabotage treatment. We couldn't agree more. Thus, in a stereotypical situation like the one noted above, the Sequential Family Addictions Model requires that the perpetrating partner receive both group and individual counseling services separate from the family. Typically the focus of the perpetrator's treatment will be specific to his battering and his addictions. We have found the most success for families when perpetrators actively participate and complete (a) a men's batterers' group experience lasting no less than 6 months, (b) a 12-step recovery group such as Alcoholics Anonymous or Narcotics Anonymous, and (c) individual counseling with goals specific to the perpetrator's abusive behaviors and his addictions.

Additionally, a restraining order can prove invaluable. Restraining orders have the potential to provide family safety, engender a physical separation and "cool-down" period, and promote perspective and possibly even helpful insight for each person within the family system.

Therefore, when domestic violence or abuse is present, the Sequential Family Addictions Model begins with only the nonperpetrating family system members. Many times mothers will readily establish such restraining orders and desire family counseling for herself and her children. In such cases, we encourage mother to "call the shots." That is to say that they immediately engage in the family counseling process with their children and seek consultation with a legal advocate to pursue a restraining order.

Given our clinical experiences in agencies and practices that often work in conjunction with family- and probate-affiliated courts as well as drug courts, we typically have close ties with judges and district attorneys. As non–mental health professionals, these judges and attorneys regularly request direction related to treatment for the addicted families and the perpetrating partners. Therefore, whenever possible we advocate that perpetrating partners participate in the aforementioned treatment regime and that family members participate in family counseling.

What If Mom Wants Perpetrator Back in the System?   Significant numbers of abused women want the perpetrating partner back in the family system immediately. Although this may at first seem illogical to the novice treatment provider, there are a multitude of reasons why these women and even their children may desire the perpetrator back in the family system. Their reasons run the gamut. We have had abused women indicate that having the perpetrator present in their home will protect them from "worse" violence occurring within their neighborhoods. Others have indicated intense anxiety related to "being alone without a man." More often than not, however, these women accurately fear the perpetrator's intense retribution or understand that without the perpetrators' income they will not be adequately able to provide for their children.

Some of the most emotionally draining cases we have experienced occur when mother wants perpetrator back in the family system and children do not. This can occur even after the most egregious acts by the perpetrating partner. Regretfully, minor children do not have the luxury of deciding if perpetrators return to the family system. Mothers and sometimes courts make these decisions.

Of course the opposite can occur, too. In the past we have encountered mothers who do not want the perpetrating partners back in the family system and accurately understand that the perpetrators remain a significant danger to her and her children. However, in an attempt to quell her children's raging anger directed toward mother for "kicking dad out" or in an attempt to do what she perceives would be best for her children, mother reluctantly allows addicted perpetrator back into the system. The cycle of domestic violence frequently continues, and mother and children are again victimized. Interestingly enough, even when the perpetrator's return is a direct result of the children's emotional blackmail of their mother, the children often accuse mother of not protecting them. This situation can be exceptionally difficult for mothers who are now revictimized by perpetrating partners and the mothers' cherished children.

Like it or not, our professional role is not to dissuade mother or children from accepting the former perpetrator back into the family system. We cannot make this decision for our clients. Nevertheless, we can provide our professional opinions when these opinions are based on our specialized graduate training, clinical judgment, and perceptions of the case. More importantly, the Sequential Family Addictions Model can be used to investigate the mothers' and children's perceptions of how treatment would be best for *them* and explore *their* wishes regarding the potential reintegration of the perpetrator back into the system near treatment's end. However, within this model, when domestic violence is present, the perpetrator is not reunited in treatment with the family until the nonperpetrating family system completes the last stage. At that time, should the mother wish to reengage with the perpetrator, family counseling sessions that revolve around this reintegration can occur. Specifically, these sessions should address issues such as safety and perceptions of safety, family expectations regarding the parenting and discipline of the children, and the reuniting of the family members.

The Model

General Model Overview

Our experience has been that a cursory overview of the Sequential Family Addictions Model's history and stages helps provide a foundation for more in-depth discussion later. Thus, we next present a very general model overview, which is visually depicted in Figure 4.1. Once the basic model has been explained, we then describe each of the stages in greater detail.

The seven-stage Sequential Family Addictions Model is a progressive, stepwise treatment model that was developed by the senior author in 1986. The model has been refined by the authors' clinical experiences and is specific to treating families in which one or more members within the system is abusing substances or is addicted. In 1989 while working in an outpatient, community agency setting, the senior author began using the model with his clinical supervisees. For the most part these clinical supervisees were counseling addicted families via treatments conducted either at the agency or at client family homes (e.g., intensive, in-home treatment). By 1991 Juhnke began using the model as a means of training his master's and doctoral students. Hagedorn and Juhnke began working together in 2000 and have utilized this model with their students ever since. The current model, then, is founded upon the authors' joint clinical and clinical supervision experiences, which span approximately 25 years.

No matter the number of substance-abusing or addicted persons in the family system, the family roles of the substance-abusing persons (e.g.,

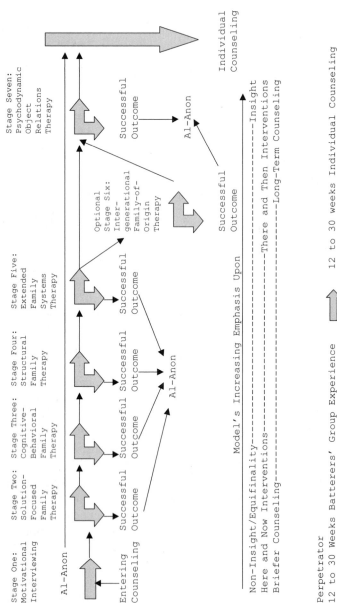

Figure 4.1 The Sequential Family Addictions Counseling Model.

mother, father, sibling), or the presence of domestic violence, Stage One of the Sequential Family Addictions Model always begins with motivational interviewing. This first stage typically lasts one or two sessions. At the conclusion of Stage One the family system's and its members' readiness for change will be clear. Based on the system's and its members' readiness to invest in change and the counseling process, it will be determined if family counseling is perceived as the best option. As previously stated, should domestic violence be present, the perpetrator is separated from mother and other family system members. Thus, perpetrator will participate in individual and group counseling separate from the family system until the nonperpetrating family members complete counseling. Thus, only mother, children, and other system members determined by mother will be involved in this motivational interviewing experience and the necessary model stages.

If family counseling is not perceived as the best option, other counseling modalities such as individual or group therapies will be presented. In the event that the family and its members are unable to perceive any valid reasons for change, the counselor may utilize motivational techniques to address the system's and its members' change ambivalence. In other words, the counselor will either help the family system move toward Solution-Focused Family Therapy, the second stage of the Sequential Family Addictions Model, or at least entertain potential reasons to consider change. This progression level might be as far as the family system can move. Counselors should not view limited progression as clinical failure. Instead, counselors should respect the family's decision to disengage from the counseling process. However, if the family system and its members are ready for change, the Sequential Family Addictions Model will continue to utilize motivational techniques to address potential treatment and commitment ambiguity. Clients will then be encouraged to move to Stage Two.

This second model stage is founded upon Solution-Focused Family Theory and encourages clients and their families to identify how things will look and be different when addictive behaviors are reduced or absent. This stage typically lasts from three to seven treatment sessions.

Depending on this theory's "family fit," the family addictions counselor may continue using Solution-Focused Family Therapy until the presenting treatment goals are achieved. However, should the family "plateau" or falter in their progression, a move to Stage Three would then follow. Additionally, the counselor may continue to utilize appropriate motivational interviewing techniques as needed during this stage. Such motivational interviewing techniques would be used to address critical issues related to goal ambiguity.

Stage Three of the Family Addictions Model is utilized only if Stages One and Two become bogged down or families fail to progress. This Sequential Family Addictions Model stage typically lasts from 3 to 11 treatment sessions and is founded upon Cognitive-Behavioral Family Theory. Emphasis here will be directly related to the identification of high-risk situations and the internal and external cues experienced by family members that encourage addictive behavior or weaken commitment to abstention.

Structural Family Therapy provides the Stage Four foundation. The intent of this stage is to create a suitable structure for the family system that will both bring stability to the addicted family members and actively contribute to the family system's ability to address addictive behaviors.

The fifth stage of the model moves the family system closer to insight-focused treatment. Unlike Stages Two through Four, which have a greater focus on the future or "here and now" strategies, this stage attempts to foster insight related to cascading intergenerational dynamics that foster addictive behaviors and addiction. This fourth stage is grounded in Extended Family Systems Theory, which is most often affiliated with Bowen's work, and typically lasts from 5 to 10 sessions on average.

Stage Six of the Sequential Family Addictions Model really bridges the gap between Stages Five and Seven. Specifically, Stage Six is an adaptation of James Framo's Intergenerational Family-of-Origin Therapy, and its emphasis is related to the adult child's reconnection with family-of-origin members as their experiences relate to addictions. Stage Six is an optional stage that may or may not fit some client families. Depending on the needs of the nonperpetrating parent, this stage typically lasts from three to five sessions. We have found this stage to be an excellent means of helping nonperpetrating partners reexperience addictions-related topics related to their families of origin. When used effectively, Intergenerational Family-of-Origin Therapy promotes the nonperpetrating partners' understanding of their addictive behaviors and insight regarding their tolerance of current family members' addictive behaviors and domestic violence.

Stage Seven is the final model stage and is founded upon Psychodynamic Family Therapy. Specifically, when client families have been unsuccessful at promoting meaningful change in the previous stages, this long-term treatment process becomes the treatment of choice. This is clearly long-term treatment that typically requires no fewer than 15 treatment sessions. Here, the counselor becomes the "transference object." Specifically, the intent is for the system's members to project onto the counselor–client relationship and internalize the counselor.

Stage One: The Change Model and Motivational Interviewing

General Overview   In 1983 Miller originally described the basic motivational interviewing concept. Unknown to him, his seminal work would forever change the face of addictions treatment. Others attempted to put their spin on Miller's motivational interviewing concept. In response, Rollnick and Miller (1995) authored an article that defined motivational interviewing as originally intended and clarified the essential "spirit" of their approach. Specifically, Rollnick and Miller (1995, p. 17) stated, "Motivational interviewing is a directive, client-centered counseling style for eliciting behavior change by helping clients to explore and resolve ambivalence."

The key to Miller's motivational interviewing concept is that counselors seek to understand the client's frame of reference through reflective listening. Counselors further express acceptance and affirmation related to both the client and the client's self-directed choices. In other words, counselors ask questions to learn how clients perceive their situation and then allow clients to make intrinsically based choices related to treatment. So, counselors listen to their clients' presenting concerns, rather than preempt the treatment by confronting clients related to their "addiction."

These motivational interviewing concepts were strikingly different from the standard addictions interventions typically utilized prior to the early 1990s. For the most part, addictions treatment prior to the early 1990s focused on confrontation. Specifically clients were confronted by addictions experts who told clients that they must both admit to their addictions and commit to abstinence. Anything other than complete willingness to admit to one's addiction and abstinence was viewed as "resistance."

Of course, to many of these early addictions counselors, such resistance required verbal confrontation. Therefore, treatment was often adversarial. Successful therapy occurred when the addictions counselor "broke" client defenses and eliminated client resistance, and clients finally agreed that they were addicted. In other words, there was an attempt by addictions counselors to use confrontation to change the client's reality so that clients would behave differently (Johnson, 1973).

Motivational interviewing provided a strikingly different framework that focused on motivation vis-à-vis confrontation. Specifically, Miller used Prochaska and DiClemente's (1982) change model. This model was founded upon six client stages (Figure 4.2). These stages included (a) Precontemplation, (b) Contemplation, (c) Determination, (d) Action, (e) Maintenance, and (f) Relapse. Each stage describes specific motivational tasks. Precontemplation describes a time when the problem drinker has not yet recognized a need to change. At this point, many addicted persons

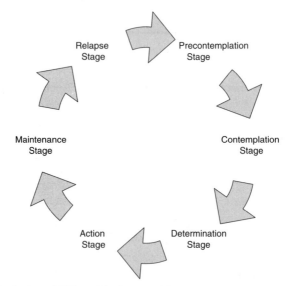

Figure 4.2 Prochaska and DiClemente's change model.

are informed that they have an addictions-related problem. The majority of the time, persons at this stage are forced into treatment via the legal system or coerced into treatment by loved ones who threaten to leave should the negatively perceived addictive behaviors continue. In this Precontemplation Stage, the person needs information related to the negative addictive behaviors to raise awareness of these behaviors.

An example of the Precontemplation Stage may be when family members confront a loved one related to her alcohol consumption behaviors and her tendency to become verbally abusive toward others when she drinks. When this person's awareness of the problem occurs, the individual moves into the Contemplation Stage. This stage is frequently marked by the addicted person's considering the information provided by others about the negative addictive behaviors. Here the person may well consider the information provided by the loved ones and "contemplate" what to do, if anything, about the voiced concerns.

At this point the addicted person potentially experiences ambivalence related to the voiced concerns and the reasons to change her addictive behaviors. For example, the person may think something like, "Well, I know that my husband and parents think that I drink too much too often. But I really don't. Certainly I'm not an alcoholic. Everyone drinks; I just drink a little more than most." In other words, the addicted person in this Contemplation Stage questions the presented information and contemplates the true need to change.

Should the addicted person believe that it is in her best interests to change or should she perceive that the presented concerns by others are legitimate and require change, she enters the Determination Stage. Here, the addicted person becomes determined to do something about her addictive behaviors. This is a fluid stage. In other words, there are times when the person becomes determined to address her addictive behaviors and there are times when her determination is diluted. At times when she is determined, the person moves into the Action Stage. Some will enter counseling during this Action Stage. However, counseling is not an Action Stage requirement. Others will continue into the Action Stage by making self-effective steps toward changing their problematic addictive behaviors. However, most will falter or slip. In other words, they will slide backward from the Action Stage to either the Determination or the Contemplation Stage.

Many nonaddicted persons can better understand Prochaska and DiClemente's stages and such a slide when the situation is placed into a dieting context. Here, for example, a person might enjoy eating without ever considering caloric intake. He eats what he enjoys and perceives no eating problem. This is similar to the Precontemplation Stage. Dieting is not yet on his radar screen. He merely eats to his heart's content with no guilt or shame.

Suddenly, he finds that he is unable to fit into his clothes and sees his rotund figure in the mirror as he exits the shower. Now, he enters the Contemplation Stage. He becomes aware of the weight problem and experiences ambivalent feelings about whether he really wants to consider dieting. He enters the Determination Stage when he no longer can shimmy into his trousers. It is during this stage that the awful truth strikes: "I can't afford a whole new wardrobe. I must start dieting."

His Action Stage begins as he enters a strict diet composed of water and two paltry meals per day. He loses five pounds the first week. Then, he slips by eating two small but tasty glazed donuts. His first thought is, "Since I've already blown my diet, I might as well satisfy my appetite." By the end of his slip he has consumed two dozen donuts, multiple nondiet sodas, and even mint chocolate chip ice cream slathered in fudge.

Thus, he slides back to the Contemplation Stage and has ambivalent feelings about whether the benefits of dieting are worth the struggle. As he again determines that he must diet and begins dieting anew, he progresses through the Determination and Action Stages. This time, however, he enters the Maintenance Stage as he implements what he had learned via his previous slip and implements new strategies that alert him to the dangers of donuts, consuming only water and paltry meals, and dieting too strictly.

So What Do Change Model Stages Have to Do with Family Addictions? Prochaska and DiClemente's Change Model Stages are unmistakably present in families facing addictions-related problems. For example, the Precontemplation Stage can be marked by a multitude of variables ranging from an adolescent consuming alcohol until she experiences blackouts to a mother whose husband has just started threatening her when he drinks to intoxication. During this Precontemplation Stage the addicted person and the family do not comprehend the problem.

However, addictive problems manifest quickly and forcefully debilitate even the strongest family system. Therefore, family addictions counselors need to be aware of the opportunities to help families entering the Contemplation, Determination, and Action Stages. It is within these stages that family addictions counselors can (a) address change ambivalence via discussions regarding the potential costs of doing nothing versus the potential benefits of addressing the addictive behaviors (Contemplation Stage), (b) identify potential courses of action to effectively facilitate change (Determination), and (c) motivate the client family toward implementing change (Action). This is where motivational interviewing is crucial in helping addicted families and their members.

Don't be fooled. Motivational interviewing is not wimpy counseling or some kind of Pollyannaish treatment. Although counselors utilizing motivational interviewing openly express empathy and acceptance of clients (which does not necessarily mean agreeing with clients), counselors are actively engendering client discomfort and discrepancy related to the client families' presented ambivalence toward change (Miller & Rollnick, 1991). An example of this would be working with a family that has experienced father's progressively worsening alcohol addiction and his increasingly more frequent violent behaviors. Here the counselor will express empathy and acknowledge the normality of change ambivalence. Then the counselor will attempt to promote discrepancy.

Mother:	"I just don't know what to do. I'd like to take out a restraining order on Bob and begin family counseling with you. Bob really hurt our son Bobby and me this last time when he was drinking and slammed us against the wall. But I really don't want to hurt Bob's feelings."
Counselor:	"It sounds as though you don't know what to do."
Mother:	"Yeah, I really don't. I want to do what is best for all of us."

Counselor: "A lot of people I counsel experience this same kind of ambivalence about filing a restraining order on their husbands and entering family counseling."

Mother: "Really?"

Counselor: Yeah, they do. These mothers want to make certain that they and their kids aren't hurt again when the husbands drink and drug. But some are too scared to get a court order to restrain their husbands from coming into their home or onto their property. Others feel really guilty about taking out a restraining order to ensure that they and their kids are safe. Still others have different reasons either for not filing restraining orders or for not starting family counseling."

Mother: "Yeah, that's me. I feel a little guilty about the whole thing."

Counselor: "So, what might happen if you don't file a restraining order and don't start family counseling for you and your kids?"

Mother: "Gee, I hate to even think of it. Bob could hurt Bobby. And Bob said he was going to kill me. Getting a restraining order on Bob and starting family counseling without him seems like a lot."

Counselor: "Ginger, it sounds as though you really think your husband could hurt your son and even kill you. What options do you have that will help ensure the safety of your son and you?"

Mother: "I guess it would be helpful to get the restraining order and for Bobby and me to get counseling without his daddy. I'm sure if Bob were there he would try to intimidate us."

As we can see, this mother is moving from Prochaska and DiClemente's Contemplation Stage to the Determination Stage. The counselor utilized motivational interviewing to "tip the balance" and provided good reasons why mother should seek a restraining order on her addicted and abusive husband and begin family counseling with her son. This is the essence of motivational interviewing. It is a method of motivating clients via their own words and wants without in-your-face confrontation.

Once ambivalence is heard, the counselor can ask crucial questions that allow the client family to explore options and move toward their treatment goals. Some of the questions suggested by Miller and Rollnick (1991, p. 117) include: "What do you think you will do?" "What's the next step?" and "What do you think has to change?" Each of these questions encourages clients to clarify their own thoughts and suggest that clients, not circumstances, control the desired outcome.

Additional Intervention Strategy In addition to expressing empathy and developing discrepancy, there are three other motivational interviewing strategies that merit review. All seem fairly intuitive, but our experiences have shown that this is not always the case. For example, Miller and Rollnick (1991) encourage counselors to avoid arguing with clients. Specifically, they report that arguing is counterproductive and can create defensiveness among clients. This seems deceptively simple. As a matter of fact, most counselors we know do not like to argue. However, during the heat of a counseling session, clients and counselors can quickly polarize and spirited arguing can ensue.

Should an argument develop, make an immediate change. One can often make a sincere apology, indicate a misunderstanding, or respond to the client's underlying concern. For example, in a recent counseling session, the senior author observed a counselor unwittingly enter an argument. Father was no longer part of the family system, and mother was in recovery. The two adolescent daughters—Adela, age 12, and Adriana, age 15—voiced concerns regarding mother's reoccurring drinking behaviors.

Mother:	"I can drink alcohol if I want."
Adela:	"Don't you remember what happened before? You and that guy started making out."
Mother:	"Shut up. I wasn't drunk. I am the adult, and I can drink if I want."
Adriana:	"Right, and you can get drunk too."
Counselor:	"Mother, I hear your daughters voicing some concerns regarding your drinking behaviors. Are you drinking to intoxication?"

Mother:	"Hey, I'm their mother and an adult. You are siding with them. Don't talk to me that way and you better give me the respect I deserve."
Counselor:	"I'm sorry; it sounds as though you felt disrespected by me. That was not my intent, and I'm very sorry for conveying any disrespect."
Mother:	"Well, you did sound disrespectful."
Counselor:	"Again, that was not my intent and I sincerely apologize. Now, when you drink, are you drinking to a point of intoxication?"

As we can see above, as soon as the counselor perceives the potential argument, the counselor sincerely apologizes and continues.

Summary Motivational interviewing provides a platform that can be continued throughout the upcoming Sequential Family Addictions Model stages. Similar to persons who are dieting, addicted families will constantly flex in and out of Contemplation, Determination, Action, Maintenance, and Relapse. The counselor's charge is multifaceted depending on the specific needs of the family and the stages of change family members currently reside in. In essence, the counselor continually challenges the system to (a) question roles, rules, beliefs, and behaviors that hinder health and abstinence, (b) secure and commit to new strategies that promote health within the system, and (c) accept relapse without blame and demoralization. Should the family system be unable to see a need for change, counseling is inadvisable and the counselor should continue to attempt to work with family members in the Precontemplation and Contemplation Stages. However, if the family members move into the Determination and Action Stages, the counselor should move into Stage Two and focus on the specific family-identified treatment goals.

Stage Two: Solution-Focused Therapy

General Overview Solution-Focused Therapy matches the adage. "What you see is what you get." Unlike psychodynamic, insight-driven theories that scour the past to identify hidden, underlying causes for problems, Solution-Focused Therapy directs the family system toward the future and provides an opportunity for the system to depict their desired "solution" (Berg, 1994; O'Hanlon & Weiner-Davis, 1989; Weiner-Davis, 1992; Weiner-Davis, 1993). Therefore, this theory views clients as kings who rule their domains via solution-seeking actions rather than as pawns driven by unconscious and unknown motives. This said, Solution-Focused Therapy assumes that families desire change and rejects the notions of resistance and deceit-filled ulterior motives.

Thus, from the very onset of treatment, Solution-Focused Therapy conveys expectations for clients and counselors alike. First, it empowers families by letting them know that they create their own solutions. Hence, clients direct their personalized pathways to solution attainment. Whatever behaviors and actions they identify as required stepping-stones for achieving their identified solutions are initiated. Given that clients establish their own markers for success and solutions, they can simply change their solutions or objectives if necessary.

Second, Solution-Focused Therapy conveys to counselors that their clients are not deceitful, resistant, uncommitted sojourners on a futile trip to nowhere. Instead, this theory demands that counselors believe in their clients and their clients' abilities to break the addictions cycle. Such counselor trust and successful expectations foster a powerful symbiotic interaction among family members and the counselor that impacts treatment.

For example, shortly after assuming the clinical directorship of a large university research and training clinic, the senior author was conducting research on the efficacy of conjoint male and female treatment teams utilizing Solution-Focused Theory with addicted couples. The overwhelming majority of couples presented with severely dysfunctional relationships, moderate to profound addiction levels, and significant treatment histories that typically spanned 10 or more years. Frankly, at the onset of the research, there was concern that treatment would be ineffective due to the limited addictions and couple's counseling experiences of the doctoral students who were facilitating treatment and the mere fact that the client couples reported little to no beneficial changes from years of previous treatment. To the senior author's surprise, many of these client couples noted remarkable improvements in their relationships and significant reductions in their drinking and drugging behaviors. When asked their perceptions regarding the favorable outcomes, most indicated something like, "Our counselors believed our marriage would improve" or "Our counselors knew we would beat my drinking." In other words, these addicted couples felt that their counselors believed their marriages *would* improve and their drinking and drugging *would* be eliminated. This expectation for positive change reportedly made a significant impact.

We believe that clients are impacted by the counselors' perceived probability of successful treatment outcome. In other words, when clients perceive that their counselors believe that successful outcomes are imminent, clients become more committed to the treatment process, work harder, and attend to markers that they believe support their perception that improvement is imminent. Conversely, when clients perceive that their counselors believe treatment is futile and the potential for positive results is nonexistent, clients become disheartened, disengage from treatment, and interpret markers that they believe support their perception that treatment is futile. Therefore, the use of Solution-Focused Therapy itself aids in establishing outcome expectations that have the potential to positively impact counselors and treatment alike.

Interventions Contrary to many theories that require one to describe the presenting symptomatology in great detail, Solution-Focused Theory immediately moves clients toward creating and focusing on a picture of the solution they seek. So, you may be asking, "What does that mean?" Well, in our family counseling courses we use the Hot Fudge Sundae Example of this solution-focused picture with our students. So, if you would be so kind as to indulge us for a moment, we would like to provide this example to you. Are you ready? OK, we merely ask that you *not* think about a hot fudge sundae. Do not think about the vanilla ice cream topped with whipped cream and nuts. Do not think about the cherry on top. Do not think about fudge cascading down the side of the ice cream, and certainly do not think about the clear parfait glass that holds that delectable and tempting hot fudge sundae itself.

How did you do? Did you *not* think about the hot fudge sundae? Of course you thought about the hot fudge sundae, right? Despite your best intentions, you probably were creating that solution-focused hot fudge sundae picture in your mind. Well, this is the exact point of Solution-Focused Therapy. Once the addicted family can identify a solution picture of what their recovery will look like, they can begin to move toward that solution. Everything they do should revolve around doing the things in their solution-focused picture that demonstrate that they are accomplishing their recovery.

This is important, so stay with us. Remember those high school physics courses where you learned that nature hates a void? As you remember, whenever nature encounters a void, nature fills the void with something. For example, if you have a bottle of soda and extract the soda, the void is filled with air. If you then submerge the soda bottle in water, the air escapes and the bottle is filled with water. No matter what you do, nature refuses to allow that soda bottle to maintain a void inside.

So what is the connection between this fundamental law of physics and the solution-focused hot fudge sundae picture? It is simple. By creating a solution-focused picture of a successful outcome, the void is filled with behaviors that will be present upon the completion of successful treatment. For example, if the client family perceives that when they have recovered dinner will be served at 6 P.M. nightly, it would be important to immediately initiate this solution-focused picture. Such a picture indicates that the family *is* in recovery. Thus, the family is filling the void of what they are currently not doing with the behaviors that they have identified as indicative of being recovered.

Of course the flip side of this example is how family systems often dwell on what is wrong and search for behavioral markers indicating that the addictive behaviors have not improved. Solution-focused counselors encourage a new perspective. Instead of focusing on pathology and behavioral markers associated with the throes of family addiction, solution-focused counselors focus the family on behaviors and markers demonstrating success. Here, for example, the counselor might use an exception question to both foil the generalization noted by the family that "Father is *always* drunk" and focus attention on father's successful abstinence. For example, here the counselor might say something like the following:

Counselor: "Help me understand. When was the last time this week when dad was not drinking or drunk?"

Oldest Son: "Oh, that's easy. He certainly wasn't drinking or drunk when he was working on his Corvette last night."

Counselor: "Dad, is that true?"

Father: "Yes, I want to be thinking clearly when I work on my baby. If I'm drinking alcohol, I can't focus and could make a mistake."

Counselor: "I'm wondering, were there other times this week when you were with your family that you wanted to be thinking clearly so you chose not to drink?"

Father: "Certainly, as a matter of fact this week when Carlos was working on his homework, I wanted to help him and didn't drink so that I could think clearly."

Counselor: "Carlos, what was that like for you when dad wasn't drinking, when he was paying attention to you and thinking clearly?"

Oldest Son: "Man, it was great. I had actually forgotten that dad had taken time with me when he wasn't drinking."

Counselor: "Tell me about other times this week when dad was sober and took time with you."

As we can see from the above exchange, the counselor eloquently expands the family's knowledge and memories of times when father was not under the influence. Again, these serve as markers denoting successful abstinence and positive intentions by father.

Additionally, at the conclusion of the counseling session, the counselor could prescribe a task that will keep members focused on father's successful abstinence. For example, the counselor could say something like the following:

Counselor: "Great session today, family. I think we've accomplished much. Listen, I have an assignment that I would like each of you to help me with. Between now and our next meeting, I would like you to keep track of times when dad is not drunk or drinking. Specifically, I want each of you to pay attention to times when dad is sober."

Again, the intervention is designed to keep the family focused not on past failures and problems but on the father's successes and improvements. Concomitantly, it notifies father that he is going to be observed this week and provides him the opportunity to "showcase" his abstinence.

Three Techniques for Generating Solution-Focused Pictures Solution-Focused Theory utilizes three general goal identification techniques to help families create and crystallize their vision of successful treatment. These techniques include the Miracle Question, the Crystal Ball Technique, and the Movie Director Technique. Each is slightly different, but the focus is the same— identify what success will look like to this family. All are exceptionally effective in helping the family system identify their counseling goals.

The Miracle Question states something like, "Let's say a miracle happened tonight while you were sleeping, and no one in your family knew the miracle had happened. However, the miracle had actually happened, and the miracle was that father was no longer addicted. What would you notice first thing in the morning that would alert you to the fact that dad's addiction was gone?" The intent here is for family members to identify what they would first notice indicating that father was addiction-free. A follow-up question would be to ask the order in which people would notice father's freedom from addiction: "So, who in the family would be the first (second, last, etc.) to notice that dad was addiction-free?" Of course, the treatment provider would follow the order until all persons in the family identified the recognition order.

On occasion, some client families become confused with the Miracle Question. Should this happen, we encourage our students to simply apologize for convoluting the instructions and move immediately to the Crystal Ball Technique. In this technique, the counselor states, "Let's pretend that I have a magic crystal ball that will show us how the future will look when dad achieves his freedom from alcohol abuse. Let's pretend to gaze into the ball. Describe what you see and tell me how things are different in your family's future." Here, the counselor is allowing the client family members to describe how things have changed.

A third option is the Movie Director Technique. Here the counselor says to the family, "If we took a movie of how your family is today, then took a movie of how your family will be when dad has achieved his freedom from alcohol abuse, and then compared the two movies to one another, how would people be acting differently?" As in the previous two techniques for generating solution-focused pictures, the counselor wants to help the family discuss how things will be different. Once these differences or changes have been identified, the counselor will begin to have people "act" in ways congruent with the positively identified difference. The following vignette provides such an example.

Chondra:	"Well, I'll know that things have really improved when Juan and I begin doing things together as a couple again."
Counselor:	"Help me understand what things you will begin doing once Juan stops his drinking."
Chondra:	"We could begin going to the movies again."
Counselor:	"Would you like to go to the movies with Juan this Friday night?"
Chondra:	"I would. You know, we haven't gone to the movies since he has had his alcohol problem."
Counselor:	"Juan, are you interested in taking Chondra to the movies?"
Juan:	"That would be cool."

Counselor:	"So what would the two of you have to do to go to the movies this Friday night?"
Chondra:	"I guess just pick a movie and a time."
Juan:	"It would be fun. Let's do it."
Counselor:	"Now another thing that you said would be different if a miracle occurred is that not only would you go to the movies, but afterward you would find yourselves talking about your marriage. Is that correct?"
Chondra:	"Yes."
Counselor:	"OK, Juan, after the movies, what are you going to do with Chondra?"
Juan:	"Well, I guess we are going to be talking about our marriage."
Counselor:	"So, help me understand where you will go to talk after the movies and what that will look like."
Juan:	"I'm cool with that. Let's see, there is a Starbucks coffee shop adjacent to the movie theater. Chondra, what do you think about us talking there after the movie?"
Chondra:	"That sounds good to me."
Counselor:	"This is what I hear Chondra and you saying. First, one indicator that you both agree will be present when you become established in your recovery and your marriage improves is that you will begin going to the movies again. Is that correct?"
Juan:	"Yup."
Counselor:	"And, Chondra, the second thing I heard you say that would indicate Juan was in recovery and your relationship was back on track would be when the two of you begin talking about your marriage. Is that correct?"
Chondra:	"Yes."
Counselor:	"So, as I understand things, both of you will be going to the movies this Friday. And, after the movie, you will go to the Starbucks coffee shop to talk."
Juan:	"This will be fun!"

We can see from the vignette that the counselor has been able to get Chondra and Juan to begin the behaviors noted as indicators of Juan's recovery and an improved marriage. Once these behaviors can become established, progress toward the overall solution picture will be noted and the couple can then either identify new solution pictures or determine that sufficient progress has been made to discontinue counseling until necessary again.

Additional Intervention Strategy Finally, it is important to note how solution-focused counselors utilize scaling questions within treatment with addicted client families. As you remember, we briefly discussed the use of scaling questions in Chapter 3 and reported how such questions could be used within the assessment process. Here, we are going to describe how to use scaling questions for intervention purposes. The intent of scaling questions used within intervention is to help family members quantify their opinions, behaviors, commitment, and intentions. We have found that a 10-point scale works well with our addicted families. In sessions, we do not wish to confuse clients, so we always make the higher score representative of something greater or larger. The following clinical vignette is used to demonstrate the use of scaling questions with addicted families.

Counselor: "Juan, on a scale from 0 to 10, with 0 meaning very little possibility of really going to the movies and 10 meaning going to the movies is a sure thing, what score would you use to indicate your commitment to taking Chondra to the movies this Friday night?"

Juan: "I'm pretty committed, and I really want Chondra to see that I'm alcohol-free for the first time in 3 years. Therefore, I would say a 10."

At this point, the counselor could ask Chondra to use a scaling question to indicate her belief that Juan will really follow through on his commitment to taking her to the movies. For example, Chondra could say something like, "I think he is pretty committed. I'd give him a 10." On the other hand Chondra might say something like, "He is all talk and no follow-through. I would only give him a 3." When such responses occur, it is important to positively reframe the client's response. One way to do this is to ask clients why they didn't provide a lower score and ask them what positive things they are noting that provided the basis of not using the very lowest available scaling score.

Counselor:	"I'm intrigued by your giving Juan a score of 3 related to his commitment to taking you to the movies. Your score indicates that you believe Juan is committed to some degree to taking you to the movies. Help me understand the behaviors you see in Juan that tell you he is committed."

Thus, we see that the counselor does not fall into the trap of asking, "Why the low score?" Instead, she eloquently keeps the focus on the behaviors that demonstrate his commitment.

Summary   Solution-Focused Therapy follows motivational interviewing exceptionally well. Specifically, it aids addicted families in continuing their commitment to sobriety and increases the probability that families that slide back into the Action Stage of motivational change reengage into Maintenance. Furthermore, solution-focused interventions help client families focus on the ultimate solutions that they wish to establish and enable client families to imagine their lives without the presence of addiction's devastating effects. Concomitantly, solution-focused interventions are time-, energy-, and cost-efficient. Based on our experiences, solution-focused interventions are highly effective with addicted families and often are sufficient to ensure goal attainment and long-term recovery. However, for families unable to gain sufficient advancement via Stages One and Two, the Sequential Family Addictions Model progresses to Stage Three.

Stage Three: Cognitive-Behavioral Family Therapy

General Overview   Cognitive-Behavioral Family Therapy comprises Stage Three of the Sequential Family Addictions Counseling Model. Given the addicted family's new understanding of how they would like things to be via their solution-focused picture and Cognitive-Behavioral Family Counseling's emphasis on identifying and addressing precipitators to addictive behaviors and sequences leading to relapse, the client family can easily follow the transition between stages. Cognitive-Behavioral Family Counseling also has significant utility for families struggling with addictions (Hedberg & Campbell, 1974; Liddle & Dakof, 1995; O'Farrell, 1999; O'Farrell & Fals-Stewart, 2003; Szapocznik et al., 1988), and via our client families' self-reports, it seems that this sequential progression— starting with motivational interviewing, moving next to solution-focused treatment, and then progressing into Cognitive-Behavioral Family Therapy when necessary—is very efficacious. In addition to the previously mentioned reasons for Cognitive-Behavioral Family Therapy's inclusion within the model, this theory's emphasis on brief, time-limited interventions directed toward immediate concerns matches the pressing needs of many addicted families.

Three primary Cognitive-Behavioral Counseling goals exist for family addictions counselors. First, family addictions counselors need to help family members understand how their thoughts and behaviors engender addictive behaviors. In other words, family addictions counselors help family members and the family system better understand what members say to themselves (e.g., "If I do drugs, others will think I'm cool and like me"), feel (e.g., anxiety, depression, anger), do (e.g., argue, fight, withdraw), and say to others (e.g., "Mother is such a witch, Dad. She is always yelling at us.") immediately before they participate in their addictive behaviors. Second, family addiction counselors promote understanding of how the family members' addictive behaviors are connected to negative consequences (e.g., feelings of failure on the job or at school, arguments with family members) and positive consequences (e.g., increased interactions among family members or friends [e.g., doing drugs with my friends], feelings of confidence). Finally, family addictions counselors help family members explore new, healthier ways of thinking and acting that reduce the probability of continued addiction.

Interventions Family addictions counselors first need to help family members recognize the triggers (e.g., thoughts, feelings, behaviors, situations, interactions) that occur immediately prior to the members' abuse. Commonly, addicted family members will be able to describe the internal dialogues they have with themselves or the physical or psychological signals that foretell of their upcoming abuse. For example, an adolescent family member might indicate that her internal dialogue immediately before using cannabis goes something like this: "I'm so stressed. There is no way I can put up with my parents yelling. I've got to smoke some weed to calm myself down." Additionally, she may describe physical feelings like an inability to relax or concentrate and physical behaviors like involuntary muscle contractions or psychomotor agitation (e.g., tapping her fingers, bouncing her leg). Psychological signals might include remembering the calm she experienced when she smoked cannabis the previous day or describing the depressed symptomatology experienced most days when she is abstinent. Furthermore, this adolescent family member might be able to identify specific family situations or circumstances that increase the probability of her cannabis abuse (e.g., when her dad teases her about being fat, the nights before her school tests, the days on which she receives her calculus quiz scores).

Once triggers are discussed and recognized by the addicted member and others within the family system, a trigger list is made. Jointly family members help the addicted members identify triggers. The triggers identified as most powerful and most frequently encountered are of primary importance. Thus, the family system, with specific input from the addicted members first, ranks the strength of the individual triggers from 10 ("When I experience this, I am inevitably going to use") to 0 ("When I experience this, I will not use at all"). Next, they rank the trigger frequency from 10 ("This trigger occurs constantly throughout my awake hours") to 0 ("I never experience this trigger"). Priority is then given to triggers identified by the addicted family members as being the most powerful and occurring most often. In other words, triggers noted as both foretelling inevitable use and constantly occurring are the triggers that warrant the most attention within the family counseling sessions.

Although some may argue that the family system jointly working with the specific input from addicted members to identify triggers is unnecessary, we disagree. Even though the primary intent is for the addicted members to identify these powerful and frequently occurring triggers, there exist three very important secondary gains by having nonaddicted family members participate in helping the addicted members rank order triggers. Specifically, this process teaches nonaddicted family members how their behaviors and actions contribute to the addicted member's triggers. Such knowledge is vitally important and can change the frequency of triggering behaviors. Therefore nonaddicted family members can learn how they can actively impact positive treatment and recovery. Second, nonaddicted family members learn that they can "check in" with recovering family members when triggers are noted. In other words, these family members can say things like,

> "Mom is yelling again. Remember Dr. Hagedorn told us to practice some of the things he taught us to do when Mom starts to yell. So, what things are you saying to yourself right now to remind you that Mom is just frustrated about Dad and not angry at you?"

Finally, by understanding how common daily stressors contribute to triggering relapse, nonaddicted family members can better understand the types of daily stress and vulnerability addicted family members experience. This can contribute additional support and encouragement from the addicted member's most treasured relationships.

Establishing Trigger Baselines The self-described severity and frequency of triggers presented by family members serves as baselines that can later be used to measure progress. In other words, these baselines allow both family members and counselors to track treatment efficacy. Should family members report a decrease in trigger severity and frequency, progress is likely occurring and the cognitive-behavioral family interventions being used should be continued. However, should the severity and frequency of triggers increase, treatment and interventions warrant revision.

Nonuse Lists In addition to the trigger list, family addictions counselors may wish to help members construct a "nonuse list." Here, the emphasis is on identifying thoughts, feelings, behaviors, and situations occurring when family members do not abuse. The purpose of this list is to help family members identify different ways of positively experiencing life without the need to incorporate addictive behaviors. Many family addictions counselors with whom we have spoken have noted that significant portions of their frequently abusing family members will be abstinent when (a) they are interacting with respected and admired family, friends, and work or school peers who do not use, (b) addicted family members are jointly participating with others in activities they are invested in and find interesting, and (c) they do not experience overwhelming anxiety related to family relationships or interactions, future performance, past arguments, or threats of danger. Thus, this list provides family members ideas on how they might better cope with experiences that commonly lead to their abuse by describing how they think, feel, and behave when they are not driven by the urge to use.

Positive Consequences Unfortunately, positive abuse consequences are often ignored or inappropriately minimized by helping professionals. This is a significant treatment error that devastates counseling efficacy and disinvests active participation.

Addicted family members frequently experience multiple positive consequences as a result of their addictions. These positive consequences can vary greatly depending on the specific addicted member and family. Perceived family and peer support provided by others, escape from pressing concerns, and pure enjoyment of being under the influence are key reasons people use. Honest discussion regarding the potential loss of these perceived positive consequences is necessary before family members can begin the abstinence process. Therefore, questions such as, "What positive things do you experience when you use?" or "What is it like drinking with your friends?" are helpful.

The intent of these questions is not to have family members romantically portray their addictive behaviors. Instead, counselors are learning "how" the addictive behaviors are pleasurable and why such experiences are important to the individual. Once the "hows" and "whys" are answered, counselors can begin working to appropriately address the void that will inevitably be created should the addicted family member eliminate his active addiction.

For example, should a 13-year-old male indicate that drinking with other teens provides him friendships, the counselor, student, and family may need to identify other ways the student can secure friendships without using. Given the importance adolescents place on peer acceptance and their desire to "fit in," this is a daunting challenge. However, failing to address this addicted family member's needs for new, nonusing friends, at best, destines the counseling process to limited success.

Negative Consequences When reviewing negative consequences resulting from the addictive behavior, it is helpful to first ask about the presenting circumstances that brought the person or family to counseling and then link the presenting circumstance to the addictive behavior. A vignette is provided below.

Counselor: "Shondra, I know that Vice Principal Myers referred you to my office. As I understand the situation, you had consumed alcohol and gotten sick last Saturday night during the homecoming basketball game. Help me understand what that was like for you."

Shondra: "It was awful. I was trying to be cool and instead I got drunk. When I got to the game, everything started spinning, and I threw up in the stands. I was so embarrassed. Now my parents know I was drinking, I'm grounded, and the people I was trying to impress laugh at me."

Counselor: "Wow, that sounds rough."

Shondra: "Yeah . . . it is."

Counselor: "What have you learned from all of this?"

Shondra: "Well, I've learned that I don't want to drink anymore."

Counselor: "Tell me about other times you had some bad things happen when you drank beer or used drugs."

Shondra: "I can't think of any."

Counselor: "Sometimes people tell me that they perform badly on tests or get bad grades, because they were under the influence of alcohol when they took their tests or because they missed a lot of school due to their drinking. Has anything like that ever happened to you?"

Shondra: "Naw, nothing like that."

Counselor: "Mother, sometimes my adolescent clients who abuse alcohol argue with family members or get into trouble at home due to their drinking. Can you think of any times that Shondra has gotten in arguments or trouble at home due to her alcohol or drug use?"

Mother: "Well, a couple weeks ago, Shondra and her friends had been out drinking and ran my car into the ditch. Shondra was really drunk. She knows better than to drive my car when she is drunk. Anyway, I had to call her dad to get the car out. He was really upset. He said Shondra had to pay the $480 to get the car fixed."

Counselor: "So, Shondra, your mother says that your drinking got you into trouble with your dad and caused you to pay the expenses for repairing your mom's car?"

Shondra: "Yeah, I guess I'm learning that drinking costs me a lot."

Within this vignette, the counselor first attempts to help Shondra to begin understanding the link between her drinking behaviors and other potential negative consequences. The counselor describes the primary reason Shondra came for counseling: the vice principal's referral. Shondra reports two specific problems resulting from this incident (e.g., embarrassment, parental punishment [grounding]). The counselor then investigates potential negative consequences of alcohol consumption related to Shondra's school experience. This is denied. Then, the counselor asks mother about other potential negative consequences of Shondra's alcohol consumption. Mother reports an accident resulting from Shondra's impaired driving. Toward the end of this session the counselor would likely summarize the problems reported by Shondra and her mother as linked to Shondra's alcohol use and ask Shondra to clarify how continued alcohol consumption is helpful.

Counselor:	"Shondra, help me understand. You say that you were terminated from Wal-Mart, because you've been too drunk to work your scheduled shift. You've said that you've gotten in trouble with your mom and dad for drinking and driving and had to pay over $400 to get your mom's car repaired. And, you've told me that you get real anxious when you buy beer, because your mom and dad told you not to drink or they would kick you out of their house. How is it helpful to you to continue drinking?"
Shondra:	"I guess it's not."
Counselor:	"Based on your trigger list, you've basically said you consume alcohol when you get bored. So, what will you do differently when you get bored in the future?"
Shondra:	"Well, I guess I'm not going to drink."
Counselor:	"OK, what will you do instead when you find yourself becoming bored or thinking that you may become bored?"
Shondra:	"I don't know."
Counselor:	"Well, on your nonuse list, you said when you are with Stacey, you don't use alcohol, because she is fun and she doesn't like beer. I'm wondering if you would be willing to call Stacey when you begin to feel bored."
Shondra:	"Yeah, I could do that."
Counselor:	"What else could you do?"
Shondra:	"I guess I could do some of the other things I said in my nonuse list, like take my dog for a walk or practice my clarinet."
Counselor:	"Mom and Dad, based on the triggers that Shondra identified as most powerful and most frequently occurring, what are some triggers that you will be watching for?"
Father:	"Boredom is the first."

Counselor: "So, what will you do if you begin to believe Shondra might be bored?"

Mother: "Well, the first thing we could do is ask her if she is starting to think about drinking. If she is, we can either help her get interested in something to do or maybe even help her do something with one of her friends or with us."

In the above vignette the counselor gently confronts Shondra's drinking by asking how continued drinking is helpful. Instead of dropping the discussion when Shondra reports that her alcohol consumption is not helpful, the counselor uses the client's trigger list to help Shondra recognize one of the primary reasons she reportedly consumes alcohol (e.g., to escape boredom). Therefore, the counselor is therapeutically using both the family member's trigger list and her nonuse list to help provide appropriate interventions. Additionally, the counselor encourages the family to begin looking for identified triggers and asks about interventions they will use should they perceive that Shondra is becoming bored. The intent here is not only to help Shondra but also to encourage her family system to address potential triggers.

Sometimes family members either are clueless regarding potential negative consequences of addictive behaviors or purposely deny any negative consequences. Under these circumstances, family addictions counselors may wish to use circular questioning. Here, the intent is to learn how family members believe they are perceived by valued and respected significant others. Thus, family addictions counselors might ask a question like, "Shondra, who is the most important person in your life?"

Once the addicted family members identify their most important significant others, counselors can ask something like, "Based on what you've told me, your mother is very important to you. Given that your mother is here, would you be willing to tell me what you think she would say some of the major negative consequences of your drinking and drugging behaviors are?" The intent here is for the addicted member to report things likely already stated by the significant family member.

It is possible that the significant family member has not reported concerns about the addictive behaviors. In this case, the counselor is still being helpful in aiding the addicted family member to cognitively understand the family's concerns. After these potential concerns have been reported by the addicted family member, the counselor then asks the addicted member to see if these in fact were the major concerns that the family members have. This might go something like this.

Counselor:	"Shondra, you've indicated that your mother and father are the two most important people in your life. What do you believe your mother would say are the major negative consequences for you as a result of your drinking?"
Shondra:	"That's pretty easy. She has told me that she is concerned that if I am drinking that I will get drunk, have sex, and get pregnant."
Counselor:	"What other negative consequences do you think she perceives from your drinking?"
Shondra:	"She really hasn't mentioned any others. However, I bet she is scared that I won't be able to get into college and have the career as a psychologist that I want."
Counselor:	"Why don't you ask your mom if these are the concerns she has about your drinking? Mother, Shondra states that you are concerned that she will get pregnant while she is under the influence of alcohol and that another concern you might have is related to Shondra not being able to make the grades to get into college and become a psychologist. Are these the concerns you have?"
Mother:	"Yes, Shondra's older sister became pregnant, because she got drunk and had sex. Then, because she had to take care of the baby, she couldn't finish school or go on to college. The truth is that Shondra doesn't have to drug. She is smart, has good grades, and can accomplish anything she puts her mind to. But, she is wasting her future, because she is not using the brains the good Lord gave to her."
Counselor:	"Shondra, what do you hear your mother saying?"
Shondra:	"She's right. I'm wasting my time drinking and partying rather than studying so I can get good grades and gain entrance into college and then graduate school."
Counselor:	"So what do you need to do differently?"
Shondra:	"I've got to stop the drinking and start studying."
Counselor:	"So what will you do when you experience those triggers you identified?"

Additional Intervention Strategy   Using cognitive-behavioral interventions to help family members more thoroughly understand their addiction sequence (i.e., triggers, nontriggers, positive consequences, and negative consequences) is helpful. However, two other adjunctive interventions warrant discussion when using Cognitive-Behavioral Family Counseling. The first is contingency contracting.

A significant number of family addictions counselors with whom we work utilize contingency contracting (Rinn, 1978) when counseling addicted family members. Contingency contracts are clearly worded contracts that describe acceptable and unacceptable addiction-related behaviors. Jointly family addictions counselors and their client family members develop an outline indicating that addictive behaviors will not be tolerated. Sanctions discussed and created within the family system are stated (e.g., losing car driving privileges, television privileges) as well as rewards for contract compliance (e.g., private time, reduced home chores, participation in athletics).

Sobriety contracts are one contingency contract type. For example, Antabuse may have been prescribed for a family member's alcohol abuse. The family addictions counselor might facilitate a meeting where mother and father speak with their alcohol-abusing son. Together the family can identify a time each day when they can meet for approximately 10 minutes or longer if necessary. During those meetings, son verbally commits to remaining alcohol-free. Thus, he might say something like, "Mom and Dad, I'm going to stay drug-free today. I promise to do my very best at learning so I can graduate from high school. And, if I start to think about using, I will call my Alateen sponsor for help." Mother and father then have the opportunity to voice any specific concerns they might have about upcoming events that day which may be identified as alcohol relapse triggers. For example, mother could say, "Charlie, I know you want to stay alcohol-free and are committed to graduating, but I also know that midterms begin today. I am concerned you might feel overwhelmed or anxious and begin using alcohol to cope."

The addicted family member then has a chance to explain how he will handle the noted concern: "Mom, I know you're worried. But, if I feel anxious or overwhelmed because of the midterms, I promise to speak with you or my sponsor. I know I can handle it, but if I can't, I've come too far to just give in and use." Once the student indicates how he will respond, the parents are not allowed to ask further questions that day. The abusing member then takes the prescribed Antabuse medications in front of mother and father and places an "X" on the Sobriety Contract Calendar for that specific day.

During the beginning of the subsequent family counseling sessions, the counselor and family identify and discuss progress made and address any changes warranted for the following week. The intent of this experience, then, is to ritualize this daily sobriety contracting experience and encourage family members to direct the maintenance and recovery process. When a relapse occurs, it is discussed in detail and the newly created contingency contract incorporates the types of things that must happen to reduce the possibility of the triggers and behaviors that sabotaged progress.

Summary   As plainly noted above, Cognitive-Behavioral Counseling builds on the Motivational Interviewing and the Solution-Focused Stages. Techniques specific to this stage, such as the identification of triggers, the implementation of nonuse triggers as means to interrupt triggers, and the use of contingency contracting, can be easily implemented by families. More importantly for counselors using the Sequential Family Addictions Model, this stage marks movement away from mere treatment goals and the creation of visual outcome pictures. Families now begin to merge their focus on problematic cognitions and behaviors. Specifically, family addictions counselors help families directly address the triggers that warn of upcoming addictive behaviors and provide ways for the individual and family to inoculate themselves from these behaviors. However, there are times when even this is not enough to address addictive behaviors. Should this be the case, the model directs movement into the next counseling stage.

Stage Four: Structural Family Counseling

General Overview   The intent of Structural Family Counseling is to bring consistent, functional, orderly structure to chaotic families (Minuchin, 1974; Minuchin & Fishman, 1981; Stanton & Todd, 1979). Similar to a blueprint describing the foundation of a house, its framework, and directions for those constructing the home (e.g., plumbers, carpenters, electricians, etc.), Structural Family Counseling organizes the larger addicted family system into distinct subsystems, each with specific boundaries, tasks, and rules (Figure 4.3). Therefore, this form of addiction family counseling is based on healthy partnerships within and between family subsystems. In other words, it helps persons within the same subsystem work effectively toward healthy self-regulation and mutually enhancing goal accomplishments. Here, the emphasis is on improving the subsystem teamwork in a manner that engenders greater satisfaction within individual subsystems. Concomitantly, Structural Family Counseling suggests that when the family's subsystems are healthy, happy, and working well, they in turn will mutually enhance the

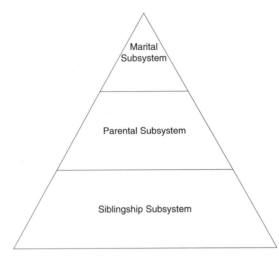

Figure 4.3 Structural hierarchy model.

entire family system and lead to a decrease in the presenting addictive behaviors. Therefore, the Structural Family Counseling view of the family system and its subsystems parallels the holistic physician's view of the human body and its many subsystems (e.g., the central nervous system, the digestive system). When the subsystems are well functioning and healthy, persons can accomplish amazing feats, from running marathons to climbing mountains. However, should one subsystem become distressed or dysfunctional, the entire body is negatively affected.

Structural Family Counseling is also concerned with the family power hierarchy. That is to say that Structural Family Counseling is concerned with establishing the Marital Subsystem, sometimes known as the Partnership Subsystem. This subsystem is at the top of the power and authority hierarchy. When the family system's adults are committed to each other, the marriage is perceived as rewarding, and the number of positively perceived behaviors outweighs the number of negatively experienced behaviors within the Marital Subsystem. Therefore, the couple can be an effective parenting team.

However, should the Marital Subsystem be in jeopardy of collapse and little marital satisfaction exist, effective parenting will be hampered. Thus, within Structural Family Counseling the intent is to strengthen the Marital Subsystem and empower its member team to have greater authority over the other subsystems. Only when this most important subsystem is adequately founded and well functioning can the second most powerful subsystem, the Parenting Subsystem, be established.

Therefore, unlike the previously described family counseling theories, Structural Family Counseling attempts to enhance the marital relationship by promoting opportunities for the couple to rekindle their previously enjoyable relationship experiences. Similar to a campfire that ultimately becomes a smoldering ash pile when neglected, marriages must be reignited and rejuvenated. Neglect in marriages is often a direct result of countless demands experienced by the couple. From the needs of children to the stressors of aging parents and finances, marriages frequently experience demise due to neglect. Structural family counselors understand that reignition can be accomplished by rekindling the embers of past positive memories and encouraging the repeat of previously satisfying experiences. Once this occurs, the marriage or coupleship becomes the glue that gives meaning and holds the Parenting Subsystem together.

The third and final subsystem is the Siblingship Subsystem. In a healthy family system, the Siblingship Subsystem should be the least powerful within the family hierarchy. In other words, this subsystem should never have authority or rule over the Marital or the Parenting Subsystems. This is not to suggest that this subsystem should be taken for granted or should be weak. A strong Siblingship Subsystem teaches children how to respect authority figures and helps children learn how to appropriately interact with peers. Clearly this is a very important subsystem that must be nurtured and respected. However, this subsystem should not unduly influence either the Marital or Parenting Subsystems. After all, the adults' relationship is the cornerstone of the family's existence and the adults are the parents.

Based on our experiences with addicted families, we have found that the power hierarchy is often pathologically inverted and children and adolescents rule the addicted family system. A few commonly encountered examples of such inverted power hierarchies are presented below. Each is equally dysfunctional and must be adequately corrected to help both the addicted family members and the addicted family system eradicate the addiction.

The first inverted power hierarchy system is when the Siblingship Subsystem stages a coup and overpowers the Marital and Parenting Subsystems. In these families the addicted members are part of the Siblingship Subsystem, and they take control via intimidation and fear. Thus, these adolescents bully their parents and become the system's authority figures.

We have worked with many family systems where addicted adolescents using a combination of alcohol, cocaine, and anabolic steroids present with significant bravado, threatening behaviors directed toward parents and siblings, and intense rage. Many of these adolescent males are disproportionately larger and more muscular than their parents and can be quite menacing in appearance even when they are not angry. However, when the volatile concoction of alcohol, cocaine, and anabolic steroid abuse occur concomitantly to comorbid rage brought about by the drug cocktail used and adolescent immaturity, the smaller-sized parents can feel utterly helpless in their attempts to establish vital parental control.

The detonation point for the coup often occurs when the parents' marriage deteriorates to a point of collapse due to the demands of the abusing adolescents. Here, the Parenting Subsystem can no longer effectively command the power required to restore necessary parental authority levels. Thus, the family system disintegrates, the addicted adolescents have no established boundaries or rules, and their addictive behaviors are rampant.

Another commonly inverted power hierarchy situation occurs when parents willingly abdicate power to their children. Earlier within the chapter we discussed the construct of homeostasis and described a situation where the eldest daughter within one addicted family system had become parentified. As you may remember, father initially gave oldest daughter control of the family system. In this situation, the power hierarchy had been willingly inverted by an addicted father who allowed the children to rule the family system. It has been our experience that these addicted parents understand that their addiction renders them ineffective parents. Therefore, the parents surrender their parenting responsibilities and often their head-of-household responsibilities, because they believe that the system can function better without them.

However, we have also experienced inverted power hierarchies when parents abdicate their parental authority to protect themselves or others from "family secrets." Such secrets can revolve around many causes including infidelity, money, and addictions. For example, we have encountered family systems where parents have attempted to "buy off" their children or spouses. Hence, these partners or parents rewarded other family members for not disclosing potentially embarrassing or hurtful secrets.

On one such occasion, the family power hierarchy was inverted as a result of sexual infidelity. Here, two of the family's adolescent children observed their intoxicated parent in a sexually compromising situation with another adult at a neighborhood pool party. In an effort to keep the children from divulging "the secret," the parent began eliminating many of the adolescents' previously required household chores and inflated their allowances to absurd levels. Furthermore, this parent refused to confront the children's alcohol use, because of the children's threats to expose the infidelity. In the end the blackmailed parent felt used and vulnerable to the children, and the secret was exposed to the other parent. Within treatment the goal was to reconnect and strengthen the Marital Subsystem so that the couple could mutually begin reestablishing their parenting efficacy. This in turn would promote the necessary boundaries for the Sibling Subsystem that would address the adolescents' abusive alcohol use and eliminate the ensuing family chaos.

In other situations, the head of the household is a single parent. In other words, the Marital Subsystem does not exist. Here, the intent is similarly related to establishing the single parent at the head of the power hierarchy, but this situation is different because there is no marriage or partnership relationship to rekindle or focus. We have found that single parents report investing "everything" into their children and saving little or nothing for themselves. Therefore, it is especially important to help single parents establish their family power hierarchy via an external support system. Specifically, we have found local churches, single-parent support groups, Al-Anon groups, extended family, and neighbors especially helpful to these single parents. As these single parents have the opportunity to be supported by other adults and experience respite, they can effectively reestablish the power hierarchy and meet the everyday demands of raising their family.

Interventions   The typical Structural Family Therapy intervention follows a standardized counseling intervention sequence. This sequence includes (a) joining the family system, (b) identifying structural patterns, (c) strengthening or loosening subsystem and system boundaries, and (d) unbalancing systems. For the family addictions counselor, joining is an important first intervention step, because the nonaddicted family members will typically be rather defensive. Nonaddicted members frequently say to themselves and to others in the treatment session, "Why am I here? I'm not the addicted person."

Given that the Sequential Family Addictions Model has already begun with motivational interviewing and progressed through Solution-Focused and Cognitive-Behavioral Family Therapy Interventions, and given that the counselor has demonstrated respect for each person within the family system, continuing to join should not pose a particularly difficult challenge. After all, the family, via each of the previous counseling interventions, has been able to tell exactly how they wish the family would be, and they have jointly identified relevant treatment goals and interventions.

However, in this fourth stage the counselor will more intentionally join each family subsystem by making certain that each family member has the opportunity to tell what life is like for them and the particular subsystem in which they participate. Particularly within this stage the family addictions counselor will identify the family structure and create hypotheses about the power hierarchies within each subsystem and within the system itself. For example, during session the counselor might formulate the hypothesis that father is both enlisting oldest son as a pseudo parent within the Parenting Subsystem and eclipsing mother as a parenting partner. To test the hypothesis, the counselor might simply ask questions about this potential behavioral pattern. Thus, the counselor might state, "Dad, it sounds as though you often rely on your oldest son to help parent the other children." The identification of such a destructive coalition between parent and child is vitally important to restoring a functional and healthy power hierarchy to the family.

Once such hypotheses are generated and tested, the family addictions counselor will begin addressing dysfunctional boundaries and unbalancing unhealthy subsystems. These can be successfully accomplished by increasingly delineating each subsystem and discussing the different roles and power levels within each subsystem of the family structure. Examples of such structural subsystems delineation would include using names that identify family members within a specific subsystem. Here, for example, the counselor might use the names "Mom" and "Dad" as a means to both join the Parenting Subsystem and amplify the Parenting Subsystem's existence within the overall family structure. Therefore, the counselor might say something like the following:

Counselor:	"Mom and Dad, help me understand what it is like to be the parents of these three teenagers?"
Mother:	"It is challenging all the time."
Father:	"Yes, very challenging. The other night, for example, we had found our two older sons drinking our beer. They always are forcing us to treat them as boys rather than enjoying them as friends. I sure wish it were different."
Counselor:	"Well, Mom and Dad, it sounds to me that you two as a parenting team are in agreement that being the parents of this family is challenging. What's really encouraging is that both of you understand that your sons are part of the kids team and, like it or not, you are the adults who first and foremost have a relationship all your own—a marriage completely separate from the kids. And secondly you are part of a parenting team whose jobs and responsibilities are to parent these nonadult children. Help me understand, as part of the adult parenting team, how the two of you as adult parents of these children jointly decide how to handle a situation such as the one you've just described."

Let's take a moment to review this vignette. The most obvious part of this intervention is the manner in which the counselor delineates the different subsystems while she continues to join the Parental Subsystem. She does this in a number of ways. First, she uses the names "Mom" and "Dad." By calling the parents "Mom" and "Dad," she names the Parental Subsystem members and notes the children's exclusion from this subsystem. Second, the counselor calls the parents a "parenting team." Doing so implies unity and common goals for the parents as they jointly address their charge. The statement further informs children and reminds parents that the parents have all corresponding parental duties, privileges, and rights to establish appropriate family rules. Third, the counselor succinctly differentiates and describes both the Parental and the Siblingship Subsystems. Again, this helps both parents and children understand the differences between the individual subsystems and notes specific subsystem members. Finally, the counselor asks the parents how they work together within the Parental Subsystem to address their children's needs. The counselor here is suggesting that the parents have jointly decided to act in unison and have discussed how they should respond to their children. Even if they haven't made such decisions to work together, the mere statement suggests that parental unity is both important and necessary to bring about favorable outcomes. In essence, then, we can see how this counselor has used titles (e.g., "Mom") and names (e.g., "Dad") to amplify the members of specific subsystems and the responsibilities of each of the subsystems.

Structural Family Counseling is also known for its enactment techniques. Specifically, within session, should the counselor observe something that weakens subsystems or blurs subsystem boundaries, she can address this via enactments. In the above example, father suggests that he would like to "enjoy" his boys as friends rather than as sons. Thus, the enactment might be for the counselor to ask mother if she heard what father just said and explain what it may be like for her when father interacts with the boys as friends and leaves her out of the sequence.

Counselor: "Wife, I am wondering if you can help me out here. Your husband just indicated that he would rather experience the boys as his friends rather than as your sons. I'm wondering, are there ever times when you feel left out by your husband, because he seems to be treating the boys more as his friends rather than acting like their father and your partner?"

Mother: "I feel left out a lot. It won't do any good to talk about it, because when I bring it up to him, he just denies it is happening."

Here, the counselor has heard statements that suggest that father at times is blurring his membership in subsystems by treating his boys as friends rather than as sons. In other words, at times father is abandoning his roles as both spouse and parent and instead is acting like a member of the Siblingship Subsystem. The counselor then creates an opportunity to discuss this perception with wife. Even if wife would have denied such boundary blurring, the counselor's discussion of the behaviors brings attention to the behaviors and suggests that it must stop. However, in this vignette, mother in fact reports that she has on occasion felt left out when father changes subsystem memberships. Wife then reports, "It won't do any good to talk about it, because . . . he just denies it is happening." Here, the counselor could say something to wife like, "Come on, now. You've got the chance to talk about it right here and now. Turn your chair toward your husband and tell him what it is like for you when he interacts with the boys as friends rather than as sons and leaves you out of the relationship." This allows wife to voice her concern to husband. It further implies to the father that these boundary-blurring behaviors are unacceptable and will be discussed in session. Concomitantly, the siblingship receives an important message: Mom's back in the power seat and Dad can't eclipse Mom's authority anymore.

Additional Intervention Strategy Structural family counselors also use *competence shaping* as a way to effectively promote a healthy family hierarchy. Continuing with the above vignette, competence shaping might be used in the following manner.

Counselor: "Way to go, Mom. I just saw you signal the boys that they were getting too rambunctious in session and that they needed to settle down. When your oldest son rolled his eyes and pulled away, you didn't even flinch. You just took the authority of being a good parent within this family and told him to settle down. Many parents who come here don't know how to be an effective parent like you or they are afraid to be a parent in their families. This clearly is not the case with you. You didn't let the children rule the family and you told them exactly what they needed to do. Excellent work, Mom. Keep it up."

Here, the counselor has accomplished three things. First, he has recognized mother for a positive behavior that most likely would have gone unnoticed by others within the family system. Second, the counselor has announced mother's competence as a parent to the other family members. In doing so, the counselor tells others that mother is competent and should be prized. Concomitantly, the counselor's statement increases the likelihood the mother will amplify such appropriate parenting behaviors.

To make this intervention even more potent, the counselor might simply ask, "Dad, how do you demonstrate your full support of Mom when she does such an outstanding job as she just did with the boys and support her as your co-parenting partner? Why don't you take just a moment and tell her that you fully support her and you appreciate the excellent co-parenting partner she is. Then, why don't you tell your oldest son how Mom and you are a team and explain to your oldest son how he can best comply with Mom's directive." This then promotes father's further joining mother within the Parenting Subsystem and signals the oldest son, who previously had been brought into the Parenting Subsystem, that mother and father are a team. In other words, son is not included in this co-parenting team. Thus, the father and mother strengthen the Parenting Subsystem boundaries, unbalance the previous coalition between father and son, and challenge dysfunctional assumptions that father and son hold the family system's power. Furthermore, should father comply, it deepens the functional chasm between the Parenting and Siblingship Subsystems.

Another Structural Family Counseling intervention hallmark is the use of *spontaneous behavior sequences*. Here, the family addictions counselor spotlights a specific behavior sequence that occurs within session. Continuing with the same vignette as above, if father said to oldest son, "Where should you and I take them [mother and the other children] out to lunch today?" the counselor might confront father for again eclipsing mother from the Parenting Subsystem. Therefore, the counselor might say, "Whoa. I can't believe you just pushed your wife out of the parent role by asking your son to join you in deciding where your wife's and your family will eat lunch." The intent here is for the counselor to draw the behavior to the attention of each family system member and to accentuate the need for mother and father to work together within the Parenting Subsystem.

The counselor may even wish to make the intervention more powerful by positioning mother to confront father regarding the behavior. Thus, the counselor might say, "Come on here, Mom. Are you going to let father get away with leaving you out of this co-parenting decision?" The intent of this confrontation is to promote vigilance related to mother's being removed from the Parental Subsystem and allow wife the opportunity to tell husband that she is not going to accept his eclipsing behaviors.

Summary   Unlike previous stages, Structural Family Counseling re-distributes power within the family system and places parental control and authority above the children's undue influence. This is done by enhancing marriage satisfaction and establishing the Marital Subsystem at the top of the family's power hierarchy. Once this subsystem is securely placed, the Parental and Siblingship Subsystems can be fully established. Only when the power hierarchy is correctly founded can functionality be restored to the entire family system.

Enactments and spontaneous behavior sequences provide opportuni-ties to modify the family structure. These in-session interventions cre-ate critical opportunities to implement solution-focused techniques such as solution pictures, which were described earlier in this chapter. Here, family members describe how the subsystems and system will look when things have improved once the power hierarchy is fully established. Con-comitantly, cognitive-behavioral techniques can be used to identify new ways of acting, responding, and coping with typical family stressors and in particular stressors related to recovery.

Finally, Structural Family Counseling promotes necessary boundaries for those in recovery and their families. In other words, addicted persons who neglected, abdicated, or lost their key roles and places within sub-systems as well as the family system itself can once again be productive. Their reentry as productive subsystem and system members can revitalize exhausted systems and can ease the demands and burdens on those already accomplishing required tasks and charges. However, should further change still be warranted by the conclusion of this stage, the family addictions counselor can move to the Extended Family Systems Counseling Stage.

Stage Five: Extended Family Systems Counseling

General Overview   Extended Family Systems Counseling is most frequently associated with Murray Bowen and encourages client families to look at pathology's cascading effects on multiple generations. Key to Bowen's theory is the *differentiation of self.* This construct was briefly described when we discussed enmeshed families in the subsection on family boundaries. Differentiation of self suggests the existence of two opposing forces that create an underlying tension in both individuals and families. These opposing forces include those that bind or fuse families together (e.g., enmeshed families) and those that individuate or drive families apart (e.g., emotional cutoffs). According to Bowen (1975), healthy and able functioning adults must be able to fully separate between thoughts and feelings both intrapsychically and interpersonally. Differentiation refers to this important process and indicates that an adult has the ability to distinguish thoughts from feelings. Stated differently, differentiated persons have the necessary self-restraint to analyze situations without emotional malaise. This, however, does not imply that differentiated persons are aloof or emotionally unresponsive. Instead, differentiated persons are balanced in their perceptions of self and others and have the ability to thoughtfully consider and respond to typical individual and family stressors.

Undifferentiated persons, on the other hand, are unable to think clearly. Typically an overwhelming rush of emotions cloud their thought processes and impede logical reasoning. Thus, undifferentiated persons are *fused* or *enmeshed* with other family members and have extreme difficulty separating themselves from their family. In other words, undifferentiated persons lack autonomy from others and say what they feel rather than what they think.

Another hallmark construct of Extended Family Systems Counseling is Triangulation. Triangulation suggests that when excessive anxiety or stressors arise within a relationship, often one person *triangulates* or seeks a third person to confide in. Or, in some cases, instead of triangulating to a third person, one of the partners turns to something such as an addiction to escape the relationship tension. Although such triangulation may initially reduce anxiety or stress within the problematic relationship, there is no final resolution. Instead the triangulation merely dilutes the presenting anxiety or stress and inhibits the persons from actually resolving the problems that initially engendered the anxiety or stressors.

A relatively frequent experience that we have encountered revolves around marital conflict and an addictions triangulation. Here, one relationship partner will begin to badger another related to common marriage-related dissatisfaction topics. These topics often include but are not limited to finances, time spent together, child rearing, or sex. Arguments ensue. The addicted partner will feel overwhelmed, helpless, anxious, or angry about the other partner's voiced complaints. In an effort to control the intensely uncomfortable feelings, the addicted partners often revert back to the addiction (e.g., cybersex) or addiction substance (e.g., cocaine) rather than invest the necessary energy and emotional expenditure to address and resolve the described dissatisfaction. For a short while the triangulation provides sufficient relief to somewhat reduce the intense negative feelings. However, by the time the addicted person realizes that the triangulation relief was merely temporary, a slip has likely occurred and the relapse cycle is in full swing. This is often a time when the non-addicted partner becomes infuriated by both the failed recovery and the nonresolution to the initial marital dissatisfaction complaint.

Another Extended Family Systems Counseling construct termed the *Family Projection Process* describes how parents transmit their failed differentiation pathology onto their children. Here, emotional fusion between marriage partners provokes distress and creates either intense marital conflict within the nuclear family (e.g., husband, wife, and children) or an emotional cutoff from the nuclear husband's or wife's parents. Emotional cutoffs occur when the nuclear couple escapes parents either by physically moving away or by becoming emotionally inaccessible. Either way, the cutoff inhibits contact between generations and results in a dysfunctional nuclear family.

Typically, emotional cutoffs result in the one partner resenting the other due to the imposed cutoff. This commonly means that the marital partner forced to abandon her family of origin becomes emotionally absent to the partner who forced the intergenerational separation. Can you anticipate the result? Exactly, the emotionally ignored marital partner who is forced to cut off from her family of origin feels alone and underappreciated. To fill this emotional absence, the ignored marital partner then overly engages with the couple's children and gains satisfaction not by being a partner to her spouse but by over-identifying and becoming the children's closest friend. In other words, this emotionally abandoned adult seeks significance and meaning via overly engaging with the couple's offspring. Thus, this parent's identity becomes the children. Such over-involvement with the children has the potential to emotionally cripple the children and prevent the children's achievement of typical developmental accomplishments.

Such was the case with Jane and Andy and their 6-year-old son, Alex. The chief presenting concerns reported by the couple related to Alex's overwhelming separation anxiety and his "tantrums" when left at school, Jane's "extreme" marital dissatisfaction, and Andy's continued alcohol abuse. Jane began by stating, "Alex is his mommy's boy. He just doesn't like it when I drop him off at school." Jane then described her intense marital dissatisfaction and her frustration with Andy's continual binge drinking episodes. Andy reported that his binge drinking episodes were a result of his anger with Jane and her unwillingness to interact with him.

According to the couple, Andy's parents had provided child care to Alex. Over the preceding 4-year period, Jane had become increasingly dissatisfied by the manner in which her in-laws "parented" Alex. The couple reportedly experienced severe arguments revolving around the in-laws providing child care. Finally, when Jane could no longer tolerate her in-laws caring for Alex, Jane made an ultimatum. Either her parents would provide child care for Alex, or Jane would take Alex and separate. Andy didn't want to "lose" his wife and feared that, as a result of his binge drinking and alcohol dependence, he would ultimately lose custody of his son. Embarrassed and angered by Jane's ultimatum, Andy conceded. He informed his parents that they could no longer be the child care providers for Alex and further indicated Jane's refusal to allow them to visit Jane and Andy's home.

Pursuant to Andy's discussion with his parents, Andy became emotionally distant to Jane and began spending time with his former drinking buddies to complain about "Jane's bullying tactics." Jane refused to interact with Andy's parents and failed to return telephone calls or allow visitation between Alex and Andy's parents. Jane's behaviors infuriated Andy to such a point that he moved out of the couple's bedroom and began sleeping in the basement. As Andy became more emotionally distant to Jane, she quit work and focused nearly all her awake time and energy on Alex. According to Andy, "I couldn't win. My wife wouldn't allow my son to enjoy his grandparents, and she hoarded all Alex's time so I couldn't be with him either. What else could I do but return to my booze and my high school buddies? She made our entire lives miserable, and she has devastated my parents."

Given your familiarity with Structural Family Therapy and your new understanding of Extended Family Systems Counseling, it likely has become apparent how the two uniquely dovetail into a sophisticated family counseling progression. Remember too that motivational interviewing, Solution-Focused Therapy, and Cognitive-Behavioral Counseling interventions can be joined within the Extended Family Systems interventions to create picture solutions and to identify and practice coping behaviors that could be helpful in both reestablishing the inverted power hierarchy and resolving the intergenerational pathology that may have negative consequences for the presenting family's children.

Interventions   The foundation of Extended Family Systems Counseling is related to the triangulation construct. Here, instead of the couple or family arguing unproductively within session and then going to a third person or addiction to triangulate, the family addictions counselor serves as the third pillar within the triangulation. The counselor's intent is to keep the family members talking with each other about meaningful concerns without allowing them to enter the unproductive chasm of emotional turmoil. The basis of this intervention follows Bowen's differentiation of self construct. In other words, the treatment key is to promote calm, logical conversation without allowing family members to become encumbered with emotions that inhibit successful outcomes. This may sound easy, but the charge is quite demanding given that so many family addictions topics and past intergenerational experiences are laden with emotional overtones.

We have found it quite helpful to enter these sessions armed with a number of techniques that help stabilize emotionally charged topics and promote insight. Thus, when emotions escalate and feelings outpace lucid and rational conversations, we temper feelings via three techniques. Specifically, we want to slow the interactions from those family members who are most actively expressing feelings and unproductively arguing. To do this we immediately redirect the focus of the dialogue into a triangulation mode. Here, we ask questions that require the family members to talk to us rather than to the members with whom they are currently arguing, and we ask questions that promote cognitive vis-à-vis feeling-based responses. Using the previously described clinical vignette with Jane and Andy, we will demonstrate this below.

Andy:	"You witch! Can't you see what you've done to my parents and Alex?"
Jane:	"Me? You are the one who can't keep your nose out of the booze."
Counselor:	"Andy, look at me for a moment. Tell me what you want for Alex."

Here, the counselor keeps the session from mushrooming. By asking Andy to look at the counselor, it breaks Andy's dialogue with Jane and encourages Andy to directly speak to the counselor. In other words, the counselor becomes the third person and facilitates a healthy triangulation with Andy and Jane. Unlike unstable, pathological triangulation, which occurs when a triangulated third person (e.g., mother-in-law, alcohol-abusing friend) is emotionally engaged in supporting one of the clients, therapeutic triangulation occurs when the counselor remains neutral and objective.

In addition to creating therapeutic triangulation, we have found it inordinately helpful to have parents redirect the conversation focus on their children's needs rather than on the marriage. This is especially helpful when arguing occurs. Most parents would do anything for their children. Discussing what Andy wants for Alex helps Andy refocus on the big family picture, not just the marriage. Furthermore, the counselor can slow the session pace. Here, the intent is to allow family members time to cool off and gain objectivity. This can be done by slowing the counselor's rate of speech and elongating vowels. In other words, the counselor simply takes more time pronouncing the vowels in each word. This surprisingly simple technique is often enough to calm the situation and help clients keep the family members focused on meaningful and objective discussion rather than on conflicting feelings.

Once self-differentiation has been accomplished and family members can rationally and thoughtfully present their chief presenting concerns without emotional hindrances, counselors can encourage family members to explore their families of origin (Bowen, 1975). Here, the counselor attempts to help clients better understand the relevance of their current concerns in relationship to previous family-of-origin experiences. Specifically, we have found that in many cases family members are quick to note that their current family problems are similar to those experienced in their personal family-of-origin experiences. The intent then is to help people understand how their emotional reactivity to the current nuclear family experience may be in part contributed to by their previous family-of-origin experiences.

Schematic diagrams known as genograms are a particularly helpful insight-producing intervention in Stage Five and help clients better understand their current relationship concerns and responses within the context of their extended family-of-origin relationships.

Genograms depict individual relationships within families and collectively depict three or more relationship generations (Figure 4.4). Important

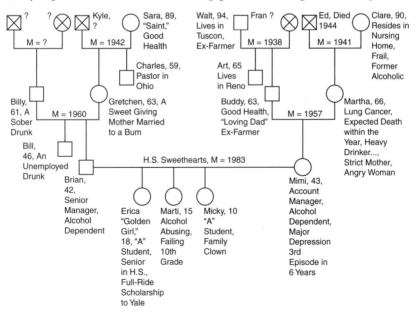

Figure 4.4 Genogram.

information is gathered related to each family member. This information includes things such as (a) birth, death, marriage, separation, and divorce dates, (b) conflictual, very close, and estranged relationships, (c) types of employment and significant employment relevant dates (e.g., date of retirement), (d) health conditions, mental health difficulties (e.g., anxiety, depression), temperament, and addictions-related concerns, and (e) geographic locations. Females are depicted as circles, men as squares, and unknown sex as triangles. Horizontal lines indicate marriages and vertical lines connect parents to children.

As a family addictions counselor, you will be specifically looking for five important themes. These include (a) important historical, familial, and relationship dates (e.g., Were grandparents born during the Great Depression? Were children born out of wedlock?); (b) gender values (e.g., Were there overt or subtle messages given to females or males that created gender-based expectations of who they should be and how they should relate to others?); (c) family secrets or cutoffs from other family members; (d) losses (e.g., Did specific family members experience chronically ill parents, economic hardships, or deaths?); and (e) family themes suggesting "who we are" or "how we behave." Should any reoccurring themes be evident, they should be discussed with the family members.

Although some family addictions counselors use genograms as independent assignments completed by individual family members outside the session, we have found greater clinical utility by actually beginning and often completing the genogram within one or two treatment sessions. Client families frequently remark that using brightly colored felt pens and large flip charts to create a "family tree" (genogram) is a refreshing break from the talk therapy that they have become accustomed to. The manners in which we introduce genograms to our addicted families vary. However, we often explain and then invite the family to create their genogram in the manner portrayed in the vignette below.

Counselor: "As you know, we have been through a lot together over these last 8 months. Many things have changed and you have made progress. For example, Marcus, you have maintained sobriety on two occasions, once to 29 days and once to nearly 70 days. Shawnette, you report that you are less anxious than ever within your marriage and that Marcus and you have a happier and stronger marriage. Is that correct?"

Shawnette: "Yes, but our marriage and Marcus's drinking still aren't where we want them to be."

Marcus: "We want things even better."

Counselor: "Given that last week and again now, I'm hearing that you want to continue to make progress, I would like to make a suggestion. Until today our primary focus has been your future goals, your immediate thoughts and feelings, and your recent behaviors within your marriage and substance use. Specifically, we have not truly emphasized your past histories within your own families."

Marcus: "What the heck does that mean?"

Counselor: "Good question, Marcus. As a computer programmer you know that a computer can only do what it is programmed to do. Humans are much more sophisticated than computers. We make daily decisions to act and behave in specific ways. In other words, we are not incapable of choosing our behaviors and feelings. However, in a way we are preprogrammed by the things we were taught or experienced in the families we grew up in. For example, we learned how we were expected to act and be, and how to communicate with siblings and people in authority such as parents."

Marcus: "OK."

Counselor: "So, as we continue in treatment, I think it would be important to see how we were programmed by the experiences of the families in which we grew up. In other words, let's see how these past experiences have impacted Shawnette and you. Many of my client couples report that by gaining knowledge of their partner's and their own families and gaining insight into how these experiences impact them, they become more understanding of their partner's behaviors as well as their own, and they learn how to best continue their recovery and enhance their marriage."

Shawnette: "I guess it makes sense."

Marcus: "How do we start?"

Counselor: "Well, the place I like to start is by making something that looks like a giant family tree for each of you. Counselors

	call this a genogram. Let's pull this flip chart over and begin. We've got lots of bright marker colors. Marcus, what color marker reminds you most of your family?"
Marcus:	"Red. We always had red-hot arguing in my family."
Counselor:	(handing Marcus the red marker): "Good, I've always liked red. It sounds like your family didn't hold things back but told people how they really felt."
Marcus:	"Yes, you can certainly say that."
Counselor:	"We start by drawing a circle like this with the red marker to represent Marcus's mother. Marcus, what was your mother's first name?"
Marcus:	"Violet."
Counselor:	"OK, let's put Violet's name in the circle. Is she still living?"
Marcus:	"Yes, she is 57 years old."
Counselor:	"OK, let's put that in the circle too. Do you remember her actual birth date?"
Marcus:	"It was March 10, 1949."
Counselor:	"Good. Did she work outside the home?"
Marcus:	"Yes, she was a waitress who worked long hours to get my brothers and me through college."
Counselor:	"What three words would you use to describe your mom? I'll write these down next to her circle."
Marcus:	"Salt of the earth, loving, and supportive."
Counselor:	"OK, let's draw a line here to your father. Since we use circles to represent women in our genogram, we use squares to represent men. Marcus, here is the red marker. Why don't you draw a square here and let's get some information related to your father in the same fashion that we did with your mother. OK? Let's write down your father's name in the square."

If we review the above vignette, we see a number of important points. First, the counselor reviewed the progress made by the clients. This reminds clients that they have accomplished major achievements via counseling.

Being reminded of such achievements promotes continued investment in the counseling process. Second, the vignette demonstrates a shift in the treatment's primary focus. Specifically, it denotes that successful interventions previously identified by the client family will continue (e.g., contingency contracting), but the counselor announces a shift in focus to the clients' family-of-origin experiences. Another important point here is that the counselor makes the analogy that, similar to computers that are programmed, clients are *influenced* by their family's programming. Note that the counselor does not state that Shawnette and Marcus are hopelessly and inescapably programmed to continue their ineffective or unwanted behaviors. Third, the counselor describes a genogram within a context that most clients are familiar—a giant family tree. Finally, the counselor engages Marcus. He does this in a couple very intentional ways. Here, the counselor has Marcus choose a marker color and hands the marker to Marcus. Then, after the counselor asks Marcus specific questions related to Marcus's mother, the counselor has Marcus draw the square representing father. Next, he has Marcus respond to and write the new responses about Marcus's father on the flip chart.

Parts of the genogram development process can be initially disconcerting to our students and clinical supervisees. Often students and novice supervisees feel as though they must prove themselves to their clients. In other words, on occasion their interventions and continued queries are less for relevant treatment purposes and more to demonstrate their clinical expertise. For example, in the vignette above, Marcus chooses the red marker. Instead of diverting into a long litany of statements and questions related to red being an indicator of hostility and fighting within families and encouraging Marcus to describe blow-by-blow descriptions of the potential hostilities experienced within his family of origin, the counselor merely reframes Marcus's statement about "red-hot arguing" in his family. This is done by stating, "It sounds like your family didn't hold things back." The counselor's response accomplishes two important tasks. It implies that there was at least one favorable outcome from the arguing (e.g., people did not internalize their anger). In addition, the response curtails potential pathologizing of Marcus's family. Such family pathologizing is enacted by some spouses as an excuse to legitimatize the reasons for their continued addictive or selfish behaviors.

Relatedly, novice counselors find it surprisingly uncomfortable to focus on one partner during the genogram development process while the other partner listens. What these counselors-in-training fail to understand is the gravity of the learning process for the nonspeaking spouse. When the nonspeaking spouse understands the spouse's problematic behaviors within the context of her family-of-origin experience, the once problematic behaviors take on new, more understandable, and often healthy meaning. One such example occurred in a rather recent family counseling session. Here, the addicted female spouse was quite loquacious. Her husband angrily indicated, "Everything revolves around Judy. When I come home from work, Judy tells me about *her* day. She never stops talking. It's as if she is the Energizer Bunny—she just talks and talks and talks. Why can't you just shut up?"

Approximately four sessions later, during Judy's genogram development, she used four word phrases to describe father. These included "hateful," "angry," "punishing," and "silent." Immediately following the use of these descriptors of her father, Judy remarked, "I never thought of it before, but I felt if I would just keep talking that sooner or later he [Father] would see who I was and like me. He never did. Later, I learned that if I kept on talking when Daddy came home drunk, he would become so perplexed by my constant talking that he would leave me alone rather than beat me like he did my sister." At the conclusion of that session, Judy's husband told the counselor, "I always thought Judy's incessant talking was because she was so self-centered that she didn't care about me or the kids. I was wrong. It [her talking] was her way of keeping safe from my anger. I reacted the same way as her father. When I came home drunk and angry, her talking drove me out of the house." Thus, such insight about one's spouse has the potential to promote more acceptable and positive behaviors toward one's spouse when the previously encountered problematic behaviors reoccur.

Concomitantly, the insight for the spouse demonstrating the problematic behaviors can be freeing. In Judy's situation, she learned that she didn't have to constantly talk to gain her spouse's attention or to be "safe." More importantly, Judy began to feel comfortable with her silence. Interestingly, at the conclusion of counseling, Judy noted that the turning point in her recovery occurred when she gained the insight that her loquaciousness was a barrier to personal happiness: "How could I possibly enjoy life? I suddenly realized why I talked nonstop. I was a chatterbox to keep danger away. But it also kept my family away. From then on when I found myself talking away, I would stop and ask, 'Why am I doing this?' Things haven't been the same since."

Thus, the genogram provides an opportunity for clients to gain insight regarding how their preprogramming occurred via their extended family system influences. Specifically, by better understanding potential reasons why parents or siblings behaved or responded to clients in the manner in which they did, clients have the potential to shed unhealthy behaviors and gain an enhanced sense of self-understanding and purpose.

Additional Intervention Strategy Another Extended Family Systems intervention that we have found helpful is the use of Guerin's "I position" (1976). As you read earlier, Bowen believed that individual and family health occurred when individuals within the system were sufficiently autonomous and independent. Again, we remind you that this did not suggest that healthy people were cold and aloof. Remember, Bowen believed that healthy persons were able to think factually without being overly encumbered with emotions. Furthermore, Bowen believed that healthy persons lived independently, without having to live their lives for others.

Guerin believed that client families could better understand such healthy differentiation when it was modeled within treatment. Thus, we encourage our supervisees to define their position and beliefs to the family within session. In other words, when the family is emotionally distraught and frazzled, we have found it helpful for our students to thoughtfully and rationally present their clinical judgment regarding discussed topics.

A few years ago, while supervising a doctoral student, the senior author observed two parents fill the treatment room with emotionally charged accusations and anger regarding the desired bedtime for their 7-year-old son. Neither was actually listening to the other. The difference in the desired bedtime was merely 30 minutes: 7:30 P.M. vs. 8:00 P.M. However, the 7-year-old was becoming quite tearful over the session's harsh emotional tone and loud arguing. As the clinical supervisor, the senior author called from the observation room telephone and told the supervisee to split the time difference to 7:45 P.M. Specifically, the supervisee was told to indicate that a 7:45 P.M. bedtime would be far superior to either of the parents' discussed times. During the following sessions, the supervisee was again encouraged to state his clinical perceptions regarding other concerns discussed by the parents. Within three sessions, the parents began to state their individual opinions without becoming encumbered in emotionally based arguing. Thus, we have found that over time the use of such I positions within multiple sessions appeared to help clients learn to calmly and unemotionally state their positions and beliefs while concurrently accepting these calmly stated partner positions. This of course encourages the healthy differentiation noted by Bowen.

Summary Within the Sequential Family Addictions Counseling Model, Extended Family Systems Theory marks the transition from the more "here and now," non-insight-based interventions to "there and then," insight-based interventions. Genograms and I positions offer therapeutically effective interventions that promote insight-based change focused on Bowen's constructs of self-differentiation. Furthermore, the theory matches the paradigm established via Stage Four's Structural Family Therapy. Should sufficient change based on insight gained within this stage not match the client family's needs, progression can then move to the next stage.

Stage Six: Modified Intergenerational Family-of-Origin Therapy

General Overview Unlike the previously described stages within the Sequential Family Addictions Counseling Model, Stage Six is optional. This new stage is founded upon Framo's (1992) Intergenerational Family-of-Origin Therapy and can serve as a transitional bridge between Extended Family Systems Theory and Psychodynamic Family Therapy. Specifically, during the previous Extended Family Systems Theory Stage, clients reexperience stories, memories, and feelings related to their family of origins that can be further addressed via this stage. In other words, the Modified Intergenerational Family-of-Origin Stage has the potential to further bring the adult clients together with their parents and siblings. This can preferably be accomplished via an actual meeting or via a conference telephone call if necessary. Moreover, the experience can be either a single meeting or a combination of meetings, depending on the adult clients' needs. We prefer face-to-face, in-person meetings. Such meetings provide counselors potential for greater session control, and counselors can respond as needed should the situation become overwhelming for any of the family-of-origin members. However, a conference call experience can be conducted should significant geographic distance or other factors inhibit such face-to-face meetings.

The actual intent of the Modified Intergenerational Family-of-Origin Therapy Meeting is twofold. First, we believe that much of the inability of our client couples to differentiate from their families of origin is founded upon childhood experiences, especially childhood roles and rules. In other words, these experiences, roles, and rules are based on the interpretations of a child's memories rather than on direct, factual adult observation. To help facilitate necessary differentiation from family, we find that clients must be able to review their experiences, memories, and feelings through the eyes of a mature, sensible, and developed adult. The Modified Intergenerational Family-of-Origin Therapy Meeting allows adults to meet, reminisce, and reexperience family members, while concomitantly differentiating themselves as adults from the other family-of-origin members. Thus, these face-to-face adult meetings aid healthy persons in seeing their family-of-origin experiences, roles, and rules within the context of their adult vision. We believe this promotes a more accurate and healthier view for adult spouses. Additionally, from a systems and circular causality perspective in particular—which suggests that every family interaction affects the behaviors and interactions of others within the system—the Modified Intergenerational Family-of-Origin Meeting has the potential to disencumber our adult spouses from their own family-of-origin enmeshments or cutoffs. Thus, our clients' more negative family-of-origin systems dynamics can be reduced or eliminated, meaning our client spouses have greater ability to engage with each other. Moreover, beyond the potential opportunity to differentiate from family, the intent is to later (e.g., after the family-of-origin meeting) allow client couples to report their adult family-of-origin experiences with their partners and create a working paradigm of how they have positively changed from the child they once were to the more fulfilled person they are becoming.

Of course, this meeting is optional and should not occur should counselors perceive the meeting as contraindicated. This seems especially true in cases where sexual, physical, or severe emotional abuse occurred, or when one or more family members seem to have long-standing, pathological histories that might suggest certain DSM-IV-TR Axis I or II disorders (e.g., bipolar disorder, schizophrenia, antisocial personality disorder, borderline personality disorder). In particular, this stage was not designed or intended to resolve past injustices among family members or to belittle or attack other family members for their previously perceived harmful behaviors. Framo (1992, p. 44) eloquently summarizes this caution, stating, "I moderate some clients' unrealistic expectations about what the sessions can accomplish. For example, clients need to be prepared for not being able to fulfill fantasies of what they can get from parents or siblings."

Interventions   Our experience has taught us that following the previous Extended Family Systems Experience, some client couples report significant changes and a desire to "reconnect" in healthier ways to their families of origin. Should we believe that this is both in the client couple's best interests and therapeutically beneficial to the client's current family system, we discuss the potential Modified Intergeneration Family-of-Origin Experience. Given that we already have a detailed understanding of the client couple's families of origin from both the Stage Four Structural and Stage Five Extended Family Systems, we begin by helping the individual spouses identify the persons who should be invited to attend the experience. Typically, this includes biological parents and siblings. Stepparents and stepsiblings can be included if they were present in the client's family-of-origin experience and if the adult spouse wishes to include them in the experience.

We believe it to be potentially disruptive to have one's spouse present during the actual Modified Intergenerational Family-of-Origin Experience. Therefore, although our client couples work together to develop agenda questions and ideas for these upcoming experiences, the actual face-to-face meeting occurs without the presence of one's spouse. In other words, the experience will include only those parents, stepparents, siblings, stepsiblings, and others identified as being part of the individual spouse's family of origin.

Additionally, unlike Framo's purest Intergenerational Family-of-Origin Model, which requires both spouses to participate in their own face-to-face Intergenerational Family-of-Origin meetings, the modified experience that we use can occur even if just one spouse wishes to participate. Basically, we do this because of our strong underlying belief in the wholeness and interconnectedness of family systems. Therefore, our guiding principle is that any positive change in one spouse has the potential to positively affect both that spouse's coupleship and the current family system.

When preparing for the Modified Intergenerational Family-of-Origin Experience, we have also found it helpful to have client couples work together to create a short, solution-focused, three-point agenda. Being believers that even minute insights from one's family of origin can create major self-perception shifts, we encourage clients to reenter their Modified Intergenerational Family-of-Origin Experience as adult anthropologists. Thus, the intent is founded upon observation and communication vis-à-vis confrontation and rebuke related to previously perceived childhood or adolescent injustices.

To this end, a three-point, solution-focused agenda is created. This agenda first creates a goal picture describing what a successful Modified Intergenerational Family-of-Origin Experience would look like. We find it important to know who will be present, the topics and family stories to be discussed, and the expected participants' behaviors and responses (e.g., our adult client, parents, siblings). Second, the agenda establishes what the client will do should the Modified Intergenerational Family-of-Origin Experience not provide the expected or desired results. Finally, the agenda clarifies how the client couple will ultimately utilize the results of the Modified Intergenerational Family-of-Origin Experience to positively impact addictions within their current family system and their coupleship.

Given your astuteness, you likely have noticed how this experience reinforces formerly used constructs and client-gained knowledge from the previous Family Addictions Counseling Model stages (e.g., Solution-Focused and Structural Family Therapies). Client couples and families that we counsel using the model find the use of previously used constructs and recently gained knowledge familiar, comforting, and helpful. On one occasion, the senior author, working with a couple who both qualified for polysubstance addictions diagnoses and whose children qualified for dual diagnoses including cannabis abuse and oppositional defiant disorder, found the interweaving of previously used constructs particularly helpful. The wife in particular noted how she had gained a better understanding of how she wanted things to be both in her immediate relationship with her husband and in her relationships with her siblings and surviving parent. To this end she stated something like, "I used to complain about how bad my family was. Now I understand them better and forgive them . . . and am free to invest my energies into my family."

After the three-point agenda is developed and discussed in detail, we address any unrealistic expectations (e.g., "My dad will beg my forgiveness for his drinking"). Then we move toward inviting family participants for the Modified Intergenerational Family-of-Origin Experience. Following Framo's (1992) recommendation, we frequently have clients telephone their parents first and follow with the statement, "I need your help" (p. 26). However, the initial call does not have to be to parents. Whoever the adult spouse believes would most likely agree to attend the Intergenerational Family-of-Origin Experience is the first contact. Once this person is identified, we enlist this family member as an ally. In other words, we have our adult spouse seek input as to how to best get the other family members to attend. Overall, family members typically make an effort to attend a conveniently scheduled and geographically close face-to-face family meeting experience.

Before describing how we begin the actual Modified Intergenerational Family-of-Origin Experience, it is necessary for us to ground the experience within the context of who we are as married, heterosexual, Caucasian males, who have doctorates in counselor education and supervision. Stated differently, due to our sex, ethnicity, and education, we are empowered members of the dominant class. We don't know what it is to be female. And, even though we both teach at Hispanic-serving institutions where the overwhelming majority of students are Hispanic and we reside in geographic locations where the majority of persons are not Euro-American, we truly don't know what it is to be a person of color or diversity living in America. Additionally, at least in the senior author's situation, he is often as old as or older than his adult clients' parents.

We state these things not to be funny. Instead we want to alert you to a very important point. Specifically related to the Modified Intergenerational Family-of-Origin Experience, we find that adult spouses and their families of origin treat us with respect and give us permission to "indirectly" direct the experience itself. Oftentimes this means that the most senior authority within the family system, often a father, temporarily yields his authority and power to us. We would like to believe that family authorities acquiesce their power to us in response to our professional expertise and the respect we demonstrate to them. However, such a perception would be too simplistic. Frankly, it is quite probable that in many cases we are given administrative control because of who we are (e.g., educated, older, Euro-American males) vis-à-vis family addiction counseling experts. Therefore, the manner in which we direct the Modified Intergenerational Family-of-Origin Experience may not be the best match for you. Adapt the experience in a manner that best benefits your adult client spouses. For example, you may wish to provide total control of the session to the adult client (e.g., providing a script and questions) or make other accommodations to best suit the particular needs of the family.

For us, once a convenient time has been scheduled and participants complete the necessary releases, we have our adult spouse introduce us to each family member. We thank the individual family member for participating and utilize a little brief chitchat to reduce the awkwardness of the moment. After introductions are completed, we again thank everyone for their willingness to participate and provide an opportunity for the adult spouse to indicate her thanks and intent for the experience. The introduction often is similar to the vignette below.

Counselor: "Luipita, would you be so kind as to introduce me to your mother and father and the family members whom they parented when you lived in their house?"

Luipita: "Sure, this is my father, Mr. Henry Price Valadez. He recently retired from the city and now is spending more time at his favorite hobby, bass fishing."

Counselor: "Mr. Valadez, thank you so much for coming. It is an honor to meet you. Bass fishing, sounds like fun. How often are you able to get out on the water?"

Henry (Father): "It is fun. I try to go fishing a couple times a week. It sure beats work."

Counselor: "Again, it is an honor having you here. I don't think this will be as fun as bass fishing, but we will try."

Henry: (smiling): "Probably not, but being here for my daughter is important."

Luipita:	(pointing to mother): "This is my mother, Mrs. Selena Valadez."
Counselor:	"Hello, Mrs. Valadez. Luipita told me how grateful she was for your coming. It is a privilege having you here today. Thank you for sharing your time to be present."

Selena (Mother): "I am happy to be here."

Luipita:	(pointing to brother): "And this is my brother, Henry Price Valadez, Jr. Henry is 18 and attends junior college."
Counselor:	"It is nice to meet you, Henry. What are you studying?"
Henry:	"I'm taking criminal justice courses and want to join the Army as an MP."
Counselor:	"I bet you're taking some really neat courses."
Henry:	"Yes, college is pretty cool."
Counselor:	"Thank you for coming, Henry." "Luipita, before we get officially started, let me thank you for your expressed confidence in the family members from your original family and for your willingness to ask them here today. I know that you love your original family very much and that today's meeting can be helpful to everyone, including members of your current family, William and Kathy, who are not here today. Mr. Valadez, Mrs. Valadez, and Henry, your being here today is very important to Luipita. Some family members don't care enough to come to a meeting like the one Luipita has called. Clearly, this is not the case with your original family. Your being here tells Luipita that she is loved and cared about. It says you want the best for her. Our purpose here today is not to change the past or to attack one another. Instead, it is Luipita's desire that she get to know you as the adult she is and take the positive lessons learned from her experiences to make her new family as healthy and happy as possible. Luipita, would you like to say anything?"
Luipita:	"Not really, just that I'm really glad you all are here."
Counselor:	"Thank you, Luipita. Mr. Valadez and Luipita, with your permission, let's begin."

The vignette provides a quick overview of the introduction. The counselor immediately attempts to help differentiate Luipita from her family of origin. The counselor does this by asking Luipita to introduce her parents and those whom they parented in Luipita's family of origin. The statement is one of many that will be used throughout the Modified Family-of-Origin Experience to emphasize the point that Luipita's parents had their opportunity to raise their family and now Luipita needs to be empowered to raise her family as she perceives best. Later, the counselor again uses a differentiation technique that emphasizes Luipita's "original" family and her "current" family. Additionally, the counselor follows the formality of the conversation based on Luipita's introductions. For example, she calls her father "Mr. Henry Price Valadez." Therefore, the counselor calls her father "Mr. Valadez." Concomitantly, matching what you've previously read about Structural Family Therapy, the counselor welcomes family members according to their roles within the family hierarchy—parents first, youngest child last.

Next we start with a simple question such as, "What was it like as a child growing up in this family?" Other questions such as, "What do you remember most about growing up in this family?" "What are some of the most memorable experiences of growing up?" and "What do you remember most about your parents and siblings?" have also proved fertile ground to start the family sessions. As you likely remember from the previous chapter, families cannot logically interact and ultimately gain insight and differentiation if they become emotionally charged. Thus, should the session plunge into a chasm of emotionally charged feelings or accusations, the family addictions counselor merely utilizes previously discussed techniques to get the focus back on the counselor until the family is once again interacting on a cognitive, Detective Joe Friday "just the facts, ma'am, just the facts" level.

As the session proceeds and facts about growing up in the family of origin are revealed, we allow the family to discuss memories and experiences through their adult vis-à-vis child lenses. Should the tempo of the session falter or the session begin to wind down too quickly, we will often follow with a question intended to allow family members to safely discuss challenges of growing up in their family of origin while reframing the experience as something that they can use to benefit them in their current life, outside their family of origin. This question typically is stated something like, "What was the most challenging part of growing up in this family and how have you used those challenges to better your current life?" Depending on time constraints, we always want to complete the session on a positive note. Thus, our concluding questions typically include one of two topic areas. The first is designed to again emphasize differentiation and reframe perceived past negative experiences into strengths: "What difficult parts of growing up in this family have best empowered you to live your life now as fully functioning and able adults?" The second question is designed to again emphasize differentiation but to further provide a period by thanking parents for what they have done: "Dad and Mom, it is clear that you invested considerable time and energy in raising your family. Before we leave, I'm wondering if your now adult children would like to thank you for being the parents that raised them and now are allowing them the freedom to be the adults they need to be in their own marriages and families?"

Additional Intervention Strategy Immediately following the Modified Intergenerational Family-of-Origin Experience, we prefer to meet our adult couple. Here, we ask the adult client who participated in the experience to describe the most powerful and then most helpful parts of the experience. Furthermore, we ask her to describe the "biggest surprises" of viewing her family of origin through her adult lenses. Many times our adult clients are mentally and emotionally exhausted, so this provides an opportunity for the adult couple to learn how to respond to each other's needs. The vignette below provides a general template for such a response.

Counselor:	"It seems as though you are emotionally exhausted, Dianne."
Dianne:	"Yes, I just need to sit and cry for a moment. I never expected talking to my family could be so overwhelming."
Counselor:	"OK, take your time, cry as much as you need, and let us know what we can do."
Dianne:	"I'm all right now. Thanks for letting me cry."
Counselor:	"Dianne, I am guessing that Bob needs to know what it is that you need from him right now. Bob, is that right?"
Bob:	"Yeah, tell me what you want me to do."
Dianne:	"I guess just be with me."
Counselor:	"Could you turn your chair toward Bob and tell him what being with you looks like and how he will know when he is doing it?"
Dianne:	"Bob, I just want you to be close to me. Hold my hand and tell me that we're going to be all right."

Summary   The above description of a Modified Intergenerational Family-of-Origin Experience demonstrates how family addiction counselors can bridge the gap between the Sequential Model's Extended Family-of-Origin Stage Five and the Psychodynamic Family Therapy Stage Seven. The described experience can provide further insight to adult client couples and build on the previous knowledge and insight gained via previously used therapies (e.g., Structural Family Therapy, Extended Family Systems Therapy). We strongly believe that healthy family-of-origin differentiation promotes increased family functioning in our addicted client families. Concomitantly, as our addicted families learn to interact more cognitively vis-à-vis emotionally, they bring new skills that have the potential to positively influence their current families.

Stage Seven: Psychodynamic Object Relations Family Therapy

General Overview   Stage Seven of the Sequential Family Addictions Counseling Model is founded in Psychodynamic Object Relations Family Theory. Here the emphasis is on increasing the members' understanding of their internalized perception of self and others (i.e., the objects in Object Relations Theory) and learning how such internalized perceptions impact their family relationships. Thus, this stage is designed to enhance intrapsychic understanding via the individual member's corrective emotional experiences with the counselor (i.e., the counseling relationship). In other words, it is the counseling relationship between counselor and individual family members that ultimately promotes healthier interpersonal interactions within the system. Thus, the family addictions counselor provides a corrective emotional experience for each person within the family system. However, unlike Bowen's Extended Family Systems Theory, which focuses on multiple generations, or Intergenerational Family-of-Origin Theory, which focuses on the impact of dynamics from within a single family-of-origin system, Psychodynamic Object Relations Family Theory focuses primarily on the unconscious perceptions of self and others and on how such personalities impact each other within the family system.

According to Psychodynamic Object Relations Theory, the residue effects from the self and other relationships (e.g., the significant caregiver's manner of interacting with the developing infant) and the ways in which these experiences are internalized by the infant create an unconscious personality lens through which the infant views self and others. This lens determines how one acts toward and reacts to others. In Psychodynamic Object Relations terms, the infant becomes "attached" to the object (e.g., the primary caregiver [most frequently mother]). In other words, the infant's personality is thereby molded by the interaction with the primary caregiver (i.e., other). This construct creates the Psychodynamic Object Relations core and suggests that the couple's current dysfunctional interactions are the result of internalized, mutual projections. Such dysfunctional interactions, then, are less the result of lucid and true experiences with one's spouse and more the result of transference—perceived distortions of others' behaviors (e.g., spouse, child, counselor) resulting from one's faulty personality lens. Thus, the individual family member's new "self–other" relationship with the family addictions counselor becomes the change agent that corrects psychic deficits from the former pathogenic experience between infant and faulty significant others (D. Schroat, personal communication, September 22, 2005).

So, what does all this mean? We think a case description will help us better explain. Paula was a 32-year-old female. She fulfilled dual diagnoses—alcohol dependence and dependent personality disorders. As you likely know, these Axis I and II diagnoses demonstrate long-term, chronic pathological patterns. For the moment, let's focus on Paula's dependent personality disorder. This disorder is marked by one's extreme need for social approval and affection. Basically this diagnosis notes Paula's willingness to live as others desire her to live. As a matter of fact, the diagnosis indicates that Paula even abandons her own desires in an attempt to gain others' acceptance and approval. Stated differently, people similar to Paula adapt their behaviors to overly please others. They do this because they fear others' disapproval. In essence, Paula was sacrificing her wants and desires so that others wouldn't reject her. According to Psychodynamic Object Relations Theory, Paula's presenting etiology is likely the result of her primary caregiver's extreme overcontrolling, authoritarian behaviors. As a growing infant and even as a toddler, Paula may have been discouraged from acting independently. Over time, she came to believe, based on her interpretation of experiences with her primary caregiver, that submissive rather than assertive behaviors ensured the greatest possible benefits. In particular, Paula's lens of the world said, "You will be abandoned by those whom you want to love you if you don't fully comply with their demands of you." Concomitantly, Paula's mother repeatedly told Paula as a child and later as a developing adult that Paula didn't have common sense and that she was "totally incapable of being successful without someone telling you what to do and when to do it!"

As an important aside, think of the type of person who would likely marry someone like Paula. And, from a systems-oriented, Psychodynamic Object Relations perspective, take a moment to consider the family system that these two personalities would likely cocreate. As you can imagine, in the best of circumstances, dependent persons like Paula search for overly nurturing spouses who will protect them from the world and life's every-day struggles. More likely, the stark reality is much less rosy. In our clinical experiences, persons like Paula often seek out controlling and domineering spouses. Many times these spouses rule their homes and their dependent spouses via verbal and physical intimidation. Thus, physical abuse by the nondependent spouse toward the dependent spouse is not atypical. Given that dependent personality disordered persons like Paula perceive themselves as totally helpless and weak, their dependent lens view of the world tells them that they cannot escape the relationship. They believe that if they try to escape, they will ultimately be abandoned and rejected by their significant others.

OK, have you identified in very stereotypical and general terms Paula's spouse's personality? Congratulations, you were correct! In very broad terms, Paula's partner, Mark, would have likely fulfilled a Diagnostic and Statistic Manual diagnosis of antisocial personality disorder. He worked on a garbage truck route and was noted within the company as "hardheaded" and "tough." Mark had a history of arrests for assault that started in junior high school and a checkered work history that suggested he had difficulties with anyone who presented as an authority figure to him. Nearly every-thing was perceived by Mark as an insult, and when he felt challenged by anyone, he believed he must respond.

From a systems perspective, both spouses were remarkably dissatis-fied. Paula's chronic and debilitating alcohol abuse was her preferred method of dulling the intense fear she had of Mark's ultimate rejection of her—especially if she did not act exactly how she believed he wanted. Often she would begin drinking by herself at their home with the intent of becoming intoxicated and "escaping" her feelings of separation and rejec-tion by Mark—especially when he was out playing cards with friends late into the evenings or when he was away on his frequent hunting or fishing trips. Concomitantly, for Mark, it was as if he was living with a needy, clingy infant who "completely failed" the charges he assigned to her. Pre-vious Sequential Family Addictions Counseling interventions were fruit-less against both Paula's dependency and her addiction. We will return to Paula and Mark's clinical vignette a little later, and hopefully you will better see how Psychodynamic Object Relations Family Therapy provided the necessary foundation to enact helpful change.

Interventions   If you have arrived at this last Sequential Family Addictions Counseling stage, your previous interventions have not been as successful as your clients want. Using Paula and Mark's aforementioned scenario, we can quickly realize that Solution-Focused, Cognitive-Behavioral, and Structural Theories can tell addicted families what they must do to bring about satisfying change. However, if the lenses through which they view themselves and others do not allow them to participate or commit to such change, failure is inevitable. Within this last model stage, we will discuss a long-term, Psychodynamic Object Relations intervention that our client families have reported as helpful.

This intervention is based on trust. Specifically, family members must trust the family addictions counselor. We would venture to guess that if the family system has continued with you until this point, they must certainly trust you. Therefore, the family addictions counselor will focus on making baby steps with each individual within this long-term counseling process. This is done by creating a holding environment for each individual within the system.

In essence such a holding environment indirectly indicates to each family member that they are valued and safe. Remember, within Psychodynamic Object Relations Counseling the change agent is the client's new remedial relationship with the counselor. The family addictions counselor's task then becomes that of metaphorically re-parenting each member and allowing the client to attach to a new object—the counselor. Clearly clients cannot return to infancy. However, counselors can provide a holding environment where the clients can feel comfortable enough to "be" and "act" without fear of the counselor's abandonment. This perceived safety net allows the client to internalize a healthier perception of self and others. Of course, gentle confrontation by the counselor occurs when behaviors, statements, and interactions intended by the client to continue their unhealthy personality exist. However, once gentle confrontation is made, the counselor works to "reconnect" with the client to demonstrate support and non-abandonment. Counseling within this stage proceeds slowly and, more times than not, includes just the spouses.

Transference is a necessary part of therapeutic change within Psychodynamic Object Relations Family Counseling. Repressed distant images from past experiences with caregivers will cascade into current spousal and family interactions, and clients will experience transference toward the counselor as well. In essence, the current skirmishes experienced by the couple result from their mutual projections onto one another. Like following the putrid odor trail of rotting meat, family addictions counselors can find such transference by listening to the couple's arguments and allowing individuals to slowly link their current argument to the past. Let's return to Paula and Mark.

Counselor:	"So, tell me about this past week."
Mark:	"Well, Paula is continuing to drink and do nothing around the house. She's an utter failure with the kids, and she is too drunk around the house to even make my breakfast or pack my lunches, so I have to use the money that I was going to use to pay down the bills to buy my lunches. She just pisses me off."
Paula:	(silently looks down at her feet and says nothing)
Counselor:	"Paula, tell me what is going on."
Paula:	"Mark is right. I'm just a drunk who doesn't do what I'm suppose to."
Counselor:	"Paula, it seems sometimes like it is very hard for you to disagree with Mark."
Paula:	(sits, silently looking away from both counselor and Mark)
Counselor:	"Paula, what is it like for you when Mark says that he is angry with you?"
Paula:	"I don't know, I guess Mark is right. I am a drunk and I don't take care of him or the kids like I should . . . I feel like I'm bad and that he is going to leave me."
Counselor:	"So, does it feel like Mark is going to leave you often?"
Paula:	(slowly responding) "Yes, because I'm not a good wife, and I don't do what I'm suppose to do."
Counselor:	"Tell me more . . ."
Paula:	"I guess it reminds me of when my mother used to get mad at me and tell me I wouldn't amount to much and that I would never be able to have a real man."

In the above vignette, we can see two strikingly different changes in the counseling application. First, unlike previous Sequential Family Addictions Counseling Model stages that begin by strategically focusing on therapeutic interventions such as solution-focused goal pictures, precipitators to the argument sequence, or changes in the family power hierarchy, the counselor uses a nebulous opening and allows clients to lead to their pressing concerns or recent arguments. Second, the counselor is now invested in exploring the clients' emotional reactions and the origins of these emotional reactions. Here, Paula doesn't verbally respond to Mark's voiced anger. The counselor then invites Paula to describe what she is experiencing. Paula then reports that Mark's anger is legitimate, because Paula is an alcoholic who fails to manage her responsibilities well. Then, her underlying feelings of being abandoned are voiced. Instead of ending the conversation here, the counselor asks a follow-up related to the frequency of her abandonment feelings. Again, the family addictions counselor does not jump to a different topic but continues to pursue Paula's underlying concerns, which link back to her experiences with her mother.

It is important to note that the intent of this final model stage is not to make things "right" or to resolve Paula's experiences with either Mark or her mother. Instead the family addictions counselor helps Paula examine the feelings beneath her expressed concerns. In the vignette presented above, the family addictions counselor allows Paula to gain her own understanding via the story that she tells regarding her mother's statements of how Paula would neither amount to much nor be able to marry or keep a husband.

Additional Intervention Strategy   Within Psychodynamic Object Relations Family Counseling, couples are encouraged to speak freely with very little guidance or direction from the family addictions counselor. However, when the conversation becomes painfully stalled and forward momentum has come to a complete halt, we typically ask a simple question related to the couple's parents to jump-start the session. One example question is, "If your mother were here today, what would she say is the reason for your continued marital disharmony and substance use?" Another question might be, "Paula, how would your mother explain your drinking?" Often these types of questions jump-start a discussion flow that is highly relevant to the couple's perceptions of self, feelings, and interpersonal histories.

Finally, we have found it vitally important to actively confront resistance. Resistance is especially relevant to addicted families. Regretfully, many addictions counselors were ineffectively trained to confront resistance or have a misperception of resistance confrontations. In particular, this is not a time to threaten clients or to turn addicted families helplessly to the streets. Contrary to saying that addicted client families must "hit bottom" before being developmentally able to begin their recovery, we believe that at this point in counseling insight and the remedial counselor–client relationship have the potential to alleviate recovery and relationship fears. In other words, if we are able to effectively help addicted families gain accurate insight into the reasons why they have unfounded recovery and relationship fears, they can begin their recovery journey.

Let's go back to Paula and Mark for a moment. As a highly dependent person, Paula would likely indicate that the problems with her marriage and family were a direct result of her. This may actually fit Mark's perception that if Paula were "fixed" of her addictions the marriage would be solid and the "biggest rock" in the marriage would be eliminated. However, these perceptions merely fit the unconscious personality lens developed by these partners to safely view their worlds. In such a case, Paula and Mark may very well be focusing on solving Paula's addiction as "the" answer to all their marital woes. In such a situation, we might respond in a manner demonstrated below.

> Counselor: "Paula, you seem to be saying that if you were only more compliant to Mark's wishes and did exactly the things he wants and in the manner he wants, then you would feel safe enough that he wouldn't abandon you and then you could begin your abstinence. Thus, you seem willing to accept all the blame in this relationship to avoid confronting your husband and avoid your own abstinence. And Mark, you seem to be suggesting that the entire problem is Paula's. You seem to think that it is easier to get angry at her than to look at your underlying feelings that you must constantly prove your superiority and your overwhelming mistrust of others. We've been working together for a very, very long time. Isn't it time you began addressing the real issues that are contributing to your personal and marital dissatisfaction and addictions?

In this situation the family addictions counselor interprets both partners' resistance to change. She respectfully confronts what is too painful or embarrassing for the individual couple members to discuss. More importantly, the counselor is actively petitioning the couple to face the fears that keep them trapped in repeating the same old patterns that are based on their flawed perceptions of self. Of course, not every hypothesis or interpretation of the addicted family member's underlying feelings warrants discussion within session. To the contrary, counselors should limit interpretations to no more than two or three per session.

Summary Psychodynamic Object Relations Counseling is based on personality change and personal insight resulting from the counselor-client relationship. Instead of focusing on behavior patterns or insight regarding the impact of multiple generations on one's family-of-origin experience, Psychodynamic Object Relations Theory encourages family addictions counselors to look at the client couples' underlying perceptions of self and others, and the fears that promote continuation of these self-perceptions. Trust and transference are necessary components of the intervention, with the intent of re-parenting the clients sufficiently so that they can adequately attach to the counselor in a manner that will free them from their internalized, unconscious false lenses, which influence how they perceive themselves and how they "must" act, and their perception of a hostile world.

Conclusion

Within this chapter you have learned why family counseling is important to those treating addicted families and you have gained an understanding of family counseling's diverse theories and structure. Furthermore, you have read about terms and constructs central to general family counseling. Most importantly, you have read about the seven-stage Sequential Family Addictions Counseling Model and learned how to implement the model with addicted families that you will likely encounter. The model builds on previous stages and allows for the continuation of techniques and interventions from previous stages to be included in the current treatment stage. The intent of the model is to provide a sequential counseling intervention plan that begins with the most time-efficient and cost-effective interventions and moves toward more costly theories as needed. Use of the model will help entry-level and experienced family addictions counselors ensure that their treatment interventions correspond with client family needs and include congruent treatment theories and interventions that do not confuse or frustrate client families. In the next chapter, we will discuss other topics of importance that arise when treating addicted families.

Skill Builder

Question 1

Describe the three commonly used family addiction counseling terms below:

Equifinality: _____

_____

_____

Homeostasis: _____

_____

_____

Chief Enabler: _____

_____

_____

Question 2

Name each of the seven stages of the Sequential Family Addictions Counseling Model and identify the stage that is optional:

Stage One: _____

Stage Two: _____

Stage Three: _____

Stage Four: _____

Stage Five: _____

Stage Six: _____

Stage Seven: _____

Question 3

If you heard an addicted family member express ambivalence to change, what two questions could you ask to encourage exploration of her options and potentially promote her successful commitment to counseling?

Question: _____?

Question: _____?

Question 4

What three techniques can you utilize within Solution-Focused Family Therapy to help your addicted families create a "solution picture"?

Technique One: _____

Technique Two: _____

Technique Three: _____

Question 5

Describe the appropriate power order of the three subsystems that compose Structural Family Therapy's "hierarchy."

Skill Builder Responses

Question 1 Responses

Equifinality suggests that instead of only one "correct" way for addicted families to attain their goals, there actually exist many ways. Thus, for family addictions counselors, equifinality suggests that if one therapeutic treatment delivery is not bringing about the desired results, they may wish to change to another rather than doing "more of the same."

Homeostasis suggests that family subsystems and members attempt to maintain the family system's status quo. When outside forces (e.g., the family addictions counselor) attempt to change stable patterns of interacting, the family members and subsystems will experience a disruption in the familiar, which can feel uncomfortable.

Chief Enabler is a dysfunctional role commonly identified within addicted families where the person attempts to protect the addicted member from assuming full responsibility or experiencing sanctions for her substance abuse.

Question 2 Responses

Stage One: Motivational Interviewing
Stage Two: Solution-Focused Family Counseling
Stage Three: Cognitive-Behavioral Family Therapy
Stage Four: Structural Family Therapy
Stage Five: Extended Family Systems Theory
Stage Six: Modified Intergenerational Family-of-Origin Therapy (Optional)
Stage Seven: Psychodynamic Object Relations Family Therapy

Question 3 Responses

Question: What do you think you will do concerning your use of alcohol?
Question: What's the next step for you?

Question 4 Responses

Three Solution-Focused Family Therapy methods that can be used with addicted families to create "solution pictures" include:

Technique One: <u>The Miracle Question</u>
Technique Two: <u>The Crystal Ball</u>
Technique Three: <u>The Movie Director</u>

Question 5 Responses

The Marital Subsystem should be at the top of the Structural Family Hierarchy, followed by the Partnership Subsystem and lastly the Siblingship Subsystem (see Figure 4.3).

References

Bennun, I. (1988). Treating the system or symptom: Investigation family therapy for alcohol problems. *Behavioural Psychotherapy, 16*, 165–176.

Berg, I. K. (1994). *Irreconcilable differences: A solution-focused approach to marital therapy* [Videotape]. New York: Norton.

Bowen, M. (1975) Family therapy and family group therapy. In H. Kaplan & B. Sadock (Eds.), *Comprehensive group psychotherapy.* Baltimore, MD: Williams and Wilkins.

Bowen, M. (1961). Family psychotherapy. *American Journal of Orthopsychiatry, 31*, 40–60.

Bowen, M. (1976). Family therapy after twenty years. In S. Arieti (Ed.), *American handbook of psychiatry.* New York: Basic Books.

Bukstein, O. G. (2000). Disruptive behavior disorders and substance use disorders in adolescents. *Journal of Psychoactive Drugs, 32*, 67–69.

Cadogan, D. A. (1973). Marital therapy in the treatment of alcoholism. *Quarterly Journal of Studies on Alcohol, 34*, 1187–1194.

Catalano, R. F., Gainey, R. R., Fleming, C. B., Haggerty, K. P., & Johnson, N. O. (1999). An experimental intervention with families of substance abusers: One-year follow-up of the Focus on Families Project. *Addiction, 94*, 241–254.

Cunningham, P. B., & Henggeler, S. W. (1999). Engaging multiproblem families in treatment: Lessons learned throughout the development of multisystemic therapy. *Family Process, 38*, 265–281.

Diamond, G. S., Serranon, A. C., Dickey, M., & Sonis, W. A. (1996). Current status of family-based outcome and process research. *American Academy of Child and Adolescent Psychiatry Journal, 35*, 6–16.

Framo, J. L. (1992). *Family-of-origin therapy: An intergenerational approach.* New York: Brunner/Mazel.

Friedman, A. S., Terras, A., & Kreisher, C. (1995). Family and client characteristics as predictors of outpatient treatment outcome for adolescent drug abusers. *Journal of Substance Abuse, 7*, 345–356.

Guerin, P. J. (1976). *Family therapy: Theory and practice.* New York: Gardner Press.

Hedberg, A. G., & Campbell, L. (1974). A comparison of four behavioral treatments of alcoholism. *Journal of Behavioral Therapy and Experimental Psychiatry, 5*, 251–256.

Jackson, D. D. (1957). Communication, family and marriage. *Psychiatric Quarterly Supplement, 31*, 79–90.

Jacobson, N. S., & Gottman, J. M. (1998). *When men batter women: New insights into ending abusive relationships.* New York: Simon & Schuster.

Johnson, V. E. (1973). *I'll change tomorrow.* New York: Harper & Row.

Kaufman, E., & Yoshioka, M. (2004). Substance abuse treatment and family therapy: A Treatment Improvement Protocol (TIP) 39. U.S. Department of Health and Human Services, Substance Abuse and Mental Health Services Administration Center for Substance Abuse Treatment (DHHS Publication No. SMA 04-3957).

Keller, M. (1974). Trends in treatment of alcoholism. In *Second special report to the U.S. Congress on alcohol and health* (pp. 145–167). Washington, DC: Department of Health, Education and Welfare.

Liddle, H. A., & Dakof, G. A. (1995). Efficacy of family therapy for drug abuse: Promising but not definitive. *Journal of Marital and Family Therapy, 21*, 511–543.

McCrady, B. S., & Epstein, E. E. (1996). Theoretical bases of family approaches to substance abuse treatment. In F. Torgers & D. S. Keller (Eds.), *Treating substance abuse: Theory and techniques* (pp. 117–142). New York: Guilford Press.

McCrady, B. S., Paolino, T. J., Jr., Longabaugh, R., & Rossi, J. (1979). Effects of joint hospital admission and couples treatment for hospitalized alcoholics: A pilot study. *Addictive Behaviors, 4*, 155–165.

Miller, R. W., & Rollnick, S. (1991). *Motivational interviewing: Preparing people to change addictive behavior.* New York: Guilford Press.

Minuchin, S. (1974). *Families and family therapy.* Cambridge, MA: Harvard University Press.

Minuchin, S., & Fishman, H. C. (1981). *Family therapy techniques.* Cambridge, MA: Harvard University Press.

O'Farrell, T. J. (1999, April/May). Systems therapy key to prevention and treatment: BCT offers good outcomes, study shows. *Family Therapy News*, p. 1.

O'Farrell, T. J., & Fals-Stewart, W. (2000). Behavioral couples therapy for alcoholism and drug abuse. *Journal of Substance Abuse Treatment, 1*, 51–54.

O'Farrell, T. J., & Fals-Stewart, W. (2003). Alcohol abuse. *Journal of Marital and Family Therapy, 29*, 121–146.

O'Hanlon, W. H., & Weiner-Davis, M. (1989). *In search of solutions: A new direction in psychotherapy.* New York: Norton.

Prochaska, J. O., & DiClemente, C. C. (1982). Transtheoretical therapy: Toward a more integrative model of change. *Psychotherapy: Theory, Research, and Practice, 19*, 276–288.

Rinn, R. C. (1978). Children with behavior disorders. In A. Hersen & A. Bellack (Eds.), *Behavior therapy in the psychiatric setting.* Baltimore, MD: Williams & Wilkins.

Rollnick, S., & Miller, W. R. (1995). What is motivational interview? *Behavioral and Cognitive Psychotherapy, 23*, 325–334.

Shapiro, C. (1999). *Integrating family-focused interventions into the criminal justices system.* New York: The Vera Institute of Justice. Retrieved February 11, 2004, from http://www.vera.org/publications/bodegafamily.htm

Stanton, M. D., & Shadish, W. R. (1997). Outcome, attrition, and family-couples treatment for drug abuse: A meta-analysis and review of the controlled, comparative studies. *Psychological Bulletin, 122*, 170–191.

Stanton, M. D., & Todd, T. C. (1979). Structural family therapy with drug addicts. In E. Kaufman & P. Kaufmann (Eds.), *The family therapy of drug and alcohol abuse.* New York: Gardner Press.

Szapocznik, J., Perez-Vidal, A., Brickman, A. L., Foote, F. H., Santisteban, D., Hervis, O., & Kurtines, W. (1988). Engaging adolescent drug abusers and their families in treatment. A strategic structural systems approach. *Journal of Consulting and Clinical Psychology, 56*, 552–557.

Walitzer, K. S. (1999). Family therapy. In P. J. Ott, R. E. Tarter, & R. T. Ammerman (Eds.), *Sourcebook on substance abuse: Etiology, epidemiology, assessment, and treatment.* Needham Heights, MA: Allyn and Bacon.

Wegscheider, S. (1981). *Another chance: Hope and health for the alcoholic family.* Palo Alto, CA: Science and Behavior Books.

Weiner-Davis, M. (1992). *Divorce-busting.* New York: Summit Books.

Weiner-Davis, M. (1993). Pro-constructed realities. In S. Gilligan & R. Price (Eds.), *Therapeutic conversations.* New York: W. W. Norton..

Zweben, A., Pearlman, S., & Li, S. (1988). A comparison of brief advice and conjoint therapy in the treatment of alcohol abuse: The results of the Marital Systems study. *British Journal of Addiction, 83*, 899–916.

Special Topics in Counseling Addicted Families

Chapter 5 Learning Objectives

After reading this chapter, you should be able to:

- Describe the social justice counseling construct and its implications for family addictions counselors
- Explain what multicultural counseling is and why family addictions counselors need to be aware of multicultural topics of importance
- Describe how to conduct a thorough suicide assessment utilizing the SAD PERSONS Scale and use information gathered from the assessment to encourage hospitalization if necessary
- Explain how to use an adapted, post-violence debriefing intervention with nonviolent parents and their children

Introduction

By this point in the book, you should be familiar with the basics of the Sequential Family Addictions Counseling Model. Throughout our clinical work with addicted families, we have found the model to be an invaluable resource to organizing our interventions with a variety of clients and presenting issues. This chapter takes the application of the model to the next level by examining how the model can be implemented with special topics and populations. Specifically, we will explore topics related to social justice, multicultural counseling, and life-threatening behaviors—that is, assessing and intervening with suicidal persons and responding to the aftermath of substance-related familial violence. Armored with this additional knowledge, you should be adequately prepared to address the multiple challenges of working with addicted families.

Social justice counseling, multicultural counseling, and life-threatening behaviors are such current, vast, and broad topics within the profession that it would be incredibly foolish to attempt an encompassing review of each within the confines of a book dedicated to family addictions. However, the topics are of such importance that our failure to both highlight them and allow you to determine your own professional growth needs related to each would be an injustice to you, our readers, and the addicted families we jointly serve.

Therefore, we will succinctly describe the topics of social justice and multicultural counseling below and ask that you self-assess your specific strengths and weaknesses related to both (questions at the end of the chapter are provided to help facilitate your self-assessment). Then, we would encourage you to use your self-assessment knowledge to seek relevant training and supervision to enhance your competence. Similarly, you are encouraged to review the resources listed in the chapter's reference section for a more thorough topic review. On the other hand, should you find that you have expertise in each, reach out to other professionals who need additional competencies and help them in their professional development. Remember, social justice and multicultural counseling competencies are not a contest. Mentoring less experienced family addictions counselors in an effort to promote and strengthen their competencies enhances the entire profession and helps ensure that the pressing needs of addicted families are successfully met. Lastly, given the frequency of life-threatening behaviors among addicted families, we will describe the SAD PERSONS Suicide Assessment Scale and offer potential interventions that can be readily used within the Sequential Family Addictions Model.

Social Justice

Stigmatization and Discrimination toward Addicted Families

Although some will undoubtedly bristle against social justice's inclusion within this book's specialized topics chapter, we believe the topic is of fundamental importance and is particularly linked to addicted families.

Given that social justice is a relatively recent construct within the helping professions, some might be asking, "What is social justice?"

In its most rudimentary form, social justice is the awareness and response to topics of unequal power, unearned privilege, and oppression (Ratts, D'Andrea, & Arredondo, 2004). Additionally, social justice seeks to balance resources and power via politically conscious methods led by professional counselors (Ratts et al., 2004). According to Ratts and co-authors (2004), the social justice paradigm actually came about because of advances within multicultural counseling itself. No matter the impetus for its genesis, social justice broadens our vision of how we *must* champion the cause of treating the addicted families we serve.

Addicted persons and their families are more often than not stigmatized, ridiculed, and discriminated against. Ultimately they are blamed by society at large and their loved ones specifically for their own dysfunctional addiction-related behaviors (Moyers & Miller, 1993). Such victim blaming has been described as "the tendency when examining a social problem to attribute that problem to the characteristics of the people who are its victims" (Levin & Levin, 1980, p. 36). From popular comedians who ridicule addicted persons and their families to unjust social policies that repeatedly victimize the addicted and inhibit their freedom to obtain basic medical, psychological, and nutritional services, the addicted are viewed within our society as an easily oppressible subpopulation unworthy of support. According to social justice, this must change, and we must lead the charge.

As counselor educators who teach addictions courses and supervisors who consult with institutions and agencies, it is not uncommon for us to hear counselors-in-training and even other helping professionals unabashedly proclaim, "How can you work with *those* [addicted] people?" or "I don't want to waste my time counseling drunks and sex addicts." Frequently, such ignorant statements are followed with comments about the *futility* of counseling the addicted and ultimately the *questionable value* of addicted persons themselves.

Such statements are a blight upon our profession and society itself. Statements of that kind simply imply that certain people and populations are unworthy of the fundamental rights and privileges. The thin line between such convoluted beliefs and endorsed genocide is merely a nanometer wide. Therefore, family addictions counselors must both be aware of such attitudes of social injustice toward the people we dutifully serve and be social advocates for their empowerment and changes within society.

Ignorance Is No Excuse

Have you ever heard the phrase "He doesn't even know what he doesn't even know"? As clinical supervisors we sometimes hear this phrase when speaking with those evaluating counselors' clinical skills. One of the last times the senior author heard this phrase, an inexperienced counselor-in-training had just told an impoverished female client to simply pack her young children and their things and "move into a hotel for a couple days" when her boyfriend's drugging behaviors again engendered violence. Although he realized her need to escape a potentially dangerous situation, he didn't comprehend the many factors that prohibited her leaving (e.g., money, boyfriend's threats).

Shamefully, this counselor-in-training did not even know what he didn't even know. In other words, his "worldview" (Sue, 1977, 1978) inhibited his ability to accurately assess the client's reality. Thus, he could not fathom someone remaining in an abusive relationship, nor could he understand why someone would live with an addicted person. Concomitantly, this neophyte family addictions counselor had never experienced poverty or an inability to readily pay for a hotel room. He had never experienced the stressors of raising young children. And, although he realized the potential dangers of remaining in this abusive and addicted relationship, he could not envision why a woman 75 pounds lighter and nearly a foot shorter than her menacing boyfriend couldn't just tell him to leave "her" trailer.

Frankly, if you can't imagine the fear of facing a drunken and enraged person hell-bent on keeping you in "his" trailer, you certainly have no right prescribing clinical directives. Yet, some counselors do exactly this, as they don't know what they don't know about addicted families or the persons who reside within them. This is a social justice topic of major importance.

So, what's the big deal about social justice, and why should counselors be concerned? Well, first we had better understand our Euro-American worldview (Sue et al., 1998)—especially the implications of perceived power differentials and disempowerment that many of our clients experience as they simply enter our offices.

Nonsense you say? Well, consider this. The authors provide clinical supervision and direct counseling at clinics located on university campuses. The vast majority of community clients entering those clinics never attended college. The clinics are climatically controlled and comfortable in comparison to sometimes brutal outside temperatures. The furnishings, although not opulent, are aesthetically pleasing. And when we are counseling or supervising, our attire is relatively "middle-class" in both appearance and cost.

In other words, we are working at places our clients may find unfamiliar at best and intimidating at worst. Additionally, the clinics where we work are likely more comfortable than our clients' very own homes. Furthermore, we wear clothes that probably are more expensive and potentially different from the clothes worn by our clients. Given the potential for such distinct differences, do you really believe addicted families are going to readily feel understood and comfortable?

Recently when the senior author sat next to a client in a counseling clinic waiting room, the mother quickly stood and apologized for remaining after the session. She explained that the motive behind staying after the session was to remain in the building's air-conditioned coolness rather than returning to the intense outside heat and humidity. When encouraged to stay and converse, this mother of two young children hesitantly sat. We watched her children play, and ever so slowly we entered into cordial but poignant conversation. Poignant because during the conversation this mother indicated that (a) the clinic's toys were the only age-related, nonviolent toys her children had access to, (b) despite the incredible heat outside, she did not have sufficient monies to run her apartment's air-conditioning, and (c) she believed that she and her children would never have the opportunity to attend this public institution as students. Strikingly evident throughout the conversation were power differential and disempowerment topics central to social justice counseling and the senior author's unearned privilege that resulted merely from being a member of the dominant, empowered society.

If client families do not perceive addictions counselors as being aware of the enormous power differential between the counselor and family or the disempowerment and marginalization that their addicted families have experienced, how can addicted persons and their family members possibly invest themselves in the counseling process? Even worse, what if the addicted family encountered a counselor who understood her privileged status and the disparate power differential between her clients and herself, but she failed to actively address these important topics throughout the course of treatment? Would you expect counseling to end successfully? Of course not. In such a situation, we can only imagine relatively unsuccessful outcomes. This is precisely why it is imperative that you gain an understanding of social justice topics. Such understanding broadens your worldview related to the power differential between yourself and many of your clients. Social justice's basic premise encourages us to proactively address such power differentials throughout the course of treatment.

In addition to counselor self-awareness is the need to advocate for clients in the public domain via educating (or reeducating) the community.

Whereas some progress has been made in destigmatizing the plight of addicted individuals, often as a result of "positive" media attention given to self-admitting celebrities and sports figures, much work remains for addicted individuals and families.

At one time the term *alcoholic* induced visions of a homeless man begging for change. Today, more often than not, individuals are given "credit" for coming forward and admitting their AOD problems. In many circles, "recovering alcoholic" embodies such concepts as strength, worldliness, and the wounded hero (especially in Hollywood movies). These are not the same attributes the junior author's clients have received upon admitting to being "recovering sex addicts." Quite the opposite—people often look at such individuals with distain, fear, and loathing and are quick to leave the room and find ways to protect their children from being exposed to such persons. Similar experiences have been reported by clients struggling with addictions to the Internet ("People actually laughed at me") and food (one client struggling with restricting her food would often hear sayings such as "She's just skin and bones—I bet a strong wind could knock her over" whereas a male overeater would have to contend with outright insults and comments such as "Why don't you just stop eating like that—where's your willpower?"). The point is that individuals are marginalized, discriminated against, and even attacked as a result of societal beliefs regarding different addictive disorders. This is where public education in the form of speaking engagements, seminars, radio and television interviews, and newsletter submissions can be effective tools at increasing social awareness, decreasing social stigmas, and maintaining justice for clients. The junior author has made numerous attempts at advocating for the addicted client population and their families and notes that there are always more opportunities for you, the reader, to do the same.

Just as important, social justice is a rallying point for all counselors to champion the cause of justice for all people via political action. When was the last time you contacted your local, state, or national governing representatives or voted on topics in a manner designed to address your addicted families' needs? On two separate occasions, while serving as the president of the International Association of Addictions and Offender Counselors and the Association for Assessment in Counseling, the senior author canvassed Capitol Hill with professional colleagues. The number of e-mails and letters he has written to legislative representatives related to social justice issues for his clients could be counted on two hands. What an abysmal record! We can't truly address social justice issues by myopically focusing merely on our clients themselves. We must actively petition our government to address the fundamental rights of the less empowered and the needy.

Multicultural Topics

Given that the vast majority of persons are raised in families and acculturated into their specific family systems' socioeconomic, ethnic, religious, gender, and value domains, it is rather understandable how some family addictions counselors erroneously assume that all families are alike. This of course seems especially true when the presenting families appear similar to those families in which addictions counselors were themselves raised. Such a perception clearly is fictitious.

Even when families are composed of similar-looking domains (e.g., third-generation, Irish American, Catholic, upper-middle-class) and there appears to be great homogeneity with other "alike" families, life events such as illnesses, job losses, career successes and failures, and car accidents impact people and families differently. Adding addictions and addictive behaviors to such families engenders further differences that ensure even more subtleties and distinctions.

An example of the impact of some of these subtleties and distinctions became remarkably apparent when the senior author counseled addicted families impacted by Hurricanes Katrina and Rita in 2005. Here, families displaced from the same geographic region and presenting with what one might initially perceive as nearly identical ethnic, religious, and socioeconomic backgrounds responded so stunningly different to the circumstances surrounding their evacuations and losses. Equally apparent, despite many observed and reported domain similarities, recovering persons and their families experienced abstinence and evacuation stressors differently.

Specifically, some recovering persons and their families promoted the notion that it was fully acceptable if not expected for addicted members to return to their former addictive behaviors because of the experienced trauma and evacuation. However, others believed that they had successfully persevered the worst nature could thrust upon them and articulated their recovery as "unshakable."

Family addictions counselors' failure to adequately understand the many subtle and distinct differences within each individual family potentially dilutes counseling efficacy and can even promote a chasm of irreconcilable treatment hindrances that render desired outcomes unattainable. Stated differently, all persons and families encountering addictions do not necessarily experience things identically, and "success" is not always measured the same way among all addicted families. However, before we can even begin the process of looking at addicted family diversity topics, we must first look at ourselves.

Self-Assessment

Many formal graduate courses in multicultural counseling as well as various professional conference programs provide students and professionals opportunities to better understand their clients by encouraging self-assessment of the participants. In other words, these multicultural self-assessment experiences can promote an enlarged worldview. Certainly, one can never know all one *could* know about multicultural counseling, diversity, and counseling addicted families from every imaginable population combination. Multicultural counseling experts spend their entire professional careers researching and developing effective multicultural counseling models. Our intent is not to advocate that family addictions counselors place their commitment to counseling addicted families on hold as they seek to become prominent multicultural counseling experts. However, we wholeheartedly believe that every family addictions counselor should possess at least minimal multicultural competencies and available multicultural resources relevant to the addicted families they serve.

We further believe that the cornerstone of such multicultural competencies begins with each individual counselor and her understanding of who *she* is among a number of very important domains. Earlier in the book we described the necessity of reporting our clinical experiences within the context of who we are: married, Euro-American, heterosexual males with doctorates in counselor education and supervision. We further suggested that although we both teach at Hispanic-serving institutions and reside in geographic areas where the majority of persons are Hispanic, Mexican American, Puerto Rican, Cuban, or Haitian, we are perceived as persons of the dominant culture with corresponding power and authority. Knowing who we are impacts how we interact with clients and helps us apply the Sequential Family Addictions Model within the context of how we are likely to be perceived. The same is true for you. Understanding who you are will help you facilitate relevant treatment to addicted families and encourage appropriate interactions that will have benefit.

Taking a racial or ethnic identity instrument such as the Multigroup Ethnic Identity Measure (MEIM) (Phinney, 1992), the Multidimensional Inventory of Black Identity (MIBI) (Sellers, Rowley, Chavous, Shelton, & Smith, 1997), the Oklahoma Racial Attitude Scale (ORAS) (Choney & Behrens, 1996), or the Racial Identity Attitudes Scale (RIAS) (Helms & Parham, 1996) is one way to learn about yourself and enhance your self-assessment. These instruments often provide information regarding positive or negative feelings regarding your race or racial identity and assimilation into the dominant culture. Depending on how they are specifically used, they have significant potential for enlightenment. Remember, the place to start your multicultural counseling journey is based on *your* self-awareness. This self-awareness can also be fostered by answering the questions at the end of this chapter.

Additionally, the Association for Multicultural Counseling and Development created an excellent monograph to help counselors operationalize multicultural counseling competencies (Arredondo et al., 1996). If you do not have it, get it. In a nutshell, this monograph describes the knowledge and skills that culturally competent family addictions counselors need and what counselors can do to gain these competencies. We especially like the monograph, because it reminds counselors that cultural competence is more than having a set of skills or knowledge about others, diversity, and multicultural counseling. More importantly, it means that counselors must possess *cultural self-awareness and sensitivity*—including an understanding of experiences, attitudes, values, and biases that may limit their own cultural competency and professional interactions. Remember, multicultural experiences, readings, interactions, and assessment instruments are simply individual road markers used along the journey, not the final destination themselves.

Multicultural Family Addictions Counseling

Finally, some might errantly believe that we should include an elaborate yet succinct diagram showing exactly how to conduct effective multicultural counseling or text describing specific "multicultural" interventions for each "type" of addicted family that presents for treatment. For example, shouldn't we discuss how to specifically treat addicted African American families, addicted Jewish families, and addicted gay families? What foolishness. We would instead argue that describing "exactly how" to provide relevant addictions counseling to each type of family perpetuates the problem that this chapter is designed to address—that is, addressing the needs of the individuals within the system by respecting the uniqueness that each individual and family system has. To do otherwise ignores the diversity within populations and mistakenly attempts to suggest that all persons from a specific population are the same.

Dana (1993) suggests that group and individual identities, beliefs, values, and languages create a means through which to interpret life-events. We believe this is especially relevant to addicted families and to the issue of multicultural counseling, because families in particular cocreate idiosyncratic cultures based on their sociocultural experiences (Schwartzman,

1983) and their collective and individual interpretations of relevant life-events (Dana, 1993). Thus, it is ultimately more important to facilitate family counseling that is sensitive to these idiosyncratic cultures developed by these families in response to their sociocultural and relevant life-event experiences than to interact in a manner focused on the general cultural and ethnic family system composition (Ariel, 1999; Schwartzman, 1983).

Stated differently, family addictions counselors should be careful not to stereotype families based on their ethnic, religious, cultural, sexual, age, or socioeconomic presentation. Instead, we must carefully ascertain the idiosyncratic and unique cultural features developed by each family system and its members. Employing terminology from previous paragraphs, we must understand the family system's worldview before we begin haphazardly utilizing interventions based on the family's misperceived stereotypical culture.

Please do not misinterpret what was just stated. We are not suggesting that family addictions counselors be dismissed from the responsibility of gaining multicultural counseling competencies and skills relevant to the multicultural diversity—especially multicultural competencies and skills related to major populations within your specific community and region. To the contrary, we believe it is imperative to have such specific knowledge. Instead, we are suggesting that it is essential to remain open to the uniqueness of the individual families that present for addiction services and to treat each person and family that you encounter with the same commitment, respect, and courtesy that you would want for your loved ones should they need addictions services.

Multicultural Resources

In conclusion, we would strongly advocate that you engage in three additional approaches to increase your multicultural sensitivity. First, access the rich resources of culturally diverse counselors and clinical supervisors who have specialized knowledge or familiarity with populations that you will likely encounter as you facilitate family addictions counseling. They are invaluable resources that can help expand your understanding of client and family behaviors, customs, and beliefs. In addition, they can help you better understand important subtleties that might otherwise go unnoticed. Second, broaden your social interactions to include individuals from a variety of cultural backgrounds. For example, it just so happens that both authors recently moved from the rich diversity of North Carolina to other parts of the country that have an abundance of diversity as well: South Texas and Miami. This has afforded both of us the opportunity to interact professionally and personally with, among others, a wealth of

Mexican American, Cuban American, Haitian American, and Caribbean American friends, colleagues, and counseling students who have lived the majority of their lives in South Texas or South Florida. These friends and students have helped acculturate both authors to some of the general customs and traditions of these regions. This in turn has allowed the authors to respond more appropriately to some client families and to connect in ways that demonstrate respect for the client families that they counsel.

And finally, we always suggest that you assume the "Colombo Approach" to understanding the impact of your clients' culture on their presenting concerns. For those of you unfamiliar with the television show *Colombo* from the 1970s, Peter Falk played a Los Angeles homicide detective whose trademark was his ability to "play dumb" with suspects who eventually led him to the answers he sought without his confronting them directly. In applying the Colombo Approach with clients, we suggest that you avoid taking an "expert approach" as it applies to culture—this is often interpreted as insensitive and tends to be inaccurate. Rather, assume ignorance: *Ask* your addicted family members to explain their culture to you, *ask* them to help you understand how their culture impacts their conceptualization of the presenting concerns, and *assume nothing* (regardless of their [or your] cultural background). We have found that clients who have the opportunity to both explore their culture with a willing audience and formulate their own hypotheses about the impact of their culture offer unique perspectives that we, the multiculturally sensitive family addictions counselors, often miss. Remember the old saying, "It is better to remain quiet and be thought a fool than to open one's mouth and remove all doubt."

Life-Threatening Behaviors

A robust correlation exists among life-threatening behaviors such as suicide and violence toward family system members and alcohol and other drug (AOD) abuse. These correlations are predominantly reoccurring within the literature and demonstrate the need for family addictions counselors to understand how to assess and intervene to ensure the family members' safety. Therefore, this chapter will describe suicide, its frequency among addicted persons, and how to conduct a thorough suicide assessment via the use of the SAD PERSONS Scale. Finally, a post-violence family debriefing model that we have found helpful will be described.

Suicide

The Event and Frequency   If you haven't yet experienced it, the probability is that you will. Your Sequential Family Addictions sessions will be progressing well, and you will find yourself successfully "dancing" with your addicted family in an almost too routine manner. Then suddenly someone unexpectedly, quietly, and nonchalantly remarks that she would "rather die than continue disappointing" her family. Your head abruptly turns toward her. You look at her, but she continues focusing her attention on her parents. Surely you misunderstood. The remark couldn't have been about suicide. Or was it?

By now the remark is long gone and lost amid new conversation and family banter. Did anyone else hear what she just said? You find yourself lost in an internal dialogue, ruminating on her words that still seem to echo in your mind. Then, it happens again. This time the alcohol- and cocaine-addicted adolescent says, "I don't want to live this way anymore." No one else seems to hear her desperate words. Then, as if her words were lost but now found, someone replies, "We don't either. Don't you realize that because of *you* and *your* alcohol and cocaine habits we have to waste our time in here?"

Boom, just like that, your clinical suspicions are founded. You stop the interactions and clarify, "Jenny, are you thinking of killing or harming yourself?" The client's affirmative response may be convoluted, disguised, or surprisingly straightforward. Suddenly you find yourself intervening with an addicted and suicidal adolescent family member. She is among the exact people she craves to be loved and comforted by. Yet, she feels helplessly rejected and abandoned by these very loved ones—those claiming to love her but treating her with disdain and making disparaging remarks about her, her loved and only true friend, cocaine, and the only way she understands coping with the stressors of an addicted family system.

Her family, too, is in pain. But they hide it well by angrily lashing out at her. They are frustrated at her inability to stop using. More likely they are scared—scared that their beloved adolescent daughter and sister can't defeat her addiction. So, the family languishes in pain, frustration, anger, fear, and disappointment.

For family addictions counselors, the rankings and numbers related to suicide and suicide attempts are markedly clear. Both are more common than many are aware. Suicide is the 11th leading cause of death among all Americans (Anderson & Smith, 2003), the second leading cause of death among Americans ages 25 to 34, and the third leading cause of death among Americans ages 10 to 14 and 15 to 24 (CDC, 2005). Annual death certificates in the United States suggest that slightly more than 30,000 persons commit suicide each year, including the 30,622 documented suicides in 2001 (CDC, 2004). These numbers likely underestimate suicide's prevalence, because many suicides are actually misidentified as accidental deaths (e.g., vehicular accidents, hunting accidents, and alcohol and other drug use) (P. F. Granello, personal communication, August 23, 2005).

Equally relevant to family addictions counselors is the suggested numbers of annual suicide attempts. Such suicide attempts are called *parasuicides*. Parasuicides negatively impact addicted families and frequently become a comorbid coping mechanism along with alcohol and other drug (AOD) abuse for family members seeking reprieve from angry others within their family system.

According to McIntosh's (1991) suicide-attempt-to-suicide-completion ratio, between 240,000 to 600,000 Americans attempt suicide annually. Such robust suicide and parasuicide numbers have particular importance to family addictions counselors, because the frequency of suicide among AOD-abusing clients is especially disproportionate to the general population of suicidal persons at large. The evidence is strikingly obvious: AOD-abusing clients are at much greater suicide risk (Flavin, Franklin, & Frances, 1990; Rogers, 1992).

Assessment   Thus, family addictions counselors must be able to thoroughly assess immediate suicide risk and appropriately respond to suicidal family members. The cornerstone to such intervention is a thorough clinical interview in combination with empirical assessment (e.g., suicide prediction scales, suicide checklists, psychological tests) (Maris, 1991; Motto, 1991). The client–counselor interview is the primary method of assessing suicide risk (Jobes, Eyman, & Yufit, 1990). Given the importance of the assessment interview, it is imperative that you understand how to conduct a thorough suicide risk interview both with individual system members and with the family itself.

Bonner (1990) suggested there are three key risk domains that should be investigated during a clinical interview and cited a number of prominent suicidologists to support his claim (Beck, Brown, & Steer, 1989; Beck, Kovacs, & Weissman, 1979; Beck, Steer, Kovacs, & Garrison, 1985; Beck, Weissman, Lester, & Trexler, 1974; Bedrosian & Beck, 1979; Bonner, 1989; Bonner & Rich, 1988a, 1988b; Motto, Heilbron, & Juster, 1985). The three domains include mental state (e.g., Are the client's mental cognitions lucid and logical?), affective state (e.g., Is the client suffering from depression or another affective disorder?), and psychosocial context (e.g., Has this individual suffered a recent loss?).

As you likely remember, the counselor used the SLAP acronym to assess Mario's suicidal potential in Chapter 2. The SLAP acronym investigates the following: Specific—how specific is the suicide plan? Lethality—how lethal is the plan? Availability—does the client have the means to carry out the plan? **Proximity**—are rescuers (e.g., supportive people) close at hand? In Chapter 2 Mario had admitted suicidal ideation and the intent was to determine his immediate self-annihilation risk.

However, if in the above scenario the adolescent female had not yet indicated suicidal intent, we might use another more comprehensive assessment. This assessment is called the SAD PERSONS Scale (SPS). As clinicians, counselor educators, clinical supervisors, and researchers, we believe that the SPS has great utility when facilitating suicide assessments and can be effectively used by master's-level clinicians assessing addicted family members' self-harm potential (Juhnke, 1996, 1994a, 1994b; Vacc & Juhnke, 1997).

The SAD PERSONS Scale   The SAD PERSONS Scale (SPS) was created by Patterson, Dohn, Bird, and Patterson (1983). The SPS is a semi-structured suicide risk assessment interview scale. It was developed to help physicians obtain a detailed investigation into the same three domains identified by Bonner (1990) as critically important when assessing suicide potential. SPS authors created the acronym SAD PERSONS from 10 literature-identified suicide risk factors (i.e., sex, age, depression, previous attempt, ethanol abuse, rational thinking loss, social supports lacking, organized suicide plan, no spouse, and sickness). Via the clinical interview process, the family addictions counselors can use the SPS to systematically investigate each of the 10 risk factors. The semistructured format of the scale aids the family addictions counselor in facilitating an interview based on specific criteria established for each risk factor. Thus, the family addictions counselor generates questions for each factor pertinent to the specific family member and her immediate clinical presentation. Absent from the SPS are stock questions that can potentially give the family member the impression of being interrogated. Instead, the SPS allows the family addictions counselor to ask multiple questions related to specific risk factors. Questioning continues until there is satisfaction that sufficient information regarding each factor has been gathered. One point is scored for each factor present; total scores can range from 0 (suggesting very little suicide risk) to 10 (suggesting very high suicide risk). Suggested guidelines for clinical actions are based on these scores.

Patterson et al. (1983) found the SPS and its acronym (SAD PERSONS) to be an easily learned memory aid for third-year medical students in psychiatry. Findings related to master's-level counseling students trained in the SPS were similar (Juhnke, 1994a). Additionally, master's-level counseling students in training self-reported an increased perception of suicide assessment competence. Thus, based on Patterson et al.'s and Juhnke's findings, the SPS appeared to aid clinicians facilitating a thorough and comprehensive suicide assessment and helped clinicians differentiate between low- and high-risk clients. Those participating in the SPS training appear to propose more appropriate clinical interventions, based on their recognition of the accurate number of present risk factors, than those who reviewed the same vignettes of suicidal persons but who did not participate in the SPS training. These findings have been consistently noted from Patterson's initial 1983 study through our in-class demonstrations and video vignette examination with our students even today.

Jenny's SAD PERSONS Scale Vignette   Therefore, let's use the earlier vignette of the addicted adolescent and see how the counselor would both ask SAD PERSONS Scale questions and then utilize the instrument to aid in the clinical disposition. Given that the counselor in this scenario knows that Jenny abuses cocaine and is not married, the fourth and ninth SPS questions (ethanol abuse and no spouse) will be scored affirmatively when summing the scale.

Counselor: "Jenny, would you mind if I focused on you for a moment and asked some questions that might help me better understand how things are going for you?"

Jenny: "Go ahead."

Counselor: "I'm trying to remember exactly how old you are."

Jenny: "I'm 16."

Counselor: "Have there been some times recently when you were feeling blue, depressed, or down?"

Jenny: "Yes, all the time. I feel like everyone is mad at me, because I keep using. I really try hard not to, but I can't seem to resist the urge to get high—especially when they are arguing and so mad at me."

Counselor: "That must be pretty rough. On a scale of 1 to 10 with 1 meaning not depressed at all and 10 meaning feeling overwhelmingly depressed all the time, what kind of depression score would you give yourself today?"

Jenny: "I don't know. I keep thinking things will get better, but they don't. My dad is mad at my mom and me. My dad is mad at me. I can't please anyone, and I feel like I'm in a black hole and just can't get out."

Counselor: "So, the depression score you would give yourself today would be a what?"

Jenny: "At least an 8 and probably a 9."

Counselor: "So, I'm wondering have you ever attempted to harm or kill yourself before or are you thinking of harming or killing yourself now?"

Jenny: (long silence) "Truthfully, this is going to sound really bad and I don't want to get Dad any angrier. But last week when I relapsed, I wanted to just end it all. I even mixed vodka and cocaine together and sat in the garage with the car running, hoping to die. But when I woke up after the car had stalled out, I just smelled like exhaust fumes."

Dad: "Oh my gosh, Princess, why didn't you tell us?"

Counselor: "So are you thinking about hurting or killing yourself now or when you go home today?"

Jenny: "I would do anything to escape this pain—especially my dad's anger."

Counselor: "Jenny, thank you for answering my questions so honestly. I've got just a few more and they might seem rather peculiar but hang with me. They are important. OK?"

Jenny: "OK."

Counselor: "Sometimes people tell me that they sometimes see things that other people don't or hear things that others don't hear. For example, sometimes people hear other people or voices telling them to do certain things. Have you ever experienced anything like that?"

Jenny: "You mean like voices telling me to kill myself and stuff like that?"

Counselor: "It could be, or it may be that you experience things that others don't."

Jenny: "I experience a lot of really strange things when I'm high, but I don't ever hear voices or see dead people or things like that."

Counselor: "How about friends, Jenny. Do you have some really close friends or family members that you truly trust and talk with about the things you are thinking and doing?"

Jenny: "I've got a lot of friends. Cheryl and Ginny are my two best school friends. However, my best friend is probably my grandma. She lives near the school and so I see her and talk with her every day. She takes a lot of time with me and she reminds me how important I am."

Counselor: "And, Jenny, how about a suicide plan. Will you tell me exactly how you were thinking of killing yourself?"

Jenny: "I don't know. I don't want to make my dad more upset and angry than he already is."

Counselor: "Dad, this is important that we understand exactly how Jenny is thinking about killing herself. My guess is that you are more scared than mad that Jenny is talking about killing herself. Can you tell her that it is OK to talk about how she was thinking about killing herself?"

Dad: "Jenny, I am so very sorry. It's not that I am mad at you. I just am really scared."

Jenny: "It's OK, Dad."

Counselor: "Jenny, do you believe your dad that he is more scared than mad?"

Jenny: "Yes."

Counselor: "Now, tell us exactly how you were thinking about killing yourself."

Jenny: "Well, given that the exhaust thing just got me sick, I've been thinking that the easiest and least painful way of dying is by using my dad's gun. It's a shotgun that he has in his bedroom. I've thought about loading it and putting the barrel under my chin and pulling the trigger with my toes. But I don't want to be barefoot when I die, so I've been trying to think of another way to pull the trigger. It's not that I want to die. It's more like I don't want to live, you know?"

| Counselor: | "Jenny, one final question for right now. Do you have any life-threatening sicknesses or illnesses like cancer or heart disease?" |
| Jenny: | "No, I had mononucleosis once, but I'm not sick much at all." |

First, let's review the scoring. As previously indicated, Jenny is female; thus, she receives no points on this factor. Had she been a male, one point would have been assigned. The second factor is age. Jenny is 16. Remember, the SPS gives one point if a client is 19 years of age or younger or 45 years of age or older. Given that Jenny's age is less than 19 years, she receives one point. Depression is the third factor. Jenny reports her immediate level of depression as either an 8 or a 9 on a 10-point scale. Thus, she is endorsing significant depression and receives a point on this factor. She receives another point for a previous suicide attempt. Jenny reports a parasuicide of significant lethality the week before. Furthermore, given her alcohol and drug abuse, Jenny receives one point on the ethanol abuse factor. Jenny denies a rational thinking loss and reports numerous social supports, so she receives no points on either factor. Strikingly, Jenny reports an organized suicide plan—using her father's shotgun. Thus, she receives one point. Jenny does not have a spouse and, therefore, receives another single point. Finally, Jenny does not endorse any life-threatening illnesses or incapacitating diseases. Therefore, she receives zero points on these factors.

Let's sum Jenny's score. Using Tables 5.1 and 5.2 in conjunction with the above paragraph, what score and corresponding clinical intervention does the SPS suggest? Did you come up with an SPS score of 6 with a corresponding clinical intervention of hospitalization? If you did, CONGRATULATIONS! If not, you may wish to review the individual 10 factors again. Remember, a person can only score "0" or "1" on each of the 10 risk factors. Thus, you merely count the number of factors that were positively endorsed by the family member and then sum the total number of scores. The possible range of scores, then, is between 0 and 10.

Four SAD PERSONS Scale Red Flags Before we proceed, four SPS factors are of critical importance and warrant discussion. These factors include depression, ethanol (or other drug) abuse, rational thinking loss, and organized suicide plan. Any client presenting with any one or more of these critical risk factors warrants immediate attention and intervention. For example, family members presenting with depression warrant evaluation for antidepressant medications. This is true whether they are

TABLE 5.1   SAD PERSONS Scale

Risk Factor	One Point Given If . . .
Sex	Male
Age	19 years of age and younger or 45 years and older
Depression	Depressed
Previous attempt	Previous suicide attempt has been made
Ethanol abuse	Substance-abusing or substance-dependent
Rational thinking loss	Rational loss is present (e.g., hallucinations, delusions)
Social supports lacking	No close friends, no social support
Organized suicide plan	Well-thought-out and constructed suicide plan
No spouse	Divorced, never married, separated, widowed
Sickness	Debilitating or life-threatening illness or disease is present

TABLE 5.2   SAD PERSONS Guidelines for Clinical Interventions

Total Points	Clinical Actions
0 to 2	Send home with follow-up
3 to 4	Close follow-up; consider hospitalization
5 to 6	Strongly consider hospitalization, depending on confidence in the follow-up arrangement
7 to 10	Hospitalize or commit

suicidal or not. Failure to minimally refer the family member to their family physician to be evaluated for potential psychotropic medications has treatment, ethical, and legal ramifications. Clearly anyone presenting depression warrants treatment.

Persons presenting with addictive disorders, AOD abuse or dependence, or AOD use below the age of majority is at increased risk of harm. Therefore, appropriate addictions interventions are *always* warranted when this risk factor is present.

The same is true of persons presenting with a rational thinking loss. Anytime a member within the addicted family has a rational thinking loss that includes delusions or hallucinations, he must be evaluated for antipsychotic medications. Persons who are floridly psychotic or not oriented to person, place, or time can be a significant danger to themselves and others.

Counseling is an excellent source of treatment with addicted families and the Sequential Family Addictions Model provides clear opportunities to aid families in the recovery process. However, talk therapies cannot be successful in instituting effective, consistent, and intentional change among persons who are distinctly out of touch with reality.

The senior author can recall occasions when counseling bipolar and schizophrenic drug-abusing persons. Although these persons might make agreements with him or embark on a recovery based on commitments to themselves and others, when they perceived the Devil or demons told them to do certain things—like kill themselves or others—their agreements and commitments where utterly useless against the hallucinations. Therefore, psychotropic mediations are very helpful to addicted persons experiencing hallucinations.

Finally, anyone with a clearly delineated and organized suicide plan warrants immediate intervention. Now this does not necessarily require that the person with an organized plan be hospitalized, although it does mean that the family addictions counselor would have to have some pretty significant reasons to think otherwise. Thus, if a family member has an organized plan, the family counselor better have a clear understanding of what steps the counselor, client, and family need to take to ensure the client's safety. Furthermore, we would strongly advocate that one seek active supervision from an experienced and appropriately credentialed clinical supervisor.

Post-SPS Score Interventions Jenny's score was high, and based on her answers she likely warrants hospitalization—especially given her current suicide plan and the lethality of that plan concomitant to her recently failed and highly lethal parasuicide. In such a case, you may wish to speak with Jenny about volunteer hospitalization. Thus, you might say something like this:

Counselor:	"Jenny, I get the feeling that you're not the type of person who lies or makes things up. Is that correct?"
Jenny:	"True, I say what I mean and mean what I say."
Counselor:	"And, if I heard you correctly, you have said that you would 'do anything' to escape the emotional pain that you are experiencing and your father's potential anger."
Jenny:	"Yup, anything."
Counselor:	"And you described how you would use your father's shotgun to kill yourself. Is that right?"

Jenny:	"Yes, things are that bad."
Counselor:	"Then Jenny, I believe you are at a point where you want to have things change and you want things to be better. Is that what I'm hearing from you?"
Jenny:	"I can't keep going on like this."
Counselor:	"Listen, given all that you are going through and your overwhelming desire to just escape, my clinical judgment is that you need to be in a safe environment until things settle down for you. Wouldn't you agree with that?"
Jenny:	"Yes."
Counselor:	"Then, what I want you to do is to help me help you. I need for you to sign yourself into the hospital as a voluntary patient."
Jenny:	"No way, I'm not going to do that."
Mother:	"That's not going to happen."
Counselor:	"Well, help me understand. This is what I've heard Jenny say. First, I've heard her say that she attempted suicide last week. That attempt was a very lethal attempt and we are just very fortunate that the car stalled. Second, I've heard Jenny say that she doesn't lie. In other words, when she says she would like to simply 'escape' and that she is concerned about her father's anger, she truly means these things. Third, I've heard Jenny describe a very well established and lethal suicide plan—she has identified the use of your shotgun, dad. As each of you likely knows, shotguns are highly lethal at such close range and Jenny has described how she would hold the gun under her chin and discharge the shotgun with her toes. It is my professional opinion that Jenny is a clear and imminent danger to herself. Therefore, in the short term, she needs to be in an environment where she can be safe and she can feel comfortable. Wouldn't you agree that ensuring your daughter's safety and, Jenny, your own safety is the very most important thing that we can do?"
Father:	"Yes, but hospitalization?"

Counselor: "Well, we are talking about a voluntary hospitalization. If Jenny admits herself as a voluntary patient, should she feel uncomfortable or not like it, she can petition to get herself out. If she is not perceived as a danger to herself, she would be free to go."

Jenny: "But I don't want to go into the hospital. I will be all right. I wouldn't kill myself and I'll promise not to drink or drug anymore."

Counselor: "Jenny, I know this sounds scary, but the truth is that you have told us that you attempted suicide last week, that you have a plan for harming yourself today, and that you just want to escape the emotional pain you are experiencing. Given your admitted risk and stated intent to harm yourself, you have two options. The first is to go with your folks and me to the hospital and admit yourself in as a voluntary patient. Or, because it is my professional opinion that you are a danger to yourself, I will complete the appropriate paperwork at the district attorney's office and petition the court to have you taken to the hospital for a psychiatric evaluation. Should that examination concur with my professional opinion, they will hospitalize you as an involuntary patient for a minimum of 72 hours and you will be ineligible to check yourself out until they believe you are no longer a potential threat to yourself. Jenny, what do you want to do? Would you be willing to have your mom and dad go with you to the hospital and admit yourself as a voluntary client? Or, do you wish for me to start the paperwork and the involuntary commitment process?"

Jenny: "I guess I have no choice."

Counselor: "I think you know what is best for yourself, Jenny. Mom and Dad, are you willing to help get Jenny over to the hospital to ensure that she remains alive?"

Father: "I think it is the right thing to do."

Jenny: "OK, I'll go, but I don't want to."

Let's discuss what happened here. First, the family addictions counselor starts by stating that she believes Jenny is a person of truth who only states what is truly believed. Jenny agrees to this. Second, the family addictions counselor repeats what Jenny has stated (i.e., that Jenny would "do anything" to escape the emotional pain currently being experienced). This includes succinctly repeating Jenny's parasuicide and the complex and intricate details of Jenny's very lethal suicide plan. After recapping Jenny's statements, the family addictions counselor attempts to empower Jenny and provide a logical reframe of hospitalization—that is, to change things for the better and ensure her safety. The family addictions counselor's proposed solution is self-admittance as a voluntary client into the hospital. Jenny and family members negatively respond to this suggestion. The family addictions counselor again simply repeats what she has heard Jenny say. Furthermore, the family addictions counselor puts Jenny's reported behaviors into the context of her past parasuicide and her current suicidal intent. Then, the family addictions counselor describes the suicide plan that Jenny has voiced and indicates the extreme lethality of the plan. She next insists that Jenny and her parents do what is best for Jenny—agree to voluntary hospitalization. When parents and Jenny hesitate, the family addictions counselor contrasts voluntary hospitalization with involuntary hospitalization and describes the potential benefits of entering the hospital as a voluntary patient.

Certainly, all hospitalizations don't go as smoothly as this. Although different states and districts have diverse means to access assessment and involuntarily hospitalize clients, the end result when suicide risk is high is that either family members or family addictions counselors petition the local courts to have the potentially suicidal person evaluated for involuntary hospitalization. This should be done only when there is clear and imminent danger of injury to self or others.

Low SPS Scores That's all great, but what do you do if the SPS and your clinical judgment both suggest little to moderate risk, and the judgment of the client and her family is that the client is not a clear and imminent danger to herself? As most of us remember from our entry-level graduate courses in ethics and law, the federal mental health system is founded upon the idea of treating patients in a "least restrictive environment." In other words, family addictions counselors do not seek involuntary hospitalization of clients when the addicted family member can be safely treated in a less restrictive environment.

Here, the family addictions counselor might ask the family member to make a "no-suicide contract" with valued family members and the counselor. A no-suicide contract cannot keep someone from killing herself and should be used only when the family addictions counselor and the other family members wholly believe that the client is not an immediate threat to self or others, and when it is perceived that the potentially suicidal client is lucid enough and willing to truly follow through with a no-suicide agreement. Stated differently, if you do not believe that the client can be adequately safe without inpatient hospitalization, do not attempt to utilize a no-suicide contract.

Although there are many ways to conduct a no-suicide contract, from written contracts to verbal commitments, we believe the best is a verbal commitment with a handshake. In this scenario, the family addictions counselor would say something like this:

Counselor:	"Jose, I'm hearing you say that you are not intending to hurt or kill yourself or anyone else, is that correct?"
Client:	"Yes, I'm not thinking about killing myself. I merely said that there have been times in the distant past like 2 years ago when I had some thoughts of hurting myself. But I'm not having those thoughts now."
Counselor:	"So, would you be willing to promise me and your family members here today that you would let us know if you had thoughts of harming or killing yourself or someone else?"
Client:	"I would let you know."
Counselor:	"So, you are promising me that you would call me or the 24-hour help-line number listed on the back of this appointment card I am giving you?"
Client:	"Like I said, I'm not thinking of killing myself. But if I was, I promise I would call the help-line number that you have given me."
Counselor:	"What do you think, family? Do you think Jose is a danger to himself or do you believe he is not a danger to himself?"

Adult Sister: "We don't think he will hurt himself. When he has gotten down in the past, he has always called me or my older brother."

Older Brother: "Hey bro, you'd call me if things got bad again, right?"

Client: "You know I would."

Counselor: "So, would you be willing to promise your brother and sister right now that you are not thinking of hurting or killing yourself and that, should you start to have those thoughts or should you begin to feel overwhelmed, you would call the 24-hour help line or both of them?"

Client: "Yeah, I would do that."

Counselor: "Do you believe him?"

Older Sister: "Yes, Jose doesn't lie to me."

Counselor: "OK, should any of you believe Jose has become a danger to himself, will you promise to call the 24-hour help-line number?"

Older Brother: "We would."

A quick review of the no-suicide contract with the addicted family system demonstrates a number of important factors. First and foremost the family addictions counselor clarifies in front of the family system that the person of concern is not actively thinking about self-harm and secures information from the client supporting the use of a no-suicide contract. This clarification provides the client an opportunity to disagree or to indicate, "No, in fact, I am actively thinking about harming myself." In this case, the counselor would seek an environment ranging from family members monitoring the person perceived at risk and ensuring that all guns and weapons are removed from that family member's access—especially weapons identified as potentially part of an organized suicide plan—to voluntary or involuntary hospitalization.

In this vignette the client reports that the previous suicidal ideation occurred 2 years ago and that he was not actively suicidal or presenting with active suicidal ideation. Because of this, the family addictions counselor asks the family member to promise both the counselor and the client's family that he would contact either the 24-hour help-line number, the counselor, or another family member should he begin to feel in jeopardy.

Even when the client verbalizes his no-suicide agreement, the counselor does not simply say, "OK, go home. Don't worry about a thing, family." Instead the counselor seeks input from those who know the family member even better than the counselor—the family.

In this vignette, the family agrees that they do not perceive Jose as an immediate danger to himself. However, the opportunity is given for family members to challenge the client if necessary or inform the family addictions counselors of further concerns. This opportunity further provides family members the chance to reach out and demonstrate their support of the person. This is done here by sister and brother. In this vignette, older brother directly clarifies that Jose would call him should Jose become a danger to himself. And Jose agrees. Then, the family addictions counselor has the family promise that should any of them perceive Jose to be a danger to himself, they would call. Again, this simply creates a system of checks and balances and distributes the responsibility evenly among everyone. Again, the emphasis is on keeping everyone safe.

Substance-Related Familial Violence

It certainly doesn't take a rocket scientist to understand the comorbidity between alcohol and other drug (AOD) abuse and familial violence. Substances that increase emotional volatility, decrease impulse control, and frequently are associated with escalating bravado and rage present a danger to all families. As previously mentioned in earlier chapters and displayed in the opening Sequential Family Addictions Model flowchart, this model encourages treatment of nonviolent family members who have been impacted by addictions within the system. Perpetrators of violence against the family are not allowed to participate in the family counseling experience, and restraining orders against such violent perpetrators are strongly encouraged.

Such a stance might be perceived by some as exceedingly rigid. However, after years of clinical practice with addicted families, we believe not. We have sometimes helplessly watched perpetually violent perpetrators continue their reign of violence, sabotage, and intimidation over nonviolent members, even though they smugly report a desire to rejoin and nurture the family to those who then mandate family-focused treatment. This is an injustice to those who are least able to defend themselves—the children within the system.

Our position is not to exclude violent perpetrators from treatment. Rather, as you likely recall, the Sequential Family Addictions Model advocates that perpetrators obtain long-term treatment outside the family system. Further, perpetrators aren't allowed to reunite with the victimized family until the nonviolent system perceives that their goals have been adequately fulfilled and further counseling is unnecessary. Thus, the post-violence family debriefing intervention we propose is only for the nonviolent parent and children.

An Adapted, Post-Violence Debriefing Intervention for Nonviolent Parents and Their Children The Adapted, Post-Violence Debriefing Intervention for Nonviolent Parents and Their Children, hereafter called the Adapted-Family Debriefing Intervention, came about as a result of the authors' Critical Incident Stress Debriefing (CISD) experiences and was developed by adapting the broadly applied CISD Model specifically to Solution-Focused Family Therapy, previously discussed in Chapter 4. As you undoubtedly recall, Solution-Focused Family Therapy emphasizes competence, strengths, and possibilities rather than deficits, weaknesses, and limitations. Remember, family addictions counselors using Solution-Focused Family Therapy respect the family's abilities and encourage the use of existing personal and familial resources to engender positive change. An expectation of successful resolution to presenting concerns is fostered within this family therapy type, and significant emphasis is placed on the family's potential to create change based on their "picture" of successful treatment.

To help you better understand the intervention—specifically how this intervention differs from CISD and how to effectively use the intervention—we will first succinctly review CISD and then compare and contrast it to the Adapted-Family Debriefing Intervention. Then, we will describe the Adapted-Family Debriefing Intervention and depict a clinical vignette that will allow you to participate in scoring the intervention.

Critical Incident Stress Debriefing CISD is a structured, one-session, small-group experience that has been reported as helpful to those who have witnessed or experienced traumatic events (Mitchell & Everly, 1993). CISD was originally developed to help emergency workers (e.g., emergency medical technicians [EMTs], firefighters, law enforcement officers) better cope with particularly distressing events encountered while on duty (Mitchell & Everly). By the early to mid-1990s, the CISD model had gained recognition as a viable aid for helping violence victims (O'Hara, Taylor, & Simpson, 1994), survivors of traumatic experiences (Vernacchia, Reardon, & Templin, 1997; Yule & Canterbury, 1994), and treatment providers working with populations that have experienced trauma (Jenkins, 1996; Matthews, 1998).

CISD is composed of seven stages. Each of the seven CISD stages (i.e., Introduction, Fact, Thought, Reaction, Symptom, Teaching, and Reentry

[Mitchell & Everly, 1993; Thompson, 1993]) is facilitated by a minimum of three "team" members (i.e., leader, coleader, and gatekeeper). A specific charge is assigned to each team member and none of the members are required to have mental health–related graduate degrees or corresponding mental health licenses. In other words, team members are often peers from within a specific profession. These CISD-trained members then aid professional peers who have encountered a significantly distressing event. Finally, the CISD process is usually limited to those adults who have experienced a *single* traumatic event (e.g., robbery).

The Adapted-Family Debriefing Intervention described within this chapter specifically adapts CISD to fit the needs of addicted families that have experienced substance-related familial violence. The intervention fits within the context of the Sequential Family Addictions Model and occurs either at the very onset of treatment or immediately following endorsed investment by the family at the conclusion of the Motivational Interviewing Stage.

In other words, this is not a stand-alone intervention but an intervention designed to fit within the Sequential Family Addictions Model itself. Stated differently, the Adapted-Family Debriefing Intervention is like an illuminating light on the Sequential Family Addictions Counseling Christmas tree. By itself, the intervention—although potentially powerful—has neither the branch to fully support itself nor the necessary context in which to understand the family "tree." Yet, when used as intended within the Sequential Family Addictions Model, the intervention provides light that both illuminates the context of the family system and then promotes the potential for healthy, normal healing.

Furthermore, unlike CISD, which uses three or more trained peers, the Adapted-Family Debriefing Intervention typically uses only one family addictions counselor to facilitate treatment. However, the family addictions counselor may wish to add a second counselor in particularly difficult cases or when addicted family systems are especially fragile or chaotic.

For example, if the perpetrator had severely injured the nonviolent spouse and the children, or if the family experienced a long-term history of violence and intimidation, it may be helpful to engage a second family addictions counselor within session. Concomitantly, should a nonviolent spouse have an Axis II personality disorder or should there exist other special concerns that make the family especially fragile, the addition of a second family addictions counselor can be potentially beneficial.

Another difference between CISD and the Adapted-Family Debriefing Intervention is that the intervention uses Solution-Focused Family Therapy's techniques to both emphasize and promote new, healthy, nonviolent, nonaddictive individual and family behaviors. Thus, unlike CISD, the Adapted-Family Debriefing Intervention promotes reliance on addicted family members' strengths and resources. In our experiences, the result is a debriefing experience that matches the sequential intent of the model and an experience that openly encourages discussion of presenting symptomatology resulting from the violence. Additionally, the process promotes attention to behavioral and cognitive markers that suggest both healthy individual and healthy family responses to the experienced substance-related familial violence.

Initial Intervention Session   As previously indicated, the initial Adapted-Family Debriefing Intervention session typically occurs either at the very onset of treatment or immediately after the nonviolent family system indicates their willingness to invest in treatment at the conclusion of the Motivational Interviewing Stage. This initial session typically lasts from 1 to 3 hours, depending on the specific needs of the addicted family system and its individual members. The intent of this initial session is to move family members through an experiential sequence that provides opportunities to discuss the violent experiences and resulting thoughts and feelings. This initial session, then, further provides family addictions counselors a means to increase understanding of both individual and family needs. It also educates family members regarding post-traumatic stress disorder (PTSD) symptoms and potentially available resources within the agency or community (e.g., support groups for battered women).

We have found that nonviolent system members from the addicted family are best served by completing the steps outlined below. Unlike nonfamilial CISD debriefings that frequently address concerns arising from a stranger's random violent acts, substance-related familial violence victims have unique concerns related to the loss of a supposedly nurturing caregiver or parent or to the victimization occurring by someone who society suggests should always be loved and accepted. Therefore, familial violence survivors want assurances that other family members will not abandon or shun them.

As is the case with CISD, it is preferred to complete all seven steps of the Adapted-Family Debriefing Intervention before ending the initial session. This sequence was established to engender movement from cognitive thoughts regarding the violent experience, to the feelings behind the familial violence, and finally to a psychoeducational model related to typical emotional responses to substance-related familial violence. Therefore, the beginning steps encourage active discussion of vivid memories and poignant feelings. Completing each of the seven steps during the initial family counseling session promotes a needed sense of safety and collective encouragement between nonviolent family members. Furthermore, it allows family members to step back from feelings and return to the safety of cognitive processing.

Seven Steps of the Initial Session

Introduction During this step, we believe it is important to remind nonviolent family members of the lack of confidentiality within session and encourage all to stay throughout the entire session. Next we generally try to engender the support of all family members by indicating something like, "Although some of you may not necessarily feel as though you need to be here today, your presence and participation will likely be helpful to other family members who especially need your family support at this difficult time." A statement like this typically inhibits family members from leaving and results in at least their minimal investment in the process.

Next we indicate that no one is to blame for the substance-related familial violence episodes, and we provide a succinct, age-appropriate discussion of how psychoactive substances often erode an addicted member's ability to self-regulate and appropriately act. The intent here is not to justify why an addicted family member became violent. Instead, it is to help nonviolent members realize that they are not to blame for somehow inciting the perpetrator's violence. Thus, when a perpetrator has been jailed, we discuss how the nonviolent members were not responsible for placing the violent family member in jail. Therefore, we attempt to help the nonviolent members understand that they were not responsible for these behaviors.

Finally, family addictions counselors indicate that the purpose of the Adapted-Family Debriefing Intervention is to help family members discuss events surrounding their victimization, including events that occurred following the violence. Concomitantly, it is important to indicate that although each family member may have witnessed the same violent events within the family (e.g., arguments between father and mother resulting in mother being struck), their recollections and experiences may dramatically differ. Failure to address the possibility of such differences may result in some family members becoming angry or frustrated that others do not recall the events or sequence of events in the same manner.

Fact-Finding The goal within the fact-finding step is to get family members talking about nonemotional facts regarding the violence. To do this, family addictions counselors elicit information from the family about the details of the events leading to the first violent experience.

Given that participation is voluntary, family members are not required to share. However, those sharing are asked to describe where they were when the first incident of violence occurred. Thus, we might ask, "Who would be willing to share when the violence began in this family or what was happening immediately before the last violent episode?" Additional questions related to the violent event's details also need to be asked. Such questions might include, "Was this the first time dad had beat Raymond?" "Did mom threaten everyone or just dad?" and "Did your brother threaten to shoot you with the gun?" Emphasis is placed on having the nonviolent family victims tell just the facts surrounding the violent experiences. The family addictions counselor should not push family members to describe feelings within this step. However, if intense feelings are reported, the counselor should emphasize that such emotions are not unusual and indicate the need to address such feelings through experiences such as the ones addressed within the Adapted-Family Debriefing Intervention.

Thoughts and Cognitions The goal within the thoughts and cognitions step is to gently encourage family members to move from discussing external, relatively safe, nonemotional facts regarding the violent episodes to their personal thoughts surrounding the family member's violent behaviors. Therefore, the thoughts and cognitions step is a *transitional step*. It helps family members discuss the thoughts and cognitions they had when they experienced the violence. The intent, then, is to safely encourage the nonviolent familial victims to move closer to the upcoming reaction step, which often has intense affective responses.

Within the thoughts and cognitions step, nonviolent family members are asked a question such as, "What was your first thought when you saw your sister hit your mother?" or "What was your first thought when you saw Pierre knock dad to the ground?" During this step, it is crucial to let family members know that their responses and thoughts are normal. Statements such as "I can understand how you thought that it wasn't really happening" validate family members' thoughts and acknowledge their concerns.

Reactions to Violence In this step, the goal is to help family members move into the affective reactions they may have regarding the violent experience. The focus should be kept on the family members' discussion of *their* reactions to the violence. Many times it is helpful to start this step with a question similar to, "What has been the most difficult thing about seeing your sister in a coma after your stepfather hit her?" or "What has been the most difficult part of your brother's arrest for beating your mom?"

Symptoms   The goal within this step is to help family members move from the affective domain back into the cognitive domain. As the emotionally charged reactions begin to subside, the counselor asks family members about any physical, cognitive, or affective symptoms such as trembling hands, inability to concentrate, or depression. As symptoms are identified, the counselor can ask if other family members have encountered similar symptoms. This interaction helps family members understand that the symptoms which they have just described are often common responses to violence.

Teaching   The teaching step goals include encouraging family members to learn about the frequent commonalities of experienced symptoms (e.g., fear, anger, depression) and teaching about typical post-traumatic stress disorder (PTSD) symptoms. Many times family addictions counselors can use the symptoms just identified by family members in the symptom step to discuss the common reactions. The counselor can also discuss other PTSD symptoms (e.g., restricted range of affect). The emphasis here is on detaching family members from the heavily affective experience and moving them into the cognitive domain.

Additionally, the teaching step can be used to help family members learn about substance-related familial violence. Specifically, family members need to again be informed that their psychoactive substances have the potential to promote violent or aggressive behaviors. However, this information needs to be balanced by noting that the family perpetrator, not the psychoactive substance, is ultimately responsible for her violent behaviors.

Reentry   Goals within this step are to help family members gain some sense of closure related to the first Adapted-Family Debriefing Intervention session and discuss any further thoughts or concerns. Finally, the counselor makes a few closing comments related to the support and caring visible among nonviolent family members who have experienced the substance-related aggression by others within the family system. A handout discussing common symptoms of PTSD and depression is distributed. This handout also includes a 24-hour help-line number and a place to write down the time and location of the next Adapted-Family Debriefing Intervention session.

Adapted-Family Debriefing Intervention Sessions 2 through 4   During Adapted-Family Debriefing Intervention sessions 2 through 4, it is critical to begin each session with solution-focused techniques designed to promote the identification of individual and family strengths, resilience, resourcefulness, and support. In particular it is important to help nonviolent family members identify behaviors that they believe suggest healing. For example, the counselor may start the second session with a statement such as,

> "Many times family members who participate in a debriefing experience like the one we had last week begin to notice one or two little things that suggest the healing and recovery process has begun. What little things have you begun noticing since our initial meeting that suggest your family is beginning the healing and recovery process?"

Once positive behaviors are identified by family members, the family addictions counselor will ask a follow-up question like, "I wonder how this family will continue these positive new behaviors?" Here, the counselor is attempting to promote a continuation of behaviors identified by the family as suggesting increased health.

In sessions 3 and 4 the family addictions counselor may wish to start the session with a discussion of behaviors previously identified by individual members or the family as a whole as suggesting healing. For example, the counselor may state,

> "Last week Claire indicated, and I believe everyone had agreed, that some noticeable changes had occurred since brother was removed from this family. Furthermore it was indicated that these changes demonstrated that this family was starting to make steps toward healing. If I'm not mistaken, these steps had to do with visible acts of supporting each other. Who would be willing to tell me which family members have demonstrated support for other family members during the past week and how their supporting behaviors have been helpful?"

As was the case in session 2, the emphasis within this opening introduction is again on identifying and promoting behaviors that the family finds helpful.

Should the family members indicate that no improvements have occurred, the counselor may find it helpful to ask the nonviolent family members to identify supporting behaviors they have observed among family members. Thus, the counselor might ask, "Charles, what things have you noticed your mother and sister doing for one another that suggest they are supporting each other since dad has left?" The counselor might then follow up with a statement such as, "Mother and Claire, Charles indicates that he has seen your support for each other by the way you are spending more time together. Is that something that has been helpful to both of you?" Such reporting by family members again promotes attention to these helping behaviors and fosters an increased sense of healing.

Remember our discussions on scaling questions? This technique can also be used to generate discussion within the debriefing. Here, the counselor might ask, "Mother, on a scale from 0 to 10, 0 indicating very little healing has occurred and 10 indicating significant healing has occurred, what score do you believe Charles would say matches the level of healing this family has experienced since dad left the family?"

Family members who continually report diminished scores or a consistent and significant increase in depressive symptomatology should undergo a psychiatric examination to determine if psychotropic medications are warranted. As in all cases, the presence of suicidal ideation by any family member warrants immediate assessment and intervention.

Positive journaling is another solution-focused technique that our client families have reported as helpful. Here, family members keep journals indicating how things have improved in the family system since the violent and intimidating member left. Specifically, we encourage family members to attend to symptom-free times. Sharing journal entries within the subsequent family sessions helps family members learn how others are experiencing relief times. Hence, these discussions encourage members to continue and amplify behaviors identified as present during symptom-free times.

The structure of sessions 2 through 4 varies according to idiosyncratic addicted families' needs. In the vast majority of the Adapted-Family Debriefing Intervention sessions, client families only need an opportunity to begin identifying behaviors that suggest improvement. Once this opportunity arises, family members often discuss means to promote or amplify the improvement continuation.

Fifth Session   The fifth session encourages a summarization regarding the Adapted-Family Debriefing Intervention experience and promotes a clearly delineated ending point (Cohn & Osborne, 1992). During this session family members report what they have learned about themselves and their family as a result of the experienced violence. Members report their renewed commitment to themselves and the other family members who survived the violence. Furthermore, family members identify helping behaviors that have fostered improvement and identify means to continue the same.

Conclusion

This important chapter has discussed three major areas of concern for all family addictions counselors. These areas include social justice counseling, multicultural topics, and life-threatening behaviors. In this chapter we learned that social justice should be of critical importance to all family addictions counselors and how addicted families in particular are stigmatized, ridiculed, and discriminated against. We further discussed how social justice ignorance can negatively impact addicted families. Proactive social advocacy was also discussed. Multicultural topics of importance were also included in this chapter, and the authors warned family addictions counselors against viewing all addicted families as being identical to the families in which the addictions counselors themselves were raised. Furthermore, family addictions counselors were implored to self-assess their multicultural competence and to reach out to less competent counselors in an attempt to increase the profession's ability to best serve addicted families. Finally, the life-threatening behaviors of suicide and substance-related familial violence were discussed. You learned how to utilize the SAD PERSONS Scale to assess potentially suicidal members within the addicted families we serve. In addition, you learned how to utilize an adapted, post-violence debriefing intervention with nonviolent parents and their children.

Skill Builder

Question 1

A. Describe how you have recently witnessed or experienced unequal power and unearned privilege.

_____

_____

_____

_____

B. Please describe what is meant by social justice and how the social justice construct has specific implications for you both as a professional and as a person.

_____

_____

_____

_____

C. What is "victim blaming" and what implications does this construct have when counseling addicted families?

_____

_____

_____

_____

D. What is the construct "worldview" and what should it suggest to us as we counsel addicted families?

_____

_____

_____

_____

E. What person(s) of political clout can you contact concerning social issues impacting the addicted client families you serve?

_____

_____

_____

_____

Question 2

A. What is cultural competence and how is the construct important to you as a family addictions counselor?

_____

_____

_____

_____

B. Describe three populations of diversity that you typically counsel and report the things that you have done to increase your cultural competence in serving addicted families within these three populations. If you find that you have not done things to increase your cultural competence with addicted families within three populations of diversity, describe what experiences might be helpful for you as you increase your multicultural competence.

_____

_____

_____

_____

C. What do the authors mean when they stress the importance of being "sensitive to [family] idiosyncratic cultures"?

_____

_____

_____

_____

Question 3

A. What four risk factors are assessed via the suicide assessment acronym SLAP?

_____

_____

_____

_____

B. List the 10 SAD PERSONS Scale risk factors.

_____   _____

_____   _____

_____   _____

_____   _____

_____   _____

C. List the four SAD PERSONS Scale risk factors that are noted as "red flags."

_____

_____

_____

_____

Question 4

List three differences between the Critical Incidence Stress Debriefing Model and the Adapted-Family Debriefing Intervention.

_____

_____

_____

Question 5

In five sentences or less, describe the most important things you gained or learned as a result of reading this chapter.

_____

_____

_____

_____

_____

_____

_____

Skill Builder Responses

Question 1

A. Describe how you have recently witnessed or experienced unequal power and unearned privilege.

Response:

Although there can be many kinds of responses to this question, we are looking for you to provide recent examples of how socioeconomic or sociocultural differences provided you opportunities that others may not have.

B. Please describe what is meant by social justice and how the social justice construct has specific implications for you both as a professional and as a person.

Response:

The social justice construct suggests that one should become aware of and appropriately respond to topics of unequal power, unearned privilege, and oppression. Additionally, social justice seeks to balance resources and power via politically conscious methods led by professional counselors. For us as family addictions counselors, the construct of social justice is vitally important, because we must become aware of how our addicted families may be negatively impacted by our socioeconomic or cultural status. Furthermore, we, both as professional family addictions counselors and as persons, must champion the cause of helping addicted families via social activism.

C. What is "victim blaming" and what implications does this construct have when counseling addicted families?

Response:

Victim blaming is the tendency to blame the very people who are victimized by a problem as the reason for the problem. Specifically, it is "the tendency when examining a social problem to attribute that problem to the characteristics of the people who are its victims" (Levin & Levin, 1980, p. 36).

D. What is the construct "worldview" and what should it suggest to us as we counsel addicted families?

Response:

Worldview is how one "sees" others and how one believes the world runs. It is a lens that filters our interactions with others.

E. What person(s) of political clout can you contact concerning social issues impacting the addicted client families you serve?

Response:

There are many people of political clout that you could have identified. Some of the persons you may have identified are the president of the United States, elected officials such as senators or representatives, local judges, mayors, city planners, and so on.

Question 2

    A. What is cultural competence and how is the construct important to you as a family addictions counselor?

Response:

Cultural competence means that one possesses cultural self-awareness and sensitivity, including an understanding of experiences, attitudes, values, and biases that may limit one's own cultural competency and professional interactions.

    B. Describe three populations of diversity that you typically counsel and report the things that you have done to increase your cultural competence in serving addicted families within these three populations. If you find that you have not done things to increase your cultural competence with addicted families within three populations of diversity, describe what experiences might be helpful for you as you increase your multicultural competence.

Response:

Here the authors were looking for presentations, experiences, and specialized supervision that you had attained related to specific populations that you commonly counsel.

    C. What do the authors mean when they stress the importance of being "sensitive to [family] idiosyncratic cultures"?

Response:

The idea of being sensitive to individual family idiosyncratic cultures was an attempt to remind family addictions counselors to be cautious about "overly stereotyping" persons who belong to certain sociocultural or economic populations. In other words, be aware of and competent in the cultures of the persons you commonly counsel (e.g., the Chicano culture, the Native American culture, etc.), but more importantly become aware of the unique culture that the family has co-created and join with *that* idiosyncratic culture.

Question 3

A. What four risk factors are assessed via the suicide assessment acronym SLAP?

Response:

Specific—how specific is the suicide plan? Lethality—how lethal is the plan? Availability—does the client have the means to carry out the plan? Proximity—are rescuers close at hand?

B. List the 10 SAD PERSONS Scale risk factors.

Response:

Sex
Age
Depression
Previous suicide attempt
Ethanol (or other drug) abuse
Rational thinking loss
Social supports lacking
Organized suicide plan
No spouse
Sickness

C. List the four SAD PERSONS Scale risk factors that are noted as "red flags."

Response:

Depression
Ethanol or other drug abuse
Rational thinking loss
Organized suicide plan

Question 4

List three differences between the Critical Incidence Stress Debriefing Model and the Adapted-Family Debriefing Intervention.

Response:

There are a number of differences. For example, the CISD Model uses professional peers such as fellow firefighters to facilitate the debriefing. Adapted-Family Debriefing Intervention utilizes graduate-level family addictions counselors who are licensed. Additionally, CISD is a one-time event typically related to a one-time trauma. The Adapted-Family Debriefing Intervention, on the other hand, has multiple meetings and often revolves around a series of substance-related familial violent episodes.

Question 5

In five sentences or less, describe the most important things you gained or learned as a result of reading this chapter.

_____

_____

_____

_____

_____

_____

_____

References

Anderson, R. N., & Smith, B. L. (2003). Deaths: Leading causes for 2001. *National Vital Statistics Report, 52*(9), 1–86.

Ariel, S. (1999). *Culturally competent family therapy: A general model.* Westport, CT: Praeger.

Arredondo, P., Toporek, R., Brown, S., Jones, J., Locke, D. D., Sanchez, J., & Stadler, H. (1996). Operationalization of the multicultural counseling competencies. *Journal of Multicultural Counseling and Development, 24,* 42–78.

Baker, S. B., Daniels, T. G., & Greeley, A. T. (1990). Systematic training of graduate-level counselors: Narrative and meta-analytic reviews of three major programs. *The Counseling Psychologist, 18*(3), 355–421.

Beck, A. T., Brown, G., & Steer, R. A. (1989). Predictions of eventual suicide in psychiatric inpatients by clinical ratings of hopelessness. *Journal of Consulting and Clinical Psychology, 57,* 309–310.

Beck, A. T., Kovacs, M., & Weissman, A. (1979). Assessment of suicidal ideation: The scale for suicidal ideators. *Journal of Consulting and Clinical Psychology, 47,* 343–352.

Beck, A. T., Steer, R. A., Kovacs, M., & Garrison, B. (1985). Hopelessness and eventual suicide: A 10 year prospective study of patients hospitalized with suicidal ideation. *American Journal of Psychiatry, 142,* 559–563.

Beck, A. T., Weissman, A., Lester, D., & Trexler, L. (1974). The measurement of pessimism: The Hopelessness Scale. *Journal of Consulting and Clinical Psychology, 42,* 861–865.

Bedrosian, R. C., & Beck, A. T. (1979). Cognitive aspects of suicidal behavior. *Suicide and Life-Threatening Behavior, 9*(1), 87–96.

Berg, I. K., & Miller, S. D. (1992). *Working with the problem drinker: A solution-focused approach.* New York: Norton.

Bonner, R. L. (1989). It's time to get back to basics in suicidology: Empathy revisited. *American Association of Suicidology, Newslink, 15*(1), 6.

Bonner, R. L. (1990). A "M.A.P." to the clinical assessment of suicide risk. *Journal of Mental Health Counseling, 12*(2), 232–236.

Bonner, R. L., & Rich, A. R. (1988a). Negative life stress, social problem-solving self appraisal, and hopelessness: Implications for suicide research. *Cognitive Therapy and Research, 12,* 549–556.

Bonner, R. L., & Rich, A. R. (1988b). A prospective investigation of suicidal ideation in college students: A test of a model. *Suicide and Life-Threatening Behavior, 18,* 245–258.

Brody, J. (1986, March 12). Child suicides: Common ingredients. *The New York Times,* pp. 42–43.

Brooks, D. K., Jr., & Gerstein, L. H. (1990). Counselors credentialing and interprofessional collaboration. *Journal of Counseling & Development, 68,* 477–484.

Cantor, P. (1987, March 17). Teenage suicide: The unheard cry for help. *The Los Angeles Times,* p. 1.

Centers for Disease Control and Prevention, National Center for Injury Prevention and Control (Producer). (2004). *Web-based injury statistics query and report system (WISQARS)* [Online]. Retrieved from http://www.cdc.gov/ncipc/wisqars/default.htm

Centers for Disease Control and Prevention, National Center for Injury Prevention and Control (Producer). (2005). *Web-based injury statistics query and report system (WISQARS)* [Online]. Retrieved from http://webappa.cdc.gov/cgi-bin/broker.exe

Choney, S. K., & Behrens, J. T. (1996). Development of the Oklahoma Racial Attitudes Scale-Preliminary Form (ORAS-P). In G. R. Sodowsky & J. Impara (Eds.), *Multicultural assessment in counseling and clinical psychology* (pp. 225–240). Lincoln, NE: Buros Institute of Mental Measurement.

Cohn, B., & Osborne, W. L. (1992). *Group counseling: A practical self-concept approach for the helping professional.* Chappaqua, NY: L. S. Communications.

Cormier, L. S., & Cormier, W. H. (1976). Developing and implementing self-instructional modules for counselor training. *Counselor Education and Supervision, 16*(1), 37–45.

Dana, R. H. (1993). *Multicultural assessment perspectives for professional psychology.* Boston: Allyn & Bacon.

Danto, B. L., & Kutsher, A. H. (Eds). (1977). *Suicide and bereavement.* New York: MSS Information Corporation.

Deutsch, C. J. (1984). Self-reported sources of stress among psychotherapists. *Professional Psychology: Research and Practice, 15*(6), 833–845.

Flavin, D. K., Franklin, J. E., Jr., & Frances, R. J. (1990). Substance abuse and suicidal behavior. In S. J. Blumenthal & D. J. Kupfer (Eds.), *Suicide over the life cycle: Risk factors, assessment, and treatment of suicidal patients* (pp. 177–204). Washington, DC: American Psychiatric Press.

Hauser, M. J. (1987). Special aspects of grief after a suicide. In E. Dunne, J. L. McIntosh, & K. Dunne-Maxim (Eds.), *Suicide & its aftermath: Understanding and counseling survivors* (pp. 57–70). New York: Norton.

Helms, J. E., & Parham, T. A. (1996). The Racial Identity Attitudes Scale. In R. L. Jones (Ed.), *Handbook of tests and measurements for Black populations* (Vol. 1, pp. 167–174). Hampton, VA: Cobb & Henry.

Jenkins, S. R (1996). Social support and debriefing efficacy among emergency medical workers after a mass shooting incident. *Journal of Social Behavior & Personality, 11*, 477–492.

Jobes, D. A., Eyman, J. R., & Yufit, R. I. (1990). *Suicide risk assessment survey.* Paper presented at the annual meeting of the American Association of Suicidology, New Orleans, LA.

Juhnke, G. A. (1994a). Teaching suicide risk assessment to counselor education students. *Counselor Education and Supervision, 34*, 52–57.

Juhnke, G. A. (1994b). SAD PERSONS scale review. *Measurement & Evaluation in Counseling & Development, 27*(1), 325–327.

Juhnke, G. A. (1996). The adapted SAD PERSONS: A suicide assessment scale designed for use with children. *Elementary School Guidance & Counseling, 30*, 252–258.

Levin, J., & Levin, W. C. (1980). *Ageism: Prejudice and discrimination against the elderly.* Belmont, CA: Wadsworth.

Littrell, J. M., Malia, J. A., & Vanderwood, M. (1995). Single-session brief counseling in high school. *Journal of Counseling & Development, 73,* 451–458.

Maris, R. W. (1991). Introduction. *Suicide and Life-Threatening Behavior, 21*(1), 1–17.

Matthews, L. R. (1998). Effect of staff debriefing on posttraumatic stress symptoms after assaults by community housing residents. *Psychiatric Services, 49,* 207–212.

McIntosh, J. L. (1991, January 12). U.S. suicides: 1988 official final data. *Michigan Association of Suicidology,* pp. 10–11.

McIntosh, J. L., & Kelly, L. D. (1992). Survivors' reactions: Suicide vs. other causes. *Crisis, 13,* 82–93.

Mitchell, J. T., & Everly, G. S. (1993). *Critical incident stress debriefing (CISD): An operations manual for the prevention of traumatic stress among emergency services and disaster workers.* Ellicott City, MD: Chevron.

Motto, J. A. (1991). An integrated approach to estimating suicide risk. *Suicide and Life-Threatening Behavior, 21*(1), 74–89.

Motto, J., Heilbron, D., & Juster, R. (1985). Suicide risk assessment: Development of a clinical instrument. *American Journal of Psychiatry, 142,* 680–686.

Moyers, T. B., & Miller, W. R. (1993). Therapists' conceptualizations of alcoholism: Measurement and implications for treatment decisions. *Psychology of Addictive Behaviors, 7*(4), 238–245.

Murphy, J. J. (1994). Working with what works: A solution-focused approach to school behavior problems. *School Counselor, 42,* 59–65.

National Center for Health Statistics. (1986). *Monthly vital statistics report.* Rockville, MD: Author.

National Center for Health Statistics. (1998, May 28). *FASTATS A to Z.* Retrieved from http://www.cdc.gov/nchswww/fastats/suicide.htm

O'Hanlon, W. H., & Weiner-Davis, M. (1989). *In search of solutions: A new direction in psychotherapy.* New York: Norton.

O'Hara, D. M., Taylor, R., & Simpson, K. (1994). Critical incident stress debriefing: Bereavement support in schools developing a role for an LEA educational psychology service. *Educational Psychology in Practice, 10,* 27–34.

Patterson, W. M., Dohn, H. H., Bird, J., & Patterson, G. A. (1983). Evaluation of suicidal patients: The SAD PERSONS scale. *Psychosomatics, 24*(4), 343–349.

Phinney, J. S. (1992). The Multigroup Ethnic Identity Measure: A new scale for use with diverse groups. *Journal of Adolescent Research, 7,* 156–176.

Ratts, M., D'Andrea, M., & Arredondo, P. (2004). Social justice counseling: "Fifth force" in field. *Counseling Today Online.* Retrieved from http://www.counseling.org/Content/NavigationMenu/PUBLICATIONS/COUNSELING-TODAYONLINE/JULY2004/SocialJusticeCounsel.htm

Reed M. D., & Greenwald, J. Y. (1991). Survivor victim status, attachment, and sudden death bereavement. *Suicide and Life Threatening Behavior, 21,* 385–401.

Rich, C. L., Young, D., & Fowler, R. C. (1986). San Diego suicide study. *Archives of General Psychiatry, 43,* 577–582.

Rogers, J. R. (1992). Suicide and alcohol: Conceptualizing the relationship from a cognitive-social paradigm. *Journal of Counseling & Development, 70*(4), 540–543.

Schwartzman, J. (1983). Family ethnography: A tool for clinicians. In C. J. Falicov (Ed.), *Cultural perspectives in family therapy* (pp. 137–149). Rockville, MD: Aspen Systems.

Sellers, R. M., Rowley, S. A. J., Chavous, T. M., Shelton, J. N., & Smith, M. A. (1997). Multidimensional Inventory of Black Identity: A preliminary investigation of reliability and construct validity. *Journal of Personality and Social Psychology, 73*, 805–815.

Sewell, J. D. (1993). Traumatic stress of multiple murder investigations. *Journal of Traumatic Stress, 6*, 103–118.

Spitzer, W. J., & Neely, K. (1992). Critical incident stress: The role of hospital-based social work in developing a statewide intervention system for first-responders delivering emergency services. *Social Work in Health Care, 18*, 39–58.

Sue, D. W. (1977). Barriers to effective cross-cultural counseling. *Journal of Counseling Psychology, 24*, 420–429.

Sue, D. W. (1978). Eliminating cultural oppression in counseling: Toward a general theory. *Journal of Counseling Psychology, 25*, 419–428.

Sue, D. W., Carter, R. T., Casas, J. M., Fouad, N. A., Ivery, A. E., Jensen, M., LaFromboise, T., Manese, J. E., Ponteroto, J. G., & Vazquez-Nutall, E. (1998). *Multicultural counseling competencies: Individual and organizational development.* Thousand Oaks, CA: Sage.

Talbot, A., Manton, M., & Dunn, P. J. (1992). Debriefing the debriefers: An intervention strategy to assist psychologists after a crisis. *Journal of Traumatic Stress, 5*, 45–62.

Thompson, R. A. (1993). Posttraumatic stress and posttraumatic loss debriefing: Brief strategic intervention for survivors of sudden loss. *The School Counselor, 41*, 16–22.

U.S. Department of Education. (1993). *Youth and alcohol, selected reports to the surgeon general* (DE Publication No. ED1.2:Y8). Washington, DC: U.S. Government Printing Office.

U.S. Department of Health and Human Services. (1989). *Report of the secretary's task force on youth suicide. Volume 3: Prevention & interventions in youth suicide* (DHHS Publication No. ADM89-1623). Washington, DC: U.S. Government Printing Office.

Vacc, N. A., & Juhnke, G. A. (1997). The use of structured clinical interviews for assessment in counseling. *Journal of Counseling & Development, 75*(6), 470–480.

Vernacchia, R. A., Reardon, J. P., & Templin, D. P. (1997). Sudden death in sport: Managing the aftermath. *Sport Psychologist, 11*, 223–235.

Weinberg, R. B. (1990). Serving large numbers of adolescent victim-survivors: Group interventions following trauma at school. *Professional Psychology: Research and Practice, 21*, 271–278.

Yule, W., & Canterbury, R. (1994). The treatment of post traumatic stress disorder in children and adolescents. *International Review of Psychiatry, 6*, 141–151.

Final Comments

We trust this book on Sequential Family Addictions Counseling will be helpful to you as you serve those who wish to begin their new existence as nonaddicted family members in well-functioning and healthy family systems. As you have read, addicted families often have relatively few healthy support systems that come to their aid. The stigma and re-victimization experienced by addicted families frequently fuels their perceptions that their addiction secrets must be kept within the family. The results promote systems designed to keep nonmembers at bay and to comply without sacrificing real change. Thus, addressing family addictions can disarm and quickly burn out entry-level counselors. Frustration is common even among the most experienced. However, the rewards are great and the appreciation of those who learn to successfully negotiate their addictive battles cannot be overly emphasized. As one recent addicted family member conveyed, "I've learned what and who matters to me . . . my family, not my drugs."

We truly wish you the very best in your professional endeavors as a family addictions counselor, and we thank you for the privilege of allowing us to describe the Sequential Family Addictions Model to you. We further wish to thank a number of others who have assisted us in countless ways as we developed and wrote *your* book. Although we can't possibly name all who provided wisdom and support, there are some very important persons who warrant special recognition.

These first include our family members, Deborah, Bryce, and Brenna Juhnke, and Olga, Mackenzie, and Logan Hagedorn. Without their support and encouragement, this book could never have been completed. They endured many long absences as we authored the book. Additionally, Dana Bliss, Jay Whitney, Mimi Williams, and Stephanie Pekarsky of Routledge have been exceptional supports who have provided input and suggestions throughout the entire publication process.

Further, Dr. Frank Miller of the SASSI Institute and Dr. Douglas Snyder, author of the Marital Satisfaction Inventory–Revised, have been exceptionally wonderful assessment experts. Both Frank and Doug provided vital, up-to-date information on their instruments and reviewed, as well as made important contributions to, the specific interpretations of their instruments for our clinical vignettes. Also, Dr. David Schroat, director of the University of Michigan–Dearborn's Counseling and Support Services and Psychodynamic Counseling expert, graciously provided feedback and suggestions on the Psychodynamic-Object Relations Family Counseling portion of the model. In addition, Drs. Paul and Darcy Granello of Ohio State University expertly provided noteworthy comments related to suicide and addicted families.

We would like to thank our professional colleagues at the University of Texas at San Antonio and Florida International University for their support, reviews, and comments. Specifically, we would like to say a special word of thanks to Dr. Marcheta Evans, Dr. Thelma Duffey, and Dr. Albert Valadez, all of whom are multicultural counseling experts and exceptional clinicians, for their thoughtful insights, comments, and suggestions.

Finally, we'd like to thank our clients and students throughout the years. The valuable input that we have gleaned from our clients who struggle with addictive disorders has truly impacted how we formulated this text. In addition, our students have helped keep the material fresh in our minds, as we are continuously reminded of how important it is to work with intentionality as we pick appropriate interventions for addicted families. It is our hope that clients and students have learned as much from us as we have from them.

Truly, we have been blessed to have so many superior experts and clinicians readily share their wisdom and knowledge regarding addicted families. Again, we thank each of these outstanding sources for their significant contributions, and we especially thank you, our readers, for your continued commitment to helping addicted family systems and their members.

Index